Innovative Applications of Knowledge Discovery and Information Resources Management

Susan Swayze
The George Washington University, USA

Valerie Ford
ISP Global Communications LLC, USA

A volume in the Advances in Library and Information Science (ALIS) Book Series

Published in the United States of America by
IGI Global
Information Science Reference (an imprint of IGI Global)
701 E. Chocolate Avenue
Hershey PA, USA 17033
Tel: 717-533-8845
Fax: 717-533-8661
E-mail: cust@igi-global.com
Web site: http://www.igi-global.com

Library of Congress Cataloging-in-Publication Data

Names: Swayze, Susan, 1968- editor. | Ford, Valerie, 1961- editor.
Title: Innovative applications of knowledge discovery and information resources management / Susan Swayze and Valerie Ford, editors.
Description: Hershey, PA : Information Science Reference, [2018] | Includes bibliographical references.
Identifiers: LCCN 2017057026| ISBN 9781522558293 (hardcover) | ISBN 9781522558309 (ebook)
Subjects: LCSH: Information resources management. | Information services. | Management information systems. | Knowledge management.
Classification: LCC T58.64 .I596 2018 | DDC 658.4/038--dc23 LC record available at https://lccn.loc.gov/2017057026

This book is published in the IGI Global book series Advances in Library and Information Science (ALIS) (ISSN: 2326-4136; eISSN: 2326-4144)

British Cataloguing in Publication Data
A Cataloguing in Publication record for this book is available from the British Library.

Advances in Library and Information Science (ALIS) Book Series

ISSN:2326-4136
EISSN:2326-4144

Editor-in-Chief: Alfonso Ippolito, Sapienza University-Rome, Italy &
Carlo Inglese, Sapienza University-Rome, Italy

MISSION

The **Advances in Library and Information Science (ALIS) Book Series** is comprised of high quality, research-oriented publications on the continuing developments and trends affecting the public, school, and academic fields, as well as specialized libraries and librarians globally. These discussions on professional and organizational considerations in library and information resource development and management assist in showcasing the latest methodologies and tools in the field.

The **ALIS Book Series** aims to expand the body of library science literature by covering a wide range of topics affecting the profession and field at large. The series also seeks to provide readers with an essential resource for uncovering the latest research in library and information science management, development, and technologies.

COVERAGE

- Diversity in Libraries
- Conservation
- Web-Based Bibliographic Instruction
- Virtual Reference Services
- Digital Library Economics
- Academic Libraries in the Digital Age
- Professional Development
- Technologies Affecting Library Services
- Digital Literacy
- User Surveys and Focus Groups

The Advances in Library and Information Science (ALIS) Book Series (ISSN 2326-4136) is published by IGI Global, 701 E. Chocolate Avenue, Hershey, PA 17033-1240, USA, www.igi-global.com. This series is composed of titles available for purchase individually; each title is edited to be contextually exclusive from any other title within the series. For pricing and ordering information please visit http://www.igi-global.com/book-series/advances-library-information-science/73002. Postmaster: Send all address changes to above address.

Titles in this Series

For a list of additional titles in this series, please visit:
https://www.igi-global.com/book-series/advances-library-information-science/73002

Changing the Scope of Library Instruction in the Digital Age
Swati Bhattacharyya (University of California – Riverside, USA) and K Rama Patnaik (Indian Institute of Management Bangalore, India)
Information Science Reference • ©2018 • 286pp • H/C (ISBN: 9781522528029) • US $175.00

Handbook of Research on Innovative Techniques, Trends, and Analysis for Optimized ...
Victor C.X. Wang (Grand Canyon University, USA) and Thomas G. Reio Jr. (Florida International University, USA)
Information Science Reference • ©2018 • 445pp • H/C (ISBN: 9781522551645) • US $275.00

Measuring the Validity of Usage Reports Provided by E-Book Vendors Emerging Research ...
Aiping Chen-Gaffey (Slippery Rock University of Pennsylvania, USA) and Heather Getsay (Slippery Rock University of Pennsylvania, USA)
Information Science Reference • ©2018 • 130pp • H/C (ISBN: 9781522532385) • US $135.00

Examining the Emotional Dimensions of Academic Librarianship Emerging Research ...
Megan Lowe (University of Louisiana – Monroe, USA) and Lindsey M. Reno (University of New Orleans, USA)
Information Science Reference • ©2018 • 168pp • H/C (ISBN: 9781522537618) • US $145.00

Handbook of Research on Managing Intellectual Property in Digital Libraries
Adeyinka Tella (University of Ilorin, Nigeria) and Tom Kwanya (The Technical University of Kenya, Kenya)
Information Science Reference • ©2018 • 461pp • H/C (ISBN: 9781522530930) • US $245.00

Digitizing the Modern Library and the Transition From Print to Electronic
Raj Kumar Bhardwaj (St. Stephen's College, University of Delhi, India)
Information Science Reference • ©2018 • 325pp • H/C (ISBN: 9781522521198) • US $195.00

For an entire list of titles in this series, please visit:
https://www.igi-global.com/book-series/advances-library-information-science/73002

List of Reviewers

R. Abirami, *Rajalakshri Engineering College, India*
Hadeel Alharbi, *University of New England, Australia*
Jaehwa Choi, *The George Washington University, USA*
K. Jayashree, *Rajalakshri Engineering College, India*
Letitia Larry, *LCDC, LLC, USA & Business Intelligence, Inc., USA*
Kamaljeet Sandhu, *University of New England, Australia*
William Anderson Von Canon Jr., *Business Intelligence, Inc., USA*
Danielle Young, *Westat, USA*

Table of Contents

Detailed Table of Contents

Identifying the precursors of turnover has been the subject of examination for the past four decades. IT professionals are a critical group of employees in the current knowledge-driven economy, and as such, they experience unique job stressors. This chapter explores recent research on the organizational stressors that influence IT turnover intentions. The goal is to provide insights on how organizations can begin to stem burnout, turnover intentions, and eventual turnover while improving work-related wellbeing. A revised model of work-related wellbeing is also presented in this chapter. Another objective is to discuss current issues in the IT domain and provide new research directions. New research for the IT turnover literature will provide information to scholars and practitioners on how they might improve and alleviate the impact of turnover on organizations.

Pre-risk governance is an extension of the risk management paradigm that allows for risk analysis prior to making a decision on whether a business objective should move forward and what the possible risks may be. Instead of making business decisions that will affect or impact technology, and the associated people, processes, and policy and then including necessary staff in systems planning after the fact, pre-risk governance allows for the inclusion of pertinent staff in the decision-making process prior to moving toward a major change or enterprise transformation effort. Historically, information technology (IT) staff have not been included in decision making as it applies to change initiatives until they are required in the overall systems/solutions development life cycle. This exclusion of IT staff has been shown to cause a higher level of risk, and actuated issues with schedule, budget, and successful implementation of or transition to a new means of doing and supporting business.

Preface

Technological advancement has become integral to almost every aspect of social life and has brought widespread changes to how we work, communicate, make decisions, learn and play. As a result, the scale and scope of technology breakthroughs are introducing change into every industry and household. For example, pervasive and rapidly evolving mobile technologies such as smart phones and tablets (and increasingly wearable mobile devices such as wrist technologies) allow people to connect and work anytime, anywhere, and on any task. Furthermore, cybersecurity, hackers, around the clock access, and 24x7 data centers are indications of an ever-changing technology landscape. Today, we are at a tipping point of a new digital paradigm in which the capabilities of technology are beginning to outpace human capabilities.

The chapters in this book represent the pervasiveness of technological change and cover a diverse set of topics ranging from the impact of permeable work-life boundaries, burnout and turnover to big data usage and computer-based learning. The chapters are the starting point for understanding and discussion regarding technological change and the social world. Also, this book aims to address some technological challenges and proposes new strategies for dealing with a variety of issues related to information technology.

INSIDE THIS BOOK

This book has three themes that make up its sections. The themes are:

- **People and Technology Issues in the Twenty-First Century:** Focuses on issues that arise when people and technology intersect
- **Knowledge Discovery and Learning:** Challenges existing paradigms in information technology to foster continuous improvement
- **Perspectives on Information Resources Management:** Discusses opportunities and issues that arise from the viewpoint of information as a shared organizational resource

ISSUES, CHALLENGES, AND OPPORTUNITIES IN INFORMATION TECHNOLOGY

The chapters in Section 1 address issues related to technological change in the workplace. In the modern world of work, organizational success depends heavily on an organization's ability to effectively apply information technology for competitive advantage or to meet strategic goals. As a result, technology has permeated industries, such as education, healthcare, security, sports, gaming, telecommunications and even accounting. However, along with the opportunities and efficiencies of information technology, come the unintended consequences, such as job stress for IT workers, lack of work-life balance due to the pervasiveness of technology, security breaches, and the uncontrolled and explosive growth of data.

In the field of education, technology is changing the relationship between educators and learners. For example, using technology for online learning makes education accessible to many who otherwise would not have access for a variety of reasons. Digital assessments are another way that technology is being applied in education. Also on the rise, are computer-based standardized assessments with automatically generated items. Traditional pencil and paper testing methods are quickly being replaced with online assessments. Section 2 discusses these topics.

In Chapter 5, innovative tools and techniques for the development and design of software systems are essential to problem solving and planning of software solutions. New methodologies and approaches are bringing together the best practices of theory and application in the software development arena. Additionally, agile methods are becoming increasingly common in application design, with their collaborative customer focus and iterative, test driven approach.

The chapters in Section 3 focus on topics and issues regarding information as an organizational resource. As technology and its application continue to grow around the world, data overload has become a critical challenge. Efficiently processing large amounts of data to produce useful information for decision making requires lots of computing power, sophisticated software and human analytical skills. Chapter 9 discusses the challenges organizations face in their attempts to decipher and use large amounts of data for knowledge discovery and decision making. Overcoming challenges with the analysis of data can help to find new correlations to spot business trends, prevent diseases, combat crime and so on.

WHO SHOULD READ THIS BOOK?

This book covers a variety of topics and has a primary aim to provide information and insights regarding the impacts of technological change in a variety of settings.

Therefore, this book is meant for academics, practitioners, IT leaders, IT professionals or anyone who is interested in examining the ways in which technology is changing the world. More specifically, this book covers the following:

- Twenty-first century challenges that affect IT professionals, such as burnout, the permeability of work-life boundaries, the impacts of technology changes on people in organizations, and information technology changes that are currently shaping our world
- How technology is increasing access to education opportunities via e-learning, distance learning, digital assessments and automatic item generation for assessments
- Best practices and new approaches to software design and development to improve performance reliability, and rapid technological growth
- How the explosive growth of data has created challenges and opportunities for industries, such as healthcare, security, sports, gaming and so on

ORGANIZATION OF THE BOOK

A brief description of each of the chapters in this book is provided below:

Chapter 1: This chapter examines boundary flexibility, home boundary permeability and work boundary permeability as separate constructs, positing eight possible boundary configurations. In this exploratory research, differences in demographics, technology usage, work-family conflict and work and life satisfaction for 65 knowledge workers who maintain different levels of boundary flexibility and permeability are examined. This research offers a new boundary configuration framework, which should guide future research and organizational policy.

Chapter 2: IT professionals are a critical group of employees in the current knowledge driven economy and as such, they experience unique job stressors. This chapter explores recent research on the organizational stressors that influence IT turnover intentions. The goal of the chapter is to provide insights on how organizations can begin to stem burnout, turnover intentions and eventual turnover while improving work-related well-being. A revised model of work-related well-being is also presented in this chapter.

Chapter 3: Pre-Risk Governance allows for the inclusion of pertinent staff in the decision making process prior to moving toward a major change or enterprise transformation effort. Historically, Information Technology (IT) staff has not been included in decision making as it applies to change initiatives until they were required in the overall systems/solutions development life cycle. This exclusion of IT staff has been shown to cause a higher level of risk, and actuated issues with schedule, budget and successful implementation of or transition to a new means of doing and supporting business.

Chapter 4: This chapter focuses on how organizations can assess the success of an ERP implementation. It contends that it is essential to evaluate how much the system has succeeded in achieving its predetermined objectives at the post-implementation stage of an ERP project. The chapter proposes an extended framework for assessing a firm's ERP post-implementation success.

Chapter 5: This chapter extends previous research which proposed the Business Process and Practice Alignment Methodology (BPPAM) to expose, manage and improve business processes based on actual work practices. The chapter describes an agile version of the BPPAM – the Agile Business Process and Practice Alignment Methodology (ABPPAM). Agility is infused in the ABPPAM through the redefinition of phases, roles and iteration cycles. A case study analysis in an actual organizational setting is used to illustrate the effects of agility for the business discovery phase of ABPPAM.

Chapter 6: This chapter introduces the concept of automated item generation (AIG) for standardized tests. It analyzes how automatically generating items affects the technology-based assessment system. In particular, this chapter illustrates how AIG's automation will affect education, professional training, and/or public policy. This chapter concludes with a discussion of the future direction of AIG's research and development.

Chapter 7: This chapter focuses on increasing the rate of adopting e-learning technologies and how it will provide educational benefits related to course access and better course delivery for Saudi citizens. Specifically, it discusses issues regarding gender-related staffing and access to educational courses. This is primarily because the e-learning technology has the capacity to adapt to dominant features in Saudi society and culture, as well as its potential to be efficiently applied in Saudi higher education settings.

Chapter 8: This chapter proposes a path forward for international assessment approaches. International assessments, such as the Trends in International Math and Science Study (TIMSS), the Program for International Student Assessment (PISA), and the International Computer and Information Literacy Study (ICILS) have traditionally relied on paper and pencil administration. These traditional assessments are being developed as computer-based tests due to advances in information and communication technologies. Computer-based assessments will eventually make traditional paper and pencil assessments obsolete. Additionally, the chapter discusses how international and other large-scale assessments can benefit from the use of Automatic Item Generation (AIG) and/or Computer Adaptive Testing (CAT) to enhance and strengthen test security and validity. The chapter discusses how to reduce costs (over the course of multiple test administrations), encourage student engagement, and efficiently measure students' abilities.

Chapter 9: This chapter explores the notion of big data and its prevalent growth in several industries. Specifically, this chapter discusses how big data has gained much attention from academia, IT, and other industries. This chapter discusses the background of big data and its various applications which include addressing future research directions for its application.

Chapter 10: Using Social Media for Healthcare Recruiting discusses how healthcare organizations have turned to social media to attract applicants for hard to fill positions. This chapter is focused on the use of social media as part of e-recruiting strategies in two healthcare organizations. One organization is located in the Rocky Mountain region and the other in the Mid-Atlantic region. Interviews with human resources recruiters and administrators provided insight into the mechanisms by which healthcare organizations are using social media to recruit top talent into their organizations.

Chapter 11: This chapter contends that a combination of Service-Oriented Architecture (SOA) and REpresentational State Transfer (REST) architectural styles can be used to deal with the fundamental problem of application coupling in distributed application integration. The chapter conducts a comparative study of these styles and argues that, while both solve basic interoperability, neither of them minimizes coupling, since data description schemas are shared by the interacting applications (symmetric interoperability). A new architectural style called Structured Services is proposed. This new style combines the best characteristics of SOA and REST (services can have structure and resources can implement application-specific services), while using asymmetric interoperability (schema compatibility is based on structural compliance and conformance) to minimize application coupling.

Chapter 12: This chapter examines information technology (IT) security in the context of current IT security scholarship, organizational management, business and complexity leadership theories. The chapter is based on well-known organizational power and politics theory as well as accounting, budget and management literature. It examines the impact of power and politics on IT security and the importance of budgetary gamesmanship as illustrated by understanding budget as a game, the politics of allocation within an organization, the influence of budgetary bias and how it shapes what Chief Information Security Officers (CISOs) must understand and master. The chapter suggests a future framework for IT security-management-budget review. The framework proposes that organizations include measures to track expenditures in addition to power alignment, and gauge the net effect on an organization's information-technology security posture.

CONCLUSION

This book examines a number of trends: an aging workforce, the proliferation of mobile devices and cloud-based applications, inexpensive internet access and the changing nature of work. Technological advancement has the potential to influence all of these trends. The chapters in this book discuss opportunities for accessibility in terms of education, best practices for quality and continuous improvement and ensuring that people, processes, and technology maintain a symbiotic relationship.

The hope is that this book provides a balanced discussion regarding the positive and negative impacts of technological change. No one knows what the future holds, but the prediction is that over the next decade, technological innovation and knowledge discovery will continue to evolve and will likely be more disruptive. This prediction presents a great opportunity as there will be no shortage of technological advancements, research opportunities and benefits to society as a whole.

Acknowledgment

The editors would like to thank each of the chapter authors who contributed their time and expertise to this book. We also wish to acknowledge the valuable contributions of the reviewers regarding the improvement of quality, coherence, and content presentation of chapters. We highly appreciate the additional effort of the authors who also served as referees.

The editors wish to thank their colleagues, friends, and family for their support during this process. Without their support, this book would not have become a reality.

Susan Swayze
The George Washington University, USA

Valerie Ford
ISP Global Communications LLC, USA

Section 1

People and Technology Issues in the Twenty-First Century

This first section highlights issues that arise when people and technology intersect. Topics such as work-life boundaries, resistance to organizational change, burnout, and turnover are discussed. People occupy many different roles in their interaction with technology. Therefore, the chapters in this section focus on information technology professionals who create and provide technology, employees who experience and adapt to technology, and leaders who must make decisions about technology that take human capital into account.

Chapter 1
Exploring the Impact of Flexible and Permeable Work–Life Boundaries in a Mobile World

Donna Weaver McCloskey
Widener University, USA

ABSTRACT

Work-life boundaries are often studied on a segmentation-integration continuum, which fails to consider that boundaries can be multidimensional. A flexible boundary allows work to be completed at different times and locations, whereas a permeable boundary allows for the integration of work and personal demands. This chapter examines boundary flexibility, home boundary permeability, and work boundary permeability as separate constructs, positing eight possible boundary configurations. In this exploratory research, differences in demographics, technology usage, work-family conflict, and work and life satisfaction for 65 knowledge workers who maintain different levels of boundary flexibility and permeability are examined. This research offers a new boundary configuration framework, which should guide future research and organizational policy.

BOUNDARY FLEXIBILITY AND PERMEABILITY

In the past the line between work and home was defined by time and location. During work hours and in the office, employees were in their work role and outside of that time/place, were in their personal life. The advent of mobile technology has all but eradicated those temporal (time) and physical boundaries. The transportability

DOI: 10.4018/978-1-5225-5829-3.ch001

of computing means that work activities can now be done at alternate times and locations. Likewise, the ubiquitous nature of communication means that personal demands can be made while working. With the breech of temporal and physical boundaries, the psychological boundary that individuals maintain between their work and personal lives becomes more important. This research seeks to further define those boundaries and explore the impact of boundary decisions on work-family conflict as well as work and life satisfaction.

The vast majority of the boundary literature utilizes a segmentation-integration continuum, positing that employees have preferences for either keeping their work and personal life separate or allowing them to overlap (Ashford, Kreiner & Fugate, 2000; Bulger, Matthews & Hoffman, 2007; Kossek, Ruderman, Brady & Hannum, 2010; Tremblay & Genin, 2008). This construct may be too simplistic. Boundaries can be flexible without being permeable and vice versa. The failure to separate flexibility from permeability has contributed to difficulties in reconciling and integrating research results (Den-Nagy, 2014). Recently researches have acknowledged that flexibility and permeability of boundaries should be examined as distinct constructs (McCloskey, 2016; Methot & LePine, 2016). This research does that by examining differences in demographics, technology use and work and personal outcomes based on boundary flexibility and the permeability of the work and home boundary.

One dimension of the work-life boundary is flexibility. The concept of flexibility is how much control the individual has over when and where work is completed. Work schedule flexibility can be a formal program, such as flex-time or telecommuting, or an informal ability to adjust work hours as needed. Work flexibility has been found to be negatively related to forms of work-family conflict (Carolson, Grzywacz & Kacmar, 2010; Kattehbach, Demerouti & Nachreiner, 2010; Porter & Ayman, 2010) since it allows employees to balance conflicting demands.

Permeability is another dimension of the work-life boundary. Boundary permeability is the extent to which we integrate the obligations of one role when in the other role. Permeable boundaries allow one to be physically located in one domain and psychologically or behaviorally involved in another role (Olson-Buchanan & Boswell, 2006). Mobile technology and the ability to communicate anytime, anywhere has made the work-life boundary even more permeable. Whether responding to a client's email at the school's chorale concert or watching the concert via Skype while in the office, technology offers employees the ability to continually cross boundaries. Researchers have addressed the issue of boundary permeability and have found that using technology to do work outside of the traditional work time to contribute to increased work-family conflict (Boswell & Olson-Buchanan, 2007; Olson-Buchanan & Boswell, 2006). Conversely, individuals with strong (i.e. non-permeable) home and work boundaries experience less work-family and family-work conflict (Hecht & Allen, 2009).

Figure 1 provides a graphical depiction of four combinations of flexible and permeable boundaries. Scenarios A and B represent inflexible borders between the work and home domain. In these scenarios there is a set, defined time for work that cannot be altered. From day to day, these employees know when they need to be in their work role and cannot readily alter their schedule. There is, however, a difference in the permeability of the borders. In Scenario A the borders between work and home are not permeable; there is little to no personal contact or tasks during work time and, likewise, little to no work contact or tasks during personal time. Conversely, in Scenario B while the work and home hours are set, there is a significant amount of communication or tasks that infringe from the other domain. Scenarios C and D represent flexible boundaries between the work and home domain. In these scenarios individuals have some control on when work is done. Called split-shift or flextime, employees can take time during the day to meet personal or family obligations and then make that time up, whether at work, home or an alternate location, at another time. In Scenario C the boundary between work and personal time are not permeable. So although the timing of work and personal tasks may shift, when engaged in one role, there are boundaries in place to limit the interference from the other role. Scenario D represents the flexible and permeable boundaries

Figure 1. Combinations of flexible and permeable boundaries

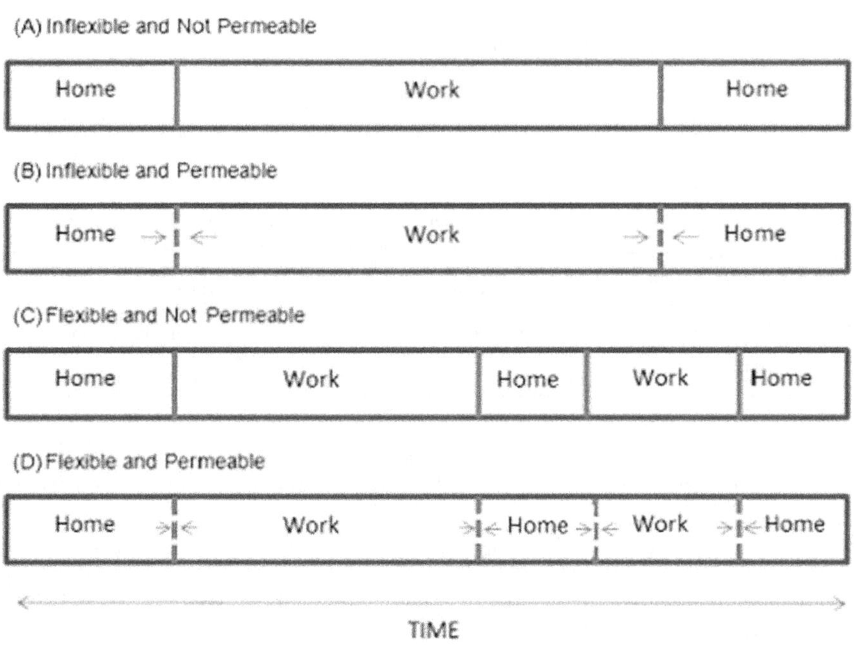

depicted by Ashford, et al. (2000) which constitutes a high level of integration. The timing of work and personal tasks may shift and due to the permeable boundaries, individuals can change their focus from one role to another.

The number of scenarios increases when we consider that there can be directionality to boundaries. Boundary flexibility is not directional. When the work boundary shifts it, by definition, shifts the non-work boundary as well. But permeability can be established for both home and work boundaries (Eagle, Icenogle, Maes and Miles, 1998; Kasper, Meyer & Schmidt, 2005). Having a work permeable boundary but a non-permeable home boundary, or vice versa, adds a layer of complexity to the scenarios depicted in Figure 1. Instead of the four scenarios, there are actually eight possible combinations of boundary flexibility and work/home boundary permeability. Table 1 presents the eight combinations of boundary flexibility and work and home permeability and offers descriptions, illustrative examples and potential mobile technology usage to support those boundaries.

Table 1. Overview of boundary configurations with regard to flexibility and work/ home permeability

	Description	Illustrative Example	Potential Technology Usage to Support Border Flexibility and Permeability
Inflexible, home and work non-permeable	At the far extreme, work and personal life are compartmentalized and work and personal times are set. Work is not done during personal time and personal demands are not met during work time	A knowledge worker has set working hours. When s/he is working, s/he does not engage in personal tasks such as personal calls/emails/texts or social media. Likewise, when not working, s/he does not engage in work activities such as work calls/ emails.	Because work and non-work times are set and rarely change, it is likely someone with an inflexible boundary would maintain separate work and personal calendars. Due to non-permeable boundaries, it is likely this person maintains separate email and mobile devices for work and home. Work devices would be shut off during personal time and vice versa.
Inflexible, home not permeable, work permeable	Work and non-work times are set and rarely altered. Home life is considered sacrosanct. While personal needs may be addressed during work time, generally work is not done during personal time.	A manager has set hours for working. Personal demands, such as a phone conference with a teacher, shopping for a birthday gift or scheduling personal appointments may happen during work time. When s/he arrives home, s/he does not check work email nor engage in work activities.	Separate work and personal calendars (see above). The home boundary is not permeable so it is likely someone with this boundary has a separate work phone/mobile device which can be turned off when not working. The work boundary is permeable so work email address may be used for personal correspondence and/or personal accounts/ devices are checked while working.
Inflexible, home permeable, work not permeable	Work occurs during scheduled time. Work life is protected with a non-permeable border. While work may intrude on personal time, the opposite does not happen.	A surgeon has set hours when s/ he must be at the hospital and does not deal with personal issues while at work. Work demands may intrude during personal/family time	Separate work and personal calendars (see above). Because the home boundary is permeable, this employee may use their personal email or mobile device for work communication or checks their work device while not working. Because the work boundary is not permeable, personal email/communication likely does not come to work accounts/ devices.

continued on following page

Table 1. Continued

	Description	Illustrative Example	Potential Technology Usage to Support Border Flexibility and Permeability
Inflexible, work and home permeable	Work and non-work times are set and rarely altered. Permeable boundaries for both work and home means that work activities are sometimes done at home and personal activities are sometimes done at work.	A supervisor may be required to be at the work location M-F from 8a – 6p. Permeability in boundaries means s/he can perform personal tasks such as a phone conference with a teacher, shopping for a birthday gift or scheduling personal appointments during work time. Likewise, work task can be done during personal time.	Separate work and personal calendars (see above). Because both the work and home boundaries are permeable, someone with these boundaries may use one mobile device and email account for both work and personal needs.
Flexible, home and work not permeable	Work and personal life are compartmentalized but the timing of work can be shifted to meet changing demands. Although time may shift, when working only work tasks are done and when not working only non-work tasks are done.	A manager can leave the office at 3 to attend after school sports but can make up those hours by working in the evening. (This is sometimes referred to as a split shift.) The work and home boundaries are not permeable, so the employee is neither responding to work emails when at the sporting event nor watching the game online while in the office.	Because work and non-work time can shift, it is likely that someone with flexible boundaries would use an integrated calendar. Because work and non-work tasks are compartmentalized, this employee may have separate work and personal email accounts as well as separate mobile devices. Personal emails/texts are not dealt with when working and work emails/texts are not dealt with when not working.
Flexible, home not permeable, work permeable	The time when work is done may shift but the home boundary is firm and work is not done during personal time. The work boundary is permeable so personal tasks may be done at work.	A manager can leave the office at 3 to attend after school sports but can make up those hours by working in the evening. S/he would not check work email while at the sporting event but may follow a youth sporting event online while in the office.[1]	Integrated calendar (see above). The home boundary is not permeable so it is likely someone with this boundary has a separate work phone/mobile device which can be turned off when not working. The work boundary is permeable so work email address may be used for personal correspondence and/or personal accounts/devices are checked while working.
Flexible, home permeable, work not permeable	The time when work is done may shift but the work boundary is firm. While work tasks may be done during personal time, personal tasks are not done during work time.	This is perhaps the category for the stereotypical workaholic. A manager can leave the office at 3 to attend after school sports but can make up those hours by working in the evening. Because the home boundary is permeable, s/he would check work email while at the sporting event. The work boundary is not permeable to s/he would not follow a youth sporting event online while in the office.	Integrated calendar (see above). Because the home boundary is permeable, this employee may use their personal email or mobile device for work communication or checks their work device while not working. Because the work boundary is not permeable, personal email/communication likely does not come to work accounts/devices.
Flexible, home and work both permeable	This combination offers the most work-life integration. The timing of work can shift and demands from one role are allowed to intrude when in the other role.	A real estate agent has flexibility as to when work is done. But having permeable boundaries means work calls are taken during family time (like dinner or a concert) and family needs (like homework help or scheduling/carpool coordination) are dealt with while working.	Integrated calendar (see above). Because both the work and home boundaries are permeable, someone with these boundaries may use one mobile device and email account for both work and personal needs.

EXAMINING THE EFFECT OF BOUNDARY FLEXIBILITY AND PERMEABILITY

Mobile technology offers workers the benefit of flexibility in completing work, which can be viewed as having positive outcomes on stress and satisfaction. But mobile technology also allows for work to intrude during personal time and for personal issues to intrude during work time. This conflict can cause stress and have a negative impact on satisfaction. This research examines the impact of boundary flexibility and home/work boundary permeability on technology usage, work-family conflict, job satisfaction and life satisfaction.

Work-family conflict (WFC) is when the stress or demands from one role interferes with the other and is comprised of three dimensions: time, psychological and behavioral. Our examination includes both the directionality and dimensions of this construct. The time based dimension of WFC is when there are pressing demands that must be met during the same time. Researchers have suggested that work-family conflict should be looked at from both sides of the relationship, the extent to which work interferes with family (work→family conflict) and the extent to which family interferes with work (family→work) (Frone, Russell & Cooper, 1992; Judge, Boudreau & Bretz, 1994). This was not done in this study for the time dimension of work-family conflict. The very concept of schedule flexibility negates directionality in this time based dimension because it assumes that there is a structured work time and non-work time. Directionality implies that a family commitment during the eight hours per day in which the employee works is family→work conflict and work commitments during "non-work" time (nights and weekends) is work→family conflict. Mobile computing and flexible scheduling allows employees to be very flexible concerning when work is completed. With the elimination of the 8-hour "shift", it is much harder to establish directionality. This research will examine the time dimension of work-family conflict but will not look at directionality of this measure.

Another dimension of work-family conflict, psychological interference, can be more insidious since it is not as obvious or as easily managed. Psychological interference is when you are physically present in one role but are distracted or consumed with needs from the other role. This conflict, which we will call the strain dimension of work-family conflict, taps into the permeability of borders and the ability to control the interference from one role when you are in the other role. The strain dimension of work-family conflict will consider the directionality of conflict, work interfering with family (work→family conflict) and family interfering with work (family →work conflict).

The third dimension of work-family conflict has to do with the different ways be behave in our work and home lives. For example, the decision-making style used in the workplace may be different from the one employed for personal decisions. While the blurring of work and home boundaries may cause increase the speed of transition, it would not eliminate it. This dimension has received much less attention in the literature and was not examined in this research.

Work-family conflict has been shown to be a contributor to many negative outcomes including depression (Frone, et al., 1992), low organizational commitment (Greenhaus & Beutell, 1985) and poor physical health (Carlson, Grzywacz & Kacmar, 2010). Since we are examining the impact of boundaries on the conflict between work and personal lives, we will also examine the resulting impact on job and life satisfaction.

Boundary flexibility refers to the degree to which the time boundary between work and personal roles can shift. Employees who maintain flexible boundaries are able to change when and where they do their job. As offered in illustrative examples in Table 1, it is likely that someone with a flexible work-life boundary would maintain one integrated calendar so that time can be managed holistically.

H1: Respondents who have flexible boundaries will use one, integrated calendar.

Researchers have found that the ability to vary work time is negatively related to work-nonwork conflict (Bulger, et. al. 2007; Carlson, et. al, 2010; Kattenbach, Demerouti & Nachreiner, 2010). Porter and Ayman (2010) found work flexibility to be negatively correlated with work interference with family measure, which is the extent to which work demands conflicted with family life. Diaz, Chiaburu, Zimmerman and Boswell (2012) found that mobile technology offered more flexibility which contributed to reduced work to life conflict. While flexibility provides agility in reducing time-based work-family conflict, it can also contribute to less strain-based work-family conflict. Knowing that we can adjust the timing and location of work to meet personal needs reduces the stress we would encounter with structured, set time boundaries. Boundary control is positively correlated with the ability to balance work and family and negatively correlated with psychological stress (Kossek, et.al, 2012). Thus, our expectation is that boundary flexibility will contribute to the reduction in the three studied forms of work-family conflict.

H2a: Respondents who have flexible boundaries will have less time based work-family conflict than those who have inflexible boundaries.
H2b: Respondents who have flexible boundaries will have less strain based work→ family work-family conflict than those who have inflexible boundaries.
H2c: Respondents who have flexible boundaries will have less strain based family→ work-family conflict than those who have inflexible boundaries.

When we're not in balance and the strain of not meeting needs in one domain conflict with another, we tend to be dissatisfied with both our job and our life (Netemeyer, Boyles & McMurrian, 1996). As prior research has supported, reduced work-family conflict contributes to other positive outcomes such as higher work and life satisfaction (Carlson, et al., 2010).

H2d: Respondents who have flexible boundaries will have higher job and life satisfaction than those who have inflexible boundaries.

Flexibility is about when and where work is completed but permeability is about the integration of work and home. As presented in Table 1, employees can maintain different levels of permeability for work and home. If an employee is interested in keeping firm boundaries, s/he would be more likely to have separate work and personal cell phones and email accounts so that those domains can be kept separate. Conversely, employees who want to integrate their work and personal life would be more likely to use one cell phone and email account for both work and personal needs.

H3: Respondents who have permeable boundaries will use one, integrated cell phone and email account.

Generally, when employees are able to establish barriers or limits between work and family, they experience less work-family conflict (Hecht and Allen, 2009) and more integration results in greater work-family conflict (DeSrochers, Hilton & Larwood, 2005). Prior research has not addressed how permeability could impact the components of work-family conflict (time, strain work→ family and strain family→ work) differently. While we hypothesized that schedule flexibility is what allows employees to minimize time-based work family conflict, perhaps permeability has an impact as well. The ability to communicate to meet a personal need, such as talking to a doctor or emailing a teacher, during traditional work time may be seen as helping to alleviate the time-based work-family conflict. While flexibility provides the ability to go somewhere during traditional work time, permeability provides the ability to communicate during traditional work hours. Because employees are able to communicate in a timely manner (i.e. not waiting until after work to return a call), they may feel a reduction in their time-based work-family conflict.

H4a: Respondents who have a permeable work boundary will have less time based work-family conflict than those who have a non-permeable work.

However the potential benefit of permeability comes at a price. Generally, integration is seen as stressful. Greater work-family integration, interruptions of one domain when in the other domain, has been associated with greater work-family conflict (Desrochers, et. al, 2005; Kossek at al., 2012) and stress (Koay, Soh & Chew, 2017). Moving from one role to another involves a rite of transition (Ashford et al., 2000). Traditionally, the commute to work or home is the transition time in which we decompress and 'change channels' from the role we are leaving to the one we are entering. Those with permeable boundaries are not afforded the time to make these transitions and must move from one role to another quickly. Hecht and Allen (2009) used a measure called boundary strength which was, in essence, the concept we are calling boundary permeability. They examined both the strength of the boundary that "protected" work from outside interference and found greater work boundary strength was related to less family→ work conflict.

H4b: Respondents who have a permeable work boundary will have more strain based family→ work conflict than those who have a non-permeable work.

When the work boundary is permeable, personal demands can intrude during work time, this leads to more strain based family→ work conflict. Increased work-family conflict is associated with negative impacts on job (Diaz, at. al, 2012) and life satisfaction (Eagle, et al., 1998).

H4c: Respondents who have a permeable work boundary will have lower job and life satisfaction than those who have a non-permeable work.

When the home boundary is permeable, work demands can intrude during non-work time. Again, while boundary flexibility is hypothesized to allow for scheduling to reduce this conflict, it is possible boundary permeability can also address the time dimension of work-family conflict. By allowing work to integrate during personal time, the employee may be able to have more personal time. For example, if there is a conference call that needs to occur on the weekend, perhaps it is better to accept that call from home (and enjoy as much of the weekend as possible) rather than scheduling time in the office and losing even more time due to commuting.

H5a: Respondents who have a permeable home boundary will have less time based work-family conflict than those who have a non-permeable work.

But the potential benefit in scheduling is likely lost when considering the strain-based dimension. Just as we argued for the permeable work boundary, when the home boundary is permeable work is allowed to intrude during non-work time. This intrusion during home time can be even more damaging because of the impact it may have on family members. Demands from a spouse or children to be engaged in family life, not just physically present, may contribute to additional strain and reduced job and life satisfaction. Hecht and Allen (2009) examined the boundary strength that "protected" home from work interference and found home boundary strength was related to less work→family conflict. Likewise, home boundary permeability had a positive impact on work-to-life conflict (Olson-Buchanan & Boswell, 2006)

H5b: Respondents who have a permeable home boundary will have more strain based work→ family conflict than those who have a non-permeable work.

Again, since we are hypothesizing home boundary permeability to result in more strain work→family conflict, we would also expect the resulting decrease in job and life satisfaction.

H5c: Respondents who have a permeable home boundary will have lower job and life satisfaction than those who have a non-permeable work.

As outlined in Table 1, there are eight combinations of boundary flexibility and work/home boundary permeability. The first and last combinations represent the segmented and integrated extremes studied by (Ashford, et. al. 2000). The other six boundary combinations have not been empirically studied.

RESEARCH METHOD

This research sought to examine the digital boundaries of professional knowledge workers making the sampling of business alumni an appropriate sampling frame. Through LinkedIn and email, the undergraduate and graduate alumni from a northeastern university were contacted and asked to complete an online survey. Of the 103 responses, 35 were eliminated due to incomplete answers, resulting in a sample of 68 professional employees. Three additional individuals were dropped because they were not full time employees leaving the final sample at 65. A summary of the demographics of the sample are presented in Table 2. While the sample size is small, it was deemed acceptable for the exploratory nature of this research.

Measures

Boundary Flexibility

Boundary flexibility was assessed with a five-point likert scale (1=strongly disagree to 5=strongly agree) on five statements regarding the individual's control over

Table 2. Demographics of total sample

	Total Sample (n=65)
Gender	Female – 31 (48%) Male – 32 (49%) Not reported – 2 (3%)
Age	20-29 yrs – 6 (9%) 30-39 yrs – 16 (25%) 40-49 yrs – 26 (40%) 50-59 yrs – 16 (25%) 60+ yrs - 1 (2%)
Marital Status	Married – 57 (88%) Divorced – 4 (6%) Widowed – 1 (2%) Single – 3 (5%)
Spouse/ Partner Work Status	Full time – 43 (66%) Part time high (20-40 hrs/wk) – 8 (12%) Part time low (<20 hrs/wk) – 2 (3%) Not employed – 4 (6%)
Parental Status	Parent – 54 (86%) Not a parent – 9 (14%)
Youngest Child	No children - 9 (14%) Infant/baby – 6 (9%) Toddler – 7 (11%) Preschooler – 3 (5%) Elementary age – 10 (15%) Middle school age – 13 (20%) High school age – 6 (9%) College age – 7 (11%) Grown/Indep – 4 (6%)
Eldercare Status	None – 44 (68%) Minimal (1-2 hrs/wk) – 13 (20%) Some (3-6 hrs/wk) – 6 (9%) Substantial (7-10 hrs/wk) – 0 (0%) Major (11+ hrs/wk) – 1 (2%) Not reported – 1 (2%)
Organizational Tenure	11.10 years (9.04 std dev)
Job Tenure	7.33 years (7.24 std dev)
# of Cell phones	1.12 (.31 std dev)
# of Email Accounts	2.75 (1.02 std dev)
# of Calendars	2.02 (.89 std dev)

whether work could be completed at different times or on different days. Statements included 'I have flexibility regarding when I complete my work.' and 'Generally, I can control the hours I work.' The responses were coded such that a higher value represents more boundary flexibility (α=70).

Boundary Permeability

Boundary permeability was assessed with a five-point likert scale (1=strongly disagree to 5=strongly agree) on a total of 16 statements regarding how strongly the individual segments or separates their work and personal life. The items were drawn from Hecht and Allen's (2009) work-nonwork boundary strength scales as well as literature recommending work-life balancing strategies (Cousins & Robey, 2015; Friedman & Westring, 2015; Golden & Geisler, 2007; Zheng, Molineux, Mirshekary & Scaparo, 2015). Eight of the items focus on the boundary that protects an employee's home or personal life from work interference, such as 'I often deal with work related issues during my non-work time' and 'I rarely turn off my mobile device so I can be available during work' (α=79). The other eight items focus on the boundary that protects work from interference from personal/home life. Statements are a mix of permeable boundaries such as 'My friends and family contact me when I am working' and non-permeable boundaries such as 'I rarely deal with personal matters when I am working.' (α=78). All items were coded such that higher scores represent a more permeable boundary.

Work-Family Conflict

This research addresses three types of work-family conflict: time work family conflict (8 items), strain work→family conflict (5 items) and strain family→work conflict (5 items). The measures used to examine these dimensions were developed by Kopelman, Greenhaus and Connolly (1983). Time-based work family conflict is when there are pressing demands from both work and family that must be dealt with at the same time (α=79). Sample items include 'My work keeps me from spending the amount of time I would like to on family related activities' and 'My home life interferes with my work responsibilities, for example starting work on time or traveling'. The strain-based component of work-family conflict arises from interference when you are physically present in one role but are distracted or consumed with needs from the other role. Stain-based work family conflict was examined with five items that addressed work→family conflict (α=80) and four items that addressed family→ work conflict (α=79). Examples include 'I am often preoccupied with my job when I am not working' and 'My family life is so demanding that I find myself thinking about family matters while working.'

Job Satisfaction

Job satisfaction was operationalized by a three-item scale developed by Hackman and Oldham (1975). Each item asked respondents to indicate their agreement or disagreement on a five-point scale ranging from (1) strongly disagree to (5) strongly agree. The items were averaged into a composite score with higher scores reflecting greater job satisfaction (α=77).

Life Satisfaction

As others have done (Carlson, et. al, 2010), the life satisfaction measures were modeled after the job satisfaction items. Life satisfaction was assessed by a three-item scale with respondents asked to indicate their agreement or disagreement on a five-point scale ranging from (1) strongly disagree to (5) strongly agree. The items were averaged into a composite score with higher scores reflecting greater life satisfaction (α=76).

Control Variables

This research sought to understand the demographic characteristics and outcomes of knowledge workers with various types of boundaries between work and home. The included demographic variables were directed by prior research and include gender (Carlson, Grzywacz & Kacmar, 2010; Powell & Craig, 2015; Tremblay & Genin, 2008), age (Zheng, et. al, 2015), and family characteristics such as marital status, spouse's work status, parental status, age of youngest child (Tremblay & Genin, 2008) and eldercare responsibilities (Friedman & Greenhaus, 2000). Additionally, job and organizational tenure (in years) were assessed so that we might examine whether boundary alignment varies with job or organizational experience.

RESULTS AND DISCUSSION

Due to the exploratory nature of this research, before addressing the proposed hypotheses, we first sought to examine whether there were differences in the demographic characteristics of those respondents who reported different boundaries. We first examined boundary flexibility. For the total respondents the average reported boundary flexibility was 3.58 with a 3.60 median. The median point was used to split the respondents into low vs. high flexibility groups. There were 40 (62%) respondents considered to have flexible boundaries and 25 (38%) who are considered to have inflexible boundaries. Once grouped into flexible and non-flexible boundaries, we examined whether there were differences in the demographic characteristics. As presented in Table 3, the flexible and non-flexible respondents were similar on gender, age, marital status, spouse work status and youngest child. In fact, the only categorical variable in which there was a significant difference for flexible vs. non-

Table 3. Demographics based on boundary flexibility

	Flexible Boundary (n= 40)	Non-Flexible Boundary (n= 25)	Sig
Gender	Female – 19 (48%) Male – 20 (50%)	Female – 12 (48%) Male – 12 (48%)	No significant difference
Age	20-29 yrs – 5 (13%) 30-39 yrs – 7 (18%) 40-49 yrs – 16 (40%) 50-59 yrs – 11 (28%) 60+ yrs - 1 (3%)	20-29 yrs – 1 (4%) 30-39 yrs – 9 (36%) 40-49 yrs – 10 (40%) 50-59 yrs – 5 (20%) 60+ yrs - 0 (0%)	No significant difference
Marital Status	Married – 33 (83%) Divorced – 3 (8%) Widowed – 1 (3%) Single – 3 (8%)	Married – 24 (96%) Divorced – 1 (4%) Widowed – 0 (0%) Single – 0 (0%)	No significant difference
Spouse/ Partner Work Status	Full time – 24 (60%) Part time high – 5 (13%) Part time low – 1 (3%) Not employed – 3 (8%)	Full time – 19 (76%) Part time high – 3 (12%) Part time low– 1 (4%) Not employed – 1 (4%)	No significant difference
Parental Status	Parent – 32 (80%) Not a parent – 8 (20%)	Parent – 24 (96%) Not a parent – 1 (4%)	*
Youngest Child	Infant/toddler – 6 (15%) Preschooler – 2 (5%) Elementary age – 7 (18%) Middle/HS age – 10 (25%) College/ Indep – 7 (18%)	Infant/toddler – 7 (28%) Preschooler – 1 (4%) Elementary age – 3 (12%) Middle/HS age – 9 (36%) College/Indep – 4 (16%)	No significant difference
Eldercare Status	None – 23 (58%) Minimal – 12 (30%) Some – 4 (10%) Substantial – 0 Major – 0 (0%)	None – 21 (84%) Minimal – 1 (4%) Some – 2 (8%) Substantial – 0 Major – 1 (4%)	**
Org Tenure	11.59 yrs (8.86 std dev)	10.32 yrs (7.80 std dev)	No significant difference
Job Tenure	7.03 years (5.99 std dev)	7.80 yrs (9.01 std dev)	No significant difference
# of Cell phones	1.11 (.31 std dev)	1.10 (.30 std dev)	No significant difference
# of Email Accounts	2.73 (1.01 std dev)	2.65 (.77 std dev)	No significant difference
# of Calendars	2.03 (.89 std dev)	2.05 (.89 std dev)	No significant difference

NOTE: Percentages do not always total 100% due to non-responses.

* Significant at the .10 level; ** significant at the .05 level; *** significant at the, 01 level

Eldercare Status: Minimal (1-2 hrs/wk), Some (3-6 hrs/wk), Substantial (7-10 hrs/wk), Major (11+ hrs/wk) – 1 (3%)

Spouse/ Partner Work Status: Part time high = 20+ hrs/wk and Part time low < 20 hrs/wk

flexible boundary respondents was parental status and eldercare responsibilities. Those employees with less flexible boundaries were more likely to be parents and reported less eldercare responsibilities. There was not a significant difference in the job or organizational tenure of those who reported flexible boundaries and those who reported inflexible boundaries nor were there any significant differences on number of cell phones, email accounts or calendars.

While the flexibility of boundaries is not directional, boundary permeability is directional. An employee could maintain a non-permeable work boundary (not letting personal tasks interfere during work time) but a permeable home boundary (letting work responsibilities intrude during non-work time). Therefore boundary permeability was assessed separately for both work and home. For the total respondents the average reported work boundary permeability was 3.29 and a 3.50 median and the average reported home boundary permeability was 3.46 with a 3.63 median. The median point was used to split the respondents into low vs. high permeability groups. Thirty six (55%) respondents are considered to have a permeable work boundary and 30 (46%) are considered to have permeable home boundary.

Once grouped into permeable and non-permeable for work and home boundaries, we examined whether there were differences in the demographic characteristics and technology usage. A comparison of the demographic characteristics of the respondents based on the permeability of their work boundary is presented in Table 4a and home boundary is presented in Table 4b.

Conventional wisdom might suggest there is a difference in the way men and women choose to integrate work and family demands. While there was no difference in the gender composition of flexible vs. inflexible boundaries or permeable vs. non-permeable home boundaries, there is a gender difference with regard to the permeability of the work boundary. Given that women are frequently characterized and depicted as multi-taskers (Powell & Craig, 2015) it was a bit surprising to find those who maintain a non-permeable boundary protecting work time are more likely to be women.

There was also a significant difference in the age of youngest child. While there was no difference on whether they had children or not, those employees who maintain a permeable work boundary tended to have younger children with 31% having a preschooler or younger compared to only 17% for the non-permeable work boundary employees. This may be because once children reach school age the structure of the school day does add a pseudo parent-child boundary. Aside from the occasional illness or school communication, the school day segments the child's day from the parent's. This separation may not occur for younger children who are not in school, thus requiring more work boundary permeability.

Table 4a. Demographics Based on Permeability of Work Boundary

	Work Boundary Permeable (n= 36)	**Work Boundary Non-Permeable (n= 29)**	
Gender	Female – 13 (36%) Male – 21 (58%)	Female – 18 (62%) Male – 11 (38%)	*
Age	20-29 yrs – 5 (15%) 30-39 yrs – 11 (31%) 40-49 yrs – 14 (39%) 50-59 yrs – 5 (14%) 60+ yrs - 1 (3%)	20-29 yrs – 1 (3%) 30-39 yrs – 5 (17%) 40-49 yrs – 12 (41%) 50-59 yrs – 11 (38%) 60+ yrs - 0 (0%)	No significant difference
Marital Status	Married – 30 (83%) Divorced – 2 (6%) Widowed – 1 (3%) Single – 3 (8%)	Married – 27 (93%) Divorced – 2 (7%) Widowed – 0 (0%) Single – 0 (0%)	No significant difference
Spouse/ Partner Work Status	Full time – 24 (67%) Part time high – 5 (14%) Part time low – 0 (0%) Not employed – 1 (3%)	Full time – 19 (66%) Part time high – 3 (10%) Part time low – 2 (7%) Not employed – 3 (10%)	No significant difference
Parental Status	Parent – 29 (81%) Not a parent – 7 (19%)	Parent – 27 (93%) Not a parent – 2 (7%)	No significant difference
Youngest Child	Infant/toddler – 9 (25%) Preschooler – 2 (6%) Elementary – 3 (8%) Middle/HS – 13 (36%) College/Indep – 2 (6%)	Infant/toddler – 4 (14%) Preschooler – 1 (3%) Elementary – 7 (24%) Middle/HS – 6 (21%) College/Indep – 9 (31%)	**
Eldercare Status	None – 27 (75%) Minimal – 5 (14%) Some – 3 (8%) Substantial – 0 (0%) Major – 1 (3%)	None – 17 (59%) Minimal– 8 (28%) Some– 3 (10%) Substantial– 0 (0%) Major– 1 (3%)	No significant difference
Organizational Tenure	9.36 years (7.75 std dev)	13.26 years (7.99 std dev)	*
Job Tenure	6.02 years (5.54 std dev)	8.95 years (8.75 std dev)	No significant difference
Number of Cell Phones	1.12 (.31 std dev)	1.10 (.31 std dev)	No significant difference
Number of Email Accounts	2.75 (1.02 std dev)	2.62 (.77 std dev)	No significant difference
Number of Calendars	2.02 (.89 std dev)	2.08 (.88 std dev)	No significant difference

NOTE: Percentages do not always total 100% due to non-responses.

* Significant at the .10 level; ** significant at the .05 level; *** significant at the, 01 level

Eldercare Status: Minimal (1-2 hrs/wk), Some (3-6 hrs/wk), Substantial (7-10 hrs/wk), Major (11+ hrs/wk) – 1 (3%)

Spouse/ Partner Work Status: Part time high = 20+ hrs/wk and Part time low < 20 hrs/wk

Table 4b. Demographics based on permeability of home boundary

	Permeable (n= 30)	Non-Permeable (n= 35)	
Gender	Female – 13 (43%) Male – 15 (50%)	Female – 18 (51%) Male – 17 (49%)	No significant difference
Age	20-29 yrs – 2 (7%) 30-39 yrs – 7 (23%) 40-49 yrs – 14 (47%) 50-59 yrs – 6 (20%) 60+ yrs - 1 (3%)	20-29 yrs – 4 (11%) 30-39 yrs – 9 (26%) 40-49 yrs – 12 (34%) 50-59 yrs – 10 (29%) 60+ yrs - 0 (0%)	No significant difference
Marital Status	Married – 26 (87%) Divorced – 3 (10%) Widowed – 0 (0%) Single – 1 (3%)	Married – 31 (89%) Divorced – 1 (3%) Widowed – 1 (3%) Single – 2 (6%)	No significant difference
Spouse/ Partner Work Status	Full time – 21 (70%) Part time high – 2 (7%) Part time low – 1 (3%) Not employed – 2 (7%)	Full time – 22 (63%) Part time high – 6 (17%) Part time low– 1 (3%) Not employed – 2 (6%)	No significant difference
Parental Status	Parent – 26 (87%) Not a parent – 4 (13%)	Parent – 30 (86%) Not a parent – 5 (14%)	No significant difference
Youngest Child	Infant/toddler – 4 (13%) Preschooler – 3 (10%) Elementary – 4 (13%) Middle/HS – 11 (37%) College/Indep – 4 (14%)	Infant/toddler – 9 (26%) Preschooler – 0 (0%) Elementary – 6 (17%) Middle/HS – 8 (23%) College/Indep – 7 (20%)	No significant difference
Eldercare Status	None – 19 (63%) Minimal – 6 (20%) Some – 3 (10%) Substantial – 0 (0%) Major – 1 (3%)	None – 25 (71%) Minimal – 7 (20%) Some – 3 (9%) Substantial – 0 (0%) Major – 0 (0%)	No significant difference
Organizational Tenure	11.99 years (7.88 std dev)	10.43 years (8.20 std dev)	No significant difference
Job Tenure	7.97 years (6.39 std dev)	6.78 years (7.95 std dev)	No significant difference
Number of Cell Phones	1.17 (.32 std dev)	1.11 (.32 std dev)	No significant difference
Number of Email Accounts	2.75 (1.04 std dev)	2.71 (.94 std dev)	No significant difference
Number of Calendars	2.02 (.89 std dev)	2.03 (.90 std dev)	No significant difference

NOTE: Percentages do not always total 100% due to non-responses.

* Significant at the .10 level; ** significant at the .05 level; *** significant at the, 01 level

Eldercare Status: Minimal (1-2 hrs/wk), Some (3-6 hrs/wk), Substantial (7-10 hrs/wk), Major (11+ hrs/wk) – 1 (3%)

Spouse/ Partner Work Status: Part time high = 20+ hrs/wk and Part time low < 20 hrs/wk

We should note there was not a significant difference in the respondents spouse/partner work status. It would seem likely that people who maintain a firm boundary between work and personal demands are able to do so because they have a spouse/partner who is able to deflect those demands. This was not found in the reported sample as there was no difference in the work status of a spouse/partner for those with a permeable versus non-permeable work boundary.

There was also a slight significant difference in the average organizational tenure between the two groups. Those employees who reported having less work boundary permeability have worked for their organizations longer, 13.26 years compared to 9.36 years for the work permeable boundary group. While we cannot assert any type of causality, those employees who keep a firmer boundary between work and their personal lives, were employed longer with their current organization.

As suggested in the vignettes in Table 1, technology can assist employees integrate or separate their work and personal lives. Centralizing all communication on one cell phone number, email account and calendar would be the epitome of integration with both work and home life managed seamlessly. The other extreme would be the setting up digital firewalls by maintaining separate work and home cell phones, email accounts and calendars. It was therefore somewhat surprising to see that there were no significant differences in the use of these technologies based on permeability of the work or home boundary. Neither of the hypotheses regarding the use of technology to support flexible (H1) or permeable (H3) boundaries were supported.

The first set of hypotheses address whether there are differences in the levels of work-family conflict, job satisfaction and life satisfaction for employees who have flexible boundaries versus those who have non-flexible boundaries. As presented in Table 5, there is no statistical difference between the flexible and non-flexible groups on the examined dimensions of work-family conflict. Despite our belief that

Table 5. Differences in study variables based on boundary flexibility

	Flexible Boundary (n= 40)	**Non-Flexible Boundary (n= 25)**	
Time Based Work Family Conflict	2.48 (.72)	2.54 (.59)	No sig diff
Strain Work→Family Conflict	2.63 (.75)	2.80 (.73)	No sig diff
Strain Family→Work Conflict	1.93 (.50)	2.14 (.66)	No sig diff
Job Satisfaction	3.79 (.76)	3.28 (.73)	**
Life Satisfaction	3.83 (.81)	3.72 (.54)	No sig diff

Mean (standard deviation)

* Significant at the .10 level; ** significant at the .05 level; *** significant at the, 01 level

flexibility would allow employees to better balance their work and family demands, there does not appear to be evidence that the flexible boundary type reduced any form of work-family conflict. We have no support for Hypothesis 2a, b or c. There was, however, a significant difference in job satisfaction. Those employees who have flexible boundaries were significantly more satisfied with their jobs than employees who did not have flexible boundaries. There is partial support for H2d since flexibility was associated with higher job satisfaction but there was no difference for life satisfaction.

The next set of hypotheses dealt with the permeability of the work boundary. It was hypothesized that individuals with permeable work boundaries would have less time work-family conflict but more strain-based family→work conflict. The strain component was thought to be so great it would impact both job and life satisfaction. As presented in Table 6, we found that employees with permeable work boundaries did have significantly less time based work-family conflict but there was not a significant difference for strain family→ work nor job and life satisfaction. Hypothesis 4a was supported but there was no support for Hypothesis 4b or c.

The final set of hypotheses dealt with the permeability of the home boundary. It was hypothesized (H5a) that having a permeable home boundary would decrease the time dimension of work-family conflict. Not only was this not the case, the opposite was significant. Those respondents who reported having a permeable home boundary also reported experiencing higher time-based work-family conflict. We also hypothesized (H5b) that having a permeable home boundary would increase the strain work → family conflict which was supported. As presented in Table 7, despite the increased time and strain work→ family conflict for those with a permeable home boundary, there was not a significant difference in their reported job or life satisfaction, thus there was no support for Hypothesis 5c.

Table 6. Differences in study variables based on work boundary permeability

	Work Boundary Permeable (n= 36)	Work Boundary Non-Permeable (n= 29)	
Time Based Work Family Conflict	2.35 (.65)	2.69 (.58)	**
Strain Family→Work Conflict	2.05 (.57)	1.96 (.58)	No sig diff
Job Satisfaction	3.67 (.80)	3.49 (.77)	No sig diff
Life Satisfaction	3.88 (.62)	3.67 (.80)	No sig diff

Mean (standard deviation)

* Significant at the .10 level; ** significant at the .05 level; *** significant at the, 01 level

Table 7. Differences in study variables based on home boundary permeability

	Home Boundary Permeable (n= 30)	Home Boundary Non-Permeable (n= 35)	
Time Based Work Family Conflict	2.80 (.59)	2.25 (.57)	***
Strain Work→Family Conflict	2.95 (.71)	2.55 (.71)	**
Job Satisfaction	3.62 (.87)	3.57 (.72)	No sig diff
Life Satisfaction	3.64 (.75)	3.91 (..66)	No sig diff

Mean (standard deviation)
* Significant at the .10 level; ** significant at the .05 level; *** significant at the, 01 level

This research posits that flexibility and permeability should be examined as distinct constructs. As summarized in Table 8, we found limited support for the proposed hypotheses. However, the hypotheses failed to address the various combinations of boundary flexibility and permeability. We found that respondents did report having flexible but not permeable boundaries and vice versa. In fact, of our 65 respondents, we had at least five in each of the eight combinations of flexible, work permeable and home permeable boundary category. ANOVA was used to examine whether there are differences in the three types of work family conflict over the eight boundary combinations. As presented in Table 9, there are significant differences. An examination of the three dimensions of work-family conflict based upon combinations of flexibility and work and home permeability doesn't point to a clear winner but does highlight a losing combination. Individuals who have an inflexible boundary but maintain both permeable work and home boundaries reported experiencing significantly more time-based work-family conflict and strain based family→work conflict. There was also bad news for individuals who have an inflexible boundary but maintain a permeable home boundary and non-permeable work boundary. They reported experiencing significantly more time-based work-family conflict and strain based work→ home conflict. When the home boundary is permeable and work is allowed to intrude, this appears to cause conflict. Conversely, those respondents who have the most separation between their work and home roles by having no flexibility and neither permeable work nor home boundaries, reported the lowest amount of strain work → home and home → work conflict.

ANOVA was also used to examine whether there are differences in job satisfaction and life satisfaction over the eight boundary combinations. The results are presented in Table 10. Despite the significant differences in the studied variants of work-family conflict, there is not a significant difference in the job or life satisfaction based on the eight combinations of flexible and permeable boundaries. Given the amount of prior research that has found such a strong negative impact of work family conflict

Table 8. Summary of hypotheses

	Result
H1: Respondents who have a flexible boundary will use one integrated calendar.	Not supported
H2a: Respondents who have flexible boundaries will have less time based work-family conflict than those who have inflexible boundaries.	Not supported
H2b: Respondents who have flexible boundaries will have less strain based work→ family work-family conflict than those who have inflexible boundaries.	Not supported
H2c: Respondents who have flexible boundaries will have less strain based family→ work-family conflict than those who have inflexible boundaries.	Not supported
H2d: Respondents who have flexible boundaries will have higher job and life satisfaction than those who have inflexible boundaries.	Partially supported Support for job satisfaction but not life satisfaction
H3: Respondents who have permeable boundaries will use one, integrated cell phone and email account.	Not supported
H4a: Respondents who have a permeable work boundary will have less time based work-family conflict than those who have a non-permeable work.	Supported
H4b: Respondents who have a permeable work boundary will have more strain based family→ work conflict than those who have a non-permeable work.	Not supported
H4c: Respondents who have a permeable work boundary will have lower job and life satisfaction than those who have a non-permeable work.	Not supported
H5a: Respondents who have a permeable home boundary will have less time based work-family conflict than those who have a non-permeable work.	Not supported The opposite was found. Permeable home boundary report significantly higher time based WFC
H5b: Respondents who have a permeable home boundary will have more strain based work→ family conflict than those who have a non-permeable work.	Supported
H5c: Respondents who have a permeable home boundary will have lower job and life satisfaction than those who have a non-permeable work.	Not supported

on satisfaction (Cloninger, Selvarajan, Singh and Huang, 2015; Frone, Russell & Cooper, 1992), this result was unexpected.

DISCUSSION

Like Kreiner, Hollensbe and Sheep (2009), the belief that the work-home boundary is a social construct that can be controlled and reshaped by the individual is the

Table 9. ANOVA results on work-family conflict differences based on flexible and permeable boundaries

	Time based Work-Family Conflict ***	Strain Work → Home Conflict **	Strain Home → Work Conflict **
Not Flexible Home – Not permeable Work – Not permeable (n=11)	2.33	2.20	1.79
Not Flexible Home – Not permeable Work – Permeable (n=12)	2.00	2.33	2.03
Not Flexible Home –Permeable Work - Not permeable (n=8)	2.98	3.33	2.13
Not Flexible Home – Permeable Work – Permeable (n=9)	3.13	2.78	2.75
Flexible Home – Not permeable Work – Permeable (n=5)	2.11	2.43	1.67
Flexible Home –Not permeable Work - Not permeable (n=8)	2.61	3.13	2.00
Flexible Home –Permeable Work - Not permeable (n=6)	2.83	3.03	1.91
Flexible, Home – Permeable Work – Permeable (n=6)	2.52	2.76	2.16

* Significant at the .10 level; ** significant at the .05 level; *** significant at the ,01 level
Lowest two are boxed and highest two are circled.

most appealing research question. Understanding boundary types and how their usage may contribute to the work and personal outcomes is the first step in helping employees consciously shape their boundaries to find the elusive work-life balance. While prior research has generally found flexibility to be positive but permeability to be negative, this research posits that flexibility, home boundary permeability and work boundary permeability are distinct constructs and should be examined as such. While few of our hypotheses were supported, this research does offer evidence that boundary flexibility and work/home permeability result in different experiences. Although flexibility did not seem to have an impact on the examined dimensions of work-family conflict or life satisfaction, the ability to have some control over when and where work is completed did result in higher job satisfaction.

The findings concerning boundary permeability were a bit surprising. As hypothesized, having a permeable work boundary was associated with less time based work-family conflict however having a permeable home boundary was associated with higher time based work-family. Addressing personal issues during work time allows individuals to balance their time demands however addressing

Table 10. ANOVA Results on Job and Life Satisfaction Based on Boundaries

	Job Satisfaction	Life Satisfaction
Not Flexible, Home – Not permeable Work – Not permeable (N=11)	3.92	3.88
Not Flexible, Home – Not permeable Work – Permeable (N=12)	3.67	4.11
Not Flexible, Home – Permeable Work - Not permeable (N=8)	3.58	3.50
Not Flexible, Home – Permeable Work – Permeable (N=9)	3.96	3.67
Flexible, Home – Not permeable Work – Permeable (N=5)	3.53	3.70
Flexible, Home –Not permeable Work - Not permeable (N=8)	3.42	3.65
Flexible, Home – Permeable Work - Not permeable (N=6)	3.17	3.33
Flexible, Home – Permeable Work – Permeable (N=6)	3.00	4.22

work issues during personal time contributed to more time stress. Similarly, a permeable work boundary did not contribute to more strain based family→work conflict but a permeable home boundary did contribute to more strain based work→ conflict. It appears that the greater source of stress comes from permeability of the home boundary. It should be noted that we examined whether boundaries were permeable but did not measure the frequency or intensity of non-role interference. It is possible that personal interferences during work time, such as a call with a teacher, were less frequent or required less time than the type of work interferences during personal time. In addition to examining work and home boundary permeability as separate constructs, future research should examine the frequency and intensity of the intervening activity.

Although the sample was small, we were able to examine differences in the eight combinations of flexibility, work permeability and home permeability boundaries. Those respondents with inflexible and both permeable work and home boundaries reported experiencing the highest time and strain home→work conflict. Those respondents who resist the boundary breeching offered by mobile technology and have neither flexibility nor permeability in their home and work boundary reported some of the lowest strain-based work→family and family→work conflict.

While this research offers evidence that flexibility and work/home permeable boundaries result in different outcomes, the limited sample size negated more in-depth analysis regarding boundary configurations. Surprisingly, technology use in the form of number of cell phones, email accounts and calendars did not vary by flexible or permeable boundary. Future research should examine the actual technology usage and the technology fit of individuals with these boundary configurations. In addition to replicating this research with a larger sample, researchers may also want to incorporate the extent to which an individual's particular boundary fits their boundary preference. While an employee may prefer work-home segmentation, their job, supervisor or organizational culture may demand a level of integration, which may contribute to negative outcomes. Other researchers have addressed boundary fit (Adkins & Premeaux, 2014; Daniel & Sonnentag, 2016; Derks, Bakker, Peters & van Wingerden, 2016; Kreiner et al. 2009; Piszczek, 2017) but have not used the expanded boundary constructs suggested in this research. Future research should address boundary fit and the impact on work and personal outcomes.

This research suggests that future work on work-home boundaries should incorporate both the permeability of the home and work boundary as a separate construct from flexibility. Permeability can also be further refined. Integrating work and home can be in the form of multi-tasking (handling tasks simultaneously) or time fragmentation (switching between tasks) (Powell & Craig, 2015) and theses forms may contribute to different stress outcomes for different individuals.

While this study and the vast majority of the boundary research has focused on the individual, there are also organizational, legislative and regulatory dimensions to the work-home interface (Piszczek & Berg, 2014). While employees may have preferences for boundary controls, their role, organization, supervisor and/or customers may have different expectations. While practitioners have given flexibility attention, the organizational perspective on permeable boundaries has not been examined. Whether through policy, cultural norms or training, organizations have the potential to help individuals use technology in a way that helps them balance work and personal responsibilities.

Mobile technology has changed the way we work and live. By eliminating temporal and physical boundaries, it is up to employees to manage their own psychological boundaries. This exploratory research offers a new work-home boundary framework. Unlike prior research, we need to think of both flexibility and permeability in our boundaries and recognize that permeability may vary for work and home. Although there were limited differences in the demographics of professionals with different boundary types, there were significant differences in their work-family conflict. Understanding and consciously choosing to right boundary configuration is a critical area of inquiry in a mobile world. The eight configurations of flexibility and work/home permeability identified in this paper should help direct future research and our continuing quest for work-life balance.

REFERENCES

Ashford, B., Kreiner, G., & Fugate, M. (2000). All in a Day's Work: Boundaries and Micro Role Transitions. *Academy of Management Review*, *25*(3), 472–491.

Boswell, W. R., & Olson-Buchanan, J. B. (2007). The Use of Communication Technologies After Hours: The Role of Work Attitudes and Work-Life Conflict. *Journal of Management*, *33*(4), 592–610. doi:10.1177/0149206307302552

Bulger, C. A., Matthews, R. A., & Hoffman, M. E. (2007). Work and Personal Life Boundary Management: Boundary Strength, Work/Personal Life Balance, and the Segmentation-Integration Continuum. *Jounral of Occupational Health Pscyhology*, *12*(4), 365–375. doi:10.1037/1076-8998.12.4.365 PMID:17953495

Carlson, D. S., Grzywacz, J. G., & Kacmar, K. M. (2010). The Relationship of Schedule Flexibility and Outcomes via the Work-Family Interface. *Journal of Managerial Psychology*, *25*(4), 330–355. doi:10.1108/02683941011035278

Cloninger, P. A., Selvarajan, T. T., Singh, B., & Huang, S. (2015). The Mediating Influence of Work-Family Conflict and the Moderating Influence of Gender on Employee Outcomes. *International Journal of Human Resource Management*, *26*(8), 2269–2287. doi:10.1080/09585192.2015.1004101

Cousins, K., & Robey, D. (2015). Managing Work-Life Boundaries with Mobile Technologies. *Information Technology & People*, *28*(1), 34–71. doi:10.1108/ITP-08-2013-0155

Daniel, S., & Sonnetag, S. (2015). Crossing the Borders: The Relationship Between Boundary Management, Work-Family Enrichment and Job Satisfaction. *International Journal of Human Resource Management*, *27*(4), 407–426. doi:10.1080/09585192.2015.1020826

Den-Nagy, I. (2014). A Double Edged Sword? A Critical Evaluation of the Mobile Phone in Creating Work-Life Balance. *New Technology, Work and Employment*, *29*(2), 193–211. doi:10.1111/ntwe.12031

Derks, D., Bakker, A. B., Peters, P., & van Wingerden, P. (2016). Work-Related Smartphone Use, Work-Family Conflict and Family Role Performance: The Role of Segmentation Preference. *Human Relations*, *69*(5), 1045–1068. doi:10.1177/0018726715601890

Desrochers, S., Hilton, J. M., & Larwood, L. (2005). Preliminary Validation of the Work-Family Integration-Blurring Scale. *Journal of Family Issues*, *26*(4), 442–466. doi:10.1177/0192513X04272438

Diaz, I., Chiaburu, D. S., Zimmerman, R. D., & Boswell, W. R. (2012). Communication Technology: Pros and Cons of Constant Connections to Work. *Journal of Vocational Behavior*, *80*(2), 500–508. doi:10.1016/j.jvb.2011.08.007

Eagle, B. W., Icenogle, M. L., Maes, J. D., & Miles, E. W. (1998). The Importance of Employee Demographic Profiles for Understanding Experiences of Work-Family Interrole Conflicts. *The Journal of Social Psychology*, *138*(6), 690–709. doi:10.1080/00224549809603255 PMID:9872064

Friedman, S., & Greenhaus, J. (2000). *Work and Family - Allies or Enemies?: What Happens When Business Professionals Confront Life Choices*. Oxford University Press. doi:10.1093/acprof:oso/9780195112757.001.0001

Friedman, S., & Westring, A. (2015). Empowering Individuals to Integrate Work and Life: Insights for Management Development. *Journal of Management Development*, *34*(3), 299–315. doi:10.1108/JMD-11-2012-0144

Frone, M. R., Russell, M., & Cooper, M. L. (1992). Antecedents and Outcomes of Work-Family Conflict: Testing a Model of the Work-Family Interface. *The Journal of Applied Psychology*, *77*(1), 65–78. doi:10.1037/0021-9010.77.1.65 PMID:1556042

Golden, A. G., & Geisler, C. (2007). Work-Life Boundary Management and the Personal Digital Assistant. *Human Relations*, *60*(3), 519–551. doi:10.1177/0018726707076698

Greenhaus, J., & Beutell, N. (1985). Sources of Conflict Between Work and Family Roles. *Academy of Management Review*, *10*(1), 76–89.

Greenhaus, J., & Powell, G. (1985). When Work and Family are Allies: A Theory of Work-Family Enrichments. *Academy of Management Review*, *31*(1), 72–92. doi:10.5465/AMR.2006.19379625

Hackman, J., & Oldham, G. (1975). Development of the Job Diagnostic Survey. *The Journal of Applied Psychology*, *60*(2), 159–170. doi:10.1037/h0076546

Hecht, T. D., & Allen, N. J. (2009). A Longitudinal Examination of the Work-Nonwork Boundary Strength Construct. *Journal of Organizational Behavior, 30*(7), 839–862. doi:10.1002/job.579

Judge, T., Boudreau, J., & Bretz, R. (1994). Job and Life Attitudes of Male Executives. *The Journal of Applied Psychology, 79*(5), 767–782. doi:10.1037/0021-9010.79.5.767 PMID:7989277

Kasper, H., Meyer, M., & Schmidt, A. (2005). Mangers Dealing with Work-Family Conflict: An Exploratory Analysis. *Journal of Managerial Psychology, 20*(5), 440–461. doi:10.1108/02683940510602978

Kattenbach, R., Demerouti, E., & Nachreiner, F. (2010). Flexible Working Times: Effects on Employees' Exhaustion, Work-Nonwork Conflict and Job Performance. *Career Development International, 15*(3), 279–295. doi:10.1108/13620431011053749

Koay, K., Soh, P., & Chew, K. (2017). Do Employees' Private Demands Lead to Cyberloafing? The Mediating Role of Job Stress. *Management Research Review, 40*(9), 1025–1038. doi:10.1108/MRR-11-2016-0252

Kopelman, R., Greenhaus, J., & Connoly, T. (1983). A Model of Work, Family and Interrole Conflict: A Construct Validation Study. *Organizational Behavior and Human Performance, 32*(2), 198–215. doi:10.1016/0030-5073(83)90147-2

Kossek, E. E., Ruderman, M. N., Braddy, P. W., & Hannum, K. M. (2012). Work-Nonwork Boundary Management Profiles: A Person-Centered Approach. *Journal of Vocational Behavior, 81*(1), 112–128. doi:10.1016/j.jvb.2012.04.003

Kreiner, G., Hollensbe, E., & Shee, M. (2009). Balancing Borders and Bridges: Negotiating the Work-Home Interface via Boundary Work Tactics. *Academy of Management Journal, 52*(4), 704–730. doi:10.5465/AMJ.2009.43669916

McCloskey, D. (2016). Finding Work-Life Balance in a Digital Age: An Exploratory Study of Boundary Flexibility and Permeability. *Information Resources Management Journal, 29*(3), 53–70. doi:10.4018/IRMJ.2016070104

Methot, J. R., & LePine, J. A. (2016). Too Close for Comfort? Investigating the Nature and Functioning of Work and Non-Work Role Segmentation Preferences. *Journal of Business and Psychology, 31*(1), 103–123. doi:10.100710869-015-9402-0

Netemeyer, R. G., Boles, J. S., & McMurrian, R. (1995). Development and Validation of Work-Family Conflict and Family-Work Conflict Scales. *The Journal of Applied Psychology, 81*(4), 400–410. doi:10.1037/0021-9010.81.4.400

Olson-Buchanan, J. B., & Boswell, W. R. (2006). Blurring Boundaries: Correlates of Integration and Segmentation Between Work and Nonwork. *Journal of Vocational Behavior*, *68*(3), 432–445. doi:10.1016/j.jvb.2005.10.006

Piszczek, M. (2017). Boundary Control and Controlled Boundaries: Organizational Expectations for Technology Use at the Work-Family Interface. *Journal of Organizational Behavior*, *38*(4), 592–611. doi:10.1002/job.2153

Piszczek, M., & Berg, P. (2014). Expanding the Boundaries of Boundary Theory: Regulative Institutions and Work-Family Role Management. *Human Relations*, *67*(12), 1491–1512. doi:10.1177/0018726714524241

Porter, S., & Ayman, R. (2010). Work Flexibility as a Mediator of the Relationship Between Work-Family Conflict and Intention to Quit. *Journal of Management & Organization*, *16*(3), 411–424.

Powell, A., & Craig, L. (2015). Gender Differences in Working at Home and Time Use Patterns: Evidence from Australia. *Work, Employment and Society*, *29*(4), 571–589. doi:10.1177/0950017014568140

Tremblay, D.-G., & Genin, E. (2008). Permeability between Work and Non-Work: The Case of Self-Employed IT Workers. *Canadian Journal of Communication*, *33*(4), 701–720. doi:10.22230/cjc.2008v33n4a1994

Zheng, C., Molineux, J., Mirshekary, S., & Scarparo, S. (2015). Developing Individual and Organisational Work-Life Balance Strategies to Improve Employee Health and Wellbeing. *Employee Relations*, *37*(3), 354–379. doi:10.1108/ER-10-2013-0142

Chapter 2
Twenty-First Century Issues Impacting Turnover of IT Professionals:
From Burnout and Turnover to Workplace Wellbeing

Valerie Ford
ISP Global Communications LLC, USA

Susan Swayze
The George Washington University, USA

ABSTRACT

Identifying the precursors of turnover has been the subject of examination for the past four decades. IT professionals are a critical group of employees in the current knowledge-driven economy, and as such, they experience unique job stressors. This chapter explores recent research on the organizational stressors that influence IT turnover intentions. The goal is to provide insights on how organizations can begin to stem burnout, turnover intentions, and eventual turnover while improving work-related wellbeing. A revised model of work-related wellbeing is also presented in this chapter. Another objective is to discuss current issues in the IT domain and provide new research directions. New research for the IT turnover literature will provide information to scholars and practitioners on how they might improve and alleviate the impact of turnover on organizations.

DOI: 10.4018/978-1-5225-5829-3.ch002

INTRODUCTION

Identifying the precursors of turnover has been the subject of examination and study for the past four decades (Dinger, Thatcher, Stepina, & Craig, 2012; Joseph & Ang, 2003; Joseph, Ng, Koh, & Ang, 2007). Historically, researchers who study employee withdrawal in the form of turnover viewed two variables as key to understanding why employees voluntarily leave organizations: job satisfaction and perceived job alternatives (Hulin, Roznowski, & Hachiya, 1985). Over the last 30 years, however, considerable research has been devoted to developing predictive models of voluntary turnover, with job satisfaction, organizational commitment, and intention to quit among the most commonly proposed reasons for dissatisfaction (Ferratt, Agarwal, Brown, & Moore, 2005; Maier, Laumer, & Echardt, 2015; Moore, 2000a; Weinert, Maier, Laumer, & Weitzel, 2015).

Information Technology (IT) professionals are a critical group of employees in the current knowledge driven economy and as such, they experience unique job stressors (Weinert, et al., 2015). Stressors are stimuli or actions encountered by an individual at work. Stressors might trigger an individual to produce different responses in the form of strain that lead to burnout (Weinert et al., 2015). There is a difference between IT professionals and knowledge workers. Information technology professionals are workers in a technology services organization (Burrell, 2014). They are in occupations that include computer programmers, systems analysts, database administrators, information security, computer support specialists, application developers, network administrators, and team members who support and maintain computer systems, other technology and related activities (Burrell, 2014; Dixon, 2016).

Recent studies have shown that the IT professional's environment – knowledge oriented work and around-the-clock service is prone to creating job stress (Chen & Karahanna, 2014; Shih, Jiang, Klein, & Wang, 2011). Additionally, as organizations continue to ask more from their IT employees (e.g. increased workload), turnover intention and job burnout also are increasing (Zaza & Armstrong, 2016). Job burnout is an extreme or advanced form of job stress and has been recognized as an occupational hazard (Maslach & Leiter, 2016). Job burnout is important to researchers and practitioners because of its association with critical psychological and behavioral outcomes, including productivity, withdrawal, turnover, and employee well-being (Maslach & Goldberg, 1998; Maslach, Schaufeli, & Leiter, 2001; Weinert, et al., 2015). Job burnout has been identified as one of the main consequences of job stress (Maslach & Leiter, 2016; Maslach, et al., 2001).

BACKGROUND

In this chapter, the authors seek to explore previous research and the most recent findings on the organizational stressors that influence the turnover intentions of IT professionals. The goal is to provide insights on how organizations can begin to stem burnout, turnover intentions and eventual turnover. Another important objective of this chapter is to provide new research directions that have not been investigated yet or have been explored less. New research for the IT turnover literature will provide information to researchers on how they might improve and alleviate the impact of turnover amongst staff.

To this end, this chapter will:

- Use previous research by the authors as the foundation upon which to explore new research directions associated with the antecedents of turnover and turnover intentions of IT professionals, such as burnout, work exhaustion and engagement.
- Make recommendations about what organizations can do to reduce stressors in the IT environment, and therefore reduce the likelihood of turnover.
- Discuss how the IT work environment and workers are changing.
- Identify retention strategies that practitioners can use to help prevent turnover as they try to remain competitive in an ever-changing, global environment.

Research presented in this chapter will contribute to scholarship and organizations by providing practical approaches that organizational leaders can use to retain IT professionals. Turnover intention and turnover is complicated, so organizations should avoid developing and implementing retention strategies without taking the time to understand the factors that influence IT employees' intentions to quit (Abii, Ogula, & Rose, 2013; Ferratt, et al., 2005).

RELEVANT QUANTITATIVE STUDY

In the article *An Exploratory Investigation of the Relationship between Disengagement, Exhaustion and Turnover Intentions Among University IT Professionals* (Ford, 2012; Ford, Swayze, & Burley, 2012), the researchers conducted a quantitative study to examine the relationship between these concepts by proposing the following research question: *To what extent is there a statistically significant relationship between disengagement, work exhaustion and turnover intentions among IT professionals in a single higher education institution in a major metropolitan area?* The researchers adapted the Job Demands-Resources (JD-R) Model of Burnout to use as the theoretical lens through which to explore work exhaustion, disengagement and how they influence turnover intentions among the selected population.

Their study and the associated outcomes and recommendations, provided insights into the unique work environment of university IT professionals and how workplace characteristics predict disengagement, work exhaustion and subsequent thoughts about quitting. Additionally, this study discussed engagement as one of the hot topics in the practitioner community. Engagement is of interest because of its perceived link to critical business outcomes like productivity, retention, loyalty and well-being (Bakker, Hakanen, Demerouti, & Xanthopoulou, 2007). Further, engagement is thought to be one of the ways that organizations can forge a path to competitive advantage (Schneider, Macey, Barbera, Young, & Lee, 2006).

Conceptual Framework

In their previous study, the authors adapted the Job Demands-Resources (JD-R) Model of Burnout as a framework to further understand work exhaustion, disengagement and their relationship to the turnover intentions of university IT professionals (Demerouti, Bakker, Nachreiner, & Schaufeli, 2001). In their quantitative study, the authors asserted that the notion of job burnout is too complex to be studied as a single entity and therefore should be deconstructed into its primary components (Ford, et al., 2012). In the literature, one theory suggests that collective burnout is comprised of two major concepts: work exhaustion and disengagement (Demerouti, et al., 2001). Schaufeli and Bakker (2004), with a sample of nearly 1,700 workers in four different occupational groups found support for the two-dimensional model with the notion that disengagement was related to job resources. However, Schaufeli and Bakker found that both demands and resources were related to work exhaustion.

Specifically, the JD-R model was recreated as depicted in Figure 1 to focus on disengagement and work exhaustion. Further, the antecedents of disengagement and exhaustion were removed from the model.

A Review of the Research on Turnover and Turnover Intentions of IT Professionals

Although researchers and managers have long explored why people leave their jobs and why they stay, there is not a complete understanding of the problem. Researchers want to ideally understand turnover behavior, but in reality, it is difficult to empirically investigate actual turnover. At the time that an employee leaves an organization it is too late to intervene, prevent or understand how they reached their decision. As a result, researchers study existing employees and ask them about their intentions to leave (Lacity, Iyer, & Rudramuniyaiah, 2008). For this reason, many studies make

Figure 1. Revised model of Burnout and Turnover Intentions

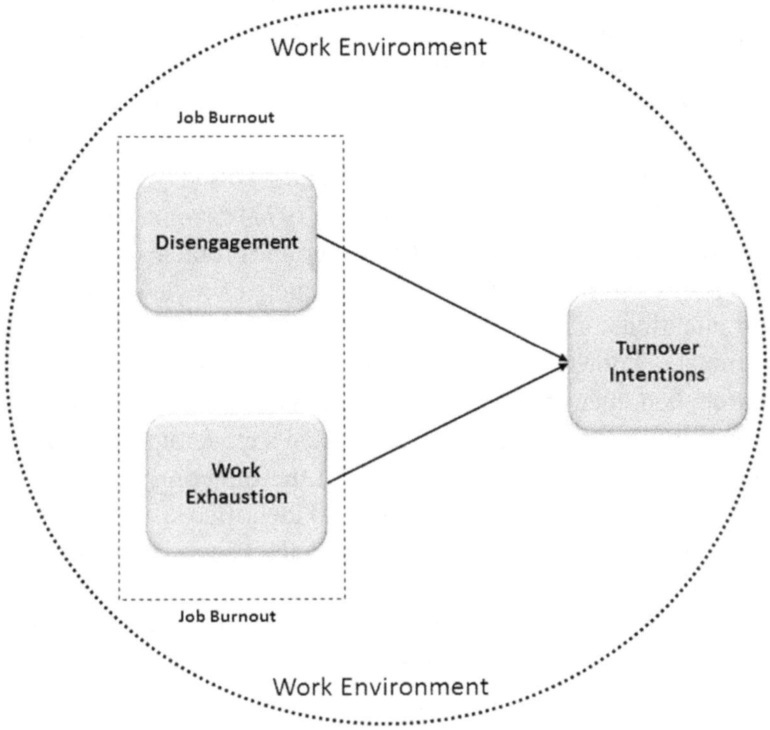

the assumption that the intention to leave is both a proxy for and predictor of actual turnover behavior (Cohen, Blake, & Goodman, 2016).

Turnover intention refers to an employee's deliberate and conscious intention to look for a new job or to voluntarily leave a current job (Joseph, et al., 2007). On the other hand, turnover is defined as the individual movement across the membership boundary of an organization and is said to occur when an employee voluntarily leaves an organization (Thwala, Ajagbe, Long, Bilau, & Enegbuma, 2012).

The notion of focusing on intentions rather than behavior is rooted in Ajzen's Theory of Planned Behavior (Ajzen, 1991), one of the best empirically supported theories of motivation. In short, this theory focuses on behavioral intentions to understand the link between attitudes and behavior. According to this theory, intention is the cognitive representation of a person's readiness to perform a specific behavior, and is considered to be the immediate precursor of behavior (Ajzen, 1991). Empirical results from turnover studies have supported the assertions that turnover intention is a stronger predictor of actual turnover compared to other antecedents like job satisfaction (Joseph & Ang, 2003).

Turnover has been a problem for the IT workforce since the early days of computing (Chang, 2010). In fact, turnover and retention of skilled IT professionals are still major issues for employers and recruiters of the IT workforce (Zaza & Armstrong, 2016). Since the beginning of the recording of statistics, the turnover of these professionals has been characterized as problematic and has been reported consistently over at least the past 40 years (Chang, 2010). One of the first reviews of IT turnover intentions was completed in the late 1970s (Willoughby, 1977; Zaza & Armstrong, 2016). In his review, Willoughby (1977) examined turnover statistics for IT professionals and concluded that it was a chronic problem (Willoughby, 1977).

Three decades later, Joseph et al. (2007) conducted a review of the literature on the turnover intentions of IT professionals from 1985-2005 to "review and reflect on our accumulated knowledge on IT turnover" and "enhance our understanding of the IT turnover phenomenon" (p. 548). In addition to exploring the direct effects on turnover intentions, Joseph et al. (2007) conducted a moderator analysis to identify possible sources of variation that could affect the direction and extent of these relationships. In their review, Joseph et al. (2007) identified six categories of factors that influence turnover intention for IT professionals. They are: desire to move (e.g., affective organizational commitment, job satisfaction), ease of movement (e.g., perceived job alternatives), job search, demographics (e.g., age, gender), human capital (e.g., organizational tenure), job-related factors (e.g., work exhaustion), and perceived organizational factors (e.g., fairness of rewards).

During the ten years since Joseph et al's (2007) meta-analysis, more than 35 new studies have been published on turnover intentions within the IT field (Zaza & Armstrong, 2016). But the research continues to identify a fragmented set of antecedents. Furthermore, many of the studies have produced inconsistent findings. For example, McKnight et al. (2009) found that work exhaustion did not predict turnover intention, whereas Shih et al. (2011) found that work exhaustion positively influenced turnover intention. Despite the number of studies on turnover intentions in the IT field within the last ten years, there has been only one attempt (beyond the Joseph et al. (2007) study) to analyze the accumulated data (Zaza & Armstrong, 2016). What is clear is that although the research has identified many important pieces in the turnover intentions puzzle as it relates to IT professionals, there is still more work to do to understand how these pieces fit together.

CHANGES IN THE INFORMATION TECHNOLOGY WORKFORCE

Despite the numerous studies on the topic of IT employee turnover and recommendations to organizations on how to retain employees, the general turnover trend for IT professionals remains high (Lo, 2015). During economic downturns, turnover rates naturally decline, but the overall turnover trend for IT professionals has not declined (Lo, 2015). In fact, recent projections show that the computer systems and related services industry will grow by nearly 4% each year through 2020, placing information technology among the fastest growing industries (Henderson, 2012). With projections like these, the demand for qualified candidates will increase. But at the same time, student enrollment in IT-related programs has declined (Lo, 2015). This finding further intensifies the need for organizations to retain qualified and skilled IT professionals.

Living in an Ubiquitous World

Cybersecurity, hackers, around the clock access, and 24x7 data centers are indications of an ever-changing landscape for IT professionals. Furthermore, globalization, outsourcing, and increasing competition, puts IT employees under growing pressure to meet deadlines and reduce response time to customer requests (Syrek, Apostel, & Antoni, 2013). Moreover, ubiquitous and rapidly evolving mobile technologies such as smart phones and tablets (and increasingly wearable mobile devices such as wrist technologies) allow people to work any time, anywhere, and on any task (Reyt & Weisenfeld, 2015). Therefore, people work all the time, everywhere, and on everything (Chen & Karahanna, 2014; Reyt & Weisenfeld, 2015; Syrek, et al., 2013). In short, technology is having the effect of diminishing time and space, rendering the lines between work demands and personal life increasingly integrated, decontextualized, and overlapping (Chen & Karahanna, 2014; Reyt & Weisenfeld, 2015).

IT professionals are likely to experience the pressures of around the clock access more acutely as advances in the connectedness of technology have blurred the boundaries between work and personal life. While the majority of knowledge workers use technology as a way to enable them to be more connected to their work, IT professionals are responsible for creating and supporting the technology that enables the ubiquitous any time, any place mentality that exists in today's society and globally connected world (Chen & Karahanna, 2014). These demands for connectedness may lead to IT employees experiencing increased job burnout, higher turnover intentions and may eventually lead to turnover.

Fear of Becoming Obsolete

Another factor leading to increased job stress among IT professionals is the fear of becoming replaceable (Van Heerden, 2015). Due to changes and advances in technology, the competencies and skills required of IT professionals is always changing. In contrast to the past, today's environment is perceived as the knowledge era where intellectual capital drives an organization's competitive edge (Syrek, et al., 2013). Many of the new generation jobs are more technologically advanced and require employees who can perform these tasks with higher demand and to perform more and varied tasks in parallel thus requiring transitory or disparate skill sets, knowledge and experience. (Van Heerden, 2015).

Information technology workers have an intense desire to keep pace with the latest technology to avoid becoming obsolete (Dixon, 2016). Falling behind technologically could easily result in reduced company marketability, the fear of the company outsourcing the function, and laying off the employee without the skill set needed to acquire another position within the IT field (Dixon, 2016). IT employees must continually learn new skills over their entire career in order to adapt to new technological development and ever changing business requirements (Dixon, 2016; Van Heerden, 2015). The sheer volume of learning required can increase work exhaustion, with a negative effect on turnover (Dixon, 2016). To retain these employees and sustain their competitiveness, organizations should design jobs to create greater autonomy over the pace and process in the hands of IT workers and to offer additional and ongoing training, education, exploration of new and future technologies in preparation for future goals and objectives (Dixon, 2016).

Retention of skilled information technology professionals is becoming increasingly important as technology is introduced into nearly every functional aspect of organizations (Burrell, 2014). Given the growing impact of technology on organizational financial and operational success, organizations depend on technology and the technical and business knowledge of IT professionals to remain competitive (Dixon, 2016; Weinert, et al., 2015). In this context, employee turnover can be a costly problem for organizations. When employees leave, organizations have to attend to the high cost of training and development, burnout of existing staff, and decreased quality of products and services due to the shortage and/or inexperience of staff (Burrell, 2014).

Around the clock access, technological uncertainty and the demands that they create for IT workers is an interesting area for future research. While, around the clock access and technological uncertainty are key stressors in the IT environment, an aging IT workforce is another factor that is contributing to the turnover of IT professionals.

An Aging IT Workforce and the Threat of Lost Knowledge

As a result of the post WWII baby boom, a large number of employees are retiring from the workforce (Van Heerden, 2015). For the information technology sector, this creates a unique issue because as these individuals retire, the knowledge that they take with them creates a void among the remaining employees. This is especially true for long-tenured employees because they create a constraint for the organization by limiting the ability to replace the employee knowledge when they leave (Shumaker, Ward, Petter, & Riley, 2017).

This problem is more serious than it seems because these retiring workers are taking with them knowledge essential to the organization that cannot easily be replaced on the open market. They take with them knowledge that can only be developed internally over a long period of time (Shumaker, et al., 2017). This knowledge is deep, contextual knowledge related to embedded business processes and how information systems are integrated (Van Heerden, 2015). Also included in this knowledge is understanding where knowledge resides within the organization and how to access it (Van Heerden, 2015). Many organizations are not prepared for the loss of this deep knowledge when these IT professionals leave the organization. Because of the aging IT workforce, retention of IT workers is even more critical.

An aging IT workforce simply means that not all turnover can be prevented. The best that organizations can do in this case is to prepare for the departure of key employees by creating succession plans for transferring knowledge and identifying critical skills. In addition, organizational leaders should create a systematic approach to identify which knowledge is most critical and where to focus their energy if several employees are nearing retirement (Shumaker, et al., 2017).

Unfortunately there is a dearth of research on age-related issues in the IT workforce (Shumaker, et al., 2017). Organizations should seek to understand the nature of potential knowledge loss as it relates to retiring employees. This is a consideration for future research.

JOB BURNOUT, WORK EXHAUSTION, TURNOVER, AND TURNOVER INTENTIONS

Previous literature demonstrates that burnout has an impact on the turnover intentions of IT professionals (Moore, 2000a; Weinert, et al., 2015). For example, research in the management and IT literature assert that turnover and turnover intentions can be an outcome of organizational factors such as, workload, time pressure and leadership, along with other antecedents that are specific to the IT profession, such as boundary spanning activities, IT (or professional) tenure, professional obsolescence, professional commitment and workplace characteristics (Demerouti, 2015; McKnight, et al., 2009; Syrek, et al., 2013). In fact, investigators claim that there are many other unmeasured variables that may be present in the IT environment to explain the phenomenon (Joseph & Ang, 2003; Lo, 2015).

Most studies on turnover and turnover intentions make explicit the causal theorizing that has always been implicit in the turnover research. Certain factors (both individual and situational) cause people to think about leaving or actually leaving their jobs (Joseph, et al., 2007; Zaza & Armstrong, 2016). Recent research therefore focuses on understanding these turnover intentions and as a result attempts to provide organizations with details for implementing successful employee retention actions (Weinert, et al., 2015). In this context, several investigations focus on work exhaustion as a source of turnover intention and acknowledge that IT professionals have a high degree of burnout, and accordingly a high degree of intention to quit their jobs (Armstrong & Riemenschneider, 2011; Moore, 2000a; Weinert, et al., 2015). The next section examines burnout and how it influences the turnover intentions and eventual turnover of IT professionals.

A Review of the Literature on Burnout

The IT research literature suggests that information technology professionals are especially vulnerable to burnout (Kalimo & Toppinen, 1995; Maier, et al., 2015; McGee, 1996; Moore, 2000a; Van den Broek, et al., 2017; Van Heerden, 2015; Weinert, et al., 2015). Burnout is a particularly tragic endpoint for professionals who entered the job with positive expectations and enthusiasm. Burnout is defined as a reaction to chronic job stress that is characterized by exhaustion and mental distancing or disengagement (Maslach & Leiter, 2016; Schaufeli, Leiter, & Maslach, 2009). Employees experiencing burnout lose the capacity to provide the intense contributions that make an impact at work (Schaufeli, Bakker, & Van Rhenen, 2009; Schaufeli, Leiter, et al., 2009). Further, research has linked job burnout to a plethora of ailments, including depression, physiological problems and family difficulties (Cropanzano, Rupp, & Byrne, 2003; Maslach & Leiter, 2016). Accordingly, IT research has begun to link job burnout to turnover intentions and eventual turnover (Kim & Wright, 2007; Moore, 2000a; Weinert, et al., 2015).

Burnout Definition and Attributes

The term burnout was first coined in the 1970s by Freudenberger to describe the gradual emotional depletion and loss of motivation he observed among people who had volunteered to work for aid organizations (Bakker, Demerouti, & Sanz-Vergel, 2014; Freudenberger, 1974). The volunteers had worked with dedication and enthusiasm for a period of time before the onset of these symptoms. On the basis of his observations, Freudenberger (1974) defined burnout as "a state of mental and physical exhaustion caused by one's professional life." Thus, individuals who burn out from their work deplete their energetic resources and lose their dedication to work.

At the same time, Maslach (2001) and her collaborators interviewed human-services workers to find out how they were coping with client-related stressors

(Maslach & Jackson, 1981). The human-services workers used the term burnout and indicated that they experienced feelings of exhaustion. They had developed negative attitudes toward their clients, and frequently felt that they lacked the professional competence needed to help their clients (Schaufeli, Bakker, et al., 2009). As an outcome of the interviews, Maslach and Jackson (1981) defined burnout as a syndrome characterized by emotional exhaustion, depersonalization, and a lack of personal accomplishment.

Emotional exhaustion refers to feelings of being emotionally drained by contact with other people, and it is the main strain dimension of burnout. Depersonalization refers to a negative or excessively detached or disengaged response toward the people who are the recipients of one's service or care. Finally, reduced personal accomplishment refers to a decline in one's feelings of competence and successful achievement at work (Maslach & Jackson, 1981; Maslach & Leiter, 2008).

Although research has confirmed that burnout is a slow process of progressive loss of energy and enthusiasm (Alarcon, 2011; Demerouti & Bakker, 2008; Maslach & Leiter, 2008; Maslach & Leiter, 2016), the notion that burnout is exclusively found in the human-services area has been rejected, and researchers now have adapted these first conceptualizations of burnout to make it applicable to workers in various occupations, including information technology (Demerouti & Bakker, 2008; Ferratt, et al., 2005; Moore, 2000a, 2000b; Weinert, et al., 2015).

The burnout models discussed in this chapter are shown in Table 1.

Table 1. Burnout Models

Burnout Model Name	Model Description
Conservation of Resources	The conservation of resources (COR) model of burnout proposes that stress and burnout occur when workers perceive a threat to that which they value (resources) (Hobfoll, 2002). That threat may come from work-related demands, the loss of work-related resources (such as unemployment) or the insufficient return of resources following an investment of resources.
Areas of Worklife	This model frames job stressors in terms of person-job imbalances and identifies six areas in which these imbalances take place. The areas are: workload, control, reward, community, fairness and values (Leiter & Maslach, 1999).
Maslach's Three-Dimensional Model of Burnout	This burnout model contends that the three key dimensions of burnout are emotional exhaustion, depersonalization, and reduced personal accomplishment (Maslach, 1982).
Job Demands-Resources	This process model of burnout asserts that burnout occurs when individuals experience incessant job demands and have inadequate resources available to address and reduce demands (Demerouti et al. (2001).

Discussion of the Burnout Models

More recently conceptual models have expanded on theories about job stress, and the notion of imbalances leading to strain. Two developmental models of the demands-resources imbalance are the JD-R model and the Conservation of Resources (COR) model (Halbesleben & Buckley, 2004). The JD-R model focuses on the idea that burnout arises when individuals experience incessant job demands and have inadequate resources available to address and to reduce those demands.

Conservation of Resources Model of Burnout

The conservation of resources (COR) model of burnout follows a basic motivational theory assuming that burnout arises as a result of persistent threats to available resources (Demerouti et al., 2001). When individuals perceive that the resources they value are threatened, they strive to maintain those resources. The loss of resources or even the impending loss of resources may aggravate burnout. The COR model of burnout proposes that stress and burnout occur when workers perceive a threat to that which they value (resources) (Hobfoll, 2002). That threat may come from work-related demands, the loss of work-related resources (such as unemployment) or the insufficient return of resources following an investment of resources (for example, if an employee spends a great deal of time assisting a coworker without any return favor from that coworker). The initial threat to resources is seen as a stressor; however the continued loss or threat to resources, particularly after a great deal of resource investment in work, is said to lead to burnout (Halbesleben & Buckley, 2004; Hobfoll, 1989, 2002). In this way, the COR model extends beyond the notion of stress to increase understanding of how chronic stress develops into burnout (Halbesleben & Buckley, 2004).

A variety of other studies have used the COR framework and found empirical support for the model (Brotheridge & Lee, 2002; Halbesleben & Demerouti, 2005). For example, Halbesleben and Bowler's (2007) study highlights an important strength of the COR model. By specifying the process underlying the investment of resources (that is, when resources become depleted, workers are more careful about the investment of those resources), the COR model provides insights into how burnout leads to such consequences as lower job performance and decreased organizational commitment (Halbesleben & Demerouti, 2005). Grandey and Cropanzano (1999) are among the first researchers to expand COR beyond work roles to examine work-family conflict (WFC). COR theory proposes that "inter-role conflict leads to stress because resources are lost in the process of juggling both work and family roles" (Hobfoll, 1989, p. 352). Moreover, COR allows for predictions about the moderating relationship of individual differences (e.g., self-esteem, positive affectivity, internal and locus of control), which may be viewed as resources. Another study that built on the COR model of burnout is the Areas of Worklife model of burnout.

Areas of Worklife Model of Burnout

A different variation of an imbalance model of burnout is the Areas of Worklife (AW) model, which frames job stressors in terms of person-job imbalances, or mismatches, and identifies six key areas in which these imbalances take place: workload, control, reward, community, fairness, and values (Maslach & Leiter, 1999). Mismatches in these areas affect an individual's level of experienced burnout, which in turn determines various outcomes, such as job performance, social behaviors, and personal well-being. The greater the mismatch between the person and the job, the greater the likelihood of burnout; conversely the greater the match, the greater the likelihood of engagement. Initial empirical support for the AW model has been provided by both cross-sectional and longitudinal studies (Maslach & Leiter, 1999).

Maslach's Three-Dimensional Model of Burnout

The most influential work on burnout was conducted by Maslach and her colleagues in the 1970s (Halbesleben & Demerouti, 2005; Schaufeli, Leiter, et al., 2009). As a result of her research, she found that the three key dimensions of burnout are emotional exhaustion, depersonalization, and reduced personal accomplishment (Maslach, 1982). Emotional exhaustion refers to feelings of being overextended and depleted of one's emotional and physical resources. Depersonalization refers to a negative, callous, or excessively detached response to a variety of aspects of the job. Reduced personal accomplishment refers to a decrease in feelings of competence or productivity at work (Demerouti, et al., 2001; Halbesleben & Demerouti, 2005; Schaufeli, Leiter, et al., 2009).

The significance of this three-dimensional model is that it clearly places the individual strain experience within the social context of the workplace and involves the person's conception of both self and others (Maslach, 2003; Maslach & Leiter, 2008).

Job Demands-Resources Model of Burnout

Demerouti et al.'s (2001) JD-R model is a revised conceptualization of job burnout that extends beyond human services workers into the corporate environment. Their model proposes that burnout is a process in which exhaustion and disengagement are separate but correlated factors that are invariant across sample work populations in different types of occupations (Demerouti, et al., 2001). In the JD-R model, burnout develops when job demands are high and job resources are limited. Job resources refer to those physical, social, or organizational aspects of the job that may: (1) reduce job demands and the associated physiological and psychological costs; (2) be functional in achieving work goals; or (3) stimulate personal growth, learning, and development and are negatively related to burnout (Bakker, Demerouti, & Verbeke, 2004; Bakker, et al., 2007). Job resources either play an intrinsic motivational role because they foster employees' growth, learning, and development, or they play an extrinsic motivational role because they are instrumental in achieving work goals. Job demands require effort and are associated with psychological costs, like burnout (Demerouti, et al., 2001; Halbesleben & Buckley, 2004). In short, job demands predict work exhaustion and job resources predict disengagement (Halbesleben & Buckley, 2004).

The JD-R model is shown in Figure 2.

In the JD-R process model of burnout, burnout has two key dimensions: (1) exhaustion, which resembles traditional stress reactions that are studied in occupational stress research such as fatigue, job related stress and anxiety and attitudinal and behavioral outcomes such as turnover intention and absenteeism and (2) disengagement which is described as a "specific kind of withdrawal or mental distancing from recipients…which may manifest itself as alienation, disengagement

Figure 2. Job Demands-Resources Model of Burnout (Schaufeli & Salanova, 2014)

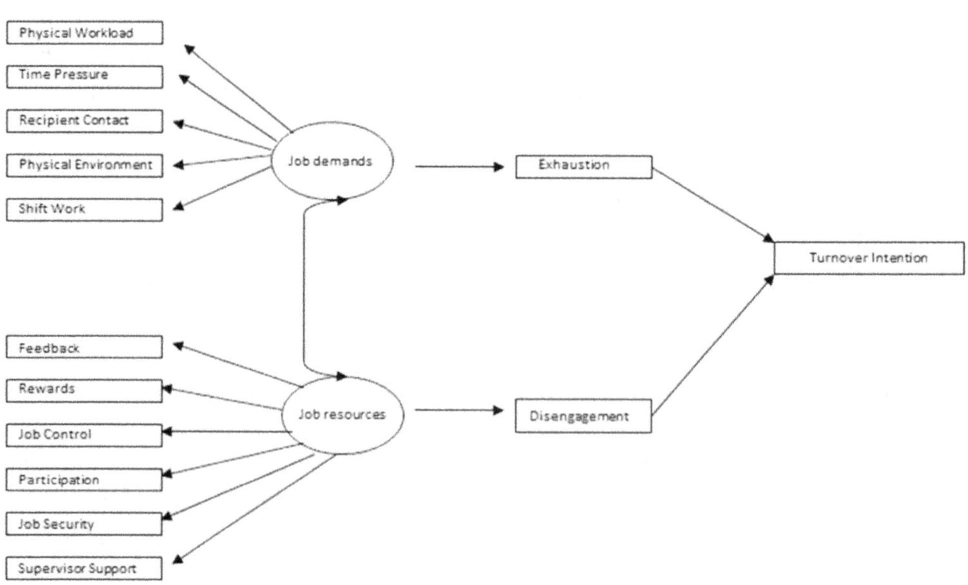

or cynicism concerning the job and the work role" (Demerouti, et al., 2001, p. 500). Table 2 describes the two dimensions of burnout as conceptualized by Demerouti et al. (2001).

The Oldenburg Burnout Inventory (OLBI) was created by Demerouti et al. (2001) and can be used in virtually every occupational context. This instrument overcomes a major psychometric shortcoming of the Maslach Burnout Inventory (MBI) and the MBI-GS, namely, the one-sided wording of the items (Demerouti & Bakker, 2008). The OLBI includes two dimensions: work exhaustion and disengagement. Work exhaustion is defined as a consequence of intensive physical, affective, and cognitive strain as a long-term consequence of prolonged exposure to certain demands. The OLBI covers not only affective, but physical and cognitive aspects of work exhaustion. This makes it more applicable to those workers who perform physical work and to those whose job is mainly about processing information, especially because there is something more related to feelings of exhaustion than just emotions—even in the service sector (Demerouti, et al., 2001). Over two decades of research on burnout have identified a plethora of organizational risk factors across many occupations in various countries (Maslach, et al., 2001). Six key domains have been identified as mentioned earlier: workload, control, reward, community, fairness sand values. The first two are in the JD-R model.

Indeed, for many IT professionals, interaction with software and hardware is more central to their work than interaction with other people (Pawlowski, Kaganer, & Cater III, 2004). Therefore, in the case of burnout in IT professionals, researchers emphasize that it is unwise to draw upon the burnout literature without first gaining a better understanding of burnout as it is understood and experienced specifically within the IT context (Pawlowski, et al., 2004). Additionally, more recent studies contend that IT environments are so complex that there are many other factors that potentially influence burnout, turnover intentions and turnover.

Employee Engagement as the Positive Antithesis to Burnout

An important development, at the beginning of the 21st century, has been that researchers have tried to broaden their understanding of burnout by expanding their

Table 2. Demerouti et al.'s two-dimensional burnout model

Burnout Dimension	Description
Exhaustion	This component refers to general feelings of emptiness, overtaxing from work and a strong need for rest and a state of physical exhaustion (Demerouti et al, 2001).
Disengagement	This component refers to "distancing one's self from the object and content of one's work and to negative, cynical attitudes and behaviors towards one's work in general" (Demerouti et al, 2001, p. 503).

attention to include its positive antithesis. This positive state has been identified as "engagement". Employee engagement is a key business driver for organizational success, is a complex concept and is influenced by many factors in the organization, such as culture, communication, and leadership (Kumar & Pansari, 2015; Maslach & Leiter, 2016). More importantly, research has suggested that engaged employees are more likely to be productive, remain with their current employer and interact positively with customers (Chalofsky & Krishna, 2009; Saks, 2006).

Although there is general agreement that engagement with work represents a productive and fulfilling state within the occupational domain, there are differences in its definition (Maslach & Leiter, 2016). For some researchers, engagement is considered to be the opposite of burnout and is defined in terms of the same three dimensions, but the positive end of those dimensions rather than the negative. By implication, engagement is assessed by the opposite pattern of scores on the three MBI dimensions (Maslach & Leiter, 2016). From this perspective, engagement consists of a state of high energy, strong involvement, and a sense of efficacy (Maslach & Leiter, 1999). In another definition, engagement is defined as the cognitive, emotional, and behavioral energy an employee directs toward positive organizational outcomes (Shuck & Reio, 2014). In yet another study, work engagement is a persistent, positive affective-motivational state of fulfillment that is characterized by the three components of vigor, dedication, and absorption (Bakker & Schaufeli, 2008). In this view, work engagement is an independent and distinct concept, which is not the opposite of burnout although it is negatively related to it (Maslach & Leiter, 2016). The Utrecht Work Engagement Scale (UWES) was developed to assess this positive state, and extensive research has been carried out in the last decade (Bakker & Schaufeli, 2008).

Since the turn of the century, work engagement has emerged as the opposite of burnout, namely a state of mental energy (Schaufeli & Salanova, 2014). From a scientific point of view, the emergence of work engagement has been fostered by the rise of positive psychology, which studies human strength and optimal functioning (Harju, Hakanen, & Schaufeli, 2016; Pfeffer, 2009; Schaufeli & Salanova, 2014). The intention of the positivist approach is to re-direct the focus of the traditional psychology field towards the building of positive qualities and valued subjective experiences reflected in the individual's experiences of well-being, contentment, and gratification (with the past), hope and optimism (for the future), and flow and happiness (during the present) (Van Heerden, 2015). Like burnout, engagement was first used in practice in business settings by human resources professionals and consultants because an organization's mental capital, that is, the cognitive and emotional fortitude and strength of its employees, is of increasing economic significance (Van Heerden, 2015). For modern organizations, employees' mental fitness rather than their mere physical fitness provides a decisive competitive advantage (Rothmann, 2008; Schaufeli & Salanova, 2014).

Employee Engagement and Work-Related Well-Being

Whereas research on burnout has produced thousands of articles during the past three decades, research on employee engagement has recently started to take shape. Because modern organizations expect their employees to be proactive and show initiative, take responsibility for their own professional development, and be committed to high quality performance standards, it only makes sense that the focus on engagement is growing. In the engagement literature, researchers continue to confirm that engagement also can make a real difference for employees and may offer organizations a competitive advantage (Bakker & Schaufeli, 2008). Overall, research has reliably demonstrated that organizations will positively benefit from the development of high levels of employee engagement. Thus, engagement is good for the organization (Shuck & Reio, 2014). The emotional well-being of employees and their satisfaction with their work and workplace affect citizenship at work, turnover and performance (J.K. Harter, Schmidt, & Hayes, 2002).

One area where employee engagement has been studied is as an aspect of work-related well-being. Work-related well-being comprises how employees feel at work (Schaufeli & Salanova, 2014). A greater part of the literature on well-being at work asserts that it is an affective state in which positive feelings occur more frequently than negative ones (Diener, 1999; Taris & Schaufeli, 2015). Further, well-being at work is partially a function of helping employees do what is right for them by allowing them to implement behaviors that positively influence engagement and other positive emotions at work (Harter, et al., 2002). In fact, according to Schaufeli (2012), a promising area of immediate exploration is the identification of the central components within a workplace climate that foster the development of engagement and stimulate well-being. However, engaging employees is just one part of the story. Improving well-being at work implies a more well-rounded approach which focuses on enabling employees to maximize their personal resources (in particular, with regard to creating a healthy work-life balance); creating an organizational structure that enables employees to flourish and take pride in what they do; supporting people to function to the best of their abilities, both as individuals and in collaboration with their colleagues; and producing a positive overall experience of work (Jeffrey, Mahony, Michaelson, & Abdallah, 2014)

Work-related well-being is conceptually grounded in the burnout literature (Maslach & Leiter, 1997; Maslach, et al., 2001; Shuck & Reio, 2014). Iverson et al. (1998) provided a research-based model of individually focused domains of well-being that include the variables of emotional exhaustion, depersonalization, and personal accomplishment. In their well-being model, the three domains represented individual, separate states of well-being rather than subcomponents of a three-component model. As part of their research, Iverson et al. (1998) suggested that employees who experienced negative psychological climates at work were more likely to report higher levels of exhaustion and depersonalization, while those who experienced positive climates reported higher levels of personal accomplishment. For example, employees who experience negative emotions as a result of their work, such as a lack of peer or managerial support, or feeling that their work is taken for granted, are far less likely to experience positive emotion (Shuck & Reio, 2014). These experiences at work are likely to influence a person's sense of psychological well-being (Shuck & Reio, 2014).

This section focused on how an employee's experience of work can positively or negatively affect their well-being. The need for new research on IT turnover has been called for, but much of the literature continues to conduct similar studies using the same search categories, and finding similar results (Lo, 2015).

RECONCEPTUALIZING THE MODEL ON JOB BURNOUT AND TURNOVER INTENTIONS: A HOLISTIC APPROACH

The study of well-being suggests that organizations are interested in it because of its impact on organizational outcomes, such as job satisfaction, engagement, organizational commitment and turnover intentions (Rothmann, 2008; Shuck & Reio, 2014). In fact, workplace well-being has been recognized as a fundamental characteristic of successful organizations, contributing to desirable results such as retention and increased performance (Harter, et al., 2002). Additionally, employees' expectations about the workplace are expanding, with many people looking for work that provides opportunities for personal development, fulfillment and well-being (Harter, et al., 2002; Jeffrey, et al., 2014; May, Gilson, & Harter, 2004). Employees are increasingly seeking to get meaning, happiness, and social connections from their work in addition to professional learning and development (Harter, 2008).

Job satisfaction, occupational stress, burnout and work engagement are all important dimensions of the psychological work-related well-being of employees (Wright & Cropanzano, 2000). Well-being could be thought of in terms of different life roles, such as marriage, family, work and housing. Work represents an important context for studying the well-being of individuals, especially because work provides a source of income that impact on various life roles, and because it demands a significant part of an individual's time and energy (Rothmann, 2008). Work also ranks high among the determinants of life satisfaction (Schaufeli & Salanova, 2014).

Unfortunately, work-related well-being has frequently been narrowly operationalized as job satisfaction (Rothmann, 2008).

Work-related well-being is of interest because of the practical and scientific interest in employee feelings at work (Schaufeli & Salanova, 2014). Historically the interest in employee feelings was solely intertwined with stress and was often defined as a physical, mental or emotional response to events or demands that cause bodily or mental tension (Maslach & Leiter, 2016). Repeatedly, studies have shown that job stress is an important factor in an employee's overall commitment, job satisfaction and decision to leave their job (Sethi, Barrier, & King, 1999). And, the research has demonstrated time and again that the organization's environment influences the psychological well-being of its employees and, as a result, the health of the organization (Vivian & Hormann, 2015). The introduction of well-being into the conversation about work expands the discussion of work to include employees' emotions. And emotions are a topic that employees are often encouraged to stay away from while at work.

Well-being also plays a central role in creating thriving societies and focusing on well-being at work presents a valuable opportunity to benefit societies by helping workers to feel happy, competent, and satisfied in their roles (Jeffrey, et al., 2014). The evidence also shows that people who achieve good standards of well-being at work are likely to be more creative, more loyal, more productive, and provide better customer satisfaction than individuals with poor standards of well-being at work (Chalofsky & Krishna, 2009; Jeffrey, et al., 2014). For decades, organizations have tried to foster these qualities through employee engagement strategies; however, the evidence demonstrates that engaging employees is just one part of the story (Jeffrey, et al., 2014). Improving well-being at work requires a more holistic approach, which focuses on helping employees to:

- Strengthen their personal resources.
- Flourish and take pride in their roles within the organization.
- Function to the best of their abilities, both as individuals and in collaboration with their colleagues.
- Have a positive overall experience of work.

Figure 3 depicts a revised model of job burnout and turnover intentions. In the authors' prior study, the model's focus was solely on the dimensions of burnout and the relationship to turnover intentions. This new, revised model suggests that an individual's physical workplace, organizational climate and job satisfaction are all a critical part of their well-being at work. Thus, well-being is at the center of the model. As job demands and resources change, the employee's emotional state is affected as well.

Figure 3. Revised Model of Burnout and Turnover Intentions to Include Well-being

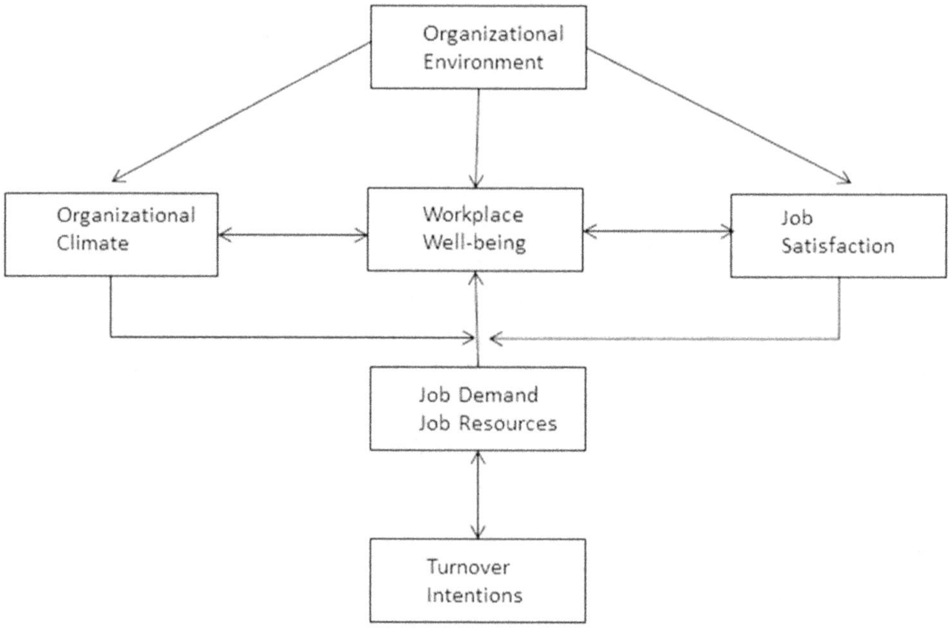

The value of research on employee well-being is that it takes a rounded view of an employee's work experience to create a state of well-being. Historically, employees have been told that feelings and emotions have no place in the workplace. However, new and growing research supports the notion that people have feelings about work at work, and that these feelings matter because they affect psychological well-being (Maslach & Leiter, 2016; Schaufeli & Salanova, 2014). Hence, issues of well-being have never been more important than they are today (Wright & Cropanzano, 2000). Up until now, the literature has largely ignored taking a holistic view and approach. Burnout and engagement researchers should focus on linking these concepts in the context of a extending the conceptualization of well-being. In Kahn's (1990) seminal work, he talks about bringing the whole self to work. If this is true, then a holistic model is what is required to advance the research—looking at the whole person at work—including emotions.

FUTURE RESEARCH DIRECTIONS

The research discussed in this chapter demonstrates that quite a bit is known about the standalone concepts of burnout and its dimensions, turnover intentions, and turnover.

Since burnout and engagement may have significant consequences for individual employees and organizations, many studies have focused on the antecedents of both concepts. Which conditions in the work environment should be targeted to prevent burnout and encourage engagement? Why are some employees prone to burnout or engagement more than others? Which of these states trigger turnover intentions and possibly turnover? These are all interesting questions for new research.

Future research also should seek to validate the revised framework in this chapter and further understanding of turnover intentions, turnover and their relationship to work-related well-being. Research on turnover as an unintended consequence of seemingly positive organizational life is another interesting research direction. The authors' future research aims to explore work-related well-being in this extended framework and how leadership might facilitate and influence work-related well-being.

Leadership is viewed as one of the "single biggest factors contributing to employee perceptions in the workplace and workforce engagement" (Wang & Walumbwa, 2007, p. 399), which makes it a potentially influential moderator of the relationship between time demands and employees' well-being. Accordingly, Bakker and Demerouti (2007) summarize studies showing that the quality of the relationship with one's leader, leaders' appreciation, support, or effective feedback may act as moderators between high job demands and employees' well-being. Building on these considerations, the authors propose that specifically leadership style is a potential moderator variable that warrants further study.

The authors also included trends and issues that are facing IT professionals in the current work environment in this chapter. One example is the issue of how to address the loss of knowledge that occurs when workers retire is a pressing one that deserves further study. Another interesting question for research is how to address the ubiquitous nature of technology. With all of the convenience that technology access has brought, unintended and often counterproductive consequences have emerged. New and interesting insights will be gained from exploring these consequences and their relationship to burnout, engagement, turnover and overall employee well-being. The fear of becoming obsolete is a real issue for IT professionals. The pace of technology change is making it difficult for IT workers to bridge the skills gap and remain competitive. Future research could identify new and creative strategies for addressing the skills gap.

A final research area is a question about the uniqueness of IT professionals. Lo (2015) asked the question and the authors agree that it is a valid one regarding whether IT workers really are unique. And if they are, in what aspects are they different from other knowledge workers? Future research is needed to confirm whether IT professionals are truly unique and if so, how will approaches to improve IT retention rates be different?

CONCLUSION AND RECOMMENDATIONS

The focus in this chapter was examining two components of well-being: employee engagement and burnout and their relationship to turnover intentions and turnover. Based on the literature, burnout is an important concept because it predicts significant outcomes like turnover and turnover intentions for employees and organizations. On the other hand, research has linked employee engagement to higher rates of profitably, growth, increased staff performance, decreased staff turnover, and improved well-being, and is considered to be an important business driver for organizational success (Rothmann, 2008; Schaufeli & Salanova, 2014; Wright & Cropanzano, 2000). A significant finding in the research is that in workplaces that are set up to nurture well-being, people tend to be more creative, more loyal, more productive and generally perform better (Jeffrey, et al., 2014).

The studies examining IT turnover have helped to cultivate this research stream. This chapter's review of the literature shows that some areas of research have matured, but other domains have yet to be explored. Key findings from the research on turnover and the turnover intentions of IT professionals assert that variables, such as job satisfaction, organizational commitment, and role stress are among the factors that cause IT professionals to leave their organizations (B. L. P. Chang, 2002; C. L. Chang, 2010). Moore (2000a) contends, however that many more factors, some that are related to the work environment and some that are related to the individual, influence an employee's commitment to the organization, and satisfaction with his or her job. Moore's study was completed nearly two decades ago, but the predictions are even more relevant today.

Recommendations

The present research also has a number of important implications for practice. As organizations become more complex and global, and demands on workers increase, fostering employee well-being could help to alleviate IT turnover by addressing key affective aspects of work life. Employees feel different at work, and these feelings matter. In this chapter, three aspects of employee well-being were discussed: burnout, exhaustion and engagement. These symptoms, which can be seen as psychological responses to overstimulation at work, represent the inability and the unwillingness to expend effort, respectively (Schaufeli & Salanova, 2014). Burnout and exhaustion are two negative patterns of employee well-being at work. What preventive strategies can organizations use to prevent burnout, curb turnover and improve well-being at work?

Robak (2013) stressed that in order to appropriately address turnover, organizational leaders must learn to face the truth about it. First, not all employees who leave an organization are unsatisfied. Some employees will leave because of low morale or due to any number of reasons (Robak, 2013). Others will move away, quit because of family concerns, change professions, even start a business of their own or retire (Robak 2013). So, staying vigilant and focused on employees is a way to stay in touch with what is happening with staff and understanding when organizational interventions are necessary. In any case, retention strategies that organizational leaders implement should focus on addressing issues that are within their control. These strategies include opportunities for promotion, creating a flexible work environment and competitive compensation. Other things that may be put in place to assist with employee retention are ongoing training/education/exploration to allow IT workers to keep up with current technologies. Additionally, interactions between IT workers and leadership may impact turnover.

Another reason employees might leave their jobs is to take jobs that allow them to reduce their commute or to work at home. Hence, one recommendation is to enact policies that allow opportunities for employees to take advantage of flexibility through telework. Additionally, providing individuals with regular opportunities to talk about their preferences about working hours with their managers and regular assessment of how working hours fit with individuals' home lives may present a sensible way to nurture well-being through work-life balance (Chen & Karahanna, 2014; Jeffrey, et al., 2014; Reyt & Weisenfeld, 2015). Having an appropriate work-life balance is extremely important when attempting to foster well-being at work. Employees who feel they have achieved this balance are shown to feel less stressed, and are likely to feel more satisfied at work, which suggests that getting the work-life balance right is likely to reduce stress and increase positive attributes, such as creativity and productivity (Jeffrey, et al., 2014).

From a global perspective, knowledge workers and IT professionals have become accustomed to new ways of working, playing, and communicating. Mobile devices and applications allow people to be alerted for every incoming phone call, text message, instant message, email, calendar event, status update notification from social networking sites like Twitter and Facebook, breaking news, and so on (Reyt & Weisenfeld, 2015). As a result, technologies create an ongoing stream of disruptions. To deal with burnout and work exhaustion due to the 24x7 connectedness, a strategy that organizations can implement includes safeguarding the boundaries between home and work by making sure that as much as possible employees are encouraged to disconnect after working hours.

A strategy for addressing the fear of obsolescence is to institute methods for improving job security via job design. Research shows that job security is also an important variable in employee well-being in terms of job design. Studies completed throughout the last three decades demonstrate that job insecurity – specifically the prospect of job loss – is associated with reduced overall and job-related well-being, even after controlling for job-related and personal factors (Jeffrey, et al., 2014). Minimizing job insecurity wherever possible is a key recommendation. Also, providing clearly defined job roles and expectations that are discussed and formalized can help in this area. In cases when ensuring job security is not possible, being transparent in communications with staff is important. Doing so will allow employees whose jobs are at risk to plan for the future.

The workplace is constantly changing and organizational leaders must rise to the challenge to ensure that employees fare well. In this chapter, the authors discussed the burnout process, work exhaustion, work-related well-being, current technology issues in the IT context, and preventing or alleviating IT turnover. Finding the balance of scientific rigor and practical application is essential for maintaining the active participation of employees and organizational leaders necessary to gain a greater understanding of these phenomena and an ability to deal effectively with them. As a final note, the authors contend that workplace well-being is a good thing. It is good for IT professionals—the group of interest in this chapter. Hence, IT professionals, their families, communities, and organizations can benefit from improved well-being and as an outcome reduced turnover rates. Additionally, it is the hope of the authors that organizational leaders take the notion of well-being to heart and become inspired to find innovative ways to nurture their employees' well-being as part of the effort to retain them.

REFERENCES

Abii, F., Ogula, D. C. N., & Rose, J. M. (2013). Effects Of Individual And Organizational Factors On The Turnover Intentions Of Information Technology Professionals. *International Journal of Management*, *30*(2), 740–756.

Ajzen, I. (1991). The Theory Of Planned Behavior. *Organizational Behavior and Human Decision Processes*, *50*(2), 179–211. doi:10.1016/0749-5978(91)90020-T

Alarcon, G. M. (2011). A Meta-Analysis Of Burnout With Job Demands, Resources, And Attitudes. *Journal of Vocational Behavior*, *79*(2), 549–562. doi:10.1016/j.jvb.2011.03.007

Armstrong, D. J., & Riemenschneider, C. K. (2011). *The Influence Of Demands And Resources On Emotional Exhaustion With The Information Systems Profession. Paper Presented At The Thirty Second International Conference On Information Systems*, Shanghai, China.

Bakker, A. B., Demerouti, E., & Sanz-Vergel, A. I. (2014). Burnout And Work Engagement: The JD-R Approach. *Annual Review of Organizational Psychology and Organizational Behavior*, *1*(1), 389–411. doi:10.1146/annurev-orgpsych-031413-091235

Bakker, A. B., Demerouti, E., & Verbeke, W. (2004). Using The Job Demands-Resources Model To Predict Burnout And Performance. *Human Resource Management*, *43*(1), 83–104. doi:10.1002/hrm.20004

Bakker, A. B., Hakanen, J. J., Demerouti, E., & Xanthopoulou, D. (2007). Job Resources Boost Work Engagement, Particulary When Job Demands Are High. *Journal of Educational Psychology*, *99*(2), 274–284. doi:10.1037/0022-0663.99.2.274

Brotheridge, C. M., & Lee, R. T. (2002). Testing A Conservation Of Resources Model Of The Dynamics Of Emotional Labor. *Journal of Occupational Health Psychology*, *7*(1), 57–67. doi:10.1037/1076-8998.7.1.57 PMID:11827234

Burrell, S. (2014). *IT Staff Turnover Intentions, Job Modification And The Effects Of Work Recognition At Large Higher Education Public Institutions* (Ed.D. Dissertation). Georgia Southern University.

Chalofsky, N., & Krishna, V. (2009). Meaningfulness, Commitment, And Engagement: The Intersection Of A Deeper Level Of Intrinsic Motivation. *Advances in Developing Human Resources*, *11*(2), 189–203. doi:10.1177/1523422309333147

Chang, B. L. P. (2002). Career Goals And Career Management Strategy Among Information Technology Professionals. *Career Development International*, *7*(1), 6–13. doi:10.1108/13620430210414829

Chang, C. L. (2010). The Study Of The Turnover Of MIS Professionals--The Gap Between Taiwanese And US Societies. *International Journal of Information Management*, *30*(4), 301–314. doi:10.1016/j.ijinfomgt.2009.11.002

Chen, A., & Karahanna, E. (2014). Boundaryless Technology: Understanding The Effects Of Technology-Mediated Interruptions Across The Boundaries Between Work And Personal Life. *AIS Transactions On Human-Computer Interaction*, *6*(2), 16–36. doi:10.17705/1thci.00059

Cohen, G., Blake, R. S., & Goodman, D. (2016). Does Turnover Intention Matter? Evaluating The Usefulness Of Turnover Intention Rate As A Predictor Of Actual Turnover Rate. *Review of Public Personnel Administration*, *36*(3), 240–263. doi:10.1177/0734371X15581850

Cropanzano, R., Rupp, D. E., & Byrne, Z. S. (2003). The Relationship Of Emotional Exhaustion To Work Attitudes, Job Performance, And Organizational Citizenship Behaviors. *The Journal of Applied Psychology*, *88*(1), 160–169. doi:10.1037/0021-9010.88.1.160 PMID:12675403

Demerouti, E. (2015). Strategies Used By Individuals To Prevent Burnout *Stichting European Society For Clinical Investigation Journal Foundation*, 1106-1112. Retrieved From www.ejci-online.com

Demerouti, E., & Bakker, A. B. (2008). The Oldenburg Burnout Inventory: A Good Alternative To Measure Burnout And Engagement. In J. R. B. Halbesleben (Ed.), *Stress And Burnout In Health Care* (pp. 65–78). Happauge, NY: Nova Sciences.

Demerouti, E., Bakker, A. B., Nachreiner, F., & Schaufeli, W. B. (2001). The Job Demands-Resources Model Of Burnout. *The Journal of Applied Psychology*, *86*(3), 499–512. doi:10.1037/0021-9010.86.3.499 PMID:11419809

Diener, E., Suh, E., Lucas, R., & Smith, H. (1999). Subjective Well-Being: Three Decades Of Progress. *Psychological Bulletin*, *125*(2), 276–302. doi:10.1037/0033-2909.125.2.276

Dinger, M., Thatcher, J. B., Stepina, L. P., & Craig, K. (2012). The Grass Is Always Greener On The Other Side: A Test Of Present And Alternative Job Utility On IT Professionals' Turnover. *IEEE Transactions on Engineering Management*, *59*(3), 364–378. doi:10.1109/TEM.2011.2153204

Dixon, S. (2016). *Retention Of Information Technology Employees.* Walden University. Retrieved From http://scholarworks.walden.edu/dissertations

Ferratt, T. W., Agarwal, R., Brown, C. V., & Moore, J. E. (2005). IT Human Resource Management Configurations And IT Turnover: Theoretical Synthesis And Empirical Analysis. *Information Systems Research*, *16*(3), 237–255. doi:10.1287/isre.1050.0057

Ford, V. (2012). *An Exploratory Investigation Of The Relationship Between Turnover Intentions, Work Exhaustion And Disengagement Among IT Professionals In A Single Institution Of Higher Education In A Major Metropolitan Area* (Dissertation). The George Washington University.

Ford, V., Swayze, S., & Burley, D. L. (2012). An Exploratory Investigation Of The Relationship Between Disengagement, Exhaustion And Turnover Intentions Among University IT Professionals. *Information Resources Management Journal*, *26*(3), 55–68. doi:10.4018/irmj.2013070104

Freudenberger, H. J. (1974). Staff Burn-Out. *The Journal of Social Issues*, *30*(1), 159–165. doi:10.1111/j.1540-4560.1974.tb00706.x

Grandey, A. A., & Cropanzano, R. (1999). The Conservation Of Resources Model Applied To Work-Family Conflict And Strain. *Journal of Vocational Behavior*, *54*(2), 350–370. doi:10.1006/jvbe.1998.1666

Halbesleben, J. R. B., & Buckley, M. R. (2004). Burnout In Organizational Life. *Journal of Management*, *30*(6), 859–879. doi:10.1016/j.jm.2004.06.004

Halbesleben, J. R. B., & Demerouti, E. (2005). The Construct Validity Of An Alternative Measure Of Burnout: Investigating The English Translation Of The Oldenburg Burnout Inventory. *Work and Stress*, *19*(3), 208–220. doi:10.1080/02678370500340728

Harju, L. K., Hakanen, J. J., & Schaufeli, W. B. (2016). Can Job Crafting Reduce Job Boredom And Increase Work Engagement? A Three-Year Cross-Lagged Panel Study. *Journal of Vocational Behavior*, *95-96*, 11–20. doi:10.1016/j.jvb.2016.07.001

Harter, J. K. (2008). Why People Change Jobs? *Gallup Management Journal*. Retrieved From Http://Gmj.Gallup.Com/Content/106912/Turning-Around-Your-Turnover-Problem.Aspx

Harter, J. K., Schmidt, F. L., & Hayes, T. L. (2002). Business-Unit-Level Relationship Between Employee Satisfaction, Employee Engagement, And Business Outcomes: A Meta-Analysis. *The Journal of Applied Psychology*, *87*(2), 268–279. doi:10.1037/0021-9010.87.2.268 PMID:12002955

Henderson, R. (2012). Industry Employment And Output Projections To 2020. *Monthly Labor Review*, 65–83.

Hobfoll, S. E. (1989). Conservation Of Resources: A New Attempt At Conceptualizing Stress. *The American Psychologist*, *44*(3), 513–524. doi:10.1037/0003-066X.44.3.513 PMID:2648906

Hobfoll, S. E. (2002). Social And Psychological Resources And Adaptation. *Review of General Psychology*, *6*(4), 307–324. doi:10.1037/1089-2680.6.4.307

Hulin, C. L., Roznowski, M., & Hachiya, D. (1985). Alternative Opportunities And Withdrawal Decisions: Empirical And Theoretical Discrepancies And An Integration. *Psychological Bulletin*, *97*(2), 233–250. doi:10.1037/0033-2909.97.2.233

Iverson, R. D., Olekalns, M., & Erwin, P. J. (1998). Affectivity, Organizational Stressors, And Absenteeism: A Causal Model Of Burnout And Its Consequences. *Journal of Vocational Behavior*, *52*(1), 1–23. doi:10.1006/jvbe.1996.1556

Jeffrey, K., Mahony, S., Michaelson, J., & Abdallah, S. (2014). The NEF Report On Well-Being. New Economics Foundation.

Joseph, D., & Ang, S. (2003). *Turnover Of IT Professionals: A Quantitative Analysis Of The Literature. Paper Presented At The SIGMIS Conference*, Philadelphia, PA. 10.1145/761849.761872

Joseph, D., Ng, K., Koh, C., & Ang, S. (2007). Turnover Of Information Technology Professionals: A Narrative Review, Meta-Analytic Structural Equation Modeling, And Model Development. *Management Information Systems Quarterly*, *31*(3), 547–577. doi:10.2307/25148807

Kahn, W. A. (1990). Psychological Conditions Of Personal Engagement And Disengagement At Work. *Academy of Management Journal*, *33*(4), 692–724. doi:10.2307/256287

Kalimo, R., & Toppinen, S. (1995). *Burnout In Computer Professionals*. Paper Presented At The Work, Stress And Health 1995: Creating Healthier Workplaces, Washington, DC.

Kim, S., & Wright, B. E. (2007). IT Employee Work Exhaustion: Toward An Integrated Model Of Antecedents And Consequences. *Review of Public Personnel Administration*, *27*(2), 147–170. doi:10.1177/0734371X06290775

Kumar, V., & Pansari, A. (2015). Measuring The Benefits Of Employee Engagement. *MIT Sloan Management Review*, *56*(4), 67–72.

Lacity, M. C., Iyer, V. V., & Rudramuniyaiah, P. S. (2008). Turnover Intentions Of Indian IS Professionals. *Information Systems Frontiers On Outsourcing*, *10*(2), 225–241. doi:10.100710796-007-9062-3

Lo, J. (2015). The Information Technology Workforce: A Review And Assessment Of Voluntary Turnover Research. *Information Systems Frontiers*, *17*(2), 387–411. doi:10.100710796-013-9408-y

Maier, C., Laumer, S., & Echardt, A. (2015). Information Technology As Daily Stressor: Pinning Down The Causes Of Burnout. *Journal Of Business Economics*, *85*(4), 349–387. doi:10.100711573-014-0759-8

Maslach, C. (1982). *Burnout: The Cost Of Caring*. Englewood Cliffs, NJ: Prentice Hall.

Maslach, C. (2003). Job Burnout: New Directions In Research And Intervention. *Current Directions in Psychological Science*, *12*(12), 189–192. doi:10.1111/1467-8721.01258

Maslach, C., & Goldberg, J. (1998). Prevention Of Burnout: New Perspectives. *Applied & Preventive Psychology*, *7*(1), 63–74. doi:10.1016/S0962-1849(98)80022-X

Maslach, C., & Jackson, S. E. (1981). The Measurement Of Experienced Burnout. *Journal of Occupational Behaviour*, *2*(99), 113.

Maslach, C., & Leiter, M. P. (1997). *The Truth About Burnout*. San Francisco, CA: Jossey-Bass.

Maslach, C., & Leiter, M. P. (2008). Early Predictors Of Job Burnout And Engagement. *The Journal of Applied Psychology*, *93*(3), 498–512. doi:10.1037/0021-9010.93.3.498 PMID:18457483

Maslach, C., & Leiter, P. L. (Eds.). (1999). Burnout And Engagement In The Workplace: A Contextual Analysis (Vol. 11). Stamford, CT: JAI Press.

Maslach, C., & Leiter, P. L. (2016). Understanding The Burnout Experience: Recent Research And Its Implications For Psychiatry. *World Psychiatry; Official Journal of the World Psychiatric Association (WPA)*, *15*(2), 103–111. doi:10.1002/wps.20311 PMID:27265691

Maslach, C., Schaufeli, W. B., & Leiter, M. P. (2001). Job Burnout. *Annual Review of Psychology*, *52*(1), 397–422. doi:10.1146/annurev.psych.52.1.397 PMID:11148311

May, D. R., Gilson, R. L., & Harter, L. M. (2004). The Psychological Conditions Of Meaningfulness, Safety And Availability And The Engagement Of The Human Spirit At Work. *Journal of Occupational and Organizational Psychology*, *77*(1), 11–37. doi:10.1348/096317904322915892

Mcgee, M. K. (1996). Hot Skills In '96: Internet, Client-Server, And Networking Experts Top Lists Of The Most Wanted. *Information Week*, 560–564.

Mcknight, D. H., Phillips, B., & Hardgrave, B. C. (2009). Which Reduces IT Turnover Intention The Most: Workplace Characteristics Or Job Characteristics? *Information & Management*, *46*(3), 167–174. doi:10.1016/j.im.2009.01.002

Moore, J. E. (2000a). One Road To Turnover: An Examination Of Work Exhaustion In Technology Professionals. *Management Information Systems Quarterly*, *24*(1), 141–168. doi:10.2307/3250982

Moore, J. E. (2000b). Why Is This Happening? A Causal Attribution Approach To Work Exhaustion Consequences. *Academy of Management Review*, *25*(2), 335–349.

Pawlowski, S., Kaganer, E., & Cater, J. III. (2004). Mapping Perceptions Of Burnout In The Information Technology Profession: A Study Using Social Representations Theory. *Paper Presented At The International Conference On Information Systems (ICIS).*

Pfeffer, J. (2009). *Building Sustainable Organizations: The Human Factor*. Stanford, CA: Foundations Of Human Ecology.

Reyt, J., & Weisenfeld, B. M. (2015). Seeing The Forest For The Trees: Exploratory Learning, Mobile Technology, And Knowledge Workers' Role Integration Behaviors. *Academy of Management Journal*, *58*(3), 739–762. doi:10.5465/amj.2013.0991

Rothmann, S. (2008). Job Satisfaction, Occupational Stress, Burnout And Work Engagement As Components Of Work-Related Wellbeing. *SA Journal of Industrial Psychology*, *34*(3), 11–16. doi:10.4102ajip.v34i3.424

Saks, A. M. (2006). Antecedents And Consequences Of Employee Engagement. *Journal of Managerial Psychology*, *21*(7), 600–619. doi:10.1108/02683940610690169

Schaufeli, W. B. (2012). Work Engagement. What Do We Know And Where Do We Go? *Romanian Journal of Applied Psychology*, *14*(1), 3–10.

Schaufeli, W. B., & Bakker, A. B. (2004). Job Demands, Job Resources, And Their Relationship With Burnout And Engagement: A Multi-Sample Study. *Journal of Organizational Behavior*, *25*(3), 293–315. doi:10.1002/job.248

Schaufeli, W. B., Bakker, A. B., & Van Rhenen, W. (2009). How Changes In Job Demands And Resources Predict Burnout, Work Engagement, And Sickness Absenteeism. *Journal of Organizational Behavior*, *30*(7), 893–917. doi:10.1002/job.595

Schaufeli, W. B., Leiter, M. P., & Maslach, C. (2009). Burnout: 35 Years Of Research And Practice. *Career Development International*, *14*(3), 204–220. doi:10.1108/13620430910966406

Schaufeli, W. B., & Salanova, M. (2014). Burnout, Boredom And Engagement In The Workplace. In M. C. W. Peeters, J. D. Jonge, & T. W. Taris (Eds.), An Introduction To Contemporary Work Psychology (pp. 293-320). John Wiley & Sons, Ltd.

Schneider, B., Macey, W. H., & Barbera, K. (2006). Employee Engagement. Academic Press.

Sethi, V., Barrier, T., & King, R. C. (1999). An Examination Of The Correlates Of Burnout In Information Systems Professionals. *Information Resources Management Journal, 12*(3), 5–13. doi:10.4018/irmj.1999070101

Shih, S.-P., Jiang, J. J., Klein, G., & Wang, E. (2011). Learning Demand And Job Autonomy Of IT Personnel: Impact On Turnover Intention. *Computers in Human Behavior, 27*(6), 2301–2307. doi:10.1016/j.chb.2011.07.009

Shuck, B., & Reio, T. Jr. (2014). Employee Engagement And Well-Being: A Moderation Model And Implications For Practice. *Journal of Leadership & Organizational Studies, 21*(1), 43–58. doi:10.1177/1548051813494240

Shumaker, J., Ward, K., Petter, S., & Riley, J. (2017). Mitigating The Threat Of Lost Knowledge Within Information Technology Departments. *Proceedings Of The 50th Hawaii International Conference On System Sciences.*

Syrek, C. J., Apostel, E., & Antoni, C. H. (2013). Stress In Highly Demanding IT Jobs: Transformational Leadership Moderates The Impact Of Time Pressure On Exhaustion And Work-Life Balance. *Journal of Occupational Health Psychology, 18*(3), 252–261. doi:10.1037/a0033085 PMID:23834443

Taris, T. W., & Schaufeli, W. B. (2015). Individual Well-Being And Performance At Work: A Conceptual And Theoretical Overview. In M. V. V. R. Peccei (Ed.), *Well-Being And Performance At Work: The Role Of Context* (pp. 15–34). London: Taylor & Francis.

Thwala, D. W., Ajagbe, A. M., Long, C. S., Bilau, A. A., & Enegbuma, W. I. (2012). Sdanese Small And Medium Sized Construction Firms: An Empirical Survey Of Job Turnover. *Journal of Basic and Applied Scientific Research, 2*(8), 7414.

Van Den Broek, A., Elst, T. V., Baillien, E., Sercu, M., Schouteden, M., De Witte, H. L., & ... . (2017). Job Demands, Job Resources, Burnout, Work Engagement, And Their Relationships: An Analysis Across Sectors., 59(4), 369-376. *Journal of Occupational and Environmental Medicine, 59*(4), 369–376. doi:10.1097/JOM.0000000000000964 PMID:28157768

Van Heerden, J. (2015). *The Impact Of Job Engagement And Job Resources On Work Engagement And Turnover Intentions Within The Information Technology Division Of A South African Bank* (Unpublished Doctoral Dissertation). University Of The Western Cape.

Vivian, P., & Hormann, S. (2015). Persistent Traumatization In Nonprofit Organizations. *OD Practitioner*, *47*(1), 25–30.

Weinert, C., Maier, C., Laumer, S., & Weitzel, T. (2015). *Extending Moore's Exhaustion Model: Including Further Dimensions Of Burnout And Investigating Their Influence On Turnover Intention Among IT Professionals. Paper Presented At The ACM SIGMIS Conference On Management Information Systems*, Newport Beach, CA. 10.1145/2751957.2751975

Willoughby, T. C. (1977). Computing Personnel Turnover: A Review Of The Literature. In *Proceedings of the 1977 Annual Conference*. Seattle, WA: ACM. 10.1145/800179.810204

Wright, T. A., & Cropanzano, R. (2000). Psychological Well-Being And Job Satisfaction As Predictors Of Job Performance. *Journal of Occupational Health Psychology*, *5*(1), 84–94. doi:10.1037/1076-8998.5.1.84 PMID:10658888

Zaza, I., & Armstrong, D. (2016). *Turnover Intention Among Information Technology Professionals: A Meta-Analytical Perspective. Paper Presented At The Thirty Seventh International Conference On Information Systems*, Dublin, Ireland.

ADDITIONAL READING

Cohen, G., Blake, R. S., & Goodman, D. (2016). Does Turnover Intention Matter? Evaluating the Usefulness of Turnover Intention Rate as a Predictor of Actual Turnover Rate. *Review of Public Personnel Administration*, *36*(3), 240–263. doi:10.1177/0734371X15581850

Lo, J. (2015). The information technology workforce: A review and assessment of voluntary turnover research. *Information Systems Frontiers*, *17*(2), 387–411. doi:10.100710796-013-9408-y

Maier, C., Laumer, S., & Echardt, A. (2015). Information technology as daily stressor: Pinning down the causes of burnout. *Journal of Business Economics*, *85*(4), 349–387. doi:10.100711573-014-0759-8

Maslach, C., & Leiter, P. L. (2016). Understanding the burnout experience: Recent research and its implications for psychiatry. *World Psychiatry; Official Journal of the World Psychiatric Association (WPA)*, *15*(2), 103–111. doi:10.1002/wps.20311 PMID:27265691

Reyt, J., & Weisenfeld, B. M. (2015). Seeing the Forest for the Trees: Exploratory Learning, Mobile Technology, And Knowledge Workers' Role Integration Behaviors. *Academy of Management Journal*, *58*(3), 739–762. doi:10.5465/amj.2013.0991

Shumaker, J., Ward, K., Petter, S., & Riley, J. (2017). *Mitigating the Threat of Lost Knowledge within Information Technology Departments* Paper presented at the Proceedings of the 50th Hawaii International Conference on System Sciences Hawaii. 10.24251/HICSS.2017.658

Van den Broek, A., Elst, T. V., Baillien, E., Sercu, M., Schouteden, M., De Witte, H., & … . (2017). Job Demands, Job Resources, Burnout, Work Engagement, and Their Relationships: An Analysis Across Sectors., 59(4), 369-376. *Journal of Occupational and Environmental Medicine*, *59*(4), 369–376. doi:10.1097/JOM.0000000000000964 PMID:28157768

Van Heerden, J. (2015). *The impact of job engagement and job resources on work engagement and turnover intentions within the information technology division of a South African bank*. Unpublished doctoral dissertation. University of the Western Cape.

Weinert, C., Maier, C., Laumer, S., & Weitzel, T. (2015). *Extending Moore's Exhaustion Model: Including Further Dimensions of Burnout and Investigating Their Influence on Turnover Intention Among IT Professionals*. Paper presented at the ACM SIGMIS Conference on Management information systems, Newport Beach, CA USA. 10.1145/2751957.2751975

Zaza, I., & Armstrong, D. (2016). *Turnover Intention among Information Technology Professionals: A Meta-Analytical Perspective*. Paper presented at the Thirty Seventh International Conference on Information Systems, Dublin.

KEY TERMS AND DEFINITIONS

Employee Engagement: Refers to the extent to which employees feel enthusiastic about their work, are committed to the organization, and put forth discretionary effort as it relates to their work.

Information Technology Professionals: Workers in a technology services organization, whether it is a standalone organization or an internal department.

Job Burnout: Burnout is a psychological syndrome that results from prolonged exposure to stressors in the workplace.

Job Demands: Aspects of a job that require continuous physical or emotional effort. Examples of demands are workload, job pressures, and emotional demands.

Job Resources: The tools, materials, and other assets that an employee can draw on at work. Examples of resources include management and peer support, training, and so on.

Turnover: The voluntary termination of employment from an organization.

Turnover Intention: Turnover intention refers to an employee's deliberate and conscious goal to look for a new job or to leave a current job.

Workplace Wellbeing: Wellbeing refers to all aspects of work life, including how employees feel about their work, their work environment, and the absence of chronic job stress and strain.

Chapter 3
Information Technology Pre-Risk Governance

Letitia Larry
LCDC, LLC, USA & Business Intelligence, Inc., USA

William Anderson Von Canon Jr.
Business Intelligence, Inc., USA

ABSTRACT

Pre-risk governance is an extension of the risk management paradigm that allows for risk analysis prior to making a decision on whether a business objective should move forward and what the possible risks may be. Instead of making business decisions that will affect or impact technology, and the associated people, processes, and policy and then including necessary staff in systems planning after the fact, pre-risk governance allows for the inclusion of pertinent staff in the decision-making process prior to moving toward a major change or enterprise transformation effort. Historically, information technology (IT) staff have not been included in decision making as it applies to change initiatives until they are required in the overall systems/solutions development life cycle. This exclusion of IT staff has been shown to cause a higher level of risk, and actuated issues with schedule, budget, and successful implementation of or transition to a new means of doing and supporting business.

INTRODUCTION

Across the span of human existence – whether talking about human mortality or shifting business models and technological systems, change is an ongoing, never-ending process (McDonough & Coghlan, 2006). As the field of information technology has evolved as a discipline and tool, there have been corresponding changes to

DOI: 10.4018/978-1-5225-5829-3.ch003

business, processes, practice, policy, and the roles and responsibilities of those who implement and support the actual change (Goodman & Loh, 2011). While change theory has traditionally concentrated on the impact that a change event exerts on an enterprise and the success or failure of the change event itself, it has not focused on the people who are responsible for the change – and their overall contribution to the change process. This misplaced, one-dimensional, focus has impacted stakeholders' acceptance of change as well as the success or failure of the intended change (Larry, 2017). By ignoring key contributors to the change, information technology (IT) staff, the probability of successful change can be undermined and may serve as a reinforcement of failure. The use of Pre-Risk Governance and inclusion of IT staff during the Pre-Risk Governance Life Cycle (P-RGLC), to provide the enterprise with a list of issues, concerns, and/or problems that may occur prior to making a decision on a new business directive and/or prior to moving forward, supports successful change (Von Canon, 2017).

BACKGROUND

"Ninety-three percent of U.S.-based multinational companies are in some phase of changing their business models," (KPMG, 2014, p. 2, paragraph 1). This percentage is particularly significant in light of the technologies upon which 21st century businesses depend for developing, redeveloping, updating, and revamping their structural frameworks, designs, communications networks, marketing and sales plans, policies, implementation practices, etc. Because organizations are continuously evolving in this way, adjustments must regularly be made to the infrastructure, systems, and roles and responsibilities of those organizations. In turn, with new systems come new modes of doing business and changes to operations (Goodman & Loh, 2011) that impact both internal and external stakeholders. Moreover, it is expected that certain Information Technology (IT) disciplines (such as solutions architecture, development/engineering, verification/testing, and technical and customer support) within an enterprise will continuously go through, promote, and support change (McDonagh & Coghlan, 2006), especially in the area of information technology driving business innovation. Planning for change prior to making a decision to change and including those subject matter experts (SMEs) that can provide relevant information on the advantages and disadvantages of moving forward increases the possibility of success upon initial implementation of a new product or service (Larry 2017). In this chapter the authors will define and discuss the use of Pre-Risk Governance prior to and/or at the onset of change projects and initiatives.

Although it may be rarely accepted as true due to fear and uncertainty, change does not have a negative connotation (Von Canon, 2017). Change is not necessarily a negative process but it may be deemed negative based on the individual experience and how change is handled. Although justifiable, changes of any sort succeed or fail based on whether the people affected are willing to do things differently and, in today's business environment, understand the primary drivers of these changes (Bridges, 2010; Goodman & Loh, 2011). The success or failure of technology changes in businesses and other kinds of organizations depends on how information technology teams handle the change and appreciate the value proposition to both the business and the individual/team. Knowledge of planned change may act as a positive influence on change agents.

Change events that occur within technology-driven organizations position IT workers as front-line staff charged with the responsibility of dealing with both people and systems in order to facilitate the mandated change and move the organization forward. Thus, tasked with handling multiple areas of technological concern and interacting with a variety of people, IT teams face intensified demands when implementing and supporting change thus positioning IT staff to provide a holistic view of the impact of change initiatives on individuals and the enterprise (Larry, 2017, pp. 139-140).

RELEVANT QUALITATIVE STUDY

In the doctoral dissertation *A Qualitative Study of the Experience of Information Technology Teams during Transition Using the Kübler-Ross Grief Construct and the Bridges Transition Model* (Larry, 2017), the researcher examined the human component of change, emphasizing the dynamics of the transition process on eight selected subjects working within an information technology environment. The qualitative study was used to provide insights and understandings to the following research question: *How are the phases of transition experienced by individuals within information technology teams during a major change effort?* The researcher used the Kübler-Ross grief construct (denial and isolation, anger, bargaining, depression, and acceptance) (Kearney & Hyle, 2003) as the theoretical lens through which to investigate the transition process in action; and Bridges' three-phased Transition theory (Ending, Losing, Letting To; The Neutral Zone; The New Beginning) (Bridges, 2010) to delve deeper into the individual experience of IT staff during change. This study, and the associated outcome and recommendations, provided insight into a best practice and approach that should be investigated to assist with how change can be successfully initiated.

Lens and Focus of the Qualitative Study

The five stages of grief, as conceived by Kübler-Ross (1969), are: (a) denial and isolation, (b) anger, (c) bargaining, (d) depression, and (e) acceptance. Following are definitions of each stage:

1. Denial is defined as "refusal to accept the diagnosis or change event" (Kearney & Hyle, 2004, p. 114; Kübler-Ross, 1969, p. 52).
2. Anger is defined as "feelings of anger, rage, envy, and resentment associated with the impending death or change event" (Kearney & Hyle, 2004, p. 114; Kübler-Ross, 1969, p. 64).
3. Bargaining is defined as "attempts to trade one action for avoidance of death or loss" (Kearney & Hyle, 2004, p. 114; Kübler-Ross, 1969, p. 94).
4. Depression is defined as "the replacement of anger with a sense of loss" (Kearney & Hyle, 2004, p. 114-115).
5. Acceptance is defined as the final stage in which "anger and depression about death or loss has dissipated; an emotionless state" (Kearney & Hyle, 2004, p. 115).

These phases are not linear, may occur cyclically and some or all may be experienced by those suffering a loss. Later, Kübler-Ross (1969) went on to determine that these very phases can be, and are, inherent to transitions of any type including divorce, changes in job, changes in responsibilities associated with a role/job/life, etc. The term "transition" was used by Kübler-Ross to describe the process of moving from one state to another in works beyond the original inception of the grief construct and this helped to show the applicability of the grief construct beyond death and dying to other life changes. The grief construct is a transition process expressing the feelings and responses associated with the transition.

The grief construct may seem dark, or morbid, based on the original application, but the applicability goes beyond death and dying to what is perceived by the individual to be highly detrimental personal transition responses that feel as if the individual is going through the phases of grief or loss. The grief construct has been revisited and/or extended since its original inception; as such, it is applied to the realm of business and other areas/disciplines involving people and change/transition processes (Bridges, 2004, 2010, 2013; Goodman & Loh, 2011; Kearney, 2003; Kearney & Hyle, 2003, 2004; McDonagh & Coghlan, 2006). An example of the application of the grief construct to technology disciplines was well expressed by Dr. William Anderson Von Canon, Jr., "The sun-setting of a project [feels] like death when completing a systems change [or transformation]" (Von Canon, 2017).

It is essential to emphasize that transition and change are not identical concepts. One is a precursor to the other; in other words, change encourages or causes transition of some sort, with transition being understood as a psychological concept and change understood as a kind of event. According to Bridges (2010),

Change is situational: the move to a new site, the retirement of the founder, reorganization of the roles on a team . . . Transitioning, on the other hand, is psychological; it is a three-phased process that people go through as they internalize and come to terms with the details of the new situation that the change brings about. (p. 4)

Specifically, Bridges' (2010) three phases of transition are:

1. Letting go of the old ways.
2. Going through an in-between time when the old is gone, but the new isn't fully operational.
3. Coming out of the transition and making a new beginning.

Per Bridges (p. 2), transition is not automatic and occurs much more slowly than change. Transition takes longer because people undergo three separate processes. In phase 1, letting go, people must let go of the way that things used to be as well as the way that they used to be. This may mean giving up the way that tasks used to be accomplished, possibly for the course of his or her career. In phase 2, saying goodbye, there is a feeling of discomfort and people may want to rush ahead into the new situation although he or she is most likely not ready to do so. It is called the neutral phase and should be experienced to ensure there is not a relapse into the previous phase. Phase 3, moving forward/new beginnings, is where people begin behaving in a new way. Phase 3 is normally only successful when enough time has been spent in phase 2 and people have put the past behind them and are ready and willing to move forward. Bridges provides a deeper dive into the actual psychologic experience and expression of transition. The Bridges Transition Model provides context, a list of feelings and an expression of the psychological phases of transition for the individual, to the Kübler-Ross grief construct stages of loss.

IT Study Participants

This study was delimited to a qualitative study of eight individuals within two IT teams in transition, situated in work settings performing software/solution architecture and development/engineering, infrastructure management/development operations (DevOps), solution verification/testing, and customer and technical support. The teams included an IT team providing technical architecture, development, testing and customer support services to a government agency; and a Health Information Technology (HIT) team within a non-profit organization providing infrastructure, solution verification and customer and technical support for insurance providers and insured consumers. Health information technology (HIT) is a subset of information technology. The focus of health information technology is the support of health systems and the associated data prescribed by the system (Brailer & Thompson, 2004), whereas information technology focuses on the systems themselves (Oxford University, 2015).

Study Purpose

This qualitative research study served to develop a better understanding of the effects of change on information technology workers, as individuals and members of teams, who were charged with supporting both internal change efforts (mandated by the firm) and the experiences of end users in adapting to the modified or new system (Larry, 2017). Typically, change efforts within the field of information technology target systems and solutions development, verification, database administration, access, and technical and customer support (Chaudry et al., 2006). Specifically, the researcher studied the effects of change and, in particular, the dynamics of personal transition processes within two selected information technology work environments: (a) a non-profit Health Information Technology (HIT) firm and (b) two IT government contracting firms with staff serving on one contract (project) within a federal agency. Across the two environments, the researcher confirmed eight study subjects, four from the HIT firm and four from the federal IT (contract) project. As to the design of this qualitative study, the researcher targeted a more unique approach by culling data specific to individual IT workers within these two work environments; in other words, data pertaining to IT contracted staff in contrast to data pertaining to HIT staff. In taking this approach, the researcher (as an experienced IT specialist) recognized that the provision of solutions and customer support would be directed toward two different perspectives or areas of priority, based on the firm type: (a) infrastructure and solutions support (IT) and (b) data management and insurer support (HIT).

Data Collection

Data collection consisted of a pre-candidacy form, per participant, providing background and experience for each individual participant as well as a list of responsibilities for their current roles; and semi-structured interviews conducted individually with each study participant (Larry, 2017). Interview data was coded and analyzed to uncover significant statements and derive meaning from participant responses. Data analysis included first-cycle and *a priori* coding processes using open coding, followed by a conceptual and theoretical theming process (Saldaña, 2013).

Recommendations for Additional Research

Based on the findings yielded by the study, the researcher offered several recommendations intended to address the following concerns: (a) how to better understand and extend knowledge on the experiences of IT staff members/teams during major change events; (b) how to expand awareness and knowledge of IT staff-based change issues among management and leadership so that they might better support staff in moving through change and transition within the organization; (c) how IT staff might better transition through change; and (d) the use of pre-risk governance for IT staff (undergoing transition due to change) (Larry, 2017, p. 157).

The recommendations, and an explanation of each, follow in proceeding subsections. These recommendations provide insight into the issues that were expressed by IT staff during interviews for the qualitative, interview-based research study. Recommendation 4 is the focus of this chapter: the initiation of Pre-Risk Governance prior to the decision to move forward with a change initiative. Pre-Risk Governance is a key area of improvement toward successful change.

Recommendation 1: Extend Knowledge on IT Staff

There is a lack of information on how leadership and management staff in IT and HIT companies prepare resources for and support IT staff members and teams through revolutionary change events (Larry, 2017). Therefore, the researcher recommends that this particular area of IT research be expanded in order to acknowledge, validate, and normalize the transition experiences of IT workers as a common phenomenon across the industry. By enlarging and adding credibility to this currently understudied area, new research could provide valuable information and insights that would support truly successful change initiatives for both human resources and the enterprises in which they work.

Recommendation 2: Enterprise Support for IT Staff

Per researcher observations, the participant descriptions (and data), for those from China the expectation is to do what is necessary and beyond; for those from India, the expectation is to work together and help one another to the advantage of the team—and normally within the culture; and for other cultures there is a variation of expression based on the individual. As an extension of recognizing and addressing the reality of change and transition issues for IT workers, findings indicated the need to conduct future research specific to how companies might best support the skills and training necessary for those individuals and IT teams directly responsible for supporting major change efforts. In other words, study participants collectively communicated the point of view that, as human resources, they are expected to have and/or be ready to apply the knowledge and expertise necessary to implement the mandated change (Larry, 2017). However, they maintained that they are, typically, not given the training or additional education needed to do so effectively and within the timelines associated with the change event.

In other words, they indicated a "learn on your own" mentality that was very apparent in the data collected from HIT staff specifically. To close the gap and respond to issues communicated during this research study, organizations should (a) include IT staff in decision making and planning as they are the experts in their fields and leadership depends on IT staff to determine how change will occur and how to best support change initiatives: (b) provide ongoing training to extend IT workers knowledge so they can complete tasking in support of change based on feedback from the IT worker on what training and education is needed; and (c) communicate the need/reason for the change and the overall impact to the enterprise often and simply to all staff concerned with the change event or initiative to ensure there is understanding and buy in from those involved - possibly aiding in keeping change initiative/event attributes (e.g., schedule, budget) in control. These three suggestions will begin to remedy the concerns shared by study participants in interviews and observed through analysis of data by the researcher.

Recommendation 3: IT Staff Vocalization/Response to Change

To better transition through change, IT workers must be vocal about what is necessary in order to support current and future change. Vocalization must be consistent and handled in multiple communication streams, verbally/orally and in writing. While IT staff is responsible for leading change as mandated by leadership and management, they must also prepare for future demands brought about in support of new company direction and updating infrastructure and solutions. Some research participants shared what they needed to support the change initiative while others did not express what was needed but did express what the problems were. One approach to getting the necessary support for change and the associated transition effort is to be clear about what is needed (training, better communication, additional resources, more experienced resources, etc.) and to map needs to what is required of the individual during change – in ongoing communications.

Recommendation 4: Pre-Risk Governance

The use of Pre-Risk Governance in the information technology arena is to plan for future change initiatives by determining possible risks to the success and on-time delivery of a solution, product or service by listing the concerns/risks and possible mitigation responses prior to the start of the change as part of the project/product/program management effort. Risks are then presented to involved technical staff and stakeholders (those who benefit from and/or consume the change). This allows for resolutions or responses to any risks prior to change initiation and continuous tracking of risk resolutions until they are complete and risks are mitigated. The researcher recommended that leadership/management and IT staff work together to utilize a pre-risk governance process to determine and address the needs of the IT organization and associated staff members prior to the start of change (Larry, 2017, p. 160).

PRE-RISK GOVERNANCE: DEFINITION AND CONTRIBUTION

One of the recommendations stands out as a relatively easy addition to the change management process, the use of Pre-Risk Governance prior to the initiation of change directives. Pre-Risk Governance does not currently exist as part of the change life cycle; it is a new concept. Pre-Risk Governance is the concentration of this chapter. Pre-Risk Governance includes IT staff in planning systems prior to initiation of change, or prior to making the business decision to make a change (Larry, 2017). Pre-Risk Governance provides the enterprise with a list of issues, concerns, and/or problems that may occur prior to making a decision on a new business directive and/or prior to moving forward (Von Canon, 2017). This allows for a better understanding of the impact of change to the enterprise as proffered by those that will have to implement and support the change initiative.

Unlike "lessons learned," historical references to issues and concerns associated with previous projects or change events, the application of Pre-Risk Governance supports the inclusion of IT staff who offer a change perspective that can bring up tactical risks and issues that are critical to change implementation and acceptance. Numerous cases of failed change initiatives have hinged on key implementation details that were either unknown or not well understood prior to program/project/change initiation. In including IT staff in preparation for decision making, there may be a savings in time, cost and the response to change by those within the enterprise and those external to the organization consuming the change. Additionally, including IT staff in pre-decision making as it relates to major changes within the enterprise may positively impact the initial and ongoing success of the project or change initiative. The Pre-Risk Governance Life Cycle phases and progression are as represented in Figure 1.

This figure illustrates the tasks and events associated with the Pre-Risk Governance Life Cycle.

The use of Pre-Risk Governance in the information technology arena is to plan for future change initiatives by determining possible risks to the success and on-time delivery of a solution, product or service at the start of the change as part of the project/product/program management effort (Larry, 2017). This allows for an (a) informed decision on whether a change initiative should be planned, (b) identification of technical risks that directly impact the business objective (Von Canon, 2017), (c) resolutions or responses to any risks prior to change initiation, and (d) continuous tracking of risk resolutions until they are complete and risks are mitigated. This is true for all forms of change to infrastructure, solutions or services; as well as the associated policy, procedures, processes, and roles and responsibilities of staff involved in the change initiative, and consumers of the change.

Figure 1. Pre-risk governance life cycle (Larry, 2017)

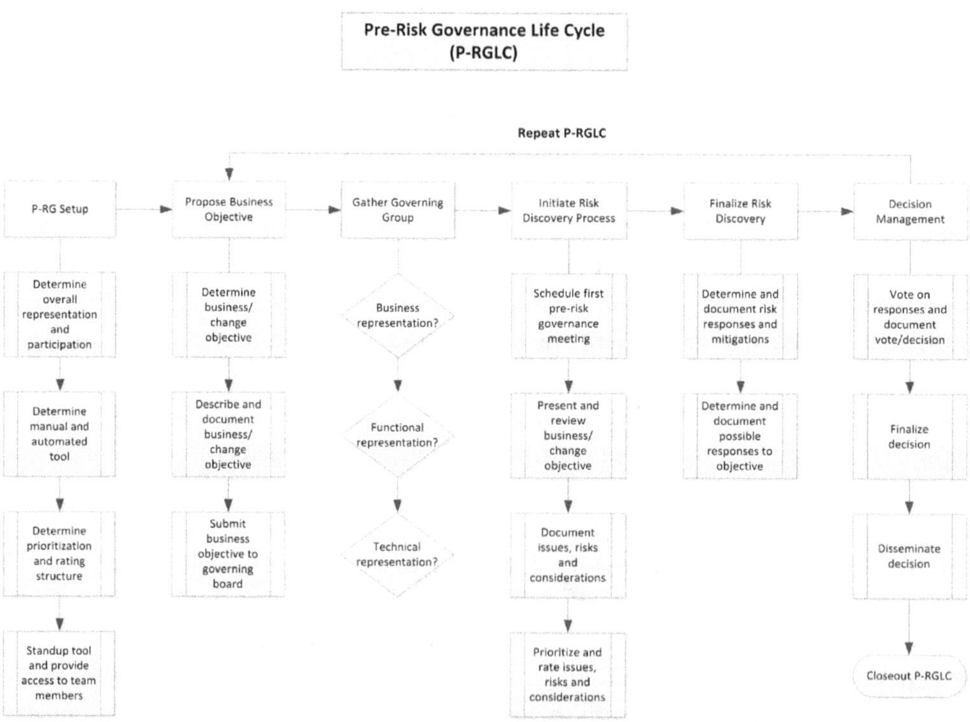

Change Management

Since the 1970s, there has been a consistent statistic regarding IT based change initiatives, 60% to 70% of change projects fail. Per Carucci (2006):

When it comes to organizational change, failure continues to be more common than success. In a survey of nearly 3,000 executives about the success of their enterprise transformation efforts, McKinsey discovered the failure rate to be higher than 60%, while Harvard Business Review conducted a study that suggested more than 70% of transformation efforts fail. (p.1, paragraph 1)

While it is a generally accepted fact that policy and technology changes directly impact consumers of products and services, policy and technology changes also impact those individuals and teams responsible for initiating and implementing such changes. However, many organizations demonstrate limited, if any, recognition and support for employees performing in the dual role of change implementers and change supporters in the workplace; on this premise, the organization, itself, remains distanced from the realities regarding how IT workers are impacted by change and the associated transition process. Furthermore, with change efforts, especially those requiring new means of operation, there is an accompanying shift in systems (i.e., infrastructure/hardware and tools) and processes. These shifts may include changes to work roles and responsibilities, including the ways in which roles are initiated and performed within information technology teams. Nevertheless, in order to support and sustain underlying infrastructure systems, IT staff must be able to work with and through the change effort while going through a transition themselves and also supporting others through transition (Venkatesh, Morris, Davis, & Davis, 2003). Otherwise, the transition process will take longer, and the change will cost more money or fail altogether (Larry, 2017, pp. 4-5).

Change events that occur within technology-driven organizations position IT workers as front-line staff charged with the responsibility of dealing with both people and systems in order to facilitate the mandated change and move the organization forward. Thus, tasked with handling multiple areas of technological concern and interacting with a variety of people, IT teams face intensified demands when implementing and supporting change while, at the same time, they are transitioning through the change event themselves.

Employee Involvement

An important study was conducted by Litwin (2010) on employee involvement (EI) with technological change, or IT, in the HIT sector (Kaiser Permanente Northwest Region's patient scheduling module). Litwin (2010) stated:

New technologies offer an important avenue by which EI can improve firm performance. Litwin also contends that those studies that do consider EI in the context of technological change may be focusing exclusively on workplace-level features of the employment relationship, ignoring variation in functional—and strategic—level aspects of employment relations. (p. 866)

Litwin (2010) discussed the association between aspects of workplace technological change and business performance. There may be a good return on investment (ROI) for new technologies, but there is an associated cost for that ROI. Cost may be associated with people, schedules/time, and effective implementation practices. He developed a study through which he aimed to explore how company performance could increase with EI if technological change is handled properly. The study site was Kaiser Permanente Northwest Region in the Portland/Vancouver metropolitan area, as well as the communities of Longview and Kelso, Washington, and Salem, Oregon where the patient scheduling module served as the study context. The study was a quantitative, employee survey-based study that ran from October 2004 through August 2007, across 16 clinics. Based on his findings, Litwin (2010) concluded, "This study offers convincing evidence that EI in implementation moderates the performance effects of IT" (p. 883). In the following passage, Litwin (2010) addressed some of the study data:

Overall, only 11% of respondents claimed that they were first introduced to the technology by a fellow member of the bargaining unit (as opposed to a manager or an IT staffer), though 18% asserted that they had, in fact, received follow-up training from a co-worker. About 40% noted the importance of "super-users"—fellow members of the bargaining unit pulled from their regular, frontline positions to assist in the development and deployment of the system—to their successful use of the scheduling module. (pp. 879-880)

Theoretically, employee involvement may be viewed as a component of the experiences associated with an organization's staff members. Through studying staff, a pattern might be found linking the individual's experience of change and transition with her/his level of participation in the process. Furthermore, the Litwin study is relevant because it reinforces the idea that possibilities for successful implementation of technological change are increased by understanding the experiences of IT staff who implement and support change efforts. This research studied the experiences of change and transition through the eyes of the IT teams who were responsible for implementation and support—of both the organization and the end user. Through this study, the researcher provided information on the psychological transition processes of IT team members and shed light on how change events might be better planned by the organization so as to support these human processes and work toward better ensuring a successful technological change.

Pre-Risk Governance includes the different components of change – people, process and infrastructure - as well as the associated risks, issues and concerns associated with the decision making process. Employee Involvement allows the people component of change to be addressed up front. IT SMEs provide additional considerations outside of and including business and functional considerations. The impact of changes to the enterprise as it applies to internal and external customers and end users, and the associated technical and customer support are also considerations that can be addressed using Pre-Risk Governance (Larry, 2017).

WHAT HAPPENS WITHOUT PRE-RISK GOVERNANCE

An excellent example of what occurs when IT Pre-Risk Governance is not used is the initial implementation of new electronic health care systems. The initial attempt at one such implementation was unsuccessful according to Scheuer and Smetters (2014). Consumers could not access the system and enroll in health care programs. The reason for the failure was attributed to lack of planning and testing. Scheuer and Smetters suggested that those responsible for supporting the systems were not ready. Information technology staff implemented and supported the new system, but planning did not include the Health Information Technology staff. Planning included only the actual infrastructure technical components: the new system, including the machines (servers and databases), and (web) access points as described in the Health Information Technology for Economic and Clinical Health (HITECH) Act (2009). Clearly, the initial problems that characterized this new electronic health care system's implementation stand as important reference points from which to assert the need for inclusion of subject matter experts (SMEs), in the form of IT staff, be included in pre-planning of the change event in order to tease out risks and issues with associated mitigation plans and practices prior to systems design, development, configuration, testing/verification and implementation.

Lessons Learned

The "lessons learned" findings that were conveyed during the study and that occur as risks, issues or concerns during change initiatives, were: (a) lack of preplanning; (b) underestimation of time, cost, schedule and/or resourcing; (c) poor, limited or no communication about the change prior to the decision to initiate change; and (d) lack of inclusion (of IT staff) in and input to decision making regarding the change. These findings can be applied across change initiatives/projects. The use of Pre-

Risk Governance and including IT staff in the pre-change initiation process begins to address the study "lessons learned" (Larry, 2017).

Solution and Project Management Life Cycles

Risk Management, as currently defined and used as part of Project Management Methodology (PMM), occurs after executive or senior management has determined that a change will be made. This is too late in the overall solutions development and project management life cycles; change should be assessed prior to initiation. The project management life cycle begins once a project has been determined (PMI, 2017). The solutions development life cycle begins at the initiation of the requirements management process (Shelly, Cashman & Adamski, 1995). The change management life cycle begins when it is determined a change needs to or must occur (Bennis, 1966; Burke, 2002). All life cycles have similarities and/or overlap and can and do occur simultaneously. All life cycles begin with a determination that some change must occur. Figure 2 illustrates the phases of each of the three life cycles (Solutions Development, Project Management and Change Management) utilized during a change initiative.

This figure illustrates the sequence of phases within each life cycle.

WHEN SHOULD PRE-RISK GOVERNANCE OCCUR?

Pre-Risk Governance should be implemented in a business "forming" stage prior to the requirements management process where requirements are verified, quantified and prioritized (Von Canon, 2017). As requirements management begins in the Planning and Project Initiation phases of the SDLC and PMLC respectively, Pre-Risk Governance should occur as early in the process as possible allowing for an informed decision regarding the way ahead for the proposed change and may be cyclical based on the possible impact to the enterprise (Larry, 2017). The earlier risks, issues and concerns are raised, the earlier a determination may be made and thus the costs associated with human capital, equipment/infrastructure, time/schedule and budget for the project or change initiative may be obfuscated early on in the associated life cycles. Figure 3 represents all of the life cycles (P-RGLC, SDLC, PMLC, and ChMLC) and when Pre-Risk Governance should occur - prior to initiation of all life cycles.

Figure 2. A Comparison of the solutions development, project management and change management life cycles (Larry, 2017)

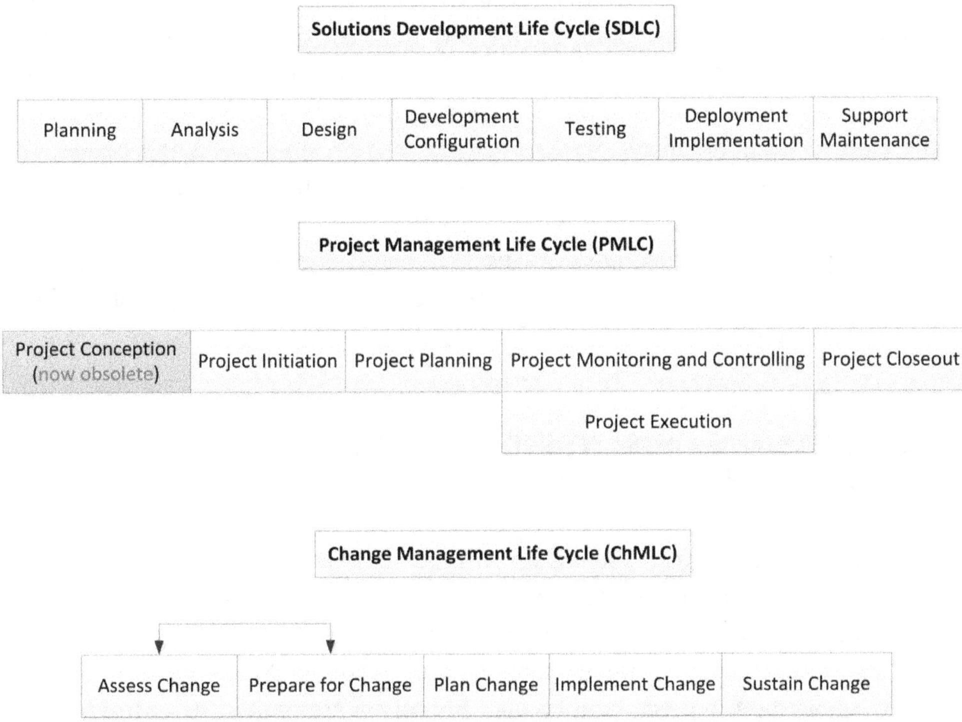

Figure 3. Pre-risk Governance in relationship to other life Cycles (Larry, 2017)

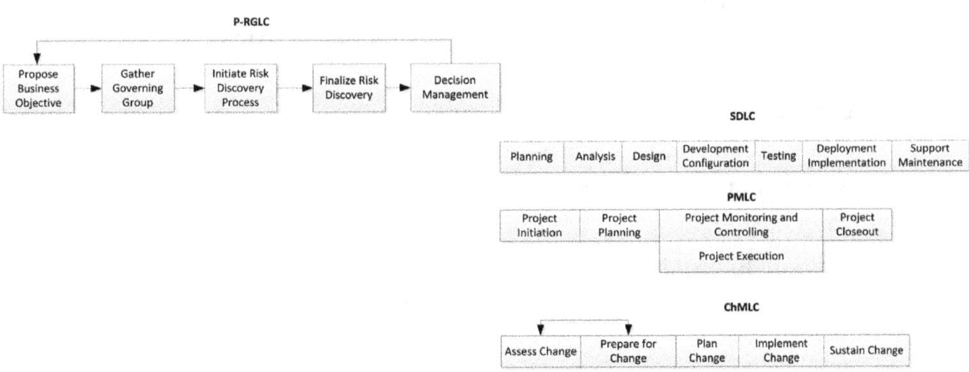

Requirements Management

A project, or change initiative, is informed by requirements to assess and help determine what needs to be built or changed and how the change may occur. A requirement is a compulsory or necessary condition for/of the change initiative or project (Lavanya & Malarvizhi, 2008). The purpose of requirements management is to ensure that an organization documents, verifies, and meets the needs and expectations of its customers and internal or external stakeholders (PMI, 2017). Requirements Management includes the gathering of business, functional and technical requirements which are prioritized to determine what and when systems (infrastructure, hardware/servers, networks, etc.) and solutions (applications and tools) will be implemented.

FUTURE TRENDS DEMANDING A PARADIGM SHIFT IN RISK MANAGEMENT

As companies and federal agencies continue to expand solution and service offerings, change projects and initiatives will increase to accommodate changes to or expansions of existing technologies. There are several trends associated with change and information technology that are continuations of existing technologies and may impact how projects and change initiatives are managed, as follows per DeMers (2016):

- Smart Technologies.
    - Interconnectedness of smart technologies.
    - Uniform user experiences (e.g., Google, Amazon and Apple technologies).
- Virtual Solutions.
    - Augmented reality systems and tools.
    - Virtual applications and games.
- Machine Learning.
    - Search engine capability expansion for electronic devices (e.g., product recommendations, improved user experience).
- Automation.
    - Robotic journalists.
- Humanized Big Data.
    - Expansion of quantitative numerical foundations.
    - Expansion of empathetic, qualitative data.
    - Visualized, accessible data.

- Physical Digital Integrations.
  - Dash button electronic devices used for ordering frequently used products (e.g., at Amazon.com).
- On-Demand Access.

With expanding technology trends, new change projects will continue to be initiated thus demanding a new more efficient and cost-effective approach, Pre-Risk Governance and the inclusion of SMEs (IT staff) to determine the feasibility of change and the possible impact to the enterprise and internal and external stakeholders prior to making the decision to make a change (Larry, 2017). The use of Project Management to manage, control and oversee solution and service extensions is the normal approach for business and technology companies today. The use of Project Management Methodology (PMM) throughout the solution development, or extension, life cycle is also part of normal operations for the enterprise or agency. This entails moving through the phases of the PMLC using a systems or solutions development methodology such as an Iterative or Agile approach (Jackson, 2012).

Current Solutions/Systems Change Methods

An Iterative approach calls for breaking down the solutions development process into small chunks and cyclically designing, developing and testing/verifying a component until the complete solution is updated and ready for implementation - use by internal and external customers (Shelly, Cashman, &Adamski, 1995). While an Agile approach is both incremental and iterative, it allows for the release and use of the component of the solution when the component is available. Components are independent in that they are stand alone or may be an upgrade to existing technologies, allowing for continued usage without bringing down the whole solution or system. Agile also allows for development of multiple components at once across Sprint teams, where a Sprint team is a standalone team including business and technical resources that can deliver a usable solution (Pressman, 2009).

Risk Management Is Not Enough

Regardless of the development methodology, risk management is a normal part of the process. But risk management in and of itself does not address what can be done if issues, concerns and problems are determined and discussed prior to making a decision to move forward with change; nor does it address the elongated schedule and increased cost implications of change as any project or enterprise transition moves forward. Including IT staff in the decision-making process prior to moving forward with a change initiative supports successful change management as defined in Pre-Risk Governance.

The Cost of Not Using Pre-Risk Governance

The additional cost of finding issues, concerns and problems while completing change is much higher than determining what they may be and avoiding them up front - or prior to the initiation of change (Pre-Risk Governance). According to solutions error and problem tracking measurements during the SDLC, the cost of finding an issue during different phases of the life cycle(s) increases as the life cycle progresses. The closer the solution is to delivery or implementation, the higher the cost of issue resolution due to the associated rework and retest as IT staff is repeating work thus driving up costs and delaying the schedule. The cost of finding and resolving a problem or error after a change/solution has been implemented is four to five times as much as one uncovered and resolved during the *Design* phase of the SDLC (Leon, 2015). Imagine the savings in finding and addressing risks, issues, concerns and problems prior to the initiation of change (Pre-Risk Governance).

CONCLUSION

The use of risk management as a part of the Project Management Methodology has been an ongoing trend over the past (almost) two decades, however, guidelines and usage of risk management and PMM has and continues to change to include best practices that have been found to aid in successful transition from obsolete systems and technologies to current and future paradigms using shared services and solutions. The use of Pre-Risk Governance should become part of the standard and we will see if this is so as the sixth edition of PMM was introduced on September 6, 2017. Pre-Risk Governance should be considered a best practice for the enterprise in any change (management) project or initiative.

Successful Pre-Risk Governance entails (a) including all manner and type of human capital in gathering information about the feasibility of making an enterprise change, and specifically IT staff; (b) recording and managing any and all issues, concerns and problems that may be discovered in discussions; (c) classifying, prioritizing and rating the issues, concerns and problems (business, functional and technical; cost/budget; schedule/time or resource; etc.); (d) providing a weight for the priority levels; (e) determining mitigation and response plans of action for each issue/concern/problem; (f) and voting on if and when a major change or transition effort should occur (Larry, 2017). All participants are provisioned with equal voting power and others may be pulled into discussions as additional information is discovered. Governance requires tracking and accountability for the enterprise. Figure 1 represents the Pre-Risk Governance Life Cycle phases and progression.

Pre-Risk Governance is not simply risk analysis, nor is it simply risk management. Pre-Risk Governance is the concatenation of risk analysis, risk management and enterprise governance to determine and address possible issues, concerns, and problems prior to making a decision to move forward with a corporate or enterprise change initiative or project that may affect or impact internal resources, stakeholders, external customers, and end users (Larry, 2017). If the cost of resolving issues during the SDLC is four to five times higher as there is progression through the life cycle (Leon, 2015), the cost of identifying and mitigating risks prior to the initiation of change is more than four or five times the savings in cost/budget, schedule/time and human capital if found prior to initiating change. In order to improve the chances for a successful change initiative involving a new solution or service, including all resources that may provide input into the possible pit falls of a transition effort in discussions prior to making a final determination to move forward with the change is an effective method toward successful transition. Pre-Risk Governance, with IT participation, should be the standard.

REFERENCES

Bennis, W. G. (1966). Changing organizations. *The Journal of Applied Behavioral Science*, *2*(3), 247–263. doi:10.1177/002188636600200301

Brailer, D., & Thompson, T. (2004). *Health IT strategic framework*. Washington, DC: Department of Health and Human Services.

Bratton, J., & Gold, J. (2012). *Human Resource Management: Theory and Practice*. Basingstoke, UK: Palgrave Macmillan. doi:10.1007/978-1-137-00095-8

Bridges, W. (2004). *Transitions: Making sense of life's changes*. Cambridge, MA: De Capo Press.

Bridges, W. (2010). *Managing Transition: Making the Most of Change*. Philadelphia, PA: Accessible Publishing Systems.

Bridges, W. (2013). *Managing Transition: Bridges transition model*. Philadelphia, PA: Accessible Publishing Systems.

Blumenthal, D. (2004). Launching HITECH. *The New England Journal of Medicine*, *362*(5), 382–385. doi:10.1056/NEJMp0912825 PMID:20042745

Blumenthal, D. (2009). Stimulating the adoption of health information technology. *The New England Journal of Medicine*, *360*(15), 1477–1499. doi:10.1056/NEJMp0901592 PMID:19321856

Blumenthal, D. (2011). Implementation of the federal health information technology initiative. *The New England Journal of Medicine*, *365*(25), 2426–2431. doi:10.1056/NEJMsr1112158 PMID:22187990

Brailer, D., & Thompson, T. (2004). *Health IT strategic framework*. Washington, DC: Department of Health and Human Services.

Buntin, M. B., Jain, S. H., & Blumenthal, D. (2010). Health information technology: Laying the infrastructure for national health reform. *Health Affairs*, *29*(6), 1214–1219. doi:10.1377/hlthaff.2010.0503 PMID:20530358

Burke, W. W. (2013). *Organization Change: Theory and practice*. New York, NY: Sage Publications.

Carucci, R. (2016). *Organizations Can't Change If Leaders Can't Change with Them*. Retrieved from https://hbr.org/2016/10/organizations-cant-change-if-leaders-cant-

Chaudhry, B., Wang, J., Wu, S., Maglione, M., Mojlca, W., Roth, E., ... Shekelle, P. G. (2006). Systematic review: Impact of health information technology on quality, efficiency, and costs of medical care. *Annals of Internal Medicine*, *144*(10), 742–752. doi:10.7326/0003-4819-144-10-200605160-00125 PMID:16702590

ConsumerReports.org. (2012). *Update on Health Care Reform; Many updates are already here, though major ones come in 2014*. Retrieved from http://www.consumerreports.org/cro/2012/06/update-on-health-care-reform/index.htm

DeMers, J. (2016). *7 Technology Trends That Will Dominate 2017*. Retrieved from https://www.forbes.com/sites/jaysondemers/2016/11/16/7-technology-trends-that-will-dominate-2017/1#95695054a51d

Goodman, E., & Loh, L. (2011). Organizational change: A critical challenge for team effectiveness. *Business Information Review*, *28*, 242–250. doi:10.1177/0266382111427087

Green, F. (2012). Employee Involvement, Technology and Evolution in Job Skills: A Task-Based Analysis. *Industrial & Labor Relations Review*, *65*(1), 36–67. doi:10.1177/001979391206500103

Hersh, W. (2010). The Health Information Technology Workforce. *Applied Clinical Informatics*, *1*(2), 197–212. doi:10.4338/ACI-2009-11-R-0011 PMID:23616836

Hoyt, R. E., & Liebenberg, A. P. (2011). The Value of Enterprise Risk Management. *The Journal of Risk and Insurance*, *78*(4), 795–822. doi:10.1111/j.1539-6975.2011.01413.x

Jackson, M. B. (2012). Agile: A decade in. *PM Network, 26*(4), 58–62. Retrieved from https://www.pmi.org/learning/library/agile-manifesto-software-development-impact-2284

Kearney, K. S. (2002). *A study of the emotional effects on employees who remain through organizational change: A view through Kübler-Ross (1969) in an educational institution.* Oklahoma State University. Retrieved from ProQuest Dissertations and Theses: http://search.proquest.com/docview/276207296?accountid=11243 (276207296)

KPMG.com. (2014). *Business Transformation and the Corporate Agenda.* Retrieved from: http://www.kpmginfo.com/Transformation/assets/pdf/business-transformation-corporate-agenda.pdf

KPMG.com. (2016). *Evolution of an industry: Spotlight on Ed-tech.* Retrieved from:https://home.kpmg.com/xx/en/home/insights/2016/02/evolution-of-an-industry.html

Kübler-Ross, E. (1969). *On death and dying*. New York, NY: Touchstone.

Larry, L. (2017). *A qualitative study of the experience of individuals within information technology teams during transition using the kübler-ross grief construct and the bridges transition model* (Order No. 10615376). Available from ProQuest Dissertations & Theses Global. (1944510678). Retrieved from http://proxygw.wrlc.org/login?url=https://search-proquest-com.proxygw.wrlc.org/docview/1944510678?accountid=11243

Lavanya, N., & Malarvizhi, T. (2008). *Risk analysis and management—a vital key to effective project management.* Paper presented at PMI® Global Congress 2008—Asia Pacific, Sydney, Australia.

Leavitt, H. J., & Whistler, T. L. (1958). Management in the 1980s. *Harvard Business Review*, *36*, 41–48.

Leon, J. (2015). *The True Cost of a Software Bug: Part One*. Retrieved from http://blog.celerity.com/the-true-cost-of-a-software-bug

Lippitt, W., & Watson, J. (1958). *Westley, the dynamics of planned change*. New York, NY: HBJ.

Litwin, A. S. (2011). Technological Change at Work: The Impact of Employee Involvement on the Effectiveness of Health Information Technology. *Industrial & Labor Relations Review*, *64*(5), 863–888. doi:10.1177/001979391106400502

McDonagh, J., & Coghlan, D. (2006). Information technology and the lure of integrated change: A neglected role for organizational development? *Public Administration Quarterly*, *30*(1), 22–55.

Oxford Press Dictionary. (2017). *Oxford Dictionaries*. Retrieved from https://www.oxforddictionaries.com/

Oxford University. (2015). *A Dictionary of Physics* (6th ed.). New York, NY: Oxford University Press.

Pressman, R. (2009). *Software Engineering: A Practitioner's Approach*. Columbus, OH: McGraw-Hill.

Project Management Institute. (2009). *Practice Standard for Project Risk Management*. Newtown Square, PA: Project Management Institute.

Project Management Institute. (2017a). *Project Management*. Retrieved from https://search.pmi.org/default.aspx?q=Project%20Management

Project Management Institute. (2017b). *Requirements Management*. Retrieved from https://search.pmi.org/default.aspx?q=Requirements%20Management

Saldaña, J. (2011). *Fundamentals of Qualitative Research*. New York, NY: Oxford University Press.

Saldaña, J. (2013). *The Coding Manual for Qualitative Researchers*. Thousand Oaks, CA: Sage Publications, Inc.

Scheuer, F., & Smetters, K. (2014). *Could a Website Really Have Doomed the Health Exchanges? Multiple Equilibria, Initial Conditions and the Construction of the Fine (No. w19835)*. National Bureau of Economic Research. doi:10.3386/w19835

Shelly, G. B., Cashman, T. J., Adamski, J., & Adamski, J. J. (1995). *Systems Analysis and Design*. Danvers, MA: Boyd and Fraser Publishing Company.

Venkatesh, V., Morris, M. G., Davis, G. B., & Davis, F. D. (2003). User acceptance of information technology: Towards a unified view. *Management Information Systems Quarterly*, *27*(3), 425–478. doi:10.2307/30036540

Von Canon, W. A. (2017). *Personal correspondence. President*. Fairfax, VA: Business Intelligence, Incorporated.

Xiong, W., Zhao, X., Yuan, J.-F., & Luo, S. (2017). Ex Post Risk Management in Public-Private Partnership Infrastructure Projects. *Project Management Journal*, *48*(3), 76–89.

Chapter 4
ERP Post-Implementation Success Assessment:
An Extended Framework

Ahad Zare Ravasan
Mehralborz Institute of Higher Education, Iran

Ali Zare
Shahid Beheshti University, Iran

Seyed Mojtaba Hosseini Bamakan
Shenzhen Institutes of Advanced Technology, China

ABSTRACT

Enterprise resource planning implementation is a costly project that tends to face serious challenges. Thus, it is essential to perform the success assessment at the post-implementation stage of an ERP project to evaluate how much the system has succeeded in achieving its predetermined objectives. This chapter proposes an extended framework for assessing a firm's ERP post-implementation success. The factors contributing to the success assessment have been adapted from the original model of Ifinedo et al., which encompasses service quality, system quality, information quality, individual, workgroup, and organizational impact surrogates. Also, a new surrogate of inter-organizational impact proposed in this research. Using this model, the firm's ERP system success can be determined and the required improvement projects can be proposed to promote the success level. The proposed model is then applied to a real international company in the field of manufacturing and supplying turbines to measure the firm's ERP post-implementation success. Finally, the results of the assessment are discussed.

DOI: 10.4018/978-1-5225-5829-3.ch004

INTRODUCTION

Enterprise Resource Planning (ERP) systems are defined as software system allowing the complete integration of information flow from all functional areas in companies by means of single database; such a system is accessible through a unified interface of communication (Davenport, 1998). In recent times, implementing enterprise resource planning (ERP) systems has become a trend across the globe and organizations are investing vast resources on it. ERP implementations are associated with a promise of benefits from automation and integration but they also carry the risk of failure. Some of the biggest failures were seen at Foxmeyer, Hershey Foods, and more recently, Avon Products. It has been suggested that new information systems (IS) often fail due to implementation weaknesses rather than technology shortcomings (Kemp & Low, 2008). Accordingly, over recent years, some researchers have provided valuable insights into the process of ERP implementation (e.g., Abdel-Kader & Nguyen, 2011; Soja, 2008; Soltani, Elkhani, & Bardsiri, 2014; Subramanianh & Hoffers, 2005; Wang, Shih, Jiang, & Klein, 2008) and others reported a set of Critical Success Factors (CSFs) or Critical Failure Factors (CFFs) in ERP projects (e.g., Amid, Moalagh, & Zare Ravasan, 2012; Hanafizadeh, Gholami, Dadbin, & Standage, 2010; Khattak et al., 2013; Kini & Basaviah, 2013; Nour & Mouakket, 2011; Rouhani, Ashrafi, & Afshari, 2013; Zhang, Lee, Huang, Zhang, & Huang, 2005).

Organizations implement ERP systems to meet predetermined corporate goals and improve functional and organizational goals (Al-Mashari, Al-Mudimigh, & Zairi, 2003; Davenport, 1998, 2000; Yusuf, Gunasekaran, & Abthorpe, 2004) and post-implementation ERP success means that these systems could help organizations to meet their goals and achieve potential benefits (Wang et al., 2008). ERP implementation is not the final goal but is an important milestone to start continuous improvements in organizations (Yu, 2005). So, organizations need to define post-implementation review (PIR) to measure ERP system success (Nicolaou & Bhattacharya, 2006). Such evaluations could determine failure factors and offer improvement projects to strengthen poor areas in the organization (Mandal & Gunasekaran, 2003); But assessing or evaluating the success of complex IT systems such as ERP in adopting organizations is difficult due to the complex nature of such technologies (Davenport, 1998, 2000; Gable, Sedera, & Chan, 2003; Ifinedo & Nahar, 2007; Markus & Tanis, 2000). Despite its importance, prior research works have overlooked these areas (Gorla, Somers, & Wong, 2010), while, it is a research interest as noted by Law, Chen and Wu (2010).

There are several models proposed by researchers for evaluating ERP systems implementation success (Delone & McLean, 1992, 2003; Gable et al., 2003; Ifinedo & Nahar, 2007; Ifinedo, Rapp, Ifinedo, & Sundberg, 2010; Zhang et al., 2005). However, these models paid much attention to the intra-organizational factors in

ERP success assessment, while overlooking inter-organizational surrogates (Zare & Ravasan, 2014). However, inter-organizational impacts and benefits of ERPs could be figured as increased customer service/satisfaction, e-government enabler, better supplier relationships, e-business/e-commerce enabler, improved service/ product delivery, improved cooperation with colleagues and so on (Davenport & Brooks, 2004; Gable et al., 2003; Gable, Sedera, & Chan, 2008; Hatzithomas, Stamelos, Fotiadis, & Mylonakis, 2011; Ifinedo et al., 2010; Su & Yang, 2010).

Hence, with this in mind, this present research effort is designed to contribute to the literature by developing a brand new and more comprehensive model for ERP success assessment. To that end, in this paper, an ERP post-implementation success assessment model has been developed based on prior models and new inter-organizational impact surrogate. It is important to mention that the purpose of this present work is not to test the previous IS or ERP success model per se, as several IS/ERP researchers (e.g., Iivari, 2005a; Petter, DeLone, & McLean, 2008) have already published works in that domain. Rather, this present effort is directed at extending and advancing previous works especially the work of Ifinedo et al. (2010) in the area of ERP system success measurement.

LITERATURE REVIEW

ERP has been proclaimed as the new information systems (ISs) paradigm (Klaus, Rosemann, & Gable, 2000) and ERP success models draw from information systems success evaluation patterns. The most famous model that emerges from IS success research projects is Delone and McLean (1992) model (D&M model). They introduced their framework as a review of 180 empirical studies in 1992. The D&M model consists of six major surrogates including system quality, information quality, use, user satisfaction, individual impact and organizational impact. Delone and McLean (1992) insisted that the above surrogates are interrelated and have a casual dependency in measuring information system success. D&M framework has been regarded as the most influential model for assessing information systems (Iivari, 2005b). After Delone and Mclean model, Seddon (1997) published an extended version of the D&M model by separating two sub models (use and success) and eliminating the process model interpretation. Delone and Mclean (2003) revised their model and replaced individual impact and organizational impact with net benefit.

The first ERP success assessment model backs to 1982 which White et al. (1982) created ABCD checklist. They classified ERP implementations into four categories. User satisfaction is also used to serve as a surrogate for ERP post-implementation success (Al-Mashari et al., 2003; Markus & Tanis, 2000; Zhang et al., 2005). White et al. (1982) proposed their ERP post-implementation success model in two surrogates:

(1) improved performance and (2) user satisfaction. One of the most accredited models that is presented in recent years is Markus and Tanis (2000) Model. They argued that the definition and measurement of ERP success depends on the point of view from which you measure it. They said that the ERP implementation cycle could be divided into three distinct phases.

The first phase is the project phase and it is related to the organization ability to successfully install and implement the system. In the second one, "shakedown phase", the model measures the extent and duration of the organizational impact caused by the ERP system. The final set of indicators which relates to the third phase is called "onward and upward" phase. Markus and Tanis (2000) showed that success in ERP implementation was derived by incremental process and could not be achieved suddenly. After Markus and Tanis (2000), Tan and Pan (2002) presented their model. They believed that in Markus and Tanis (2000) model, little attention was paid to the soft side of ERP systems. So, they offered a new model that defined ERP success as an infrastructure success, info-structure success and knowledge success. This model includes both sides of technical and strategic values in ERP post-implementation success assessment.

Another prominent research in this area is the Gable et al. (2003) model that has been validated and widely considered in the literature (Ifinedo & Nahar, 2007). The Gable et al. (2003) model rooted in the D&M model but they asserted that several measures in the D&M model were redundant, unsuitable and inappropriate to measure the success of ERP systems. Furthermore, they concluded that user satisfaction was not a distinct surrogate and then omitted user satisfaction from their proposed model. They also pointed out that D&M measures of organizational impacts focus on financial factors and do not cover business process improvement and organizational change. Therefore, Gable et al. (2003) proposed their model in four surrogates including system quality, information quality, individual impact, and organizational impact which was also considered as a foundation for latter models. System quality is related to system flexibility, reliability, responsibility, integration and sophistication. Therefore, this surrogate is an intrinsic property of ERPs that is relevant to system design and development process and also is more considered by IT staff. Information quality is the second surrogate in Gable et al. (2003) list that is related to the quality of outputs and could be founded in forms of reports and screens.

Information quality guaranties ERP usefulness and should be represented in relevance with user needs (Kwahk, 2006). Additionally, it should be presented in an easy-to-use format, available in desired time and contain frequent updates. ERP usage has significant impacts on individual works such as improving personal productivity and daily business activities, increasing the quality and decreasing the time of individual decision making and facilitating knowledge sharing between system users (Zhang et al., 2005). Individual impact affects users' satisfaction and encourages them to use or disuse the system (Chien & Tsaur, 2007). Employees are more willing to use the ERP system if it can support their daily activities, reduce reworks and release more time to think. The last one but not the least surrogate is organizational impact. An ERP package is considered successful at the post-implementation phase, if it enhance potential benefits through organizational cost reductions, higher operational productivity, increased customer satisfaction levels, and so forth (Gable et al., 2003).

Studies show that one of the most powerful managerial expectations to implement ERP systems is to improve organization competiveness (Yu, 2005). Competitive advantages could not be achieved without improving core processes. The main benefits of ERP implementation stand in processes and people. Meanwhile, system implementation in itself, does not improve anything (Kumar, Maheshwari, & Kumar, 2003). So, another important factor that affects success in ERP projects is business process re-engineering. ERP systems improve organization efficiency in terms of saving labor costs, better use of resources and supporting decision making with better accessibility to large amount of information (Botta-Genoulaz & Millet, 2005; Hsu & Chen, 2004; Olhager & Selldin, 2003). Therefore, Gable et al. (2003) introduces five factors of competitive advantage, customer service/ satisfaction, facilitating business process change, supporting decision making and better use of organizational data resource to evaluate organizational impact.

After Gable et al. (2003), Zhang et al. (2005) presented a model based on Ives et al. (1980) and D&M models. Their case studies were in home appliances and electronics industries in China. Zhang et al. (2005) developed a conceptual research framework to guide the relationship among organizational environment, user environment, ERP system environment, ERP vendor environment and ERP post-implementation success. Nevertheless, the Zhang et al. (2005) model has been recognized more as a guidance framework to implement ERP system successfully rather than a practical model to measure ERP post-implementation success. So, it attracted less attention than Gable et al. (2003) model in the latter literature.

Based on Gable et al. (2003) model, Ifinedo and Nahar (2007) tried to develop their work. They continued their work by asking this question: "Is the Gable et al. (2003) ERP success measurement model comprehensive? If not, can the model be extended to incorporate other relevant surrogates of success?" In this way, Ifinedo and Nahar (2007) added workgroup impact to the Gable et al. (2003) model. They argued that the philosophy of ERP is to improve the performance of sub-units in organizations and then it should be considered in success assessment. To justify this development, they referred to previous works in which the significant effect of information technology investments occurred at operational level of organizations. They identified improved workers' participation, improved organizational-wide communication, creation a sense of responsibility, improved efficiency of sub-units and solution effectiveness as the factors for assessing workgroup impact. Another surrogate that was added to Gable et al. (2003) model was vendor and consultant quality. Selecting the appropriate vendor is one of the key critical success factors in ERP implementation. Earlier, other researchers found that the vendor quality had an important role in achieving success through ERP implementation (Markus & Tanis, 2000; Sedera, Gable, & Chan, 2004; Wu & Wang, 2006).

Ifinedo and Nahar (2007) argued that the quality of external providers (vendor and consultant) had also a significant influence in ERP success. They represented adequate technical support, credibility and trustworthiness, good relationships, experience and good communication as the factors to assess vendor and consultant quality. Ifinedo et al. (2010) replaced aforementioned vendor and consultant quality surrogate with service quality and operationalized that by reliability, dependability, quality of expertise, and so forth. Moalagh and Zare Ravasan (2012) proposed their model which strived to highlight the importance of considering the nonlinear relationships among surrogates and subsequent factors as well as unique organizational goals in ERP success assessment. They used fuzzy ANP method for weighting Ifinedo and Nahar (2007) model's surrogates and related factors. Besides, they broke down the construct of ERP success into three main parts, including "managerial success", "organizational success", and "individual success" as figure 1.

Figure 1. ANP framework for ERP success implementation (Moalagh & Zare Ravasan, 2012)

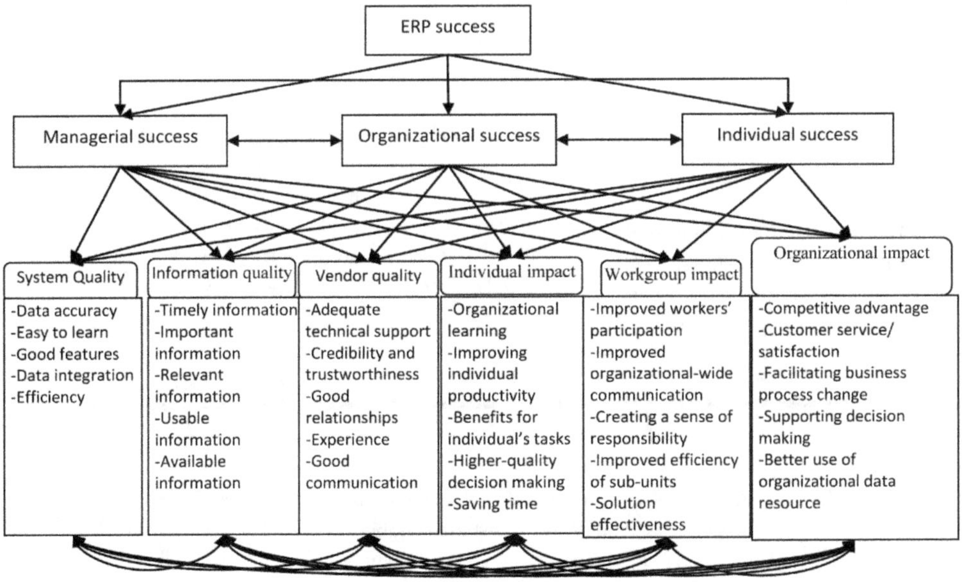

Zerbino et al. (2017) formulated ERP Success from an Information Systems Failure Perspective and defined ERP success as success in the four following dimensions, contextualized within the ERP environment: process, correspondence, interaction, and expectation. These categories are actually four-level classification of IT project failure modes a) Process failure, when the project is not completed within time and/or budget. b) Expectation failure, when the IT systems do not live up to user expectations. c) Interaction failure, when users' attitudes towards the IT are negative. d) Correspondence failure, when there is no match between IT systems and the planned objectives (Amid, Moalagh, & Ravasan, 2012). The authors claimed that their approach dynamically considers all the most relevant dimensions of success in different points in time; it keeps into account ERP peculiarities; it gathers, integrates, and formally improves the extant definitions of ERP success;

Nizamani (2017) proposed an ERP success model for universities of Pakistan. The theoretical foundation of this model was based on DeLone and McLean (1992) IS success model which incorporated system quality, information quality, service quality, user satisfaction, and organizational impact

Gollner and Baumane-Vitolina (2016), based on a survey data of 300 companies located in Austria and Germany, proposed that characteristics of ERP success factors can be summoned up to five different dimensions, namely project management, user satisfaction, time and budget, ERP system quality and economic value. They implied that some of the dimensions suggested by other scholars are coherent and redundant, and, therefore, an extra measurement of these aspects is misleading.

The evolution of ERP post-implementation success assessment models in the previous years along with a description of the surrogates was mentioned above. The summarized timeline of emerging models is illustrated in Figure 2.

Figure 2. The timeline of major emerging ERP post implementation success models

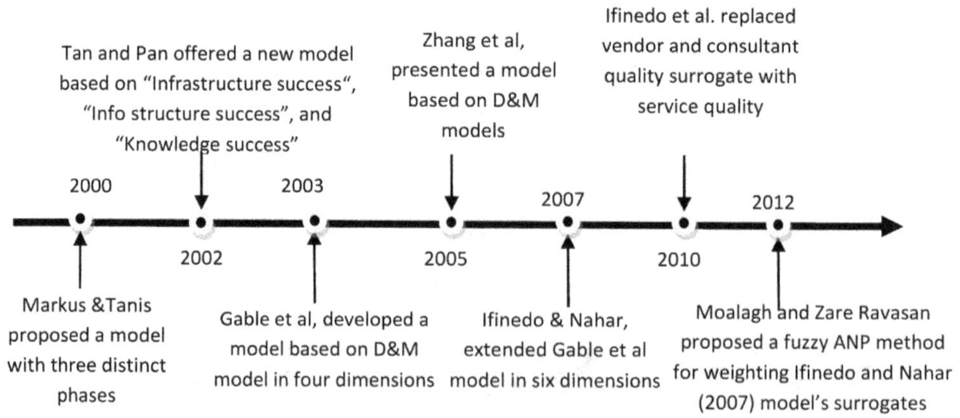

RESEARCH CONCEPTUAL MODEL

An ERP system could potentially enhance transparency across the supply chain by eliminating information asymmetry and increase information velocity. Hence, there is reason to believe that ERP adoption could be associated with significant gains in supply chain effectiveness and inter-organizational communications (Akkermans, Bogerd, Yücesan, & Van Wassenhove, 2003). According to Kalakota and Robinson (2001), the evolution of ERPs can be divided into four phases: manufacturing integration, enterprise integration, customer-centric integration, and inter-enterprise integration. The industrial trend between ERP and SCM -the integration of supply chain capabilities with ERP systems- was enhanced in a few recent years. One of the main reasons for such trend is that cross enterprise integration will continue to be one of the major organizational goals, especially for those whose business success is directly dependent upon the success of their supply chain.

Then, inter-organizational impacts can be considered as another important surrogate in ERP post-implementation success assessment which has also been proposed as a research interest in previous research (e.g., Moalagh & Zare Ravasan, 2012). The inter-organizational impacts of ERPs can be evaluated through increased customer service/satisfaction, e-government enabler, better supplier relationships, e-business/e-commerce enabler, improved service/ product delivery, improved cooperation with colleagues and so on (Davenport & Brooks, 2004; Gable et al., 2003, 2008; Hatzithomas et al., 2011; Ifinedo et al., 2010; Su & Yang, 2010). Thus, our proposed ERP system success measurement model has seven surrogates as system quality (SQ), information quality (IQ), service quality (ServQ), individual impact (II), workgroup impact (WI), organizational impact (OI), and finally inter-organizational impact (IOI) as depicted in Figure 1. Also, Table 1 highlights the measurement item sources for each surrogate. It should be noted that the measurement items of all the constructs were borrowed directly from Ifinedo et al. (2010) except for the new proposed inter-organizational impact (IOI) surrogate which encompass six new measurement items.

RESEARCH METHOD

The questionnaire used for data collection contained scales to measure the various factors of the research model. The survey instrument asked the respondents to rate the impact of factors on ERP post-implementation success using a 5 point scale with items ranged from 1 (strongly low) to 5 (strongly high). Content validity of the questionnaire -the extent to which the items on a test adequately reflect the domain of the content for which they were written (Nunnally, 1978)- is conducted through the

Figure 3. Research conceptual model

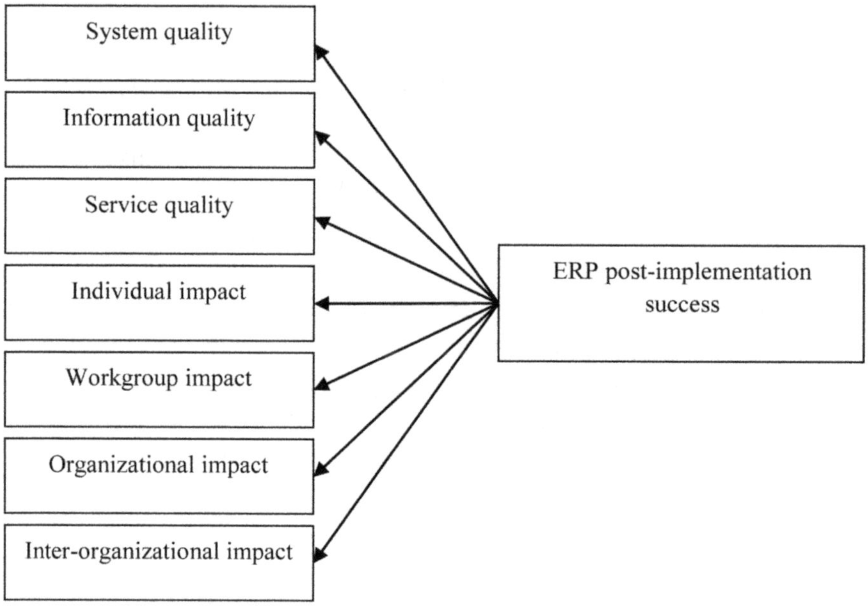

Table 1. Model surrogates and related sources

Surrogates	No. of measures	Sources for measures
System quality	11	(Ifinedo et al., 2010)
Information quality	7	(Ifinedo et al., 2010)
Service quality	7	(Ifinedo et al., 2010)
Individual impact	6	(Ifinedo et al., 2010)
Workgroup impact	7	(Ifinedo et al., 2010)
Organizational impact	8	(Ifinedo et al., 2010)
Inter-organizational impact	6	(Davenport & Brooks, 2004; Gable et al., 2003, 2008; Hatzithomas et al., 2011; Ifinedo et al., 2010; Su & Yang, 2010)

literature review and experts judgment (Straub, 1989). Also, to ensure face validity, at first six ERP project managers of high academic levels and more than eight year experience reviewed the questionnaire. They had some comments on the length and the clarity of each question. For instance, since the original English questionnaires were translated to Persian (Farsi); we refined the items in the language, wording, and clarity of the instrument based on some feedback from these experts. Also, their comments motivated authors to assess the translation validity of the instrument.

For checking this, a back-translation technique was employed, whereby a different translator changed the Persian questionnaire back into English. A high degree of correspondence between the original English questionnaire and its back-translated version assured us that the translation process is adequate.

Also, test-retest method was used to assess instrument clarity, question wording, ease of understanding and validity, logical consistencies, sequence of items, and contextual relevance. Test-retest determines whether an instrument will produce the same scores from the subjects every time (Cronbach, 1951; Nunnally, 1978). For conducting test- retest method, 16 ERP experts with more than eight year experience were asked to participate in the study in a 14-day interval. The estimated Cronbach's Alpha coefficient was 0.852 that implies good reliability of the instrument (Nunnally, 1978). The questionnaire items are appeared in Appendix A.

Since success assessment factors are diverse in organization, human, and technical contexts, it needs experts familiar with these surrogates to do data gathering. It seems that project managers involved in business and technical issues in ERP projects are so familiar with success and failure causes of these projects and have the highest merit to participate in the research. Hence, the target of this study was ERP project managers in organizations that had adopted an ERP system located in Iran. In order to gather data from the eligible experts, the following procedure was performed: first, the eligible firms and related project managers were identified and their contact information were gathered; second, authors asked their project managers to participate in the study; third, the questionnaire were sent to them, and finally, they filled the questionnaire. Totally, 430 questionnaires were sent, 287 questionnaires were gathered and 204 usable questionnaires were used for the analysis. The response rate was 0.47. To obtain such relatively large number of respondents, authors paid visits to the offices of some of the respondent organizations and contact them personally to fill the questionnaire. Table 2 and 3 lists the demographic information of the respondents and organizations, respectively.

Results

The Structural Equation Modeling (SEM) approach was used to validate the research model. SEM is a powerful multivariate data analysis tool that estimates a complete model incorporating both measurement and structural considerations (Kelloway, 1998). Confirmatory Factor Analysis (CFA) is a widely used application of SEM to test the constructs. It is one of the most prevalent SEM techniques in the evaluation especially in the social and behavioral sciences (Mueller, 1996). Here, CFA using LISREL 8.54 (Jöreskog & Sörbom, 1989) is employed to perform the analysis. Prior to factor analysis, a test was conducted to verify the adequacy of the data for CFA.

Table 2. The demographics of the respondents (number of respondents = 204).

Demographic Characteristics		Percent
Gender	Male Female	68% 32%
Age	<30 31–40 >41	49% 43% 8%
Education	BSs MSs PhD	38% 58% 4%
Tenure in firm	<2 year 2–5 6–10 >10	35% 30% 27% 8%

The Kaiser-Meyer-Olkin (KMO) measure of sampling adequacy is a popular measure for assessing the extent to which the indicators of a construct belong together. The KMO is 0.861 which is above the mediocre threshold of 0.5 (Kaiser, 1974). Large values for the KMO indicate that a factor analysis of the variables is a good idea. The research model shown in Figure 1 has been analyzed in two steps. The first step involves the analysis of the measurement model, while the second step tests the structural relationships among latent constructs.

Measurement Model

CFA has been performed for assessing measurement model, construct validity, convergent validity, and discriminant validity using LISREL 8.54. The concern of construct validity is that the instrument items selected for a given construct are, considered together, a reasonable operationalization of the construct (Cronbach & Meehl, 1968). It can be examined by observing the factor loading of each item. A high loading implies that the shared variance between a construct and its measurement is higher than the error variance. A factor loading higher than 0.7 can be viewed as highly reliable while a factor loading of less than 0.5 signifies a lack of reliability, in which case the item should be dropped. In Appendix A, all loading values appear to be acceptable.

Convergent validity means the items measure the variable are indeed theoretically related to each other and the relation is confirmed if the items within the construct are significantly correlated with another one, particularly when compared to items in other constructs. The convergent validity of the scales was verified by using the three criteria suggested by Fornell and Larcker (1981): (1) all indicator loadings should

Table 3. The demographics of the firms (number of organizations = 204).

Category	Percent
Industry type	
Automobile Dealership	6.4%
Bank, Insurance, Investment	7.8%
Chemical & Pharmaceuticals	4.9%
Dairy, Food, & Meat Products	5.9%
Electrical & Electronics	4.9%
Medical & Healthcare	2.9%
Information Technology (IT)	2.0%
Manufacturing	24.5%
Retail/Wholesale/Distribution	13.2%
Telecommunications	3.9%
Transportation, Logistics, & Courier	7.4%
Construction	3.9%
Other	12.3%
Revenue ($ billion Million)	
Over 1000	22.1%
501–1000	10.3%
251–500	17.6%
101–250	15.7%
Less than 100	32.4%
Missing data	2.0%
Number of company employees	
Less than 50 employees	21.1%
51–100 employees	12.3%
101–500 employees	20.1%
501–1000 employees	21.6%
1001–10,000 employees	25.0%

be significant and exceed 0.7, (2) construct reliability (CR) should exceed 0.7 (Hair, Black, Babin, & Anderson, 2010), and (3) average variance extracted (AVE) by each construct should exceed 0.50. As shown in Appendix A, factor loadings for most items (belonging to latent constructs) in the CFA model are significant at $p = 0.05$, and most items have factor loadings greater than 0.70. However, some items have a loading below 0.70, which are also deemed acceptable as they are above 0.60 (Hair

Table 4. Discriminant validity: AVEs versus squared correlations.

	SQ	IQ	SerVQ	II	WI	OI	IOI
SQ	**0.75**						
IQ	0.68	**0.74**					
SerVQ	0.72	0.63	**0.73**				
II	0.71	0.51	0.68	**0.71**			
WI	0.50	0.47	0.52	0.67	**0.72**		
OI	0.71	0.60	0.65	0.54	0.70	**0.76**	
IOI	0.47	0.51	0.46	0.44	0.50	0.51	**0.75**

*The diagonal line of the correlation matrix is the square root of AVE.

et al., 2010). Composite reliability of all constructs exceeded 0.70. Furthermore, all AVEs exceeded 0.50. Thus, convergent validity is established.

In addition for adequate discriminant validity, the square root of AVEs should exceed the correlations of the constructs (Chin, 1998; Fornell & Larcker, 1981; Gefen & Straub, 2005). From the inter-factor correlations in Table 4, we can see that the square root of AVEs range from 0.71 to 0.76, and each one is much larger than the corresponding squared inter-construct correlations.

Structural Model

Having established the reliability, convergent validity, and discriminant validity of the constructs, the next step is the structural model test. The results of measurement model test imply that identified factors are good measures for success assessment surrogates. The goal of structural model test is to assess whether success assessment surrogates are good measurements for ERP post-implementation success construct or not. To this end, structural model test or second order CFA has been conducted. Perhaps the greatest advantage of CFA using LISREL is that it offers an index of how well the proposed model fits the given data set (Greenspoon & Saklofske, 1998). The result of the analysis is shown in Figure 4.

As can be seen from the figure, all loading values are exceeding the threshold value of 0.4. Regarding Figure 2 and Table 5, it can be implied that all parameter estimates for the structural model are significant. Furthermore, a total of 81% of the variance of ERP system success construct is explained by all the preceding surrogates. Considering the complexity of the model, eight fit indices were used as goodness of fit index (GFI), adjusted goodness of fit index (AGFI), comparative fit index (CFI), normed fit index (NFI), non-normed fit index (NNFI), p-value, root mean square error of approximation (RMSEA), and $\chi 2$/df which are very common

Figure 4. The Results of Second Order CFA

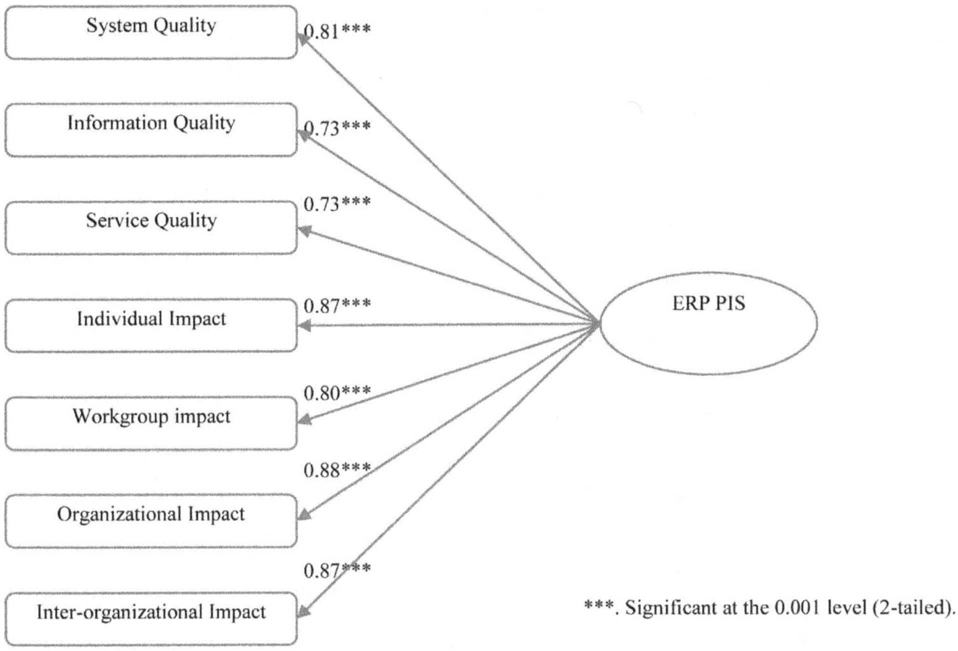

in the literature (Moeini, Farahani Farmahini, & Zare Ravasan, 2013). The results of the analysis and accepted thresholds are summarized in Table 5 suggesting that the model fits the data well.

The accepted threshold of p-value (>0.05) should be interpreted cautiously. According to Hair et al., (2010), an important difference between SEM and other

Table 5. The results of goodness of fit assessments and accepted thresholds

Fit indices	Observed values	Accepted thresholds	Source
GFI	0.92	> 0.90	(Chau, 1997; Segars & Grover, 1993)
AGFI	0.89	> 0.80	(Chau, 1997; Segars & Grover, 1993)
CFI	0.93	> 0.90	(Hatcher, 1994)
NFI	0.92	> 0.90	(Bentler & Bonett, 1980; Chau, 1997)
NNFI	0.93	> 0.90	(Chau, 1997)
p-value	0.09	> 0.05	(Hair et al., 2010)
RMSEA	0.054	< 0.06	(Hu & Bentler, 1998)
$\chi2/df$	2.74	< 3.00	(Chau, 1997; Segars & Grover, 1993)

multivariate techniques stands in the fact that in other techniques, we typically looked for a smaller p-values (<0.05) to show that a significant relationship existed. But, with the SEM, we make inferences in a way that is in some ways exactly opposite. When we find a p-value for the $\chi 2$ test to be small and statistically significant, it indicates that the two covariance matrices are statistically different and indicates problems with the fit. So, in SEM we look for a relatively large p-value indicating no statistically significant differences between the two matrices, to support the idea that a proposed theory fits reality.

AN ILLUSTRATIVE EXAMPLE

The first significant ERP system implementation in Iran dates back to implementing Oracle E- business suite in Isfahan steel company. Since then, several large enterprises tried to use such solutions. Based on a report that published in 2008, 42 vendors were active in Iran ERP market as a solution provider or implementer. 43 percent of these companies were agent of international and famous ERP providers and other ones were the local companies that have their own solutions. Although there is no clear report about the activity of international solution providers or their third party agents in Iran, but some famous enterprises in automotive, mining, oil, gas, mill and consumer products have implemented and used such solutions. SAP, Oracle, IFS and Sage take the majority of international ERP market share in Iran. On the contrary, there are many local vendors that have deployed their own solutions in Iranian companies. But, there are some considerations about ERP solutions of these companies. At first, they were developed around local practices and suffer from lack of best practices. Lack of proper integration and knowledge of business process reengineering are other problems of local solutions. Most of these ones don't include important modules in ERP systems like Production Planning and Material Requirement Planning. In addition, they don't provide multicurrency and multi lingual support (Nikookar, Yahya Safavi, Hakim, & Homayoun, 2010).

The proposed model has been applied in an Iranian international company in the field of manufacturing and supplying turbines and auxiliary equipment to measure the firm's ERP post-implementation success. Having produced over 300 power gas and steam turbines supplied to international markets up to the end of 2016, the company is now considered as an international player in the turbine industry. To sustain the company's competiveness in the market and improve efficiency, executive managers of the company decided to implement SAP R/3. This company has about 500 employees and is composed of six different functional departments. Following SAP implementation for production planning (shop floor), finance, controlling, material management, sales distribution, logistic execution, project system modules in stage one on March 2007, the remaining modules, that is plant maintenance, quality management, fund management, document management system, customer service, production planning (capacity planning) were implemented in the company on October 2016. The proposed model is applied here in order to assess the firm's ERP post-implementation success. Each item is assessed using linguistic values as appeared in Table 6.

The result of the assessment is represented in Appendix B. According to the final scores, the overall success is at a medium to high level with the lowest score in inter-organizational impact with just 0.25 gained value.

The results of the assessment depicted that the company gained a relatively good success rate in some factors such as system quality. This is due to the fact that implemented system (SAP R/3) in the company is one of the most reputable ERP systems and best practices that have been widely implemented in similar industries and competitors such as Siemens and Rolls Royce. Given these experiences, SAP R/3 has a high level of capability in mapping business requirements with system functionalities in the field of manufacturing and supplying turbines and auxiliary equipment.

In the case of good scores gained in information quality surrogate, it can implied that one of the major advantages of ERP systems over traditional information systems is the integrated, centralized database that "dramatically streamlines flow of information throughout a business" (Davenport, 1998). Regarding this advantage, it is expected that the system provides timely, relevant and accurate information which is also achieved in the studied case. As a result, the score of IQ sounds quite satisfactory.

One of the main reasons for achieving high scores in service quality surrogate is highly concerned with using top tier international ERP vendors in the implementation process, while the service costs of such a company were three to four times higher than regional ones. It is owing to the fact that the top management was more interested in implementing the system with the aim of heightening the quality rather than reducing costs.

Table 6. Linguistic values and scores for assessing items

Linguistic values	Scores
Very high (VH)	1.00
High (H)	0.75
Medium (M)	0.50
Low (L)	0.25
Very low (VL)	0.00

In the case of individual impact surrogate, we know that ERP implementation can be considered as an organizational learning process (Davenport, 2000). In the studied company, high levels of communication and cooperation are required between R&D and shop floor departments to improve product design and development. ERP system in the company helped it by facilitating knowledge transfer among engineering designers and shop floor staff. Also, ERP system enables organizations to reduce the transaction costs of the business and improve employees' productivity (Beheshti & Beheshti, 2010). ERP system facilitated workflows in the studied case. So, each employee in this company is familiar with his/her work and also the others'. Therefore, people spend most of their times to do the job done, appropriately; instead of wasting their time in tracking or coordinating activities.

The next surrogate in the model is workgroup impact surrogate. Implementation of ERP systems in organizations could accelerate communication between internal and external parties (Al-Mashari & Zairi, 2000). In this case, efficient communication between sales, engineering, inventory management and job shop is critical. Hence, ERP system minimized reworks or misunderstanding and lessen time to market. In addition, each working group is informed about revisions made by other groups, so they could follow-up the changes more accurately.

The achieved score for organizational impact surrogate is almost low. Although, ERP systems exert a positive impact on competitiveness (Holsapple & Sena, 2005), there have been failures of ERP systems in organizations such as FoxMeyer Drug and Hershey which serves as a challenge to this claim. The company under study has not gained a considerable competitive advantage via implementing EPR system, because the company is operating in a high-tech industry and the international competitors in the field have just implemented such a system. So, the company did not gain "competitive advantage" by implementing the system. As a result, lower levels of success scores are observed in this item. To promote a sustained competitive advantage, the company must be able to use ERP in distinctive ways; that is, people must change their attitude toward their work, processes and their enterprise. They should alter their feelings about their organization and ERP system and finally the type of relationships they develop within and across organizational boundaries. Similarly, the company should incorporate new modules into the system to improve business performance and gain a competitive advantage over its rivals. The ERPs decision-making benefits includes enhancing decision makers' ability to process knowledge, shortening the time and costs associated with decision-making, the reliability of decision processes or outcomes, and so on (Holsapple & Sena, 2005). But, it was observed in the studied case that the system could not have a considerable effect on these items. Such a limited effect is believed to be the result of system weakness in providing a user-friendly report generator and customizable data fields in the provided reports by the end users. Such inflexibility in the system to provide reports and information required for making decisions reduced the decision support capabilities of the system.

As with ERP systems, real time visibility of processes can be achieved and business process improvement options can be identified (Gargeya & Brady, 2005). In recent years, the company endeavored to improve its business processes. But, the efforts prior to the ERP implementation failed to achieve acceptable results. However, implementation of SAP R/3 which has been adapted with several leading companies in the same industry, promoted business processes to world class. Another factor in OI is "supporting decision making" which gained a medium level. It can be inferred that the ERP system cannot succeed in helping managers to make proper organizational decisions in the company. Just as decision-making weakness in the individual impact surrogate, the source of the problem arises from weak report generator capability of the system along with poor system users. On one hand, managers' weaknesses in using system's reporting features, and on the other hand, the lack of clearly defined strategic and operational goals and priorities in the company, made decision-making a real challenge for managers. Hence, training the users in ERP system's reporting capabilities as well as defining strategies, goals, and priorities in the company along with adding new modules such as Business Intelligence (BI), Advanced Planning Systems (APS) or other similar Add-on solutions can help improve this item's score.

The low score of inter-organizational impact surrogate is noticeable. The company lacks implemented customers' side modules in its ERP system; therefore, the "customer service/ satisfaction" score is low. This can occur for the reason that most of company implementation team efforts focused on internal processes rather than external ones. So, the processes associated with customers' side were neglected. It has been claimed that CRM applications could fulfill undeniable roles in providing customer-based services through the integration of CRM with ERP (Xu, Yen, Lin, & Chou, 2002). Hence, it seems that the purchase of CRM applications or modules and their integration with the current ERP system would improve customer service/ satisfaction. The same argument could be true for supplier relationships and supporting applications to enable e-business or e-commerce initiatives with business partners. Also, regarding the low maturity of governmental organizations in terms of developed information technology tools and e-government enablers, as it is common in the majority of developing countries, the score of related measure is very low.

IMPLICATIONS FOR RESEARCH AND PRACTICE

This paper has two main research implications for ERP literature. The multidimensionality of ERP success is not challenged adequately in the previous research. In fact, the assessment of ERP success through a snapshot from a single perspective is partial and little useful: in the best case, such an approach may only highlight a local sub-optimization. With this in mind, this research at first, contributes to the ERP literature by introducing a new surrogate of inter-organizational impacts in the ERP post- implementation assessment. In particular, our research effort extends the ERP system success model proposed by Ifinedo et al. (2010). Second, as this endeavor is among the few to discuss ERP system success with organizational level data in developing countries, our effort enriches the IS literature accordingly.

This research has useful implications for practitioners. Once the ERP project goes live, enterprises should evaluate its implementation result to see what the ERP system could do to improve their business performance in that the ERP project is a large program that involves many people, money, and time investment. With correct evaluation of the ERP project, enterprises could find where they should spend more time and effort to improve and what places they succeed so that they could elevate their firm's operational performance. As this study is partly motivated by such need, we hope that our list of ERP success surrogates and measures could be used as an assessment tool in success evaluations of such packages. In order to gain a fuller appreciation of ERP system success, it is important to analyze success at multiple levels in an organization, from multiple perspectives. Then, this research provides some implications for implementing and managing ERP systems.

ERP vendors, consultants and IS managers should pay attention not only to improve the organizational impacts of ERPs, but also to improve inter organizational aspect. The study model and instrument have explicitly been designed to work for all levels inside and outside the organization. Having gathered these multiple perspectives, it becomes possible from the model items and surrogates mean scores to usefully describe and compare these various perspectives. The identified surrogates/items used in this study can be used to assess the effectiveness of the system for the individual, their work group, the entire organization, and their inter-organizational relationships. If the proposed measurement evaluation tool is utilized appropriately and periodically, management could use it to obtain timely feedback about the success of the ERP package in their setups. Practitioners can compare satisfaction levels of their ERP systems with the expected levels to understand relative goodness or badness and to take necessary corrective actions to improve them.

LIMITATIONS AND FUTURE RESEARCH DIRECTIONS

Although the numerical example demonstrated the applicability of the model, we believe that more studies are expected in this area of research. For example, this study can be replicated in other settings to fine tune the model. It is impossible to establish the validity of findings on the basis of a single study. Further testing of the proposed model should seek to establish its validity in other contexts. Our data is cross-sectional in nature; future studies could consider using longitudinal data to facilitate insight regarding ERP success evaluation over its life cycle in adopting organizations. Also, investigating inter-relationships among success assessment surrogates is proposed as another future research interest.

Previous models did not pay much attention to the inherent characteristics and individual goals of each business because every organization runs its business through different goals and strategies and needs an ERP system that meets its specific requirements (Ayag & Özdemir, 2007). By reviewing recent research projects, we come up with different objectives pointed out by researchers. Some researchers indicate that the integration of information, the increase in the speed of communication between organizational units, the reduction of raw materials, production costs, and speeding to the delivery of the final product to market are the main objectives of ERP implementation (Botta-Genoulaz & Millet, 2005; Hsu & Chen, 2004; Olhager & Selldin, 2003). Meanwhile, another group of scholars concluded in their research projects that improving decision-making and increasing flexibility in knowledge generation are the primary goals of ERP implementation (Holsapple & Sena, 2005; Spathis & Ananiadis, 2005; Spathis & Constantinides, 2003).

Other studies indicate that ERP implementation goals change business by business. For example, in manufacturing industries, lessening bottlenecks and waste, improving supplier relationship and real-time calculation of final product costs are the most important primary goals to implement ERP systems (Bendoly & Schoenherr, 2005). While, in service industries, other goals such as customer care and human resource management are of high significance (Botta-Genoulaz & Millet, 2006). So there is a crucial need for ERP post-implementation success assessment models that recognize these differences in various kinds of organizations. Hence, as another research avenue, investigating the differences between ERP success surrogates/ items in industrial sectors and public/service sector could be of interest for future researchers.

Furthermore, the underlying surrogates in the proposed model should provide a basis for further standardized application of ERP post-implementation success assessment. The measured success of ERP implementation can be seen as the dependent variable in further models, as the output can be influenced by various factors during different phases of the project. Furthermore, regarding recent ERP implementation approaches in the form of Software as a Service (SaaS) and Application Service Provider (ASP), it is suggested that future research should study to what extent ERP implementation approach might calls for specifications in the assessment models.

CONCLUSION

In this paper, an attempt was done to elaborate on the importance of ERP post-implementation success assessment and an extended model is proposed for such assessments. Using this model, the state of ERP project success can be determined. The factors contributing to the post-implementation success assessment have been adapted from the original model of Ifinedo et al. (2010) encompasses service quality, system quality, information quality, individual impact, workgroup impact, and organizational impact surrogates. Also, a new surrogate of inter-organizational impact proposed in this research. The proposed model was then applied to an international company in the field of manufacturing and supplying turbines and auxiliary equipment to measure the firm's ERP post-implementation success. The results indicated that the company gained a satisfactory level of success, but weaknesses have been observed in some items. Therefore, some improvement projects were suggested to overcome these poor areas.

REFERENCES

Abdel-Kader, M., & Nguyen, T. P. (2011). An investigation of enterprise resource planning implementation in a small firm: A study of problems encountered and successes achieved. *International Journal of Enterprise Information Systems*, *7*(1), 18–40. doi:10.4018/jeis.2011010102

Akkermans, H. A., Bogerd, P., Yücesan, E., & Van Wassenhove, L. N. (2003). The impact of ERP on supply chain management: Exploratory findings from a European Delphi study. *European Journal of Operational Research*, *146*(2), 284–301. doi:10.1016/S0377-2217(02)00550-7

Al-Mashari, M., Al-Mudimigh, A., & Zairi, M. (2003). Enterprise resource planning: A taxonomy of critical factors. *European Journal of Operational Research*, *146*(2), 352–364. doi:10.1016/S0377-2217(02)00554-4

Al-Mashari, M., & Zairi, M. (2000). Supply-chain re-engineering using enterprise resource planning (ERP) systems: An analysis of a SAP R/3 implementation case. *International Journal of Physical Distribution & Logistics Management*, *30*(3/4), 296–313. doi:10.1108/09600030010326064

Amid, A., Moalagh, M., & Ravasan, A. Z. (2012). Identification and classification of ERP critical failure factors in Iranian industries. *Information Systems*, *37*(3), 227–237. doi:10.1016/j.is.2011.10.010

Amid, A., Moalagh, M., & Zare Ravasan, A. (2012). Identification and classification of ERP critical failure factors in Iranian industries. *Information Systems*, *37*(3), 227–237. doi:10.1016/j.is.2011.10.010

Ayag, Z., & Özdemir, R. (2007). An intelligent approach to ERP software selection through fuzzy ANP. *International Journal of Production Research*, *45*(10), 2169–2194. doi:10.1080/00207540600724849

Beheshti, H. M., & Beheshti, C. M. (2010). Improving productivity and firm performance with enterprise resource planning. *Enterprise Information Systems*, *4*(4), 445–472. doi:10.1080/17517575.2010.511276

Bendoly, E., & Schoenherr, T. (2005). ERP system and implementation-process benefits: Implications for B2B e-procurement. *International Journal of Operations & Production Management*, *25*(4), 304–319. doi:10.1108/01443570510585516

Bentler, P., & Bonett, D. (1980). Significance tests and goodness of fit in the analysis of covariance structures. *Psychological Bulletin*, *88*(3), 588–606. doi:10.1037/0033-2909.88.3.588

Botta-Genoulaz, V., & Millet, P. A. (2005). A classification for better use of ERP systems. *Computers in Industry*, *56*(6), 573–587. doi:10.1016/j.compind.2005.02.007

Botta-Genoulaz, V., & Millet, P. A. (2006). An investigation into the use of ERP systems in the service sector. *International Journal of Production Economics*, *99*(1-2), 202–221. doi:10.1016/j.ijpe.2004.12.015

Chau, P. (1997). Reexamining a model for evaluating information center success using a structural equation modeling approach. *Decision Sciences*, *28*(2), 309–334. doi:10.1111/j.1540-5915.1997.tb01313.x

Chien, S. W., & Tsaur, S. M. (2007). Investigating the success of ERP systems: Case studies in three Taiwanese high-tech industries. *Computers in Industry*, *58*(8-9), 783–793. doi:10.1016/j.compind.2007.02.001

Chin, W. (1998). Issues and opinion on structural equation modeling. *Management Information Systems Quarterly*, *22*(1), 7–16.

Cronbach, L. (1951). Coefficient alpha and the internal structure of tests. *Psychometrika*, *16*(3), 297–334. doi:10.1007/BF02310555

Cronbach, L., & Meehl, P. (1968). Construct validity in psychological tests. *The Foundations of Science and the Concepts of Psychology and Psychoanalysis*, 174-204.

Davenport, T. (1998). Putting the enterprise into the enterprise system. *Harvard Business Review*, *76*(4). PMID:10181586

Davenport, T. (2000). *Mission critical: Realizing the promise of enterprise systems*. Harvard Business Press.

Davenport, T., & Brooks, J. D. (2004). Enterprise systems and the supply chain. *Journal of Enterprise Information Management*, *17*(1), 8–19. doi:10.1108/09576050410510917

Delone, W., & McLean, E. (1992). Information systems success: The quest for the dependent variable. *Information Systems Research*, *3*(1), 60–95. doi:10.1287/isre.3.1.60

Delone, W., & McLean, E. (2003). The DeLone and McLean model of information systems success: A ten-year update. *Journal of Management Information Systems*, *19*(4), 9–30. doi:10.1080/07421222.2003.11045748

Fornell, C., & Larcker, D. (1981). Evaluating structural equation models with unobservable variables and measurement error. *JMR, Journal of Marketing Research*, *18*(1), 39–50. doi:10.2307/3151312

Gable, G., Sedera, D., & Chan, T. (2003). Enterprise systems success: a measurement model. *Proceedings of the 24th International Conference on Information Systems*.

Gable, G., Sedera, D., & Chan, T. (2008). Re-conceptualizing information system success: The IS-impact measurement model. *Journal of the Association for Information Systems*, *9*(7), 377–408. doi:10.17705/1jais.00164

Gargeya, V. B., & Brady, C. (2005). Success and failure factors of adopting SAP in ERP system implementation. *Business Process Management Journal*, *11*(5), 501–516. doi:10.1108/14637150510619858

Gefen, D., & Straub, D. (2005). A practical guide to factorial validity using PLS-Graph: Tutorial and annotated example. *Communications of the AIS*, *16*(5), 91–109.

Gollner, J. A., & Baumane-Vitolina, I. (2016). Measurement of ERP-Project Success: Findings from Germany and Austria. *The Engineering Economist*, *27*(5), 498–508.

Gorla, N., Somers, T., & Wong, B. (2010). Organizational impact of system quality, information quality, and service quality. *The Journal of Strategic Information Systems*, *19*(3), 207–228. doi:10.1016/j.jsis.2010.05.001

Greenspoon, P., & Saklofske, D. (1998). Confirmatory factor analysis of the multidimensional students' life satisfaction scale. *Personality and Individual Differences*, *25*(5), 965–971. doi:10.1016/S0191-8869(98)00115-9

Hair, J. F., Black, W. C., Babin, B. J., & Anderson, R. E. (2010). Multivariate data analysis (Vol. 7). Prentice Hall.

Hanafizadeh, P., Gholami, R., Dadbin, S., & Standage, N. (2010). The core critical success factors in implementation of enterprise resource planning systems. *International Journal of Enterprise Information Systems*, *6*(2), 82–111. doi:10.4018/jeis.2010040105

Hatcher, L. (1994). *A step-by-step approach to using the SAS system for factor analysis and structural equation modeling*. SAS Publishing.

Hatzithomas, L., Stamelos, I., Fotiadis, T., & Mylonakis, J. (2011). Quality And Effectiveness Of Enterprise Resource Planning–Customer Relationship Management Systems: Implications For Information Systems Marketing Strategies. *Journal of Applied Business Research*, *23*(3). doi:10.19030/jabr.v23i3.1389

Holsapple, C. W., & Sena, M. P. (2005). ERP plans and decision-support benefits. *Decision Support Systems*, *38*(4), 575–590. doi:10.1016/j.dss.2003.07.001

Hsu, L. L., & Chen, M. (2004). Impacts of ERP systems on the integrated-interaction performance of manufacturing and marketing. *Industrial Management & Data Systems*, *104*(1), 42–55. doi:10.1108/02635570410514089

Hu, L., & Bentler, P. (1998). Fit indices in covariance structure modeling: Sensitivity to underparameterized model misspecification. *Psychological Methods*, *3*(4), 424–453. doi:10.1037/1082-989X.3.4.424

Ifinedo, P., & Nahar, N. (2007). ERP systems success: An empirical analysis of how two organizational stakeholder groups prioritize and evaluate relevant measures. *Enterprise Information Systems*, *1*(1), 25–48. doi:10.1080/17517570601088539

Ifinedo, P., Rapp, B., Ifinedo, A., & Sundberg, K. (2010). Relationships among ERP post-implementation success constructs: An analysis at the organizational level. *Computers in Human Behavior*, *26*(5), 1136–1148. doi:10.1016/j.chb.2010.03.020

Iivari, J. (2005a). An empirical test of the DeLone-McLean model of information system success. *ACM SIGMIS Database*, *36*(2), 8–27. doi:10.1145/1066149.1066152

Iivari, J. (2005b). An empirical test of the DeLone-McLean model of information system success. *The Data Base for Advances in Information Systems*, *36*(2), 8–27. doi:10.1145/1066149.1066152

Ives, B., Hamilton, S., & Davis, G. (1980). A framework for research in computer-based management information systems. *Management Science*, *26*(9), 910–934. doi:10.1287/mnsc.26.9.910

Jöreskog, K., & Sörbom, D. (1989). *LISREL 7: A guide to the program and applications*. Chicago: SPSS.

Kaiser, H. F. (1974). An index of factorial simplicity. *Psychometrika*, *39*(1), 31–36. doi:10.1007/BF02291575

Kalakota, R., & Robinson, M. (2001). *E-business 2.0: Roadmap for Success*. Addison-Wesley Professional.

Kelloway, E. (1998). *Using LISREL for structural equation modeling: A researcher's guide*. Sage Publications, Inc.

Kemp, M., & Low, G. C. (2008). ERP innovation implementation model incorporating change management. *Business Process Management Journal*, *14*(2), 228–242. doi:10.1108/14637150810864952

Khattak, M. A. O., She, Y., Memon, Z. A., Syed, N., Hussain, S., & Irfan, M. (2013). Investigating Critical Success Factors Affecting ERP Implementation in Chinese and Pakistani Enterprises. *International Journal of Enterprise Information Systems*, *9*(3), 39–76. doi:10.4018/jeis.2013070103

Kini, R. B., & Basaviah, S. (2013). Critical Success Factors in the Implementation of Enterprise Resource Planning Systems in Small and Midsize Businesses: Microsoft Navision Implementation. *International Journal of Enterprise Information Systems*, *9*(1), 97–117. doi:10.4018/jeis.2013010106

Klaus, H., Rosemann, M., & Gable, G. (2000). What is ERP? *Information Systems Frontiers*, *2*(2), 141–162. doi:10.1023/A:1026543906354

Kumar, V., Maheshwari, B., & Kumar, U. (2003). An investigation of critical management issues in ERP implementation: Emperical evidence from Canadian organizations. *Technovation*, *23*(10), 793–808. doi:10.1016/S0166-4972(02)00015-9

Kwahk, K. (2006). ERP acceptance: organizational change perspective. In R. H. Sprague Jr. (Ed.), *Proceedings of the 39th Hawaii International Conference on System Sciences*. Hawaii, HI: IEEE Computer Society Press.

Law, C. C. H., Chen, C. C., & Wu, B. J. P. (2010). Managing the full ERP life-cycle: Considerations of maintenance and support requirements and IT governance practice as integral elements of the formula for successful ERP adoption. *Computers in Industry*, *61*(3), 297–308. doi:10.1016/j.compind.2009.10.004

Mandal, P., & Gunasekaran, A. (2003). Issues in implementing ERP: A case study. *European Journal of Operational Research, 146*(2), 274–283. doi:10.1016/S0377-2217(02)00549-0

Markus, M., & Tanis, C. (2000). The enterprise systems experience-from adoption to success. *Framing the domains of IT research: Glimpsing the future through the past, 173*, 207-173.

Moalagh, M., & Zare Ravasan, A. (2012). Developing a practical framework for assessing ERP post-implementation success using fuzzy analytic network process. *International Journal of Production Research, 51*(4), 1236–1257. doi:10.1080/00207543.2012.698318

Moeini, A., Farahani Farmahini, A., & Zare Ravasan, A. (2013). The Consistency of Virtual Organizations Enabling Capabilities and Improvements in Knowledge Management Performance. *International Journal of Enterprise Information Systems, 9*(2), 20–43. doi:10.4018/jeis.2013040102

Mueller, R. (1996). *Basic principles of structural equation modeling: An introduction to LISREL and EQS*. Springer Verlag. doi:10.1007/978-1-4612-3974-1

Nicolaou, A. I., & Bhattacharya, S. (2006). Organizational performance effects of ERP systems usage: The impact of post implementation changes. *International Journal of Accounting Information Systems, 7*(1), 18–35. doi:10.1016/j.accinf.2005.12.002

Nikookar, G., Yahya Safavi, S., Hakim, A., & Homayoun, A. (2010). Competitive advantage of enterprise resource planning vendors in Iran. *Information Systems, 35*(3), 271–277. doi:10.1016/j.is.2009.09.002

Nizamani, S., Khoumbati, K., Ismaili, I. A., Nizamani, S., Nizamani, S., & Basir, N. (2017). Testing and validating the ERP success evaluation model for higher education institutes of Pakistan. *International Journal of Business Information Systems, 25*(2), 165–191. doi:10.1504/IJBIS.2017.083682

Nour, M. A., & Mouakket, S. (2011). A classification framework of critical success factors for ERP systems implementation: A multi-stakeholder perspective. *International Journal of Enterprise Information Systems, 7*(1), 56–71. doi:10.4018/jeis.2011010104

Nunnally, J. (1978). *Psychometric theory*. McGraw-Hill.

Olhager, J., & Selldin, E. (2003). Enterprise resource planning survey of Swedish manufacturing firms. *European Journal of Operational Research, 146*(2), 365–373. doi:10.1016/S0377-2217(02)00555-6

Petter, S., DeLone, W., & McLean, E. (2008). Measuring information systems success: Models, dimensions, measures, and interrelationships. *European Journal of Information Systems*, *17*(3), 236–263. doi:10.1057/ejis.2008.15

Rouhani, S., Ashrafi, A., & Afshari, S. (2013). Segmenting critical success factors for ERP implementation using an integrated fuzzy AHP and fuzzy DEMATEL approach. *World Applied Sciences Journal*, *22*(8), 1066–1079.

Seddon, P. (1997). A respecification and extension of the Delone and McLean model of IS success. *Information Systems Research*, *8*(3), 240–253. doi:10.1287/isre.8.3.240

Sedera, D., Gable, G., & Chan, T. (2004). *A factor and structural equation analysis of the enterprise systems success measurement model.* Paper presented at the 25th international conference on information systems, Washington, DC.

Segars, A., & Grover, V. (1993). Re-examining perceived ease of use and usefulness: A confirmatory factor analysis. *MIS Quarterly Executive*, *17*(4), 517–525. doi:10.2307/249590

Soja, P. (2008). Examining the conditions of ERP implementations: Lessons learnt from adopters. *Business Process Management Journal*, *14*(1), 105–121. doi:10.1108/14637150810849445

Soltani, S., Elkhani, N., & Bardsiri, V. K. (2014). The Effects of Perceived Organizational Support and Organizational Citizenship Behaviors on Continuance Intention of Enterprise Resource Planning. *International Journal of Enterprise Information Systems*, *10*(2), 81–102. doi:10.4018/ijeis.2014040105

Spathis, C., & Ananiadis, J. (2005). Assessing the benefits of using an enterprise system in accounting information and management. *Journal of Enterprise Information Management*, *18*(2), 195–210. doi:10.1108/17410390510579918

Spathis, C., & Constantinides, S. (2003). The usefulness of ERP systems for effective management. *Industrial Management & Data Systems*, *103*(9), 677–685. doi:10.1108/02635570310506098

Straub, D. (1989). Validating instruments in MIS research. *MIS Quarterly Executive*, *13*(2), 147–169. doi:10.2307/248922

Su, Y., & Yang, C. (2010). A structural equation model for analyzing the impact of ERP on SCM. *Expert Systems with Applications*, *37*(1), 456–469. doi:10.1016/j.eswa.2009.05.061

Subramanianh, G., & Hoffers, C. (2005). An exploratory case study of enterprise resource planning implementation. *International Journal of Enterprise Information Systems*, *1*(1), 23–38. doi:10.4018/jeis.2005010102

Tan, C., & Pan, S. (2002). *ERP success: the search for a comprehensive framework.* In R. D. Banker, H. Chang & Y-C. Kao (Eds.), *Proceedings of the 8th. Americas Conference on Information Systems*. Dallas, TX: AMCIS Press (AIS e-Library).

Wang, E., Shih, S., Jiang, J., & Klein, G. (2008). The consistency among facilitating factors and ERP implementation success: A holistic view of fit. *Journal of Systems and Software*, *81*(9), 1609–1621. doi:10.1016/j.jss.2007.11.722

White, E., Anderson, J., Schroeder, R., & Tupy, S. (1982). A study of the MRP implementation process. *Journal of Operations Management*, *2*(3), 145–153. doi:10.1016/0272-6963(82)90002-X

Wu, J., & Wang, Y. (2006). Measuring ERP success: The ultimate users' view. *International Journal of Operations & Production Management*, *26*(8), 882–903. doi:10.1108/01443570610678657

Xu, Y., Yen, D. C., Lin, B., & Chou, D. C. (2002). Adopting customer relationship management technology. *Industrial Management & Data Systems*, *102*(8), 442–452. doi:10.1108/02635570210445871

Yu, C. S. (2005). Causes influencing the effectiveness of the post-implementation ERP system. *Industrial Management & Data Systems*, *105*(1), 115–132. doi:10.1108/02635570510575225

Yusuf, Y., Gunasekaran, A., & Abthorpe, M. (2004). Enterprise information systems project implementation: A case study of ERP in Rolls-Royce. *International Journal of Production Economics*, *87*(3), 251–266. doi:10.1016/j.ijpe.2003.10.004

Zare, A., & Ravasan, A. Z. (2014). An extended framework for ERP post-implementation success assessment. *Information Resources Management Journal*, *27*(4), 45–65. doi:10.4018/irmj.2014100103

Zhang, Z., Lee, M., Huang, P., Zhang, L., & Huang, X. (2005). A framework of ERP systems implementation success in China: An empirical study. *International Journal of Production Economics*, *98*(1), 56–80. doi:10.1016/j.ijpe.2004.09.004

APPENDIX 1

Table 7. Confirmatory factor analysis results of measurement models

Measurement Items	Item Loading
SQ: Cronbach's Alpha = 0.84; Composite Reliability = 0.90; AVE= 0.56	
Data accuracy	-
System flexibility	0.78
Easy to use system	0.63
Easy to learn system	0.91
System reliability	0.75
Allowing for data integration	0.67
System efficiency	0.77
Allowing for customization	-
Good database content	-
Allowing for integration with other IT systems	0.68
Meeting users' requirements	-
IQ: Cronbach's Alpha = 0.83; Composite Reliability = 0.88; AVE= 0.55	
Providing timely information	-
Providing understandable information	0.82
Providing important information	0.63
Providing brief/concise information	0.76
Providing relevant information	0.69
Providing usable information	0.83
Providing available information	0.70
SerVQ: Cronbach's Alpha = 0.81; Composite Reliability = 0.87; AVE= 0.53	
Providing prompt information to users	0.71
Providing good interface	0.84
Providing visually appealing features	0.67
Providing right solution to requests	0.76
Dependable service provider	0.71
Up-to-date facilities of service provider	0.68
Experienced service provider and providing quality training and services	-
II: Cronbach's Alpha = 0.81; Composite Reliability = 0.85; AVE= 0.51	
Enhancing individual creativity	-
Enhancing organizational learning and recall for individual worker	0.84
Improving individual productivity	0.61
Benefit for individual's tasks	0.77
Enhancing higher-quality decision making	0.73
Saving time for individual tasks/duties	0.65
WI: Cronbach's Alpha = 0.86; Composite Reliability = 0.88; AVE= 0.52	
Helping to improve workers' participation in the organization	0.80
Improving organizational-wide communication	0.72
Improving inter-departmental coordination	0.86
Creating a sense of responsibility	0.62
Improving the efficiency of sub-units in the organization	-
Improving work-groups productivity	0.76
Enhancing solution effectiveness	0.65

continued on following page

Table 7. Continued

Measurement Items	Item Loading
OI: Cronbach's Alpha = 0.83; Composite Reliability = 0.89; AVE= 0.58	
Reducing organizational costs	0.82
Improving overall productivity	0.77
Providing competitive advantage	0.89
Facilitating business process change	0.73
Supporting decision making	0.64
Allowing for better use of organizational data resource	-
IOI: Cronbach's Alpha = 0.85; Composite Reliability = 0.89; AVE= 0.57	
Increasing customer service/satisfaction	0.71
Enabling e-government	0.91
Better supplier relationships	0.84
Enabling e-business/e-commerce	0.74
Improved service/ product delivery	0.67
Improved cooperation with colleagues	0.63

Note: The measurement items marked with (-) were dropped from subsequent analysis.

APPENDIX 2

Table 8. Performance measured by using the proposed model

Factors	Measurement items	Success score
SQ		***0.82***
	System flexibility	0.75
	Easy to use system	0.75
	Easy to learn system	0.75
	System reliability	1
	Allowing for data integration	1
	System efficiency	0.75
	Allowing for integration with other IT systems	0.75
IQ		***0.75***
	Providing understandable information	0.75
	Providing important information	0.75
	Providing brief/concise information	0.75
	Providing relevant information	0.75
	Providing usable information	0.75
	Providing available information	0.75

continued on following page

Table 8. Continued

Factors	Measurement items	Success score
SerVQ		***0.75***
	Providing prompt information to users	0.75
	Providing good interface	0.75
	Providing visually appealing features	0.75
	Providing right solution to requests	0.75
	Dependable service provider	0.75
	Up-to-date facilities of service provider	0.75
II		***0.60***
	Enhancing organizational learning and recall for individual worker	0.75
	Improving individual productivity	0.75
	Benefit for individual's tasks	0.50
	Enhancing higher-quality decision making	0.50
	Saving time for individual tasks/duties	0.50
WI		***0.62***
	Helping to improve workers' participation in the organization	0.75
	Improving organizational-wide communication	0.75
	Improving inter-departmental coordination	0.75
	Creating a sense of responsibility	0.50
	Improving work-groups productivity	0.50
	Enhancing solution effectiveness	0.50
OI		***0.50***
	Reducing organizational costs	0.50
	Improving overall productivity	0.50
	Providing competitive advantage	0.25
	Facilitating business process change	0.75
	Supporting decision making	0.50
IOI		***0.25***
	Increasing customer service/satisfaction	0.25
	Enabling e-government	0.00
	Better supplier relationships	0.25
	Enabling e-business/e-commerce	0.25
	Improved service/ product delivery	0.50
	Improved cooperation with colleagues	0.25
Success Score		**0.62**

Section 2
Knowledge Discovery and Learning

In the spirit of better, cheaper, faster, this section challenges existing paradigms in information technology to foster continuous improvement. The chapter on agile business processes examines traditional approaches to managing business requirements and proposes a methodology to improve this approach. In addition, this section discusses how to make learning accessible across the globe and how using technology to administer traditional pencil and paper assessments is one path to providing access via e-learning, distance learning, and electronic assessment.

Chapter 5
Agile Business Process and Practice Alignment Methodology:
A Case-Study-Based Analysis

Marielba Zacarias
University of Algarve, Portugal

Paula Ventura Martins
University of Algarve, Portugal

ABSTRACT

Business process management (BPM) encompasses the discovery, modelling, monitoring, analysis, and improvement of business processes. Traditional BPM limitations in addressing changes in business requirements have resulted in a number of agile BPM approaches that seek to accelerate the redesign of business process models. In a previous work, the authors proposed the business process and practice alignment methodology (BPPAM) to uncover, supervise, and improve business processes based on actual work practices. BPPAM aims at enabling business process modeling, supervision, and improvement through the distinction of two dimensions: (1) business processes and (2) work practices. This chapter describes an agile version of the methodology (ABPPAM). Agility is infused in ABPPAM through the redefinition of phases, roles, and iteration cycles. The chapter illustrates the effects of agility for the business discovery phase of ABPPAM through a case study analysis of a real organizational setting.

DOI: 10.4018/978-1-5225-5829-3.ch005

1. INTRODUCTION

Business Process Management (BPM) encompasses the discovery, modelling, monitoring, analysis and improvement of business processes. Traditionally, business processes are developed by creating a detailed model of a business process in question, acquiring an IT-system to support it, and then implementing it in the organizational practice (Bider & Jalali, 2016). Business Process (BP) modeling specializes on describing how activities interact and relate with each other, and how activities interact with other business concepts such as goals and resources, where resources may be material and informational entities, as well as human or automated actors. Current BP modeling methodologies are supported by data collection techniques including interviews, surveys, text/document analysis, among others. BP modeling emphasizes process notions (workflow, decision, information, activities) as the dominant dimension (Hollingaworth, 2004).

However, BP modeling would benefit from a better understanding of other elements that contribute to process execution such as *people* and *human interactions*, *products* or *tools* used, specific *vocabularies*, *preferences*, *habits* and *rules*. Moreover, it has been argued that existing BP modeling methodologies offer little guidance in keeping up-to-date the continuously evolving knowledge coming from business process execution (Castela, Dias, Zacarias, & Tribolet, 2012). Business processes are executed through human and automated activities. Whereas many business processes are fairly static only at a high level, at finer-grained levels such as activities, are more agile and unpredictable. Indeed, many organizations do not know their end-to-end processes accurately or in detail, since the knowledge required for its execution is tacit and decentralized (Verner, 2004). Recent research in BP modeling is aiming to address the unpredictability of business processes (Mutschler, Weber, & Reichert, 2008; Reichert, Dadam, Jurisch, Kreher, & Goser, 2008), but there is yet little help in addressing the problem of tacit knowledge and business process model maintenance.

From our point of view, what appears to be unpredictable behavior does not mean chaos. Indeed, it follows certain rules. The rules followed in the execution of activities and tasks can be uncovered by capturing work practices. Work practice is a concept that originates in socio-technical systems, business anthropology, work systems design, and management science (Sierhuis, Clancey, Hoof, & Hoog, 2000). Work practices are behaviors of specific individuals, performing specific activities, in specific circumstances, exhibited as *action patterns*. Work practices involve people engaging in activities over time, not only with each other, but also with machines, tools, documents, and other artifacts.

The importance of discovering work practices to improve user support has been acknowledged in (Brezillon, 2003; Pomerol & Brézillon, 2011; Sierhuis, Clancey, van

Hoof, & de Hoog, 2000). Work practice modeling is also important in (1) providing a deeper understanding of the human activities composing business processes, and (2) assessing the alignment between process models and actual execution (Zacarias, Serendero, Pinto, & Tribolet, 2008).

This paper describes an agile version of the Business Process and Practice Alignment Methodology (BPPAM) proposed in (Zacarias & Martins, 2014). BPPAM allows business analysts to discover, supervise, analyze and improve business processes, paying attention not only to the process dimension but also to product, information and human dimensions that become visible in actual work practices. The Agile Business Process and Practice Methodology (ABPPAM) aims at faster and more frequent delivery of business process models through the integration of phases and roles, as well as defining more focused iteration cycles.

ABPPAM was developed following a design research approach (Hevner, March, Park, & Ram, 2004). Design research enables building and evaluating artifacts such as models and methodologies. Design-science research involves two processes; (1) *build* and (2) *evaluate*. Both processes are used to create and/or improve four kinds of artifacts; (a) *constructs*, (b) *models*, (c) *methods*, and (d) *instantiations*. Purposeful artifacts are built to address unsolved problems. They are evaluated with respect to the utility provided in solving those problems. Constructs provide the language in which problems and solutions are defined and communicated. Models use constructs to represent a real- world situation. Models enable exploring the effects of design decisions and changes in the real world. Methods provide guidance on how to solve problems. Instantiations show that constructs, models or methods can be implemented in a working system.

The remainder of this paper is organized as follows; section 2 summarizes related work about traditional and agile business processes and work practice modeling. Section 3 summarizes the ABPPAM methodology, emphasizing the Discovery (BPD). Section 4 illustrates the BPD phase of ABPPAM through an analysis of a case study analysis of a real organizational setting. Section 5 outlines our conclusions and outlook.

2. RELATED WORK

Business processes represent business operations in terms of sequences of activities, as well their inputs, outputs and the actors that perform them. Several BP modeling frameworks describe the ways of building business process representations. Some approaches are systematic and detailed methodologies encompassing a set of procedures, techniques and tools to support the business process model construction.

BP modeling (Bider & Jalali, 2016) methodological procedures involve of several steps and include descriptions of the inputs and outputs of each step (Spewak & Hill, 1993; The Open Group, 2011).

Improving business processes, conforming to existing approaches, do not always give a quick response to business needs. In some cases, it is indispensable to adopt agile approaches to business processes improvement. Nevertheless, the agile business process definition is not consensual since several proposals have been issued in the literature. So, the authors start presenting definitions for the main concepts in this paper, namely agile business process and agile business process methodology. The authors also intend to describe the relationships established between them. The focus of our work is business process improvement in order to be adapted to organizational changes. In this paper, the authors consider agility in business process methodologies. Our approach concerns the cycles of the methodology and modelling principles applied to business processes.

The Manifesto for Agile Software Development (Beck, 2001) introduces the core principles of the agile philosophy in the domain of software development. This section discusses the principles behind the agile software development and how they can be adapted to BPM. However, Agile Business Process does not have a manifesto, neither a consensual definition accepted by practitioners and researchers. The first goal of this section is to clarify the differences between traditional and agile Business Processes (BP); traditional and agile BP methodologies.

Traditional Business Process (TBP) follows a strict action sequence, creates a detailed business process model and implements it in the organization. This approach may not be suitable for organizations classified as dynamic because of the high degree of changes. The adjustment to new requirements is a complex and arduous procedure (Alexopoulou et al., 2010). With regard to the definition of Agile Business Process (ABP), it concerns the ability to discover changes and new opportunities, reacting quickly to them. In software development, the authors can consider BPMS a special case of a software system. So, it is possible to consider BPM methodologies also a subclass of software development methodologies. In the domain of agile approaches, the sequential life cycle associated with a TBP will require a change to a new BPM lifecycle.

From our point of view, the traditional BPPAM (Zacarias & Martins, 2014) should be configured in order to address all the features related with agility. The approach will be adapted to include the following principles of the agile manifesto for software development:

- Individuals and interactions over processes and tools: collaboration between involved stakeholders and developers; Enable face-to-face interactions.

- Working software over comprehensive documentation: frequent delivery of working software; working software is the primary measure of progress.
- Responding to change over following a project plan: accommodate changing requirements; simplicity.

In the following section, an adaptation of the BPPAM methodology will be presented. The agile BBPAM will preserve the most important features related to the alignment between work practices and business process descriptions. Following the principles of the agile manifesto, the traditional BPPAM will be readapted.

3. AGILE BUSINESS PROCESS AND PRACTICE ALIGNMENT METHODOLOGY (ABPPAM)

The purpose of adapting traditional BPPAM to the agile philosophy is to provide a mechanism to react quickly to changes in business processes with the simplicity necessary to non-expert users since they will collaborate to describe daily practices. The authors reinforce that before a business process description starts, the team must identify the complexity level involved in the business process improvement.

The agile BPPAM (ABPPAM) differs from the traditional approach in four subjects:

- For small or micro enterprises, in the first phase, Business Process Discovery, when is possible to analyse the behaviour of individuals and the effect on the organisation, it is advisable an agile approach with short cycles and quick response to changes in business processes.
- The second and third phases are merged into one phase – *Business Process Change*.
- The structure of the *Business Process Change* phase reshapes against the practices of the two old ones (*Business Process Supervision* and *Business Process Assessment and Improvement*). It consists in transferring knowledge gathering directly from business stakeholders. Providing a simple language, similar to user stories from agile software development methodologies, to describe observed changes. The big cycles of the phases, *Business Process Supervision and Business Process Assessment and Improvement*, are replaced by smaller cycles and shorter iterations length. The reaction to changes is immediate, the change in the BPMS is made iteratively and following the three principles of the agile manifesto described in the previous section.
- Integrating multiple roles and assigning them to one person (stakeholder) is important to simplify the review and approval of business processes described by business stakeholders.

ABPPAM proposes a two-dimensional approach, encompassing two phases: (1) Business Process Discovery and (2) Business Process Changes. The Business Process Discovery of the Traditional BPPAM provides an initial process specification through interviews and collaborative methods. For large enterprises, the authors propose an initial stage that includes a description of all organisational processes, an agile approach is not advisable. In this case, the traditional methodology should be applied. For small or micro enterprises, where it is possible to analyse the behaviour of individuals and their effect on the organisation, it is advisable an agile approach. Business Process Changes assures that daily practices follow base business process models and allows analyzing performance measures to improve and refine business process models.

Each phase integrates two dimensions: (1) Process and (2) Practice. The Practice dimension explores day-to-day work based on individual actions and practices. This dimension captures and represents on-site information needed to systematically validate business process models, eliciting the knowledge of operational actors (represented by individuals or groups). At this level, knowledge is local and frequently tacit, thus it is hard to formalize. However, it encompasses information needed to validate process execution. In the Process dimension, business analysts discover, review and improve business process descriptions, based on information from the Practice dimension. The process dimension addresses knowledge that crosses functional divisions and organizational boundaries (clients, suppliers). Therefore, it is not confined to particular individuals or groups. The process dimension also addresses the need of continuous business process supervision and improvement as a reaction to fast-changing environments. These two dimensions, Practice and Process, will ensure the proper structure to articulate individual, group and organizational knowledge with the knowledge of business analysts.

3.1. Business Process Discovery

The main goal of a Business Process Discovery (BPD) is to get personal descriptions of business processes from work practice descriptions. BPD phase aims at developing an organizational profile of people, activities, technology, and information in order to capture actual business processes. This phase includes two main sub-phases: (1) Learning (Eliciting) Business (LB) and (2) Modeling Business (MB).

3.1.1. Learning Business Phase

The Learning Business phase encompasses three activities; (1) kickoff meeting, (2) eliciting information of practice and process, and (3) elaborating preliminary practice and process descriptions. The kickoff meeting communicates operational actors the goal and procedures of the BPD phase. Information elicitation is accomplished according to the nature of each dimension.

Initially, for large organizations, the sub-phase Learning Business includes interviews where the business analyst interacts with operational actors as key to the success of business discovery. For small or micro enterprises, it is advisable an approach with short cycles and quick response to changes in business processes. At an organizational level, the methodology proposes to assist organizations in their effort to assess and manage problematic situations based on daily actions and implement solutions related to these problems. Table 1 lists the tasks performed for each of the activities performed by involved actors.

The ABPPAM methodology was designed for explicitly addressing the social dynamics of business process specification. It is based on social interactions as proposed in a two-dimensional space. The Practice dimension covers information needed to systematically support or reject many process decisions based on the result of daily experiences. The exact process representation concerns activities, resources, decision points and work flows (topology). In the Process dimension, business analysts capture best practices from the practice dimension that leads to business process description. The dynamic interplay between these two dimensions (practice and process dimensions) shows the synergy between activities performed by key operational actors and activities described by business analysts involved in Business Process Discovery. In ABPPAM there are several roles that represent the different responsibilities, which occur during learning business process (see Table 2). The outcome of this sub-phase is preliminary descriptions of both work practices and business processes.

Practice Dimension

In our framework, work practices are defined in terms of action and interaction patterns. Due to its local nature, work practices vary according the context of execution. Moreover, operational actors are often unaware of their recurrent action patterns. Hence, instead of conducting standard interviews and workshops, the approach to elicit work practices is accomplished as follows: (1) Capturing daily

Table 1. Learning Business Process Activities

Activity	Tasks performed in this activity
Kick-off meeting	Discuss the BPD program issues with operations actors, since the focus are daily experiences
Information elicitation	Collect data, interact with operational actors to identify problematic situations
Preliminary specifications	Create initial description of work practices and business processes

Table 2. Learning Business Process Roles

Role	Responsibility
Business analyst	Responsible for operational actors' relationship and learning business process features
Operational actors	Responsible for reporting their daily actions and determining the priority of business process

actions, (2) Identifying action and interaction contexts created by related actions, and (3) discovering recurrent action patterns within contexts. Figure 1 depicts the concepts that support this dimension.

Capturing daily actions creates action repositories, where each action is registered as *<actor, action, resource>* triples. Actions refer to fined-grained operations of actors' daily work. Actions are identified with verbs taken from the vocabulary shared among operational actors. Resources may involve information, tools, materials or even human knowledge not yet externalized in external sources. Resources are described with nouns or nominal phrases using actors' own vocabulary. Actions may be communicative or not communicative. Communicative actions involve two actors; a sender and a receiver.

Understanding the meaning of actions requires situating them in a particular context. Action contexts are defined as situations created by action sequences

Figure 1. Practice dimension meta-model

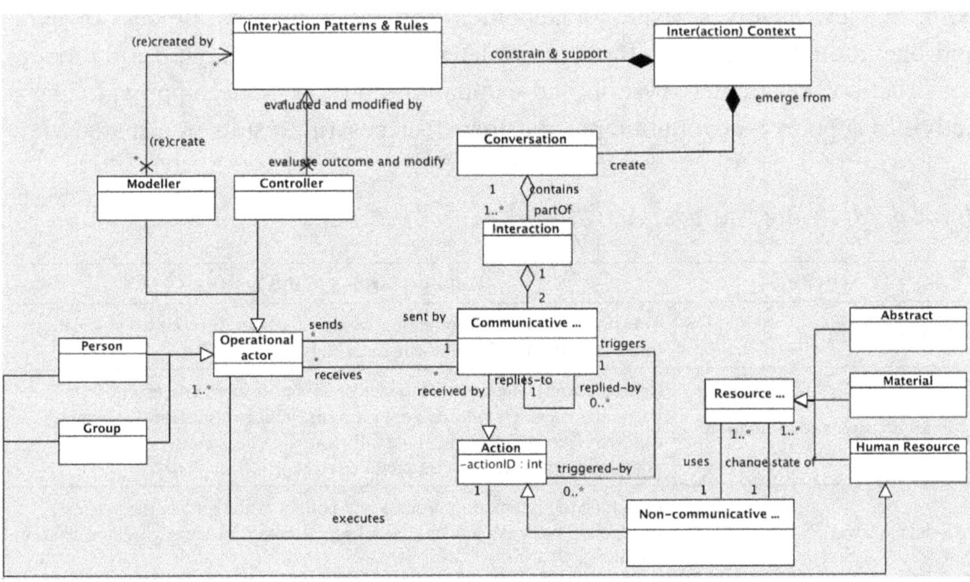

performed by one or more operational actors. Action sequences performed by a single individual create personal action contexts. Interaction sequences i.e. communicative actions exchanged between two or more actors that are part of a single conversation, create interaction contexts. Conversations are sequences of interactions around a given business topic that tell a story about that topic. Conversations are supported and constrained by interaction patterns and rules. Under this definition, recurrent action and interaction patterns are uncovered using conversations as units of analysis. Recurrent interaction patterns and rules represent work practices. It is noteworthy that such patterns are not generic. Rather they refer to specific people, places a time periods.

Process Dimension

The action patterns discovered at the practice dimension are then analyzed and discussed by operational actors and business analysts in order to define business processes, as well as the business activities and resources, composing business processes. This discussion entails an aggregation process that is accomplished in a bottom-up fashion. However, a top-down application of high-level knowledge such as organizational goals and strategies is required to complete business process definitions.

3.1.2. Modeling Business

After an initial business process definition, business analyst starts modeling business processes. The sub-phase Modeling Business, from the knowledge management point of view, involves several stakeholders (business analysts, process owners, and operational actors) into three interrelated activities (see Table 3): (1) model construction; (2) model revision and evaluation and (3) model approval. These activities support a negotiation process that if successful, results in a shared view

Table 3. Modeling Business Activities

Activity	Tasks performed in this activity
Model construction	Transforms tacit and implicit knowledge and specific contextual situations into more structured and documented forms
Model revision and evaluation	Critical review of existing knowledge about business processes. Participants present alternative proposals, which result from associating different facts and new meanings. Business process model discussions and negotiations to correct these models
Model approval	Conclude the interaction process and collaboration among the parties involved in business process model specification by approving or rejecting the model

of the process. Finally, the model approval activity concludes when the participants approve or reject the model.

All participants may present alternative proposals that result from associating different facts and new meanings. The updating process provides support to business process model discussions and negotiations to correct represented activities and other aspects. Finally, the model approval activity concludes the interaction process and collaboration among the parties involved in a business process model specification by approving or rejecting the model. At the process level, model revision and evaluation activity uses the annotation as a mechanism to capture the update proposals made by business actors. Annotations are used mainly to make proposals to correct the model (corrective maintenance), to capture changes in action or interaction contexts (adaptive maintenance), to make free comments that could anticipate problems (preventive maintenance) and promote continuous process improvement (perfective maintenance). If business actors detect any misalignment between the model and their knowledge of activity current states-of-affairs, they can make a textual or graphic annotation with the correction proposal.

Table 4 describes roles involved in the Modeling Business sub-phase. At practice dimension, in order to infuse agility by rapidly identify and reacting to changes in work practices, the authors draw on the idea of using dynamic control systems to address enterprise transformations (Abraham, Tribolet, & Winter, 2013). Thus, the authors adopt a notion of work practice management in terms as a cyclic feedback loop that comprises *defining, executing, evaluating*, and *redefining* work practices. That means regardless of the operational role played, actors evaluate the results of their actions and interactions. Upon changes on requirements, and depending on the frequency, dimension and degree of unpredictability of the change, actors may redefine their goals, change their pattern of behavior or even defining a totally new behavioral pattern. In the former case, actors apply control measures and thus, play the role of a *controller.* When they change their patterns of behavior or create new ones, they play the role of a *modeler.*

Table 4. Modeling Business Process Roles

Role	Responsibility
Modeler (operational actor)	At practice dimension, this actor changes the patterns of behavior or creates new ones
Controller (operational actor)	At practice dimension, this actor applies control measures when he changes or defines new behavioral patterns
Process owner	At process dimension, modeling responsibilities are attributed to process owners
Business analyst	At process dimension, this actor concludes the interaction process and collaboration among the parties involved in business process model

Practice Dimension

The action and patterns identified within particular contexts in the previous phase are shared, discussed among operational actors (playing the role of controllers) involved in similar activities in order to identify which practices represent deviations causing problems, and which practices yield better results. In the former case, the same operational actors discuss and may change those practices (thus changing their role to modelers).

Process Dimension

The process representation concerns activities, resources, decision points and work flows (topology). In the Process dimension, business analysts only use the best practices that lead to business process reviews and improvement. Business analysts then define business process models based on previously identified best practices. Agility at this dimension is reflected by defining several but shorter process modeling cycles. Each cycle addresses the patterns uncovered within one or several inter-related action and interaction contexts.

3.2. Business Process Change

In the Business Process Change (BPC) phase, formal control mechanisms are designed in order to ensure that operational actors carried out real business activities as described by business models. Business Process Assessment is a mean for organizations to identify their strengths, weakness, and key areas for improvement. It enables organizations to determine the current state of their business processes and to develop improved models. In the end of the BPC phase, the business analyst analyzes change proposals and through a comparison between base business process models and proposed changes, a new set of models is built to correct work that is not proceeding well, by showing where adjustments need to be made. The results gathered during assessments enable improvements and consistent refinements in order to produce an improved set of business process models. This phase ends when all the involved actors agree that the objectives set during BPD (and modified throughout the second phase) have been met and especially if all participants are satisfied with the new business process model version.

Three main purposes of Business Process Change measurement have been identified: understanding proposed changes, controlling BPC programs, and improving business processes and its work products. In ABPPAM, the Business Process Change phase is accomplished at both dimensions. Whereas at the practice dimension, data is analyzed, interpreted and used in at the level of work practices, at the process dimension it is accomplished for business processes. Work practices are an essential input for BPC measurements. Work practices can also use measurement data from related business process in order to make decisions regarding changes proposed.

Normally, business process success is evaluated in terms of staff productivity, service quality, service time, and cost of the service or product provided. However, these organizational keys indicators may change and evolve, as well as the key indicators applied in Business Process Change. Over time, process changes can impact the way measurements are defined, the way measurements are collected, or the frequency of measurement collection and analysis activities.

The initial control mechanisms of the BPC phase consist in three main activities: (1) compare real business activities with base business models (2) annotations/reviews and (3) identify new business descriptions. To facilitate the evolution and ensure that measurements and indicators continue to provide meaningful information to business analyst and process owner, periodically capturing daily actions information is important to: (1) facilitate the analysis and interpretation of measurements over time; (2) to establish links between process and practice measurement data sets and (3) to understand exactly how both measurement levels are evolving. Process owner and business analyst should check collected data and the metrics set because they have to make decisions and take corrective actions based on the same data and rules. Table 5 lists the tasks performed for each of the activities performed by involved actors.

The main purpose of the Business Process Change is to verify if work practices are conforming to the business process identified in the previous phase. The practice dimension covers information needed to systematically support or reject many process decisions based on the result of daily practices. In this dimension, operational actors register their daily actions. Registered actions are used to identify modified or new work practices. This is achieved using the notions of personal and interaction contexts defined in section 3.1.1. Coordination and monitoring activities performed at the practice dimension allow detecting misalignments with the base business process, discuss if these misalignments are negative or positive for business performance (they could represent innovations). In the process dimension, business analysts capture best practices from the practice dimension that leads to business process reviews and improvement. In the process dimension, work practices collected from personal and interactions contexts are linked with roles, activities and resources defined by the business process model. Business processes are then annotated or reviewed to reflect the newly identified best practices. Each annotation/review should be adding or validating new features to improve the business process.

When changes in business process activities are introduced, a validation period is necessary for monitoring its fitness and performance in the organization. A new

Table 5. Business Process Change Activities

Activity	Tasks performed in this activity
Compare real business activities with base business models	Coordination and monitoring activities performed at practice dimension, allow detecting misalignments with the base business process, and discussing if they entail negative or positive results.
Annotations/reviews	Operational actors register their daily actions, which are used to uncover updates and new adopted practices. Business processes are annotated and reviewed to add new features to improve the business process.
Identify new business descriptions	New work practices are analyzed to determine if base business process should be updated. The process owner introduces new activities, modifies or deletes activities from the process.
Analyze proposed changes	Business analyst monitors and controls change proposals made by operational actors. In the future, process owner uses that data to support decision making when implement an improved business process.
Improve business process based on key indicators	The detailed assessment report with multi-level conclusions refines findings and supports the improvement program.
Analyze metrics evolution	Process owner and business analyst should check collected data and the metrics set because they have to make decisions and take corrective actions based on the same data and rules.
Iteration Feedback meeting	Process owner present and discuss with operational actors the improved version of the business process.
Final Feedback meeting	In the final feedback meeting, if involved actors approve the new business process, the organization has a new base business process to apply in future services.

base business process is defined once the business process is validated. When refining the business process, outcomes and results described in the assessment report should be made concrete through a set of activities with the main goal to refine the organizational base business process. This methodology will use measures at business process and work practices level to generate a variety of improvement ideas. Some of the ideas and the candidate improvement actions arise in discussions the process owner and operational actors during practical and business process assessment meetings. Additional improvement actions are derived from indicator ratings of the assessed business process. An assessment report with conclusions refines assessment findings and supports the improvement planning and activities over a period of time. Business process improvement must be analyzed in a final feedback meeting. The main goal is to analyze all improvement opportunities identified in the practice dimension, and validate all the BPC actions accepted in previous meetings. In the final feedback meeting, participation of the process owner, business analyst and operational actors is advisable. Final version of the report can be released after the feedback meeting, which enables corrections and modifications of the report to promote later improvements in business process work products such as business practices and business process documents. As ABPPAM proposes, a new business process version will be the final work product. Table 6 describes roles involved in the Business Process Change phase.

4. TESTING THE BPD PHASE: A CASE STUDY

4.1. Organizational Setting

The case study involved a software development team of 4 programmers (Gonçalo, Carla, Catarina, Alexandre), the project leader (Mariana), who performs both programming and project management tasks, and Mariana's boss (Antonio). The team develops web applications for a commercial bank. Team members perform systems analysis, design, programming, test and maintenance tasks. Thus, they played the role of *operational actors*. During the observation period, the team worked on the following applications; (1) Suppliers, (2) Claims, (3) Clients' Mail Correspondence (called Mail application), (4) Evictions and (5) Marketing Campaigns. Since this case study had a reduced dimension, the team leader role was two-fold: she played the role of an operational actor and business analyst. As all actors, Mariana's boss is an operational actor but also plays the role of owner process.

Table 6. Business Process Change Roles

Role	Responsibility
Modeler (operational actor)	At practice dimension, this actor changes the patterns of behavior or creates new ones. Identifies candidate improvements actions. Participates in iteration/final feedback meetings.
Controller (operational actor)	At practice dimension, this actor applies control measures when he changes or defines new behavioral patterns. Participates in iteration/final feedback meetings.
Process owner	At process dimension, modeling responsibilities are attributed to process owners. This actor validates the new proposal of the business process and prepares iteration/ final feedback meetings. Coordinates iteration/final feedback meetings.
Business analyst	At process dimension, this actor coordinates the interaction and collaboration between all participants. This actor analyzes change proposals and through a comparison between base business process models and proposed changes, a new set of models is built to correct work that is not proceeding well. Controls effects of change in business processes.

4.2. Business Process Discovery Results

4.2.1. Kickoff Meeting

The research goal and data collection methods were discussed in a briefing session. In order to achieve some standardization regarding the terms used, the meeting also served to discuss typical action names and resources. Templates and indications for data collection were also discussed. Indications included registering actions in active voice sentences, mandatory inclusion of the subject performing the action and registering the action date, as well and all possible relevant action details. According to the methodology (see Table 2), it was defined that operational actors (team members) were responsible for collecting actions, coordinated by the business analyst (team leader).

4.2.2. Information Elicitation and Preliminary Specifications

As aforementioned, information elicitation and preliminary specification activities are accomplished at practice and process dimensions. Results of both activities for each dimension are described below:

Learning Phase: Practice Dimension

A set of 534 actions was manually collected through a three-week observation period. Figure 2 shows an extract of an action log that illustrates the structure defined for actions. Due to human multitasking, grouping actions in personal contexts is essential to distinguish related from unrelated actions. This discrimination use is achieved with the notion of personal contexts.

Figure 2. Some registered actions

nº	day	Actor/Sender	Receiver(s)	action type	description	*tools*	*documents| information*	*human*
1	**6**	Carla	team members	propose	a team meeting at 15h	e-mail	team member addresses	
2	**6**	Pproduction area	Mariana, Catarina	inform	error in automatic table updates	e-mail	error message	
3	**6**	Carla	Catarina	command	find a solution to the automatic table update problem	e-mail	Catarina' address	
4	**6**	Carla	CG team	propose	test claims application (integration tests)	telephone	CG team tlf. number	
5	**6**	CG team	Mariana	accept	test claims application (integration tests)			
6	**6**	Carla		prepare	prepare claims application test environment	claims application	test data	claims application knowledge (testing procedure)

Personal action contexts were discovered grouping together registered actions performed by a single operational actor and related to a given situation, subject, problem or task. Action groupings were analyzed by each operational to identify most recurrent action types and resource-related items, label the grouping as a personal context and select *context features* or *keywords*. Figures 3, 4 and 5 depict the personal contexts identified by operational actor Carla after grouping her collected actions, as well as the keywords characterizing each context. Operational actor Carla labeled these contexts as *Common Services Application* (Figure 3), *Development Support* (Figure 4), and *Team Meetings* (Figure 5). The *Common Services Application* context is characterized by the following keywords: program (action); common services application (information items); and visual studio .net, sql server, msdn, google (tools). The *Development Support* context is characterized by the keywords *answer, help (actions), suppliers application, mail application, web services (information items), mail application software (tools);* and *alexandre, catarina (human resources).* The *Team Meetings* context is characterized by the keywords *accept, assist* (actions); *team meeting* (information items); *e-mail* (tool); and *goncalo, catarina, mariana, alexandre* (human resources).

Table 7 shows the personal contexts identified for Carla, Alexandre and Mariana (the team leader). Notice that the number of contexts identified by Mariana is at least twice greater. Indeed, all operational actors identified between 3 and 6 contexts. This difference is consistent with the diversity of her tasks as programmer and team leader.

Personal contexts are the basis to uncover individual action patterns. Nonetheless, to properly understand collective practices, it is not enough to analyze personal contexts. Indeed, practices are typically executed by several individuals. Thus, it is

Figure 3. Carla's Common Services Application context

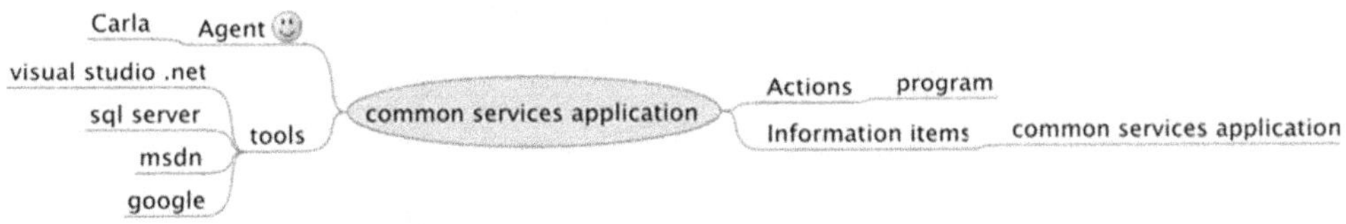

Figure 4. Carla's Development Support context

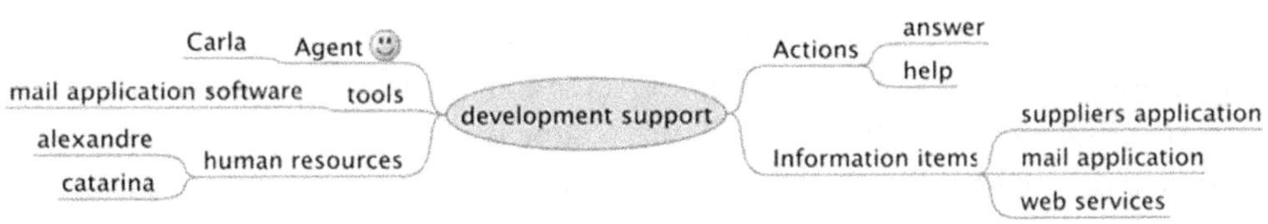

Figure 5. Carla's Team Meetings context

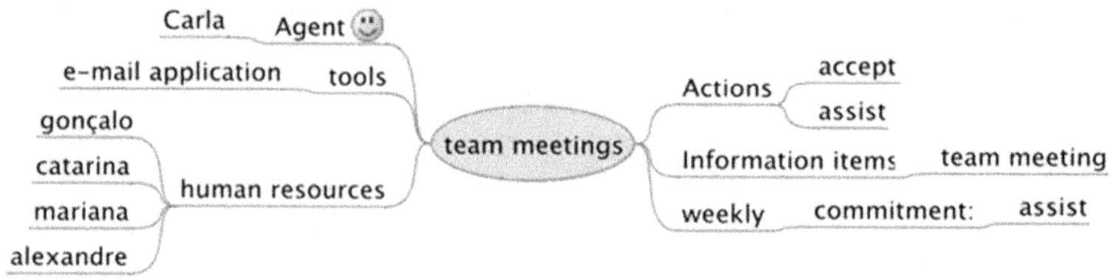

Table 7. Personal contexts of Alexandre, Carla and Mariana

Operational Actor	Context ID	Context Description
Alexandre	a1	Data Collection for Mail Application
Alexandre	a2	Mail Application Programming
Alexandre	a3	Evictions Web Service Problem
Alexandre	a4	Team Meetings
Carla	c1	Common Services Application Programming
Carla	c2	Programming Support
Carla	c3	Team Meetings
Mariana	m1	Project Management Reports and Meetings
Mariana	m2	Automatic Table Update Problem
Mariana	m3	Integration Tests
Mariana	m4	User Support
Mariana	m5	Document Association Function
Mariana	m6	Evictions Web Service Problem
Mariana	m7	Script Execution Problem
Mariana	m8	Suppliers Application
Mariana	m9	Web Components Programming

essential to identify and characterize not only personal contexts but also, interaction contexts. The analysis of interaction contexts allows capturing which actions and resources are shared (and how) between different individuals.

Whereas personal contexts are identified from action sequences of a single individual, the identification of interaction contexts is made from action sequences from *two* or more given individuals. Interpersonal contexts relate two specific personal contexts of interacting individuals. Figure 6 depicts an action sequence created by a problem detected on the ''evictions web service''. This action sequence involves

Figure 6. Evictions Web Service Action Sequence

Nº	day	ent (send	ctxt	agent (receiver)	action	description item keywords
1	9	evictions-v	-	alexandre	request	solve problem, evictions web service
2	9	alexandre	a3	NULL	solve	solve problem, evictions web service
3	9	alexandre	a3	mariana	request	publication in quality environment, evictions web service
4	9	mariana	m6	publication team	request	publication in quality environment, evictions web service
5	9	publicatio	-	mariana	inform	publication, evictions web service
6	9	mariana	m6	alexandre	request	test, web service, quality environment
7	9	alexandre	a3	NULL	test	evictions web service, quality environment
8	9	alexandre	a3	mariana	request	publication, production environment, evictions web service
9	9	mariana	m6	publication team	request	publication, production environment, evictions web service
10	9	mariana	m6	publication team	ask	evictions web service, production environment
11	9	publicatio	-	mariana	answer	evictions web service, published, monday
12	9	mariana	m6	alexandre	inform	evictions web service, published, monday
13	9	alexandre	a3	evictions-ws user	inform	evictions web service, published, monday
14	17	evictions-	-	alexandre	request	test, evictions web service, development environment
15	17	alexandre	a3	mariana	request	publication, evictions web service, quality environment
16	17	mariana	m6	publication team	request	publication, evictions web service, quality environment
17	17	publicatio	-	mariana	inform	publication, evictions web service, quality environment
18	17	mariana	m6	alexandre	inform	publication, evictions web service, quality environment
19	17	alexandre	a3	NULL	test	evictions web service, quality environment
20	17	alexandre	a3	mariana	request	publication, evictions web service, production environment
21	17	mariana	m6	publication team	request	publication, evictions web service, production environment
22	17	publicatio	-	mariana	inform	publication, evictions web service, production environment
23	17	mariana	m6	alexandre	inform	publication, evictions web service, production environment
24	17	alexandre	a3	NULL	test	evictions web service, production environment
25	17	alexandre	a3	web service user	inform	evictions web service, in production environment

several interactions between Alexandre's personal action context **a3**, and Mariana's personal action context **m6**. This action sequence shows a set of communicative actions exchanged mostly between Alexandre and Mariana in day 9 and day17. This action sequence starts when Alexandre receives a request to solve a problem in the "evictions web service". After solving the problem, Alexandre requests Mariana to publish the modified web service in the quality environment. This action sequence shows the interaction context created by the actions related to the Evictions web service software publication.

Table 8 illustrates some interaction contexts identified by analyzing action sequences as described for the Web Service action sequence illustrated in figure 4. Each interaction context is identified with a code, the personal contexts associated to it, and a description. The action sequence in figure 4 corresponds to the interaction context **ic3,** is composed by the personal contexts **a3** and **m6** (see Table 7) and is described as the "evictions web service problem".

Identifying interaction contexts allows uncovering recurrent actions sequences or patterns. Identifying action patterns allows assessing how different groups execute activities and how they differ from pre-defined activities composing business process models. With the data collected, it was possible to identify action patterns within some interaction contexts (Table 9). It is important to notice that actions in italic represent actions that do not appear within some but not all sequences. Its

Table 8. Some interaction contexts

Interaction Context	Personal Contexts	Description
ic1	<a1- x>	Data collection for mail application
ic2	<a1-m011>	Cards information collection
ic3	***<a3- m6>***	***Evictions web service problem***
ic4	<c2 - a5>	Web services and mail app. Support
ic5	<c2 - m8>	Suppliers app. Support
ic6	<g2 - t3>	Suppliers app. Support
ic7	<g3 - m8>	Suppliers app. support
ic8	<m1 - a4/c3/g5/t6>	Team meetings
ic9	<m1 - António>	Project management reports
ic11	<m3 – Integration team>	Integration tests
ic16	<m4/m51/m6/m7/m8/m10 – Publication Team>	Software publication

Table 9. Some action patterns

ID	Context Name	Action Pattern
ic5	suppliers application support	1.request (help) - 2.help
ic6	suppliers application support	1.ask - 2.answer
ic7	suppliers application support	1.request (help) - 2.help
		1.request (solve) - 2.solve
ic8	team meetings	1.propose - 2.accept - 3.assist
ic9	project management reports	1.request (update) - 2.update-3.send
ic11	integration tests	1.request (test) - 2.test
		1. inform(test results) - 2. test
ic16	software publication	1.request (publication) - 2.perform (publication)
		3.*test* - 4.inform (publication)
		5.inform (publication)- 6.*inform(publication)*

presence was inferred from on the fact that they needed to be executed in order for the remaining actions to take place.

Learning Subphase: Process Dimension

Action patterns uncovered at the Practice Dimension can be used in a bottom-up fashion to discover actual business activities, processes, and resources. However, in this case, the organization had previously accomplished a business process modeling initiative, having already identified a list of pre-defined activities composing business processes. Some pre-defined activities related to the interaction contexts and action patterns identified in Tables 8 and 9 include: *Software Programming, Software Testing, Software Publication, User Support, Project Management.* In this case, action patterns were associated to those activities. The activities related to the action patterns identified in Table 9 are: (1) Application Testing (**ic11**), (2) User support (**ic5, ic6, ic7**), (3) Project management (**ic8, ic9**), and (4) Application Publication (**ic16**). Following an agile approach for this case, whereas the Application Testing and Application Publication activities are addressed first in a single modeling cycle, the User support and Project management are respectively addressed in a second and third modeling cycles. This section illustrates the results of the first modeling cycle.

Action repositories include descriptions of the information items, tools, materials or knowledge used or produced by each action. However, at the process dimension those items need to be linked with formally defined resources already associated to given business activities or processes. In this case, a list of such resources was pre-defined together with business activities. The table depicted in Figure 7 shows the association made by operational actors and the process owner between most frequently found items within the personal and interaction contexts included in the first cycle (ic11 and ic16), and formally defined resources that are used or produced by the Application Testing and Application Publication activities. The left column in the table depicted in Figure 7 shows the most recurrent items found within action descriptions, the middle column shows its frequency, and the right column, the resource to which that item is related. Some description items -such as application names- were they are resources themselves (e.g. common services application). In other cases, the item relationship with a resource was obvious (e.g. relating evictions web service with the evictions application). In some cases, however, relating a description item with a resource required knowledge of the organizational setting (e.g. relating automatic table updates with the message application).

In summary, action object descriptions within repository provided information about items, which are part of, or related to the following information resources: *Application Status, Suppliers application, Mail application, Common services application, Claims application, Message application, Evictions application, Cards application, Marketing application*

Modeling Subphase: Practice Dimension – Cycle 1

The remainder of this section illustrates the results of the first cycle of the modeling phase. Action patterns found in specific contexts allows uncovering work practices of

Table 10. Relating context items to formal resources

Description Item	Frequency	Formal Resource
quality environment	33	application status
suppliers application	32	suppliers application
suppliers application web component	28	suppliers application
mail application	28	mail application
suppliers application data management class	24	suppliers application
common services application	23	common services application
suppliers application application class	22	suppliers application
claims application integration test	18	claims application
application integration test	17	claims application
claims application	17	claims application
message application	16	message application
evictions web service	16	evictions application
Production environment	16	application status
evictions web service problem	9	evictions application
document association function	9	claims application
automatic table update problem	8	message application
cards information	8	cards application
campaigns application adjustment	7	marketing application
claims application file upload component	7	claims application
cards application maintenance	7	cards application
claims application problem	6	claims application
automatic table update solution	6	message application
updated evictions web service	6	evictions application
claims application document association	5	claims application
suppliers class	5	suppliers application
development environment	5	application status

specific individuals or groups. For example, figure 7 depicts a software publication practice. This practice was uncovered from the action pattern found in interaction context **ic16.** Notice how practices are related to particular persons and tools, rather than generic roles or actors. It is also noteworthy that a practice can be related to more than one formally defined activity. The publication practice includes actions belonging to two pre-defined business activities; (1) Software Testing (2) Software

Figure 7. Publication practice

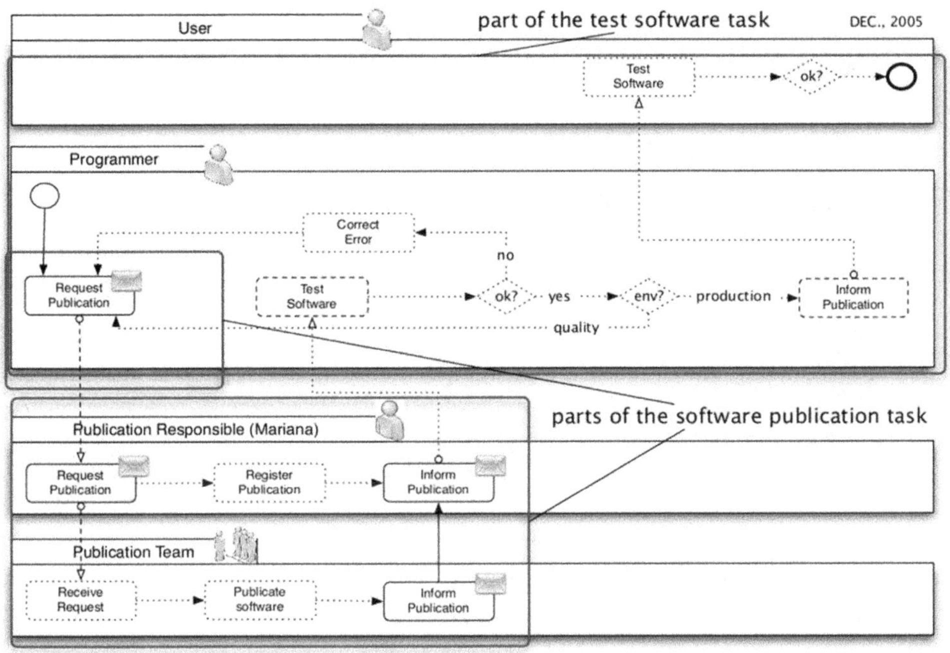

publication. Actions depicted in solid-line boxes are actions found in the action log. Traced-line boxes represent actions not always present but presumed to be performed always. Dotted-line boxes are actions never registered but inferred from registered actions.

Interaction context **ic11** uncovered two action patterns (request test – test, inform test results test), that after analysis reflected the practice of software testing and keeping the team informed of all test results.

Modeling Subphase: Process Dimension

After collecting diagrams representing several practices, the team discussed them and selected the best practices. Best practices were then used to build a software development process shared by all development teams. Figure 8 depicts a process model resulting from this phase. In this case, the resulting process reflects the publication practice depicted in figure 8 as this was considered a good practice by all teams. As the test practice is a standard practice shared by all teams, it was simply confirmed and kept in the model.

Figure 8. Generic Software Publication Process

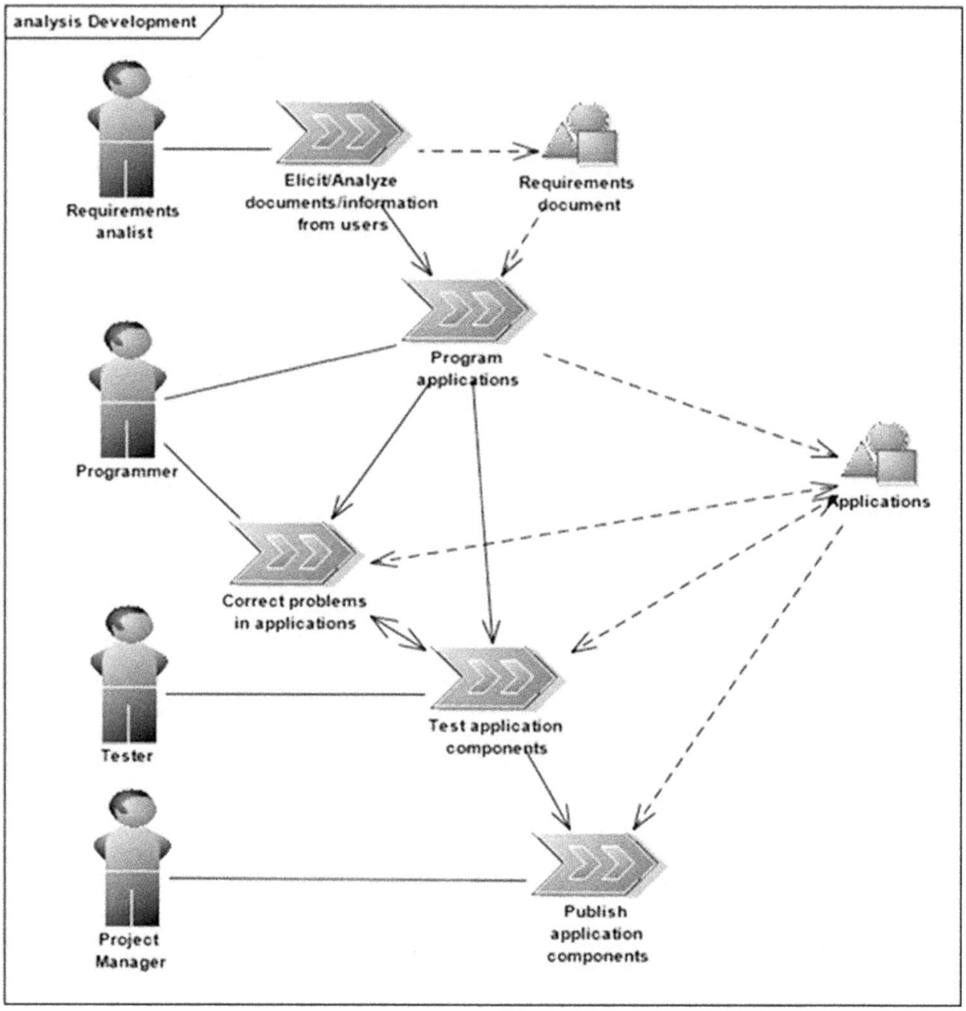

5. CONCLUSION AND OUTLOOK

This paper describes how to infuse agility in a previously developed methodology that aims at modeling and supervising business processes aligned with work practices. We argue that agility requires (1) grouping together roles and (2) defining shorter cycles with smaller scopes. In this paper, the case study is used as analytical tool to understand the effects of introducing the aforementioned adaptations. Departing from information previously collected, we aimed at assessing if it was to possible to accelerate the learning and modeling subphases.

Our results suggest that whereas at the learning phase the benefits are not evident, at the modeling subphase and practice dimension, acknowledging that the same operational actors alternate among different roles (controller and modeler) could accelerate discussions and avoid delays due to bureaucratic activities before triggering any formal process change effort. Moreover, at the modeling subphase it is possible to define smaller and more focused cycles to address more frequent and faster improvements. Nonetheless, it is necessary to conduct further case studies for empirical validation of the proposed changes to our approach.

REFERENCES

Abraham, R., Tribolet, J., & Winter, R. (2013). Transformation of multi-level systems: Theoretical grounding and consequences for Enterprise Architecture Management. In D. Aveiro & K. Galoul (Eds.), Advances in Enterprise Engineering VII (Vol. 146). Springer Berlin.

Alexopoulou, N., Nikolaidou, M., Kanellis, P., Mantzana, V., Anagnostopoulos, D., & Martakos, D. (2010). Infusing agility in business processes through an event-centric approach. *International Journal of Business Information Systems*, *6*(1), 21. doi:10.1504/IJBIS.2010.034005

Beck, K. (2001). *Manifesto for Agile Software Development*. Retrieved from http://www.agilemanifesto.org/principles.html

Bider, I., & Jalali, A. (2016). Agile business process development: Why, how and when—applying Nonaka's theory of knowledge transformation to business process development. *Information Systems and e-Business Management*, *14*(4), 693–731. doi:10.100710257-014-0256-1

Brezillon, P. (2003). Using context for supporting users efficiently. *Proceedings of the 36th Annual Hawaii International Conference on System Sciences.*

Castela, N., Dias, P., Zacarias, M., & Tribolet, J. (2012). Collaborative maintenance of business process models. *International Journal of Organisational Design and Engineering*, *2*(1), 61–84. doi:10.1504/IJODE.2012.045903

Hevner, A., March, S., Park, J., & Ram, S. (2004). Design Science in Information Systems Research. *Management Information Systems Quarterly*, *28*(1), 75–105. doi:10.2307/25148625

Hollingaworth, D. (2004). The Workflow Reference Model: 10 Years On. In L. Fischer (Ed.), *Workflow Handboook 2004* (pp. 295–312). Future Strategies Inc.

Mutschler, B., Weber, B., & Reichert, M. (2008). Workflow management versus case handling: results from a controlled software experiment. *Proceedings of the 2008 ACM symposium on Applied computing*. 10.1145/1363686.1363711

Pomerol, J. C., & Brézillon, P. (2011). About some relationships between knowledge and context. *Proceedings of the Third International and Interdisciplinary Conference on Modeling and Using Context.*

Reichert, M., Dadam, P., Jurisch, M., Kreher, U., & Goser, K. (2008). *Architectural Design of Flexible Process Management Technology.* Paper presented at the PRIMIUM Subconference at the Multikonferenz Wirtschaftsinformatik (MKWI), Garching, Germany.

Sierhuis, M., Clancey, W. J., Hoof, R. V., & Hoog, R. D. (2000). *Modeling and simulating work practices from Apollo 12*. Paper presented at the International Workshop on Simulation for European Space programmes, ESTEC.

Sierhuis, M., Clancey, W. J., van Hoof, R., & de Hoog, R. (2000). *Modeling and simulating human activity*. Paper presented at the AAAI Fall Symposium on Simulating Human Agents, North Falmouth, MA.

Spewak, S. H., & Hill, S. C. (1993). *Enterprise architecture planning: developing a blueprint for data, applications and technology*. QED Information Sciences, Inc.

The Open Group. (2011). *TOGAF® Version 9.1.* Van Haren Publishing.

Verner, L. (2004). BPM: The Promise and the Challenge. *Queue*, *2*(1), 82–91. doi:10.1145/984458.984503

Zacarias, M., & Martins, P. V. (2014). Business alignment methodology: The discovery phase. *Information Resources Management Journal*, *27*(1), 1–20. doi:10.4018/irmj.2014010101

Zacarias, M., Serendero, P., Pinto, H. S., & Tribolet, J. (2008). Capturing and modeling work practice: A context-based approach. *Revue d'Intelligence Artificialle*, *5*(22), 669–688. doi:10.3166/ria.22.669-689

Chapter 6
Roles and Impacts of Automatic Item Generation on Assessment Research, Practice, and Policy

Jaehwa Choi
The George Washington University, USA

ABSTRACT

The development of science and technology will have widespread impacts throughout society, and the "assessment" will also be a sensitive area to the impact of scientific and technological developments. Especially information communication technology, or intelligent communication technology (ICT), which has developed rapidly in the twenty-first century, has had a sudden and even destructive effect on various studies and the field. The assessment, which has the most central function of collecting, processing, and analyzing data, would be one of the most rapidly changing areas under the influence of this ICT. This chapter deals with the following four topics about automation of AIG. Firstly, this chapter will introduce the meaning/implication of automation in AIG and analyze how automation of AIG affects the technology-based assessment system. In particular, this chapter will illustrate how AIG's automation will affect education, professional training, and/or public policy. Finally, this chapter concludes with a discussion of the future directions of AIG research and development.

DOI: 10.4018/978-1-5225-5829-3.ch006

INTRODUCTION

The development of science and technology will have widespread impacts throughout society, and the 'assessment' will also be a sensitive area to the impact of scientific and technological developments. Especially information communication technology, or intelligent communication technology (ICT), which has developed rapidly in the 21st century, has had a sudden and even destructive effect on various studies and the field. The development of ICT, called the fourth science and technology revolution of the 21st century, differs from the previous scientific and technological revolutions. The key difference is the "smartness" or "intelligence" based digitalized data. Therefore, studies or industries that are highly associated with computerized data are significantly affected by the development of these ICTs, and the changes are expected to be sharp in the future. The assessment, which has the most central function of collecting, processing, and analyzing data, would be one of the most rapidly changing areas under the influence of this ICT. In this paper, I will deal with "Automatic Item Generation (AIG; Embretson & Yang, 2007; Gierl &Haladyna, 2013; Irvine & Kyllonen, 2002; Choi, 2017a)" science and/or technology, which has recently received a great deal of attention in the assessment field.

Modern researchers, psychometricians, item writers, and assessment service providers increasingly find themselves facing a new paradigm where the assessment item production process is no longer manual, but rather can be a massive production systematic and automatized by technology, that is, AIG. AIG is an emerging research and technology area where an innovative assessment tool where cognitive and psychometric theories are integrated together into a comprehensive assessment development framework for the purpose of generating assessment items using state-of-the-art technology, especially in ICT environments. With AIG technique, parent model or item templates once developed by experts (i.e., item model or item template writers) are utilized in producing (or generating) clone items (also called isomorphs) via computer-based applications. The number of content areas (e.g., K-12 education, licensure and certification), and the number of applications (e.g., workbook, homework, or exam, etc.) of AIG are exploding (Choi, 2017a). As such, this new reality raises important issues in effective and scientific item development with ICTs.

Choi (2017a) argue that, although AIG has been initiated and developed on the basis of automatic generation of assessment items, we should note that an interesting and important phenomenon that automation in AIG can affect the automation of other assessment components/processes (e.g., grading, testing, or reporting), rather than merely automating item generation. What's even more interesting is that AIG's automation role can have a profound impact on its upper realm, education and society as a whole (for example, education, training, teacher evaluation, and public policy, etc.). In this paper, I will deal with the following four topics about automation of AIG. First, I will introduce, in detail, the meaning/implication of automation in AIG via ICT development in. Second, analyze how automation of AIG affects the intelligence of the technology-based assessment system which is composed of various assessment components, that is, Assessment Engineering (AE) framework. Third, I introduce how AIG automation affects/interacts with other components of an AE system. In particular, I will introduce how AIG's automation will affect education, professional training, and/or public policy. Finally, I will discuss the future directions of AIG research and development.

AUTOMATIC ITEM GENERATION

Traditionally, item writing has been done manually by item writers and content experts. For these items to be administered to test-takers, they would have to go through item review and editing, field testing, item analysis, revision, editing, formatting, etc. During this process, many items are either discarded or revised and only a small number of them survive to be put into operational use. When the cycle for test administration is long (e.g., once a year), there seems to be little need for changing this approach.

However, there is a growing need to administer tests frequently and continuously, with more and more assessments being delivered digitally. This creates a need for large item pools to be created and replenished continuously to address the issue of test security. The demand for large numbers of items to be generated rapidly poses a great challenge to large-scale testing programs. The limitations of manually producing items become obvious—they are both expensive and time-consuming, which prohibits their use and motivates test developers to seek for more efficient ways of generating items. AIG (Bejar, 1993; Choi, 2017a; Embretson & yang, 2007; Gierl & Haladyna, 2013; Irvine & Kyllonen, 2002) can be a solution to this problem. With the aid of computer technology, AIG can generate large number of items in an efficient manner. Efficiency in generating items has the potential to bring down the cost significantly in developing items, which may be one of the core factors for its quick development in recent years. However, as we will argue later in this chapter, AIG has more advantages than its efficiency in item generation.

Nowadays, tests of all kinds are being administered much more frequently than before. With the rapid development of computer technology and the wide use of the Internet, a growing number of tests are administered on computers, tablets, on the Internet, and even cell-phones. The need for high-quality tests to be administered at a quicker pace demands that more quality items be generated in an efficient manner and items banks need to be refilled rapidly and constantly. This brings a huge challenge to test developers.

Traditionally, items were developed *manually* by item writers, and researchers have pointed out the drawbacks of the traditional way of item development. The process of developing items typically began with a test specification detailing item formats, content to be covered, scoring rules, etc. Based on the test specification, content experts and test writers used their expertise and experience to develop items to measure the intended content. However, in the absence of a cognitive theory to guide test development and without a clear understanding of the underlying cognitive processes underlining item responses and other item features that might have an influence on item difficulty, content experts often rely on their experience, personal judgment and intuition to develop items. Due to subjectivity in item writing, the quality or psychometric characteristics of items (e.g., difficulty) are often hard to predict and control. Items for the given construct are intended to measure the same content, but development by different item writers often leads to differences in item characteristics and results. After items are drafted, they also have to go through long and costly processes: they need to be field-tested and then selected for operational use, revised, or discarded.

With the rapid development of Computer-based Testing (CBT) or Internet-based Testing (iBT), the traditional way of manually developing items can hardly meet the demands of replenishing the item bank. Of course, test developers can hire a large group of test writers to constantly produce test items in this way. However, the cost for this approach is also substantial. For example, Gierl and Haladyna (2010) stated that using the traditional approach to develop one item in high-stakes testing program, the cost can range from $1,500 to $2,000 per item. If we multiply this cost by the number of items needed for each administration, this approach of generating items can be quite expensive.

AIG researchers argue that AIG is a potential solution to this problem of the traditional item development (Lai, Gierl, & Alves, 2009). Instead of focusing efforts on developing individual items manually and treating them as if they are independent unit, the AIG approach develop item templates (item models) to generate isomorphic items (i.e., items which have the same psychometric characteristics and measure the same construct). This means that in AIG, content experts and item writers still need to be trained to develop item templates. However, once an item template is developed, it can generate hundreds, even thousands of unique items. This can serve as a good solution for the demand for larger number. For example, Lai, Alves and Gierl (2009) conducted a study in which they were able to generate 64,280 items using only 34 models. Other mathematics based AIG projects (Choi, Kim, & Yoon, 2016; Choi, Kim, & Yoon, 2017) demonstrated that more than two million unique math items can be generated by 350 item templates at the 6th or 7th grade level.

Generating items in such an efficient manner brings along another obvious benefit: cost reduction. Though there have not been studies conducted to compare the actual cost involved creating the same number of items using AIG and using traditional approach, it is widely acknowledged that item model development is more effective (Wainer & Kiely, 1987). If we suppose that the same amount of effort and money is invested in developing item templates, then the cost of developing individual items will be reduced considerably since many more items can be generated using one item template. Furthermore, item models, unlike individual items, are supposed to be reused once they are developed and well-calibrated. If there is a need to make changes to individual items, such as the wording of questions, the order of options, or translating items to different languages, then we only need to make changes to a few handfuls of item models instead of large number of individual items.

Although AIG is gaining in popularity, it is primarily known for its advantages in terms of production speed and unit price reduction of items (Choi & Li, 2016; Choi, 2017a). However, "the benefits of AIG are not limited to mass production, and the benefits of this mass production must also be considered along with the cost and time required to deploy AIG" (Choi, 2017a). For example, the time and cost of training AIG template writers, along with the costs associated with developing AIG templates should be carefully evaluated before adaptation of AIG in an assessment practice (Choi, 2017a). Choi (2017a) also emphasizes the fact that many researchers have already argued that the benefits of AIG have been above and beyond mass production. In this regard, the following sections will clarify the role of AIG and its impact on assessment research, policies, and practices, so that researchers, policy-makers, and the public can fully understand AIG's significant implications in a variety of ways.

ROLES AND IMPACTS OF AIG TO ASSESSMENT THEORY

As mentioned in the above section, the advantages of AIG are highlighted in terms of mass production of items. However, Choi (2017a) points out that AIG's theoretical, practical, and technical implications can be overlooked when focusing on AIG's mass production. In this section, I will briefly summarize the advantages and implications of the theoretical aspects of AIG (Choi, 2017a).

Construct Preservation

AIG presents a new concept for traditional test security and offers a variety of options to address the threat of test security. Using AIG, test builders and administrators can effectively and differently handle test security concerns and improve instruction-assessment alignments via AIG.

Construct Representation

AIG provides several options for further improving construct representation. The process of generating an item using AIG is to further objectify and strengthen the link between empirical evidence measured by item responses and the construct that the item is measuring. Moreover, it enables the physical access to the "principal" that is the basis for the specific item that the item developer has generated, making item development and review possible in a more clear and verifiable way.

Scientific Test Design

AIG plays a key role in recent scientific test design approaches. (i.e., Evidence-centered Design [Mislevy, Almond, & Lukas, 2004], Cognitive Design System [Embretson, 1998] and Assessment Engineering [Luecht, 2014]). The scholars argue that AIG is a very useful tool of transitioning the traditional item development process, which has heavily relied on the experience and intuition for item developments, into a more scientific and systematic process.

Item Calibration

The traditional item or test development process requires an item calibration or validation process that heavily depends on empirical data, collected via field tests. This process leads to many constraints and difficulties in the production of test items because of the high cost, especially the item and test production time and security. AIG provides several strategies to improve item calibration and validation more efficiently. AIG further reduces the dependence of the field test and offers the possibility of generating high quality items by performing calibration and validation even without a field test.

Equating and Linking

AIG can increase the efficiency of test equating and linking by allowing it to produce superior quality common items or tests. The homogeneity or equivalency of assessments that are systematically developed and controlled by AIG templates enables effective treatment of the interaction between the item and the person, particularly the "memory or instrument effect," in equating and linking (Choi, 2017a).

In sum, AIG has several advantages and implications in theory. Additionally, the theoretical implications presented above are directly related to the validity of items and tests. It is therefore clear that AIG could be a useful tool for improving validity of assessments beyond the point of simply mass-producing questions and tests and lowering unit costs.

ROLES AND IMPACTS OF AIG TO ASSESSMENT PRACTICE

In addition to the theoretical advantages and implications described above, AIG also plays various roles and brings impacts in assessment practices (Choi, 2017a). In this section, I will briefly summarize the advantages and implications of AIG on the practical aspects as follows.

Item Management

AIG will provide efficiencies in storing, delivering, editing, and revising items. In particular, AIG provides an excellent option for creating and managing global assessment contents.

Learner-Centered Assessment

AIG can be used as a valuable tool to transform existing assessments into more learner-centered assessments, such as diagnostic and/or formative assessment. AIG strengthens the links the skills to be measured with interpretations of test scores. AIG helps probe deeply into an examinee's weakness, and is useful in diagnostic classification. In formative assessment settings, AIG provides consistent, timely,, and individualized feedback and diagnoses.

Intelligent Assessment

We can utilize and fuse various ICT technologies (big data analysis, virtual or augmented reality, simulation based inferences, blockchain, etc.) to develop existing assessments into more intelligent assessments beyond the traditional paper-pencil or computer-based assessment. A series of these theoretical and technical efforts can be abbreviated as Assessment Engineering, and AIG plays a central role in building such intelligent system.

We have just briefly reviewed the fact that AIG has several advantages and implications from a practical point of view. Now one can understand that AIG can develop more efficient and effective assessments in practice. In addition, AIG plays a crucial role in creating and implementing a variety of assessments for various purposes, especially learner-centered assessments, as seen in the characteristics mentioned above.

ROLES AND IMPACTS OF AIG TO ASSESSMENT TECHNOLOGY

In this section, we will look at AIG's roles and impacts for Assessment technology. Choi (2017a) called the "Assessment Engineering (AE) framework" a form that combines the latest technologies and theories to develop the assessment. In this section, I will introduce AE first and explain how AIG plays a central and integral role in the AE framework.

Assessment Engineering

The 4th industrial revolution represents a change in the industrial environment that maximizes automation and connectivity due to the development of Artificial Intelligence (AI) and Machine Learning (ML). The field of education will not be an exception to this revolutionary change. In this section, I would like to introduce Assessment Engineering (AE), which is emerging in the field of education, in line with this 4th industrial revolution.

Definition

AE (Assessment Engineering) is a discipline that analyzes statistical analysis tools, services, and information related to assessment using Information/Intelligent and Communication Technology (ICT). The assessment related information, services, and models related to measurement, diagnosis, and prediction in various educational fields such as K12 education, higher education, and professional trainings.

Usages

There are two main uses of Assessment Engineering. First, there is "analytical purpose" to statistically analyze the assessment related data, and to improve the quality of utilization, understanding, prediction, and decision making of this information. Second, it is a "development purpose" that develops and advances assessment services by integrating state-of-the-art mathematical/statistical (psychometric) methods and ICTs in educational institutions, such as schools, academies, and educational enterprises.

History

The early introduction of AE can be called CBT or Computer Adaptive Testing (CAT), which has been studied in Educational Statistics and/or Educational and Psychological Measurements since the early 1970s. The concept of AE, especially CBT and CAT, became widespread in the real world in the 1990s. This is because the utilities of CBT, CAT and Internet-based testing (IBT) have been verified due to the rapid developments of various ICT technologies, especially Internet-related technologies and infrastructure. Since then, advanced assessment theories and technologies have been developed and applied in various fields. In the US, most of the large scale standardized tests are being implemented as CBT or IBT in 2017.

Academic Backgrounds

AE is a convergent discipline that combines education, applied statistics, and applied computation. In addition to CBT or CAT, which are the traditional focuses of AE, there are many topics, such as AIG, Automatic Scoring, and Assessment Platform. Teaching and Learning Analytics is also regarded as a branch. AE differs from traditional Educational Technology, which focuses primarily on instructional design in that it is centered on assessment models and data.

Figure 1. A Concept Model for Assessment Engineering Framework

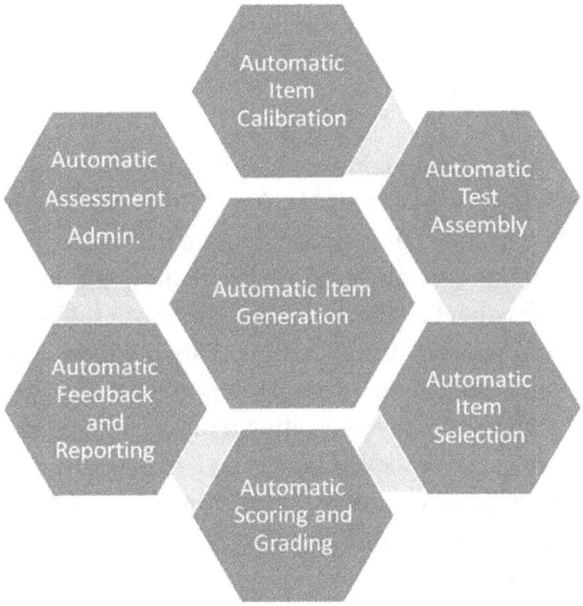

Components of AE Framework

As seen in above figure, AE contains several assessment components, and each component can be automated. As a result of the nature of the assessment system or application (i.e., a typical assessment is composed of items), AIG's role is particularly dominant in this AE framework. In this AE framework, AIG plays a crucial role in ensuring that each component is efficiently functional by supporting large quantities and high-quality items.

Technological Characteristics

AE aims to develop assessment system maximizing automation, intelligence and connectivity that can be characterized by the era of the 4th Industrial Revolution, and has the following distinctions with existing technologies or academic fields:

Automation/Intelligence

The main trend pursued by AE is the automation or intelligence of repetitive, human-oriented evaluation tasks. It is a key characteristic of AE to pursue automation, mechanization, or intelligence throughout assessment processes, such as item development, assessment assembly, measurement modeling selection, feedback and report generation, and assessment analysis. In the future, the marginal cost of production and consumption of assessment services will be significantly lowered, and accessibility will be enhanced by AE.

Cloud Assessment Platform

A characteristic of AE systems compared to existing assessment systems is the transition from individual assessment services to the Assessment Platform. The assessment platform is a cloud computing paradigm specialized in assessment. And the platform is for enabling network access to a scalable and elastic pool of shareable physical or virtual assessment resources and services with self-service provisioning and administration on-demand (Choi, 2017a). This platform enables a variety of assessment services and applications to be interconnected to share assessment-related resources and information, thereby preventing redundant investment in the services and enabling efficient service development and management. The Assessment Platform, which is a fusion of various assessment services, supports the ubiquitous assessment environments which enable various types of on-demand assessment services anytime, anywhere.

Strategic Goals and Potential Benefits

AE aims at developing the evaluation system using the technologies of the fourth industrial revolution era (for example, artificial intelligence, blockchain, or machine learning), and aims at the following strategic goals in this development direction.

Individualizing or Tailoring

Unlike existing single or group-based assessment services, AE aims at individualized assessment that is appropriate to each person type and characteristics. AE adapts advanced technology to plan and implement individualized assessment services to meet the varying needs of individual differences. In particular, AE focus on automation, mechanization, and intelligence of individualization in order to minimize human and time cost of personalization.

Learner-Centered Assessment

AE focuses on learner-centered diagnosis/formative assessment rather than the decision-maker-oriented summative assessment. In particular, AE aims to maximize the effectiveness of teaching and learning by providing immediate feedback and analysis of the assessment information through automation and intelligence, and to overcome various problems caused by the existing summative-oriented assessment environments. For example, AE studies the directions of developing classroom assessments using advanced technologies such as the Teacher Empowered Assessment (TEA; Dardick & Choi, 2016) framework.

Alignment

AE aims to enhance the integration of the three elements of Curriculum, Instruction, and Assessment using advanced technology. For example, AoT (Assessments on Textbook; Choi, 2017a; Choi 2017b) is a good example of AE pursues the alignment in which attempts to integrate assessment systems into digital textbooks to reduce inconsistencies between curriculum/instruction and instruction/assessment. Stealth Assessment or Game-based Assessment are also examples of AE to complement the shortcomings of existing assessments using advanced technology and to improve integration.

ROLES AND IMPACTS OF AIG TO ASSESSMENT POLICY

The strategic goals and potential benefits of AIG within AE framework (i.e., Individualized or Tailored, Learner-centered, and Aligned Assessment) have several important implications on the assessment related public policy (Choi, 2017a). In this section, I will articulate a few public policy related points which are possibly influenced by adapting AIG within AE framework.

Atoms to Bits for Assessment Economy

Note that the most obvious consequence of a successful AIG implementation will produce a massive amount of high-quality assessment items. Especially AIG within AE framework, entire assessment services will be much more accessible, coherent, and intelligent. Note that all of these assessment resources and services can be in a digitalized form, in other words, the assessment recourses and services are in the bit's world (e.g., digitalized test) instead of atom's world (e.g., paper pencil test) (Choi, 2017a). Consequently, AIG within AE will drop costs for creating, processing, duplicating, and delivering the assessment resources and services. In other words, the price of these digitized assessment goods (items) and services (tests) will fall towards to zero. Once these technologies are fully implemented, the current assessment industry and its associated economy may undergo a major transformation. In order to cope with these rapid changes, especially the change of the tasks and the work environments of the traditional psychometricians, the training programs or companies in the field of measurement will have to thoroughly prepare it by fully understanding the potential impacts of the assessment technology such as AIG.

Ubiquitous Assessment (Longitudinal)

AIG within the AE framework will enable ubiquitous assessment beyond individualization in a society where interconnectivity is maximized through the Internet as it is now. This ubiquitous assessment not only connects and uses various assessment services at one point, but also supports diversity of measurement occasions for a subject. In other words, continuous assessment services are implemented from the cradle to the grave.

Public Concerns on Testing-Driven Educational Reform

The successful implementation of the AE-based services (which is aiming for Learner-centered assessment and Curriculum-Instruction-Assessment alignment; Choi, 2017a; Choi, 2017b) will ease various public concerns (e.g., Teaching to

Test, Test Anxiety, and Abandonment) related to testing-driven educational reform. Therefore, the training site will not be a place to improve students' test scores anymore, but will become a place where student learning is the main focus. At this time, information and data about the quality of education will be also measured and analyzed sufficiently and effectively.

FUTURE DIRECTIONS OF AIG RESEARCH AND DEVELOPMENTS

This section discusses AIG's future research and developments. Specifically, I will discuss what research, developments, and awareness shifts are needed to ensure that AIG strengthens the more theoretical foundation, is technologically advanced, and is more widely disseminated. What I would like to emphasize here is that the AIG theoretical work must be well integrated with high-tech development. Also, it is necessary to consider enough about the impact of AIG research and development on actual education and human development. AIG researchers should be able to explain thoroughly to the public how AIG can solve the various problems of the current system, then the future AIG research and development will proceed smoothly. In this regard, some of the areas of AIG research and development that we wish to proceed with are as follows.

Validating Validity Arguments

Researchers in the AE field should note that AIG and AE were promoted as scientific approaches to improve quality of assessment outcomes and processes, and therefore the validity of the assessment is expected to be improved by adapting AIG (and/or AE). It should be noted that it is an unfavorable argument to enhance the assessment validity, especially in solving the quantity and quality of assessments simultaneously, through advanced technology. It is imperative to know in detail what kind of situation, which process, and how to improve the quality of the assessment. A diverse and rigorous empirical evaluation study is required in this area.

Pathway to Smart Assessment

AI and machine learning have already been applied to various fields and are changing our lives dramatically. This change is not simply a conversion to a computer-based or Internet-based assessment, but rather a so-called "smart" assessment using artificial intelligence or augmented intelligence. However, in the field of education, it is very rare to use these techniques to effectively solve various problems in the actual education field. The field of education seems to be immune to the introduction of these advanced technologies. In order to intelligence the education measurement services through advanced technologies, much research and developments are needed with step-by-step roadmap to implement

"Machine for Human" Instead of "Machine vs Human"

The development of AIG within AE may have a devastating effect on existing assessment, evaluation or measurement related industries through mechanization/automation of assessment service, and it will have a big influence on educational environments. There are voices that concern the development of the 4th Industrial Revolution, especially after the confrontation between Lee Sedol and Alpha-Go, but they should not be regarded as a "human vs. machine" confrontation. Rather than being a substitute for machines by person (e.g., teachers or item developers), it is better to say that the machine helps complement the human ability. In particular, note the socioeconomic effect of reducing the cost of assessment services through the development of convergence technologies such as AIG and maximizing the accessibility to educational services. For example, it is necessary to change social understanding and recognition such as "AE can effectively reduce teachers' burden/burnout" by automating the tedious and labor intense assessment tasks instead of "AE would replace teachers with robots".

Assessment Data Security and Privacy

As the disclosure and sharing of assessment information becomes more active, the debate about personal privacy and personal information protection will deepen. It should be noted that high-tech (such as blockchain technology), which is believed to be a tool for democratization of assessment services, can also be an indiscriminate and widespread means of public surveillance. Broad dialogue is needed between expert groups and political leaders, especially evaluation-related stakeholders, about what to adapt and accept.

This chapter demonstrates how the assessments are changed and included by the new ICTs focused on AIG which has recently received a great deal of attention in the field assessment. We reviewed the fact that one can use AIG as an innovative assessment tool where cognitive and psychometric theories are integrated together into a comprehensive assessment development framework, and automatically generating assessment items using state-of-the-art ICTs. Furthermore, AIG within AE framework also enables us to support and/or enhance automation of other assessment components/processes (e.g., grading, testing, or reporting). I also illustrated how

AIG's automation can affect education, professional training, and/or public policy. Finally, I discussed the future directions of AIG research and development. In this article, we have looked at how the development of technology evolves (in particular, automates) the assessment, and how this assessment developments ultimately may have implications for future research, practice, and policy of assessment.

REFERENCES

Bejar, I. I. (1993). A generative approach to psychological and educational measurement. In N. Frederiskson, R. J. Mislevy, & I. I. Bejar (Eds.), *Test theory for a new generation of tests* (pp. 323–359). Mahwah, NJ: Lawrence Erlbaum Associates.

Choi, J. (2017a). Next Generation Item and Test Development: A Practical Introduction to Automatic Item Generation. Washington, DC: Assessment, Testing and Measurement Technical Report Series, The George Washington University.

Choi, J. (2017b, April). *Assessments on Textbook: Psychometric Implications on Next Generation Digital Textbook based on Automatic Item Generation.* Paper presented at the 2016 meeting of the Korean Society for Educational Evaluation, Seoul, South Korea.

Choi, J., & Li, L. (2016). *Automatic item generation: Beyond cost efficiency*. Presented at *Annual Meeting of Korean-American Educational Researchers Association*, Washington, DC.

Choi, J., Kim, S., & Yoon, K. (2016). *K-Math Workbook Grade 6*. Clarksville, MD: CAFA Lab, Inc.

Choi, J., Kim, S., & Yoon, K. (2017). *K-Math Workbook Grade 7*. Clarksville, MD: CAFA Lab, Inc.

Dardick, W., & Choi, J. (2016). Teacher Empowered Assessment System: Assessment for the 21st Century. *Journal of Applied Educational and Policy Research, 2*(2).

Embretson, S. E. (1998). A cognitive design system approach to generating valid tests: Application to abstract reasoning. *Psychological Methods, 3*(3), 380–396. doi:10.1037/1082-989X.3.3.380

Embretson, S. E., & Yang, X. (2007). Automatic item generation and cognitive psychology. In C. R. Rao & S. Sinharay (Eds.), *Handbook of statistics: Psychometrics* (vol. 26, pp. 747-768). North Holland, UK: Elsevier. doi: 26023-110.1016/s0169-7161(06)

Gierl, M. J., & Haladyna, T. M. (2013). *Automatic item generation: Theory and practice*. New York, NY: Routledge.

Irvine, S. H., & Kyllonen, P. C. (Eds.). (2002). *Item generation for test development*. Mahwah, NJ: Lawrence Erlbaum Associates.

Lai, H., Gierl, M. J., & Alves, C. (2009, June). *Development of an item model taxonomy for automatic item generation in computer adaptive testing*. Poster presented at the GMAC Conference on Computerized Adaptive Testing, Minneapolis, MN.

Luecht, R. (2014). Assessment Engineering Task Model Maps, Task Models and Templates as a New Way to Develop and Implement Test Specifications. *Journal Of Applied Testing Technology*, *1*(1), 1–38. Retrieved from http://www.jattjournal.com/index.php/atp/article/view/45254

Mislevy, R. J., Almond, R. G., & Lukas, J. F. (2004). *A Brief Introduction to Evidence-Centered Design (CSE Report 632)*. Center for Research on Evaluation, Standards, and Student Testing.

Wainer, H., & Kiely, G. L. (1987). Item clusters and computerized adaptive testing: A case for testlets. *Journal of Educational Measurement*, *24*(3), 185–201. doi:10.1111/j.1745-3984.1987.tb00274.x

Chapter 7
E-Learning and Information Communications Technologies (ICT) in Saudi Arabia:
An Overview

Hadeel Alharbi
University of New England, Australia

Kamaljeet Sandhu
University of New England, Australia

ABSTRACT

This chapter argues that increasing the rate of e-learning technological adoption will provide educational affordances related to access to courses and better course delivery for Saudi citizens. Specifically, issues related to gender-related staffing issues and access to education courses. This is primarily because the e-learning technology has the capacity to adapt to dominant features in Saudi society and culture, as well as its potential to be efficiently applied in Saudi higher education settings. However, despite the widespread adoption of information communication technology (ICT) in society, Saudi Arabians have yet to fully experience the transformative effects of this medium, particularly in relation to e-learning. This is evidenced in a lack of deep understanding on how best to implement e-learning and distance learning applications.

DOI: 10.4018/978-1-5225-5829-3.ch007

INTRODUCTION

This chapter presents a model for initial acceptance and adoption of E-Learning in the Saudi Arabian education sector. Furthermore, this chapter broadens the contextual focus of information technology uptake and the contribution of E-Learning and Information Communication Technologies (ICTs) in the Saudi Arabian higher education sector. This chapter has two main sections. First, an examination of the contribution of E-Learning and ICTs in the Saudi Arabian context begins with a discussion of E-Learning systems. Further, an overview of the increasingly integral role of E-Learning systems to academia and corporate training, and the characteristics and functions of the different systems available to educational institutions is presented. Second, an examination of the relationship between social networking sites and developments in E-Learning platforms, particularly the ways in which these sites can encourage student learning will be undertaken. The main points to emerge from these two sections are then positioned within the Saudi Arabian context. Specifically, the initiatives undertaken by the Ministry of Education in recent years to upgrade ICTs are discussed and the implications are explored. This chapter then concludes with an examination of the adoption rates of E-Learning in Saudi Arabia. Particular focus is given to the increasing rate of adoption and the implications this holds for significant changes to the way higher education services are provided to different gendered students in Saudi Arabia.

In the context of Information Technology (IT) usage, the user experience of IT is considered to be of paramount importance for technology adoption and success. Users draw on their direct experiences with IT to develop their future behavioural intentions. However, despite the important role of user experience in technology usage, few studies have investigated the implication of this construct for continued IT usage in Saudi Arabia (Deng et al., 2010) in general and E-Learning tools in particular. To address these issues, this research will seek to explore the factors of the acceptance and the continuance usage intention of E-Learning recommender systems in Saudi universities. The model developed in this chapter will help to investigate the relationships between the different experiences of students and instructors filling the knowledge gap between service quality and user experience of E-Learning recommender systems. Thus, the factors of acceptance (such as service quality and user experience) should be considered in the E-Learning system because these factors are viewed as a determinant of student/instructor/university satisfaction. Consequently, a number of dimensions have been taken into account for facilitating the relationship between the student and instructor, and the university via electronic means such as electronic services.

E-LEARNING

The term *E-Learning* refers to the adoption of electronic information, multimedia, and ICTs in education. E-Learning is a largely inclusive term incorporating of all forms of educational technology utilised in training, learning, and teaching. E-Learning is a form of elastic learning that utilises ICTs as connections and delivery instrument between persons and communities, to sustain students, enhance E-Learning management, and offer flexible learning (Xu, 2011). However, there are issues with some conventional E-Learning systems, such as Blackboard and Moodle, which are not appropriate enough to support the educational process at schools since they provide less collaboration, and less learner's participation than traditional education and limited memorable change (Ebner, 2007). Moodle is an open-source tool that has been adopted as an E-Learning system by many universities around the world.

The Moodle concept is based on a learner-oriented philosophy which offers social sharing among the learners with the goal of engaging students in constructing their own knowledge and sharing it with colleagues (Mohd Said et al., 2005; Tasir et al., 2011). Of the systemic failings of the courses offered via Moodle and similarly designed E-Learning platforms is the content is fully controlled by the lecturers. Consequently, there is a need to make social E-Learning systems more inclusive of all stakeholders to improve effectiveness in learning outcomes, and this can be accomplished by studying and analysing the contents of students' comments and posts on social media. The use of social media provides an opportunity for insights into the development of an evolving system of educational delivery to be developed that considers the individual accounts of users then tailors learning activities to the individual's specific needs.

A personalised E-Learning application can be achieved with the use of a mobile social network (Moodle) and integrating data mining applications. Applying data mining to social platforms will enhance the development of new correlations, the identification of patterns, and the manifestation of trends that will allow the generation of pattern recognition techniques that can enhance E-Learning (Kalina, 2013). However, data mining at present has limitations with content-based recommendation algorithms needing to be improved on in order to support learning behaviour (Paul 2004). One of the major issues in algorithm design is web-based learning in the context of social networks and E-Learning is a very dynamic and personalised, particularly when the learning is self-directed.

The Personalised Learning Framework is being used to connect formal education providers with personal web hosting and social networks. This arrangement has made it possible to publish as well as aggregate knowledge. This recognised that the learner is also able to not only consume but also produce learning resources.

This has led to a paradigm shift where fostering student engagement in learning involved a two-way process such that there is "a transfer of content and knowledge to the production of content and knowledge" (Kim, 2010).

Notwithstanding the problems with the application, the multiplicity of advantages E-Learning brings makes the adoption of new technology in the Saudi Arabian context increasingly more attractive. These advantages include increased flexibility and convenience, greater geographical reach, the ability to overcome the problems of inadequate classroom space and limited facilities, as well as cost-effectiveness in course delivery and its management (Al-Gahtani, 2016). Consequently, there has been a steady expansion uptake of ICTs in Saudi Arabian educational institutions and professional organisations (Al-Gahtani, 2016).

ICT IN SAUDI ARABIA

Saudi Arabian Government has recently set goals to building a knowledge-based society and digital economy (Al-Gahtani, 2011). This goal was highlighted in the *Ten Year Plan* (2004-2014) with the prioritisation of upgrading the existing digital structure within educational intuitions to match the trend towards integrating new technological developments into the Saudi Arabian educational sector (Saudi Ministry of Education, 2005). The adequate financial resources, strategic push from the government, privatisation and the subsequent opening of the telecommunications market to competition have placed Saudi Arabia among the fastest developing ICT markets in the Arab Region (CITC, 2009).

The spread of broadband internet has played a major role in the development of Saudi Arabia economy. In 1997, Internet services were officially made available in Saudi Arabia for business and individuals (Al-Ghaith et al., 2010). According to the Saudi Communications and Information Technology Commission (CITC), the internet penetration rate in Saudi Arabia has rapidly grown from 5% in 2001 to 55% in 2013 (CITC, 2013). Business organisations in Saudi Arabia are also increasingly recognising the importance of the adoption of ICT technologies and high-speed broadband internet in their operations. As a result, computer ownership among businesses has moved up significantly from 76% in 2007 to 82% in 2009 (CITC, 2009). Internet adoption rates in Saudi Arabia are still significantly lower than in other Western countries even though the GDP per capita is at comparable levels (CIA, 2015; CITC, 2013). This move towards technological advancement has increased the potential for growth in the Saudi ICT market. However, adoption rates of ICT applications, such as E-Learning solutions, are still limited (Alenezi et al., 2012; Al-Gahtani, 2016; Asiri et al., 2012). Therefore, the explanation for the decision and behaviour of individuals toward the acceptance and continual usage of E-Learning in academic settings in Saudi Arabia is an important area in need of further research.

E-LEARNING ADOPTION IN SAUDI ARABIA

The shift in Saudi government attitudes and the uptake of internet usage has led to a rapid adoption of E-Learning technology in educational settings. This shift is a consequence of the recognition of the benefits these new technologies offer to students, teachers and education systems administrators (Hussein, 2011). Recently, there has been a rapid increase in the Saudi Arabian student population in higher institutions (Alamri, 2011). At the same time, academic institutions suffer from a shortage of qualified faculty members on the physical campus. Therefore, E-Learning technology could offer a valuable option that helps to increase the numbers of available staff and reduces the dependency on local faculties (Alzamil, 2006).

In addition, due to the dominant Islamic culture in Saudi Arabia, the higher education institutions have to separate students and teaching staff based on gender. For this reason, these institutions provide isolated buildings and different faculty members for their female and male students. This issue raises the challenge of wasting the financial and the academic resources especially with the noted shortage of female faculty staff in Saudi Arabia (Asiri et al., 2012). E-Learning and its various tools are regarded as fruitful solutions to overcome this issue. Accordingly, higher education institutions are highly encouraged to introduce E-Learning technology as a cost-effective and culturally accepted solution wherein male faculty is able to teach female students remotely (Al-Sarrani, 2010).

Factors Influencing E-Learning Adoption in Saudi Arabia

Long-term E-Learning adoption is dictated by the rates of initial acceptance. Initial acceptance reflects the likelihood that a potential user will use an IS/IT system either for one-time or an infrequent manner (Davis et al., 1989). Indeed, the initial acceptance of an E-Learning system is a significant first step toward achieving E-Learning success (Dağhan, and Akkoyunlu, 2016; Lee, 2010; Lin 2011). There are five key variables that impact on the initial acceptance, and later adoption, of an E-Learning system.

User Experience

The User Experience contributes IS/IT research by providing guidelines for designing successful IS/IT systems and strengthen the design and development process for user-centric systems (Djamasb et al., 2016). Users usually develop their experience with an IT system by repeatedly interacting and using them. Researchers have also recognized the importance of user experience for the continuous usage as a determinant of IT success (Deng et al., 2010). Previous studies have shown a significant relationship between experience and user acceptance and post-adoption IT usage (Davis et al., 1989, Taylor and Todd, 1995a; Karahanna et al., 1999; Agarwal and Karahanna, 2000; Hsu and Lu, 2004; Castaneda et al., 2007; Deng et al., 2010). As users' experiences develop over time, their familiarity with IT systems would increase and one would expect them to experience less frustrating practice (Karapanos, 2013). In addition, effort saved due to the improved experience with an IT system may enable a user to accomplish more tasks with the same effort and thus improve her/his performance (i.e. perceived usefulness).

Service Quality

The concept service quality has been widely studied in many fields of study, including marketing, commerce, management, and IT/IS. Service quality was introduced and further developed in many different ways. For example, Web quality, system quality and information quality were introduced to predict users' acceptance and usage of Web-based systems (Fang et al., 2016; Al-Debei et al., 2015; Zheng et al., 2013; Lin and Lee, 2006). Many studies have investigated the relationship between service quality and perceived ease of use. Previous studies (Rana et al., 2015; Ahn et al., 2007; Cheong and Park, 2005; Liaw and Huang 2003) found service quality had a positive effect on individual perceived ease of use of information systems.

Perceived Usefulness

Adding to the traditional benefits of any E-Learning management system, the E-Learning recommender system provides students more personalized content and services according to their needs and preferences. This is an important addition to the valuable advantages that an E-Learning system offers to learners and instructors. Students are expected to enjoy more usefulness as these systems help them to identify the most interesting and relevant learning content/materials from a large number of possible alternatives (Sikka et al., 2012; Thai-Nghe et al., 2010). By using such systems, students can automatically receive applicable and personalized content on demand rather than providing them with all educational materials at once. Therefore, it could be argued that the characteristics of the E-Learning recommender system could improve the learning performance of students (Sikka et al., 2012; Chen et al., 2005). When improving users' performance, it would positively influence their perception toward the system use (Davis, et al., 1989).

Perceived Ease of Use

Preserved ease of use simultaneously showed a strong direct effect on behavioural intention to use E-Learning technologies (Al-Gahtani, 2016), and prior research found a positive relationship between perceived ease of use and continuance usage intention (Roca et al., 2006; Shih, 2004). If learning how to use a system is made easy, this may offer students with greater experience in the interactions with the system (Novak et al., 2001). When users have sufficient experience they perceive that less effort is required to use an E-Learning system and are more likely to use and continue using it (Roca et al., 2006). The E-Learning recommender system prevents the learner from becoming lost in the course materials as it offer them a personalized learning guidance, minimize search's time and effort and filtering out inappropriate content to reduce cognitive loading (Chen et al., 2005).

User Acceptance and Continued Use of the E-Learning Recommender System

The literature distinguished between the initial acceptance and the continuous usage of an E-Learning system (e.g. Dağhan, and Akkoyunlu, 2016; Lee, 2010; Terzis et al., 2013). While the initial acceptance of an E-Learning system is a significant first step toward achieving E-Learning success, long-term success still requires continued usage (Dağhan, and Akkoyunlu, 2016; Lee, 2010; Lin 2011). In other words, the success of an E-Learning service depends on both its initial acceptance and its continued usage. Hence, understanding the factors affecting users' intention to continue using E-Learning is very noteworthy for a successful implementation of E-Learning recommender systems as it will assist vendors and developers to provide better services for learners and teachers.

Modeling Factors of E-Learning Adoption in Saudi Arabia

Based on the five factors, there are five key hypothesised relationships that are used to generate the model for E-Learning acceptance and adoption:

- **H1:** The Perceived recommender system usefulness affects E-Learning recommender system acceptance.
- **H2:** The perceived recommender system ease of use affects E-Learning recommender system acceptance.
- **H3:** The E-Learning recommender system acceptance affects the continued use of recommender system.

- **H4:** The recommender system service quality affects perceived recommender system ease of use.
- **H5:** The recommender system user experience affects perceived recommender system usefulness.

These relationships are modelled and conceptually based on the integration of the technology acceptance model (TAM) (Figure 1). This model has two external variables: user experience and service quality (Davis et al., 1989). The constructs, perceived ease of use and perceived usefulness, were adopted from TAM (Davis et al., 1989). In the proposed framework, the first external construct is the user experience variable. This variable includes elements that assist us to measure the user experience which is critical for the success of E-Learning recommender systems in Saudi universities. The process of using an E-Learning recommended system as an innovative technology requires user experience in interacting with this system. Users need to have enough skills such as using toolbars, navigation, searching for information, and switching between different functions. The second external construct is service quality which is associated with the information quality that the electronic university information system delivers to its users, and is measured in relation to currency, accuracy, format, and completeness. Service quality determines the success of a website design (Wixom & Todd, 2005).

CONCLUSION

This chapter presents a model that relatesAuser experience, service quality, perceived usefulness and perceived ease of use as a means to understanding acceptance and use of the E-Learning recommender systems in the Saudi Arabian context. Thus, the model presented herein is consistent with previous research that tests and

Figure 1. A proposed conceptual model of E-Learning recommender system acceptance

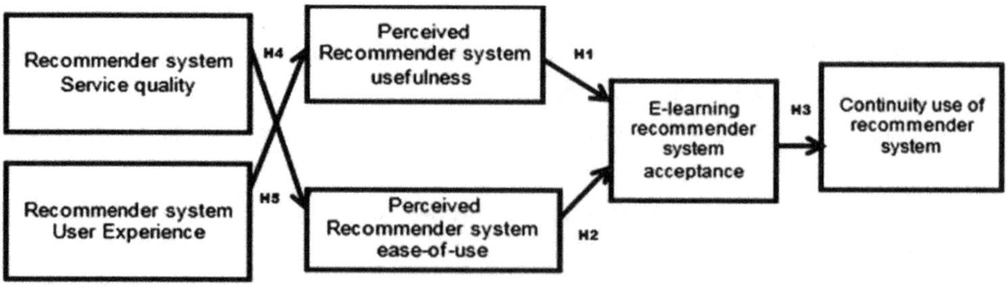

validates the consistent relationships between service quality and perceived ease of use (Rana et al., 2015; Ahn et al., 2007; Cheong and Park, 2005; Liaw and Huang 2003). Based on this result, it can be also argued that an E-Learning recommender system with higher service quality, that is, with more reliable, relevant, accurate, complete, precise, concise, and current information will be perceived by students as an easy to use interface. This model rationalises that designers of the E-Learning recommender systems need to pay more attention to the service quality issues including accuracy, relevance, reliability and timeliness of the content provided by such systems. In addition, officials who are responsible for E-Learning systems should regularly update the system and the information to avoid any misperception regarding the use of the system.

Furthermore, several studies have confirmed the significant relationship between the user experience and the usefulness of E-Learning systems (e.g. Lee et al., 2013; Purnomo and Lee, 2013; Martin, 2012). Individuals who enjoy higher computer-related experience, such as those who are skillfully using computers, Internet and E-Learning systems, are more likely to have more favourable perceptions towards the usefulness of an E-Learning system (Lee et al., 2013; Purnomo and Lee, 2013). Given that E-Learning recommender system technology is newly adopted in Saudi universities, the model presented indicates that educational institutions need to provide proper and adequate training programs about these systems for their students. Online tutorials, awareness programs as well as an efficient technical support may also help students to develop their experience with these systems.

REFERENCES

Agarwal, R., & Karahanna, E. (2000). Time flies when you're having fun: Cognitive absorption and beliefs about information technology usage. *Management Information Systems Quarterly*, *24*(4), 665–694. doi:10.2307/3250951

Ahn, T., Ryu, S., & Han, I. (2007). The impact of Web quality and playfulness on user acceptance of online retailing. *Information & Management*, *44*(3), 263–275. doi:10.1016/j.im.2006.12.008

Alamri, M. (2011). Higher education in Saudi Arabia. *Journal of Higher Education Theory and Practice*, *11*(4), 88.

Al-Debei, M. M., Akroush, M. N., & Ashouri, M. I. (2015). Consumer attitudes towards online shopping: The effects of trust, perceived benefits, and perceived web quality. *Internet Research*, *25*(5), 707–733. doi:10.1108/IntR-05-2014-0146

Alenezi, A. M. (2012). *Faculty members' perception of E-Learning in higher education in the Kingdom of Saudi Arabia (KSA)* (Doctoral dissertation). Texas Tech University.

Al-Gahtani, S. S. (2011). Modeling the electronic transactions acceptance using an extended technology acceptance model. *Applied Computing and Informatics*, *9*(1), 47–77. doi:10.1016/j.aci.2009.04.001

Al-Gahtani, S. S. (2016). Empirical investigation of E-Learning acceptance and assimilation: a structural equation model. *Applied Computing and Informatics, 12*(1), 27e50. 10.1016/j.aci.2014.09.001

Al-Ghaith, W., Sanzogni, L., & Sandhu, K. (2010). Factors influencing the adoption and usage of online services in Saudi Arabia. *EJISDC: The Electronic Journal on Information Systems in Developing Countries,* (40), 1.

Al-Harbi, K. A. S. (2011). E-Learning in the Saudi tertiary education: Potential and challenges. *Applied Computing and Informatics*, *9*(1), 31–46. doi:10.1016/j.aci.2010.03.002

Al-Hujran, O., Al-Lozi, E., & Al-Debei, M. M. (2014). "Get Ready to Mobile Learning": Examining Factors Affecting College Students' Behavioral Intentions to Use M-Learning in Saudi Arabia. *Jordan Journal of Business Administration*, *10*(1).

Al-Sarrani, N. (2010). *Concerns and professional development needs of science faculty at Taibah university in adopting blended learning* (Doctoral dissertation). Kansas State University. Retrieved Mar 9th, 2016 from: http://krex.kstate.edu/dspace/bitstream/2097/3887/1/NauafAl-Sarrani2010

Alzamil, Z. A. (2006). Students' perception towards the E-Learning at the GOTEVOT and the Arab Open University in Riyadh. *Journal of King Saud University: Educational Sciences and Islamic Studies*, *18*(2), 655–698.

Al-Zamil, O. A. (2003). *High School Social Studies Teachers' Attitudes and Usage of Instructional Technology in Saudi Arabia* (Unpublished doctoral dissertation). University of Arkansas.

Asiri, M. J. S., Mahmud, R. B., Abu Bakar, K., & Mohd Ayub, A. F. B. (2012). Factors influencing the use of learning management system in Saudi Arabian higher education: A theoretical framework. *Higher Education Studies*, *2*(2), 125. doi:10.5539/hes.v2n2p125

Chen, C. M., Lee, H. M., & Chen, Y. H. (2005). Personalized E-Learning system using item response theory. *Computers & Education, 44*(3), 237–255. doi:10.1016/j.compedu.2004.01.006

Central Intelligence Agency (CIA). (2015). *The world factbook.* Retrieved from https://www.cia.gov/library/publications/resources/the-world-factbook/index.html

Communications and Information Technology Commission (CITU). (2013). *Electronic newsletter*. Retrieved from http://www.citc.gov.sa/English/MediaCenter/Newsletter/Documents/PR_ENL_017.pdf

Communications and Information Technology Commission (CITC). (2012). *Internet Usage Study in Saudi Arabia*. Retrieved from http://www.internet.sa/en/internet-usage-study/#more-120

Dağhan, G., & Akkoyunlu, B. (2016). Modeling the continuance usage intention of online learning environments. *Computers in Human Behavior, 60*, 198–211. doi:10.1016/j.chb.2016.02.066

Davis, F. D., Bagozzi, R. P., & Warshaw, P. R. (1989). User acceptance of computer technology: A comparison of two theoretical models. *Management Science, 35*(8), 982–1003. doi:10.1287/mnsc.35.8.982

Djamasbi, S., Strong, D., Wilson, E. V., & Ruiz, C. (2016). *Designing and Testing User-Centric Systems with both User Experience and Design Science Research Principles*. Academic Press.

Garrison, D. R. (2011). *E-Learning in the 21st century: A framework for research and practice*. Academic Press.

Hsu, C. L., & Lu, H. P. (2004). Why do people play on-line games? An extended TAM with social influences and flow experience. *Information & Management, 41*(7), 853–868.

Deng, L., Turner, D. E., Gehling, R., & Prince, B. (2010). User experience, satisfaction, and continual usage intention of IT. *European Journal of Information Systems, 19*(1), 60–75.

Hu, P. J.-H., Clark, T. H. K., & Ma, W. W. (2003). Examining technology acceptance by school teachers: A longitudinal study. *Information & Management, 41*(2), 227–241. doi:10.1016/S0378-7206(03)00050-8

Hussein, H. B. (2011). Attitudes of Saudi universities faculty members towards using learning management system (JUSUR). *TOJET: The Turkish Online Journal of Educational Technology, 10*(2).

Karahanna, E., Straub, D. W., & Chervany, N. L. (1999). Information technology adoption across time: A cross-sectional comparison of pre-adoption and post-adoption beliefs. *Management Information Systems Quarterly*, *23*(2), 183–213. doi:10.2307/249751

Karapanos, E. (2013). User experience over time. In Modeling Users' Experiences with Interactive Systems (pp. 57-83). Springer Berlin Heidelberg. doi:10.1007/978-3-642-31000-3_4

Kim, T. (2010). A self-directed dynamic web-based learning environment: Proposal for personalized learning framework. *Journal of Security Engineering*, *9*(2), 177–187.

Lee, Y., Hsieh, Y., & Chen, Y. (2013). An investigation of employees' use of E-Learning systems: Applying the technology acceptance model. *Behaviour & Information Technology*, *32*(2), 173–189. doi:10.1080/0144929X.2011.577190

Lee, M. C. (2009). Factors influencing the adoption of internet banking: An integration of TAM and TPB with perceived risk and perceived benefit. *Electronic Commerce Research and Applications*, *8*(3), 130–141. doi:10.1016/j.elerap.2008.11.006

Liaw, S. S., & Huang, H. M. (2003). An investigation of user attitudes toward search engines as an information retrieval tool. *Computers in Human Behavior*, *19*(6), 751–765. doi:10.1016/S0747-5632(03)00009-8

Lin, H. F., & Lee, G. C. (2006). Determinants of success for online communities: An empirical study. *Behaviour & Information Technology*, *25*(6), 479–488. doi:10.1080/01449290500330422

Lin, H. F., & Lee, G. C. (2006). Determinants of success for online communities: An empirical study. *Behaviour & Information Technology*, *25*(6), 479–488. doi:10.1080/01449290500330422

Martin, R. G. (2012). Factors affecting the usefulness of social networking in elearning at German university of technology in Oman. *International Journal of e-Education, e-Business, e-Management and e-Learning,* *2*(6), 498–502.

Ministry of Education. (2005). *The executive summary of the Ministry of Education ten-year plan*. Ministry of Education in Saudi Arabia.

Mohd Said, M. N. H., Ali, M. F., Sidek, R. Z. H., & Md Noor, N. (2005). *The application of e learning in supporting teaching and learning: An overview*. The 3rd International Seminar on Learning and Motivation Enhancing Student Engagement, Langkawi, Malaysia.

Novak, T.P., & Hoffman, D.L. (2001). *Profitability on the Web: Business Models and Revenue Streams*. Owen Graduate School of Management, Vanderbilt University, eLab Position Paper, January.

Purnomo, S. H., & Lee, Y. (2013). E-Learning adoption in the banking workplace in Indonesia: An empirical study. *Information Development*, *29*(2), 138–153. doi:10.1177/0266666912448258

Rana, N. P., Dwivedi, Y. K., Williams, M. D., & Weerakkody, V. (2015). Investigating success of an e-government initiative: Validation of an integrated IS success model. *Information Systems Frontiers*, *17*(1), 127–142. doi:10.100710796-014-9504-7

Roca, J. C., Chiu, C. M., & Martinez, F. J. (2006). Understanding E-Learning continuance intention: An extension of the technology acceptance model. *International Journal of Human-Computer Studies*, *64*(8), 683–696. doi:10.1016/j.ijhcs.2006.01.003

Shih, H. P. (2004). An empirical study on predicting user acceptance of e-shopping on the web. *Information & Management*, *41*(3), 351–368. doi:10.1016/S0378-7206(03)00079-X

Sikka, R., Dhankhar, A., & Rana, C. (2012). A survey paper on E-Learning recommender system. *International Journal of Computers and Applications*, *47*(9), 27–30. doi:10.5120/7218-0024

Tasir, Z., Al-Dheleai, Y., Harun, J., & Shukor, A. N. (2011). Students perception towards the use of social networking as an E-Learning platform. *Proceeding of the 10th WSEAS International Conference on Education and Educational Technology '11*.

Taylor, S., & Todd, P. A. (1995). Understanding information technology usage: A test of competing models. *Information Systems Research*, *6*(2), 144–176. doi:10.1287/isre.6.2.144

Terzis, V., Moridis, C. N., & Economides, A. A. (2013). Continuance acceptance of computer based assessment through the integration of user's expectations and perceptions. *Computers & Education*, *62*, 50–61. doi:10.1016/j.compedu.2012.10.018

Thai-Nghe, N., Drumond, L., Krohn-Grimberghe, A., & Schmidt-Thieme, L. (2010). Recommender system for predicting student performance. *Procedia Computer Science*, *1*(2), 2811–2819. doi:10.1016/j.procs.2010.08.006

Wixom, B. H., & Todd, P. A. (2005). A theoretical integration of user satisfaction and technology acceptance. *Information Systems Research, 16*, 85.

Xu, G. (2011). *Social networking sites, Web 2.0 technologies and E-Learning* (Master thesis). Retrieved from http://hdl.handle.net/10652/1864

Zheng, Y., Zhao, K., & Stylianou, A. (2013). The impacts of information quality and system quality on users' continuance intention in information-exchange virtual communities: An empirical investigation. *Decision Support Systems*, *56*, 513–524. doi:10.1016/j.dss.2012.11.008

Chapter 8
Information and Computer Technologies for Improving International Assessment

Danielle Young
Westat, USA

Jaehwa Choi
The George Washington University, USA

ABSTRACT

International assessments such as the trends in international math and science study (TIMSS), the program for international student assessment (PISA), and the international computer and information literacy study (ICILS) have traditionally relied on paper and pencil administration. These assessments are rapidly transforming into or have been developed as computer-based tests due to advances in information and communication technologies of the past decade. These computer-based assessments will eventually make traditional paper and pencil assessments obsolete. Specifically, international and other large-scale assessments can benefit from the use of automatic item generation (AIG) and/or computer adaptive testing (CAT) to enhance and strengthen test security and validity, as well as reduce costs over the course of multiple test administrations, encourage student engagement, and efficiently measure students' abilities.

INTRODUCTION

International assessments, such as the Trends in International Math and Science Study (TIMSS) and the Program for International Student Assessment (PISA), have traditionally relied on paper-and-pencil administrations. These assessments have been redesigned as computer-based tests due to advances in information and communication

DOI: 10.4018/978-1-5225-5829-3.ch008

technologies of the past decade. Computer-based assessments will eventually make traditional paper-and-pencil assessments obsolete. The International Computer and Information Literacy Study (ICILS), a new, computer-based assessment, could also benefit from various advanced digital technologies as described.

International assessments can benefit from the use of digital assessment technologies, such as automatic item generation (AIG) and/or computer adaptive testing (CAT), to enhance and strengthen test security and validity. Additional benefits include cost reduction over the course of multiple test administrations, increased student engagement, and efficient measurement of students' cognitive abilities.

AIG is a process of generating unique items based on a template and item modeling approach. CAT is a process in which the assessment device chooses an individual's assessment items based on their ability level and performance on previous test items. TIMSS is in the process of converting from a traditionally paper-and-pencil test to a computer-based assessment. PISA has already converted to a digital format and will be introducing CAT in the 2018 cycle.

Purpose

The purpose of this chapter is to demonstrate the various benefits of AIG and other assessment technologies on large-scale, international assessments. As previously mentioned, these benefits include, but are not limited to, cost effectiveness, increased validity, security, global content, advancement in cognitive assessment, and accessibility. Educational assessments must continue to advance at the same rate as the average student's technological savvy. AIG and other technologies will keep students engaged with the assessment, giving educators and international leaders a clearer image of their respective country's student population knowledge. This chapter contains background information for international assessments, AIG, and other technologies. Developments include an a priori, theoretical cost benefit analysis and sample items.

SIGNIFICANCE OF THE CHAPTER

These developing technologies have several important benefits relating to educators, students, and policy makers. As previously stated, the advance in assessment technology has the potential to keep students more fully engaged throughout the process, capturing an accurate account of the students' cognitive abilities. Unlike the traditional paper-and-pencil assessment, an AIG computer adaptive assessment more efficiently and accurately determines a student's ability by adapting questions based on a student's response. This timesaving benefit could greatly reduce the overall amount of classroom time dedicated to assessment, which is one of the great burdens of contemporary education.

More broadly, AIG will change the overall practice of international assessment. Presently, development of thousands of new items is required for every new assessment. Following this process is an intensive series of adaptations and translations for each country participating in the assessment. The advancement and utilization of AIG lends itself to a streamlined process of assessment development, translation, and administration. Item models, the foundation of an AIG assessment, can produce thousands of unique instances, or items, and will not need updating as frequently as paper-and-pencil items (Choi, 2017b).

It is important to note that the initial cost of training master item model writers and item model developers would likely be higher than the cost of a traditional paper-and-pencil assessment or a basic digital assessment. However, the money savings and timesaving benefits of using AIG over multiple test administrations greatly outweigh the cost of the initial investment (Choi, 2017a).

INTERNATIONAL ASSESSMENT BACKGROUND

TIMSS has measured math and science achievement of fourth- and eighth-grade students in approximately 50 countries worldwide every 4 years since 1995. A pilot of the new, digital TIMSS assessment, called eTIMSS, was conducted in spring of 2017 in the United States. Test developers and partners have already invested a substantial amount of money to convert and pilot a digitally formatted assessment for the TIMSS 2019 assessment. Investing the time and money to implement AIG and CAT for the 2023 main assessment is a logical next step to receive the maximum benefit of the financial investment (TIMSS 2015, 2017).

Even with the upcoming digital assessment administration for its main study in 2019, TIMSS is limited. Items have been traditionally developed and converted to a digital format, which is expensive and time consuming. It also limits all students to the specific number of items that were developed. This means that many students will see the same items, making the items vulnerable to security leaks. Instead of converting the assessment to a simple digital format, it would be more beneficial to convert the items directly into an AIG item template, thus allowing the production of thousands or millions of items. This method of development would ease the requirements on future item writers, assuming items are successful (TIMSS 2015, 2017).

PISA, first administered in 2000, measures the reading, mathematics, and science abilities of 15-year-olds every 3 years in up to 80 countries. PISA allows for international comparisons of student performance, and provides data about participating education systems' ability to prepare their students for continuing education and careers. In their "Beyond PISA 2015" report (2017), the Organisation for Economic Co-operation and Development (OECD) emphasized that they intend to incorporate computer adaptive technologies and innovative item formats into future PISA administrations.

PISA has historically concentrated on the three previously mentioned domains, with one domain per cycle assessed as the major domain, and the other two identified as minor domains. Results have historically been unavailable at the subdomain level because the minor domains are not given as much time as the major domain. The introduction of CAT increases the efficiency of the assessment, allowing more time across all domains, thus negating the need for major and minor domains. This allows for reporting the results for all measured domains at every administration ("Beyond PISA 2015: A Longer-Term Strategy of PISA," 2017).

ICILS, first administered in 2013, is a digital assessment measuring eighth-graders' preparation for academic and professional futures in the digital age. ICILS is preparing for its second cycle in 2018, with approximately 15 countries participating. Data from the 2018 cycle will link directly to the 2013 results. Computer and information literacy, or "the ability to use computers to investigate, create, and communicate in order to participate effectively at home, at school, in the workplace, and in the community" (Fraillon, Schulz, & Ainley, 2013), is a new addition to domains assessed by the international consortium. Computational thinking, a domain assessed in ICILS, requires higher caliber assessment items. Test developers could meet this requirement by incorporating an adaptive test format and AIG. ICILS contains four small modules containing multiple choice, constructed response, drag and drop, and linear and nonlinear skills task items. Students complete two randomly assigned smaller modules in preparation for one large, final task (Fraillon et al., 2013).

In addition to these advancements, the National Assessment for Educational Progress (NAEP) will be implementing AIG-developed items for their 2018 geography assessment, setting a precedent in large-scale assessment for the utilization of advanced assessment technologies in the United States and, eventually, elsewhere around the world (Carr, 2017).

THEORETICAL BACKGROUND

Overview of AIG

Technology is a key factor in today's assessment. Students in many countries take multiple tests throughout the school year. With traditional paper-and-pencil-formatted tests, it could take several months for the return of test results when accounting for shipping, scanning, analyzing, and releasing results. Now, with the invention of AIG and other automatic components, such as scoring and reporting, it is possible for schools to work on a more flexible schedule. This provides a unique option for researchers and test developers. Traditionally, researchers and test developers needed to wait for data to return and go through cleaning and processing prior to performing any analysis. Automatic scoring provides immediate results, allowing researchers and test developers to begin analyzing data shortly after an assessment administration, saving additional time and money. Additionally, this innovation allows teachers to review content with students while the test is still fresh in their minds. Standardized tests could become more valuable as a teaching tool and give purpose to the hours of preparation that occur in classrooms across the globe (Drasgow, Luecht, & Bennett, 2006).

History of AIG

Automatic item generation has a somewhat disjointed history, as Haladyna describes in *Automatic Item Generation: Theory and Practice* (2013). There is a "lack of cohesion" among the historical and contemporary contributors to the AIG field. In 1970, Bormuth and Menzel suggested that item generation in its current form was too subjective and inefficient. They proposed a theory of "item generation from prose" – meaning that item specifications would be developed so that multiple item writers using these specifications would develop items similar in quality and difficulty. There were some challenges to this theory of item generation – namely, that the algorithms proposed were too complicated. Effective items must be written clearly and concisely.

Contemporary AIG relates to the concept of item forms, originally proposed by Osburn in 1968. An item form generates items with a specific, fixed structure containing multiple variable elements. For example, a test developer creates a sentence containing a few blanks, or spaces for missing words. The developer provides a set of specific words or numbers that could fill in the blanks, to develop multiple individual items from the item form (Gierl & Haladyna, 2013).

Theories of AIG

Automatic item generation is "the process of using item models to generate statistically calibrated items, with the aid of computer technology" (Choi, 2017a). These item models, which look a lot like Osburn's item forms, measure a specific construct. Figures 1-4 are examples of item models based on the TIMSS 2011 assessment (TIMSS 2011 Assessment, 2013). The Computer Adaptive Formative Assessment - Automatic Item Generation (CAFA AIG) tool was used for these examples. (Choi, Kim, & Yoon, 2012).

Figure 1. CAFA AIG model development window for a TIMSS Grade 4 math question

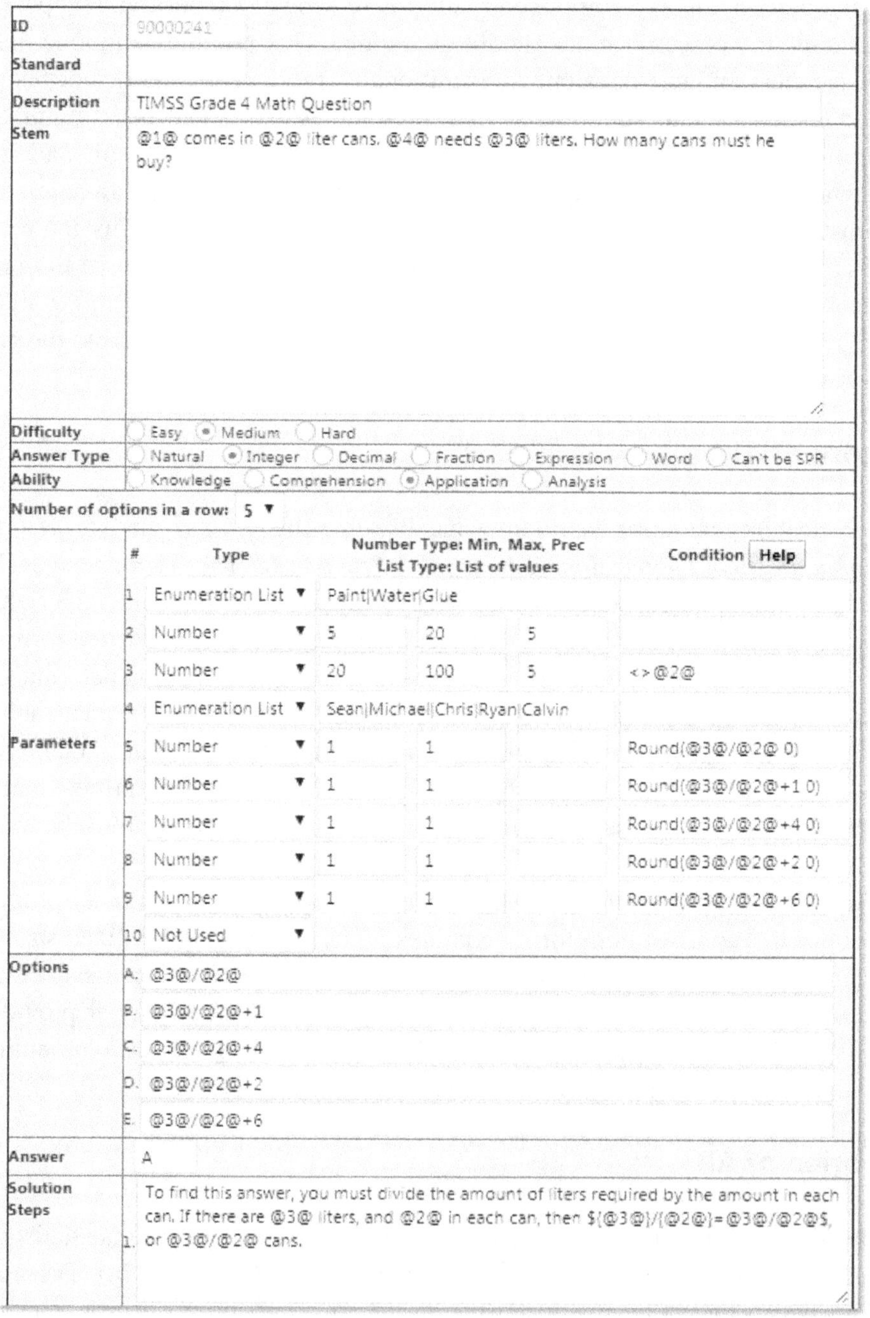

Figure 2. CAFA AIG item output example for a TIMSS Grade 4 math question

Item Test Result

Item instance with seed 100 []
Question: Glue comes in 15 liter cans. Sean needs 75 liters. How many cans must he buy?
A. 5
B. 6
C. 9
D. 7
E. 11
Answer Key: A
Solutions
1. To find this answer, you must divide the amount of liters required by the amount in each can. If there are 75 liters, and 15 in each can, then $75/15 = 5$, or 5 cans.

Item instance with seed 102 []
Question: Water comes in 20 liter cans. Sean needs 60 liters. How many cans must he buy?
A. 3
B. 4
C. 7
D. 5
E. 9
Answer Key: A
Solutions
1. To find this answer, you must divide the amount of liters required by the amount in each can. If there are 60 liters, and 20 in each can, then $60/20 = 3$, or 3 cans.

Item instance with seed 103 []
Question: Water comes in 5 liter cans. Sean needs 30 liters. How many cans must he buy?
A. 6
B. 7
C. 10
D. 8
E. 12
Answer Key: A
Solutions
1. To find this answer, you must divide the amount of liters required by the amount in each can. If there are 30 liters, and 5 in each can, then $30/5 = 6$, or 6 cans.

Figure 3. CAFA AIG model development window for a TIMSS Grade 8 science question

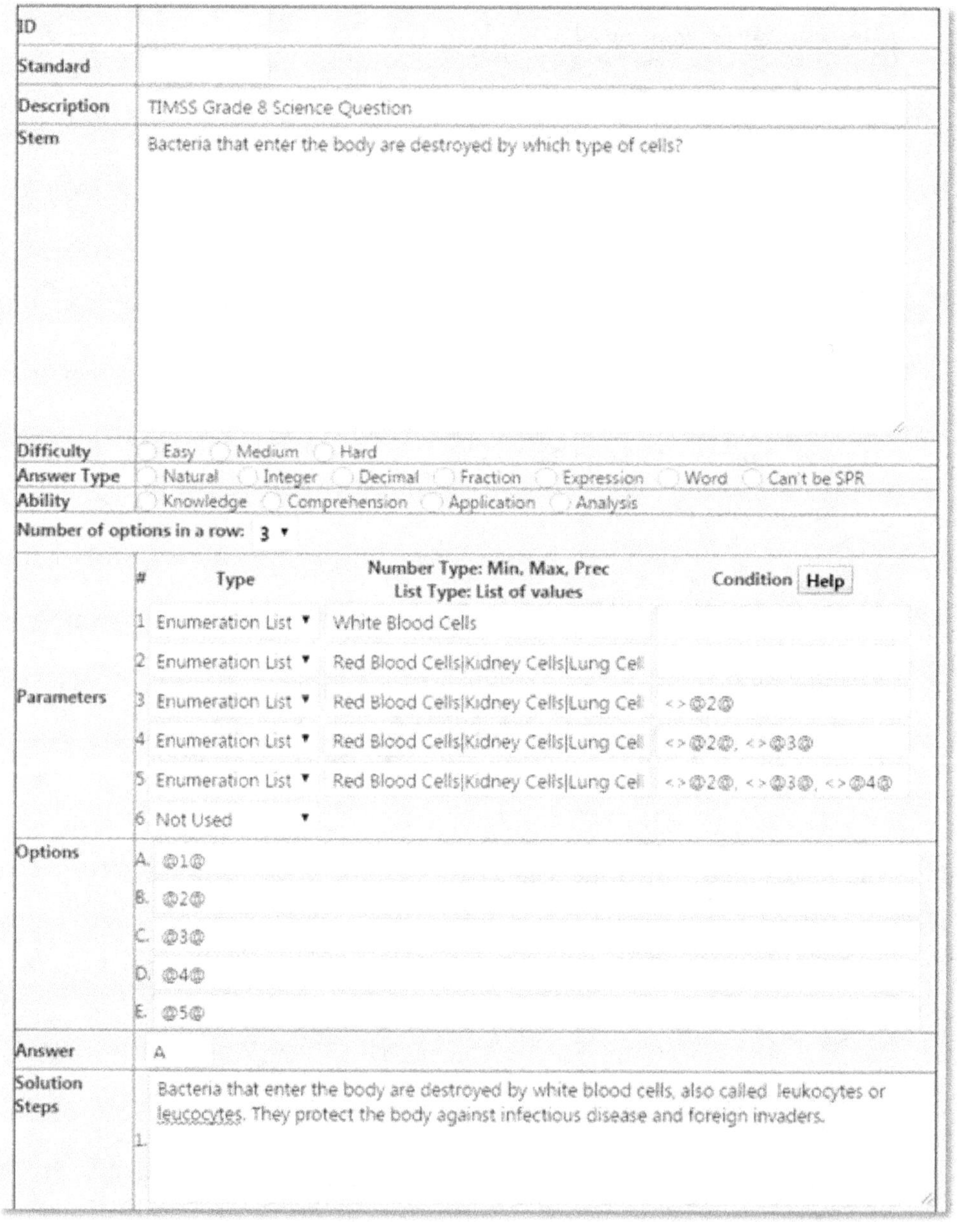

ID	
Standard	
Description	TIMSS Grade 8 Science Question
Stem	Bacteria that enter the body are destroyed by which type of cells?
Difficulty	○ Easy ○ Medium ○ Hard
Answer Type	○ Natural ○ Integer ○ Decimal ○ Fraction ○ Expression ○ Word ○ Can't be SPR
Ability	○ Knowledge ○ Comprehension ○ Application ○ Analysis
Number of options in a row: 3 ▾	

Parameters	#	Type	Number Type: Min, Max, Prec List Type: List of values	Condition Help
	1	Enumeration List ▾	White Blood Cells	
	2	Enumeration List ▾	Red Blood Cells|Kidney Cells|Lung Cel	
	3	Enumeration List ▾	Red Blood Cells|Kidney Cells|Lung Cel	<>@2@
	4	Enumeration List ▾	Red Blood Cells|Kidney Cells|Lung Cel	<>@2@, <>@3@
	5	Enumeration List ▾	Red Blood Cells|Kidney Cells|Lung Cel	<>@2@, <>@3@, <>@4@
	6	Not Used ▾		

Options	A. @1@ B. @2@ C. @3@ D. @4@ E. @5@
Answer	A
Solution Steps	Bacteria that enter the body are destroyed by white blood cells, also called leukocytes or leucocytes. They protect the body against infectious disease and foreign invaders. 1.

Figure 4. CAFA AIG item output example for a TIMSS Grade 8 science question

Item Test Result

Item instance with seed 100 []
Question: Bacteria that enter the body are destroyed by which type of cells?
A. White Blood Cells
B. Microglial Cells
C. Lung Cells
D. Red Blood Cells
E. Alpha Cells
Answer Key: A
Solutions
1. Bacteria that enter the body are destroyed by white blood cells, also called leukocytes or leucocytes. They protect the body against infectious disease and foreign invaders.

Item instance with seed 101 []
Question: Bacteria that enter the body are destroyed by which type of cells?
A. White Blood Cells
B. Lung Cells
C. Red Blood Cells
D. Alpha Cells
E. Microglial Cells
Answer Key: A
Solutions
1. Bacteria that enter the body are destroyed by white blood cells, also called leukocytes or leucocytes. They protect the body against infectious disease and foreign invaders.

Item instance with seed 102 []
Question: Bacteria that enter the body are destroyed by which type of cells?
A. White Blood Cells
B. Alpha Cells
C. Kidney Cells
D. Red Blood Cells
E. Lung Cells
Answer Key: A
Solutions
1. Bacteria that enter the body are destroyed by white blood cells, also called leukocytes or leucocytes. They protect the body against infectious disease and foreign invaders.

As the item models are developed, we will have better documentation about the item model's purpose from the item model developer, making the items more valid. Item difficulty is modeled on the model's difficulty, so we do not need to empirically validate individual items anymore.

Item model development using weak theory relies on design guidelines to develop item models that generate isomorphic instances. Per Bejar (2012), isomorphic (or equal) items are those having the same "psychometric attributes." Put simply, items are equal in their measurement attributes. A "parent item" is developed – either brand-new, or from a previous iteration of the assessment in question. This parent item outlines the structure of the model, generating items in its image. Generally, the goal of using weak theory for item development is to produce statistically calibrated items. The content specialist working with the item must then alter the elements of the parent item that will allow for production of similar items (Choi, 2017a).

Drasgow et al. (2006) describe the strong theory process as a process that utilizes cognitive models to specify and manipulate elements that affect difficulty levels of items using "a theoretical account of test performance." Cognitive theory allows test developers to examine the test takers' knowledge and skills base, as well as the content in each item that affects the item's difficulty. Drasgow et al. further state that in modeling the interactions between the test taker and test content, it is "possible to predict and therefore control the psychometric characteristics of the generated items." When the strong theory approach is successful, it exposes a strong link between test takers' performance in the tested content area and the interpretation of their score.

AIG AND DIFFERENT TYPES OF ASSESSMENT

AIG and Diagnostic Assessment

Diagnostic assessments, also called pre-assessments, determine an examinee's knowledge prior to a lesson. AIG is a great tool for diagnostic assessment and for examining the validity of such assessments. Good diagnostic assessments have large, well-defined item banks. AIG gives more opportunities for larger item banks, because individual models can create many individual items. A valid model produces many valid items. The number and depth of items available in an automatically generated test allow diagnostic assessments to get a closer look at an examinee's real mastery or ability (Choi, 2017a).

AIG and Formative Assessment

Formative assessments expand on the outcomes of diagnostic assessments. Formative assessments are often administered but never fully utilized to move an examinee beyond the level at which they are measured in that assessment. Where diagnostic assessments measure an examinee's strengths and weaknesses, formative assessments measure what they must do to improve. The diagnostic process determines which skills are bottlenecks, whereas the formative process, also called the "treatment process," determines what treatments will maximize the student learning outcome (Choi, 2017a).

The use of AIG for diagnostic and formative assessments, or "Learner Centered Assessments," will lead to teachers gaining a clearer understanding of their students' abilities. Teachers can use this knowledge to create a clear path forward in their classroom, allowing them to provide guidance and additional work that is appropriate to the individual student and their level of knowledge (Choi, 2017b).

OTHER ASSESSMENT TOOLS

Artificial Intelligence

Artificial intelligence (AI) is a very useful tool for AIG. The first two uses of AI are talking and listening. The examinee can talk to the AI, and the AI can estimate input and respond by talking to the examinee (Choi, 2017b).

AI is useful for scoring. Automatic scoring can go beyond simple multiple-choice items and into the realm of short-answer, essay-length responses and technologically based math items. Using AI for scoring these types of assessment responses requires a large initial monetary investment and data. The training data required to develop a properly working AI automatic scoring system includes items, answers, and grading rules. Automatic item generation can support this process by providing developers with the data needed — items, responses, and grading rules — to train the AI in scoring assessments. Because the item model, and all items generated from it, are valid, then the AI can understand what good, valid data is. Training AI with this data always provides an expedited method of populating an item bank without waiting for item model developers to be trained over the course of 1 or 2 years. AI can support a master item model writer in writing models after just a few weeks (Choi, 2017a).

Assessment Platform

An assessment platform is a service that provides an accessible method of developing, administering, and managing assessments and scores. It works similarly to a train platform, which designates a space for the passenger to remain while waiting for a rail car to arrive. Because the platform exists, the person knows where to wait, and the driver or train conductor has a scheduled pick-up location, resulting in convenience for both parties. It is important to consider digital platforms for assessments, considering the rapid advance in technology (Choi, 2017b).

A digital platform works the same way as a physical platform does. A producer and a consumer can meet in the same virtual space so that the producer can administer the assessment and the examinee can take the assessment. Another benefit to using an assessment platform is that all aspects of a course's requirements can be accessible via a platform. For instance, a course may have a formative assessment, some quizzes, classwork, midterm, and final exam. Instead of having these assessments developed separately and stored in individual locations, they could all be developed and loaded onto a single platform, so that teachers and students have easy access to all the assessments. This allows for all parties involved to become familiarized with the assessment process, and the platform could eventually assist in reducing any assessment-related stress that students experience because of lack of familiarity with the process and content (Choi, 2017b).

The assessment platform is designed by loading the necessary curriculum, tasks, and assessment items, which can be accessed by teachers as needed for in-class assessment purposes. The item types and formats may also vary using an assessment platform, offering a wide range of digital assessment resources. The platform can store student data for longitudinal observation. Ultimately, the assessment platform serves as a centralized engine that can provide on-demand assessments, item banks, scoring, feedback, etc. (Choi, 2017b).

Assessment on Textbook

Textbooks are one of the most widely used educational tools. They are chosen according to standards, instructional needs, and assessment components. The "Assessment on Textbook" (AoT) framework focuses on the development and utilization of digital textbooks in conjunction with the assessment platform. The AoT textbook contains resources to prepare assessments, which makes these books and assessments more accessible to teachers. Pairing the AoT textbook with the assessment platform provides on-demand, digital curriculum content and assessments, which leads to lower costs, more efficiency in the classroom, and fewer security issues. With instant assessment results, teachers can begin working with students on their problem areas immediately. The items developed on the assessment platform, when paired with the AoT textbook, can also be accessed during class. This means that students will be familiar with the assessment item style, and they will be tested on what is taught, reducing the mystery of the test and leading to fewer test anxiety issues (Choi, 2017b).

Speech to Text

Speech to text and AIG listening tests are two simple methods to incorporate AIG into more language-based assessments. Speech to text, specifically, can receive student input beyond just multiple choice. These dynamic voice files are created and saved on demand. AIG speech to text can record lengthy responses – many sentences or paragraphs, for essay or short-answer responses. This allows the assessments to become more literacy and disability friendly, as some students may not be reading proficiently but can still understand and communicate material by listening and speaking. This adds an element of fairness, another important element of digital assessment, as well as validity that may have been missing from some more traditional methods of assessment (Choi, 2017a).

AIG AND TEST SECURITY

Test security is a very sensitive topic in our technologically driven world. As assessments become more technologically advanced, it is very important that security measures be carefully considered during test development. AIG can drastically lessen or eliminate security concerns, for the simple reason that there are so many items developed from one model. The chances of an examinee getting a leaked item on their test is very slim because of the number of items generated from that item's model. In the event that a student does view a leaked test item, they would need to learn how to solve the type of problem to answer it correctly on their version of the test. This is not necessarily a bad thing, because it ultimately leads to student learning (Choi, 2017a).

Other measures to ensure test security include fingerprint biometrics, testing in a web-lock environment, and e-monitoring. The fingerprint biometrics method would pair an examinee's fingerprint to his or her assessment with the intent of prohibiting another individual from taking the test. Testing in a web-lock environment, which is the method used for the eTIMSS pilot, requires the assessment to display in full-screen mode, preventing examinees from accessing the tablet's browser and other features. E-monitoring occurs via the use of a webcam built directly into the assessment device. This method might be financially impractical if there are also in-person proctors monitoring the assessment (Al-Saleem & Ullah, 2014).

VALIDITY ARGUMENT

As previously mentioned, assessments that are products of AIG have the potential to be highly validated tests. Assuming the item model is a good model, and items that are developed are isomorphic instances, or isomorphs, we can trust that these items are already calibrated and do not need to undergo piloting or pretesting (Gierl & Haladyna, 2013). Eliminating the necessary pilot and/or pretest saves a substantial amount of time and money.

Additionally, an item cannot be thoroughly validated if the intention is unknown. It is much easier to understand the intention of an item that is automatically generated, thereby enhancing the item's validity. Item model developers might be tasked with developing 40 models instead of 2,000 individual items. It would be much more manageable to document and understand the intention behind those 40 models, and, by default, their generated isomorphs, than it would be for 2,000 individual items. This idea of having a connection between the item and the principle/intention of the item—also referred to as "construct relevance"—makes AIG even more useful for large-scale assessment and its validation (Choi, 2017a).

STUDENT PERCEPTION

Computer-based assessments can include traditional multiple choice and free response questions, along with interactive graphics and games. There are complications with graphically intricate test designs. They are very expensive and can be difficult to develop, because each graphic requires a unique layout and method of response. More research is needed to measure the value of these methods. See Figures 5 and 6 for two example items based on the TIMSS 2011 assessment (TIMSS 2011 Assessment, 2013), created in CAFA AIG (Choi, Kim, & Yoon, 2012).

Student feedback about these types of assessments has been generally positive (Cheng & Basu, 2009). In addition to improving students' engagement and their perception of assessments, digital assessments, including standard digital assessment and computer adaptive testing, have proven beneficial in other areas. In one study, students had the opportunity to participate in a linear and a computer adaptive test utilizing a mobile device and a laptop. Results of paired *t*-tests indicated that the estimation of students' ability was not statistically significantly different between

Figure 5. CAFA AIG item output example for a graphics-based TIMSS Grade 4 math question

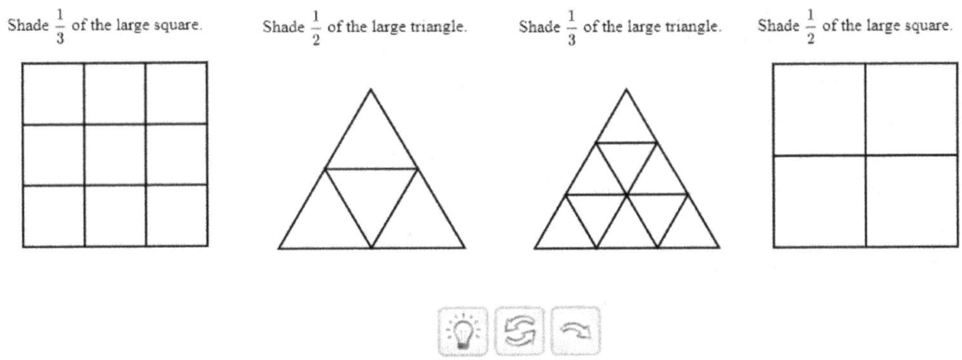

Figure 6. CAFA AIG item output example for a graphics-based TIMSS Grade 8 math question

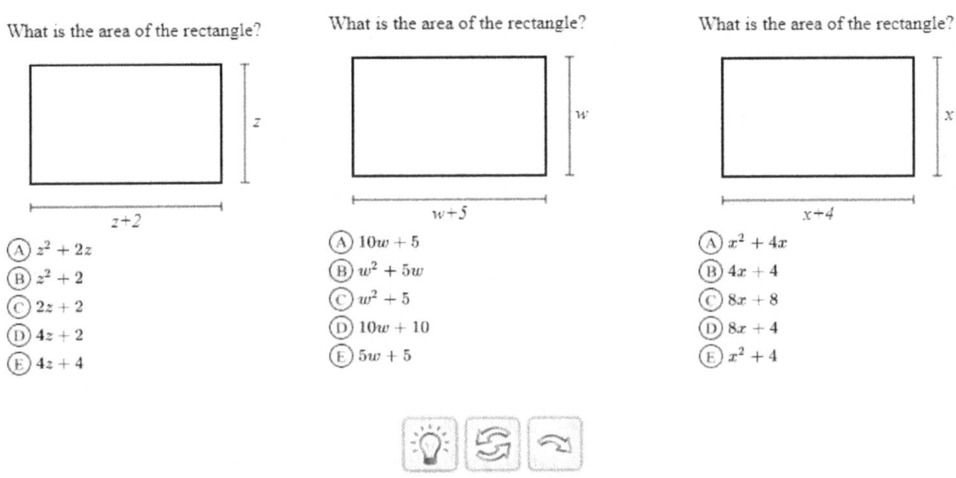

the computer-based assessment and the traditional paper-and-pencil assessment. This means that the computer-adaptive and paper-and-pencil assessments are interchangeable when used to determine a student's ability. There was a statistically significant difference in the time used and length of the test required to assess a student's ability. The computer-adaptive assessment was much more efficient in assessing a student's ability, because students could answer fewer items to achieve their result. Interviews with the assessed students in this study revealed that they were very pleased with this type of assessment, and the students felt that they had a better understanding of their own abilities when using the computer-adaptive assessment rather than the paper-and-pencil assessment (Huang, Lin, & Cheng, 2009).

These are great benefits to computer adaptive assessments, but there are some factors, such as fairness, to consider as this type of assessment becomes more widely utilized. In one study about the fairness of CAT assessments, researchers investigated students' attitude toward computer adaptive assessments, their computer self-efficacy, and test anxiety. The only variable that had a significant negative influence on the assessment results was test anxiety. Students with a high level of test anxiety could be disadvantaged when taking a computer-adaptive assessment, although this may be true for paper-and-pencil assessment as well. The other variables had an insignificant positive result. Additionally, there were significantly different technology facilities available to students in different areas (urban vs. rural, for instance). There was some concern that this difference in facilities may have a negative influence on the computer self-efficacy of the students, but the results showed that this might have been a negligible concern (Lu, Hu, Gao, & Kinshuk, 2016).

IMPORTANCE OF THE MULTIMEDIA COMPONENT

Cheng and Basu (2009) noted that current literature focuses primarily on the use of multimedia elements for learning but not assessment. This is because AIG and other digital technologies have historically shown to be ideal for "algorithmic items with a minimum amount of supplementary information" (Lai & Gierl, 2013) such as math and science, but limited for cognitive assessment and content rich domains, such as writing, reading, and language.

Cognitive abilities and subject knowledge can be assessed together only when using a multimedia-based assessment. Paper-and-pencil tests can be displayed on a monitor, but that does not take advantage of the potential scope of digital assessment.

Mayer and Moreno's Cognitive Theory of Multimedia Learning (CTML; 2005) describes how people learn from multimedia. The assumptions of this theory are: (1) people have separate channels for processing visual and verbal information, (2) the capacity of these two channels is limited, and (3) connecting these channels leads to significant learning.

The dual channel assumption, relating to Paivio's dual-coding theory (1986) and Baddeley's model of working memory (1986), indicates that information absorbed via the eyes is processed through the visual channel, while information absorbed through the ears is processed through an auditory channel. It is important to note that information enters through one of the two channels but can process again through the other channel. For example, a person can read a sentence, process through the visual channel, and imagine the sounds of those individual words if spoken aloud, which processes through the auditory channel. Similarly, a person may hear the sentence "This dog has spots" with their auditory channel, which causes their visual channel to process a mental image of a dog with spots (Mayer, 2005).

Mayer's second assumption states that each channel processes a limited amount of information. When a person reads a large wall of text, they may remember only the gist of the paragraph or some key phrases, but rarely can they recall the entire body of text without actively working to commit it to memory. Memory span tests estimate a person's cognitive capacity, usually by requiring the subject to recite back a number of items in a specific order. A person's memory span can be said to be equal to the largest amount of items that person can list without making a mistake. People may work to process items in chunks, rather than individually, allowing them to remember more of the original list of items (Mayer, 2005).

The final assumption of CTML states that using both channels leads to significant learning. In so doing, humans combine their visual and auditory channel processing with other cognitive processes to capitalize on their current knowledge and to acquire and store new knowledge. Active learning requires access to relevant and well-organized material that integrates with current knowledge, as well as continuous processing of both channels (Mayer, 2005).

COST AND BENEFITS ANALYSIS

As previously stated, the use of AIG can result in the development of thousands of unique items produced by just a few item models. This process saves test developers a significant amount of time and money because they no longer need to develop multiple items on several test forms to measure the same concept. Gierl and Haladyna (2013) estimate that, as of 2010, the standard large-scale, 40-question assessment should have a 2,000-question item bank. As of 2010, each of those items cost between \$1,500 and \$2,000 to develop. The cost for this type of standard assessment, for items alone, would be upwards of \$3,000,000. The use of a basic, hypothetical AIG model shows significant cost reduction, as the cost of one model can be as low as \$500. If this \$500 model generates 2,000 individual items, the individual item cost reduces from \$2,000 to only 25 cents.

Traditional item development in paper-and-pencil format can cost an estimated \$1,000 – 2,000 per item. For our purposes, we will assume the new digital format for the TIMSS 2019 administration will cost \$1,500-2,000 per item. A well-developed AIG template, with item models based on the original 2,000 items, and with the capability of producing a minimum of 100 unique instances, can drastically reduce the per-item cost to \$50-200 for the TIMSS assessment (Choi, 2017a). Table 1 contains the breakdown of this cost and benefit analysis.

Table 1. Theoretical cost/benefits of different item types, assuming a traditional 40-item test with a minimum 2,000-question item bank

Item type	Items	Total for all items or item models	Additional cost overall	Cost per item instance in first year of administration*	Additional benefits
Traditional Base Items	2,000	$4 million	N/A	$1,000 – 2,000+	Traditional paper-and-pencil format in which item writers are currently trained (N/A)
Updated Digital Items (2019 TIMSS administration)	2,000	Additional $4 million (total 8M)	$4 million	$1,500 -2,000	Improved student engagement; more complex, technologically based items; assesses students' abilities more efficiently
Automatically Generated Item Models	2,000 x 100 (unique instances per model, total 200,000 unique instances)	Additional $2 million (total 10M)	$6 million	$50**	Same benefits as above, plus: improved test validity and test security; formative and diagnostic assessments; cost effective over several test administrations

*Assumes costs of software development and staff training over 2 years

**Assumes each item model template will produce a *minimum of 100 unique instances*

There are potentially significant upfront costs when implementing AIG, particularly in acquiring software, training item model developers, and developing the items. Software that has already been developed includes Computer Adaptive Formative Assessment AIG (CAFA AIG), which is best utilized for math and science items, and IGOR for word-based items. The development of a new AIG software would take approximately 2 years to complete and cost an additional $2-5 million. Staffing and training is critical when planning an assessment using AIG. A staff for traditional paper-and-pencil assessment might include 2-3 psychometricians, 20-50 item writers, and 2-3 administrative assistants. A staff for an AIG assessment could include as few as five item model developers and one administrative assistant (Choi, 2017a).

The first step in staffing the AIG team is to train two to three item model developers. These developers will train 2 years to reach mastery in item model development using the chosen or developed software. An ideal candidate for this position would have an undergraduate background in hard sciences (50%), with some basic psychometric (20%) and content background (30%). These master item model developers would be full-time employees who can train an additional one or two template writers immediately or as needed. Entry-level template writers require a minimum of two weeks of intensive workshop training. The ideal template writers would work part time and have strong content background (80%), along with some basic hard science (15%) and psychometric knowledge. One administrative assistant can round out the team. Assuming a schedule of 3 years and salaries of $75,000 each per year for two master developers, $45,000 each per year for two item writers, and $30,000 per year for one administrative assistant, the cost of staffing could range from $675,000 to $1 million (Choi, 2017a).

The most significant advantages of using AIG—the financial benefits and potential time saved—can also be a significant drawback because of the upfront costs and time needed for training item model writers. It is commonly believed that it takes 10,000 hours to master any skill, and mastery of AIG should not be an exception (Ericsson, Krampe, & Tesch-Römer, 1993). Because AIG is a new and evolving technology, there are not many fully trained item model developers. Once trained, item model writers must also collaborate effectively with content and IT experts (Choi, 2017a).

Item model development is another consideration, in addition to the training of item model writers and their collaboration with content experts. As previously stated, the development of item models may start at a much lower rate than traditionally developed individual items. However, models that are more complex will cost more money and require more training to develop. Well-designed item models will be useful for multiple administrations with only minor adjustments made by the item model developers, but the up-front costs and the cost of updates and adjustments are important considerations (Choi, 2017a).

Overall, the use of AIG for international assessments can prove to be a very valuable option, assuming time and money are available to implement these changes to current assessments as the technology advances. As the technology becomes more popular, more trained item model developers and additional software models will become available. These advances will drive down the cost of using AIG and make the technology more accessible to different types of users, including but not limited to large-scale education and assessment companies, businesses, and teachers. The advancement of this and other digital technologies represents very exciting steps for assessment technology. TIMSS, PISA, and other international assessments potentially could be ideal pioneers for AIG.

LIMITATIONS AND FUTURE WORKS

Automatic item generation is a new and evolving technology. At present, there are not many psychometricians trained to the level of mastery required to tackle the requirements of implementing AIG into a large-scale, international assessment. As AIG becomes a more prominent fixture in American and international assessment, there will be more software in development, and more master psychometricians will be trained and available to implement the work, and to train others for AIG.

As various assessment companies begin using AIG and developing their own software, the overall cost will become less hypothetical and more concrete, allowing a better understanding of overall cost and benefit comparisons. The availability of more software options to assessment developers and the public will help lower the overall cost of implementing AIG, making it a much more reasonable option for future large- and small-scale assessments.

There are also potential benefits to developing AIG software for use by educators. The addition of this type of software could make classroom planning much simpler and allow teachers time to focus on important classroom activities besides assessments. Other educational and workplace tools, such as Blackboard and various Learning Management Systems (LMS), will benefit from the integration of AIG assessments. I imagine that this type of small-scale software would be simpler for development than for large-scale, more complicated assessments.

REFERENCES

Al-Saleem, S., & Ullah, H. (2014). Security considerations and recommendations in computer based testing. *The Scientific World Journal, 2014*, 1–7. doi:10.1155/2014/562787 PMID:25254250

Baddeley, A. (1986). *Working memory*. Oxford, UK: Oxford University Press.

Bejar, I. (2012). Item generation: Implications for a validity argument. In M. Gierl & T. Haladyna (Eds.), *Automatic item generation: Theory and practice* (pp. 40–56). New York: Routledge.

Bormuth, J. R., & Menzel, P. (1970). *On the theory of achievement test items*. Chicago: University of Chicago Press.

Carr, P. (2017). *NAEP Special Interest Group Business Meeting*. Presented at the *annual meeting of the American Educational Research Association*, San Antonio, TX.

Cheng, I., & Basu, A. (2009). Interactive graphics for computer adaptive testing. *Computer Graphics Forum, 28*(8), 2033–2045. doi:10.1111/j.1467-8659.2009.01427.x

Choi, J. (2017a). *Introduction to assessment engineering lectures*. Washington, DC: Personal Collection of J. Choi, The George Washington University.

Choi, J. (2017b). Next generation item and test development: A practical introduction to Automatic Item Generation. Washington, DC: Assessment, Testing, and Measurement Technical Report Series, The George Washington University.

Choi, J., Kim, S., & Yoon, K. (2012). CAFA automatic item generation: Vol. 1. *0 beta) system: Computer adaptive formative assessment client application for automatic item generation* [computer system]. CAFA Lab, Inc.

Drasgow, F., Luecht, R. M., & Bennett, R. E. (2006). Technology and testing. In S. H. Irvine & P. C. Kyllonen (Eds.), *Educational measurement* (4th ed.; pp. 471–516). Washington, DC: American Council on Education.

Ericsson, K., Krampe, R., & Tesch-Römer, C. (1993). The role of deliberate practice in the acquisition of expert performance. *Psychological Review*, *100*(3), 363–406. doi:10.1037/0033-295X.100.3.363

Fraillon, J., Schulz, W., & Ainley, J. (2013). International Computer and Information Literacy Study assessment framework. Amsterdam: International Association for the Evaluation of Educational Achievement (IEA).

Gierl, M., Lai, H., & Turner, S. (2012). Using automatic item generation to create multiple-choice test items. *Medical Education*, *46*(8), 757–765. doi:10.1111/j.1365-2923.2012.04289.x PMID:22803753

Gierl, M. J., & Haladyna, T. M. (2013). *Automatic item generation: Theory and practice*. New York, NY: Routledge.

Huang, Y., Lin, Y., & Cheng, S. (2009). An adaptive testing system for supporting versatile educational assessment. *Computers & Education*, *52*(1), 53–67. doi:10.1016/j.compedu.2008.06.007

Lai, H., & Gierl, M. J. (2013). Generating items under the assessment engineering framework. In M. J. Gierl & T. Haladyna (Eds.), *Automatic item generation: Theory and practice* (pp. 77–101). New York, NY: Routledge.

Lu, H., Hu, Y., Gao, J., & Kinshuk. (2016). The effects of computer self-efficacy, training satisfaction and test anxiety on attitude and performance in computerized adaptive testing. *Computers & Education*, *100*, 45–55. doi:10.1016/j.compedu.2016.04.012

Mayer, R. (2005). *The Cambridge handbook of multimedia learning*. New York: University of Cambridge Press. doi:10.1017/CBO9780511816819

Organisation for Economic Co-operation and Development. (2017). *Beyond PISA 2015: A Longer-Term Strategy of PISA*. Retrieved from http://www.oecd.org/pisa/pisaproducts/Longer-term-strategy-of-PISA.pdf

Osburn, H. (1968). Item sampling for achievement testing. *Educational and Psychological Measurement*, *28*(1), 95–104. doi:10.1177/001316446802800109

Paivio, A. (1986). *Mental representations*. New York: Oxford University Press.

TIMSS. (2017). *International Association for the Evaluation of Educational Achievement (IEA)*. Retrieved 12 September 2017, from http://www.iea.nl/timss-2015

TIMSS 2011 Assessment. (2013). *International Association for the Evaluation of Educational Achievement (IEA)*. TIMSS & PIRLS International Study Center, Lynch School of Education, Boston College, Chestnut Hill, MA and International Association for the Evaluation of Educational Achievement (IEA), IEA Secretariat, Amsterdam, The Netherlands.

KEY TERMS AND DEFINITIONS

Artificial Intelligence: Computer systems programmed to perform tasks that require human-level intelligence.

Automatic Item Generation: A digital process of generating multiple assessment items using item models.

Computer Adaptive Testing: A digital assessment that adapts its questions based on the examinee's ability level and responses.

Diagnostic Assessment: An assessment used to determine a student's knowledge, skills, and abilities prior to instruction.

Formative Assessment: An assessment used mid-instruction to determine a student's level of comprehension and learning needs.

Isomorphs: Automatically generated items containing the same psychometric properties.

Item Models: Template used in automatic item generation to generate items.

Psychometrics: The study and theories of psychological measurement, including the measurement of skills, knowledge, attributes, and personality traits.

Section 3
Perspectives on Information Resources Management

The chapters in this section discuss information as a shared organizational resource and include discussions of big data for decision making and knowledge discovery, using social media for healthcare recruiting, creating a new and improved architecture based on SOA and REST. The final chapter proposes a new framework for IT security management budget review.

Chapter 9
Big Data Technologies and Management

Jayashree K.
Rajalakshmi Engineering College, India

Abirami R.
Rajalakshmi Engineering College, India

ABSTRACT

Developments in information technology and its prevalent growth in several areas of business, engineering, medical, and scientific studies are resulting in information as well as data explosion. Knowledge discovery and decision making from such rapidly growing voluminous data are a challenging task in terms of data organization and processing, which is an emerging trend known as big data computing. Big data has gained much attention from the academia and the IT industry. A new paradigm that combines large-scale compute, new data-intensive techniques, and mathematical models to build data analytics. Thus, this chapter discusses the background of big data. It also discusses the various application of big data in detail. The various related work and the future direction would be addressed in this chapter.

1. INTRODUCTION

Big data is the new approach that is used for analyzing large amount of data-set. Data-set can be from different sources which includes both structured and unstructured data, be it a sensor data or emails or social media (Hiba et al., 2014). The standard method used for analyzing and processing the structured data using Relational Databases is no longer satisfactory due to several challenges. Big data deals with high Volume, Velocity, Variety, Veracity and Value of data.

DOI: 10.4018/978-1-5225-5829-3.ch009

As the amount of data grow day by day, the cost of storage and management became a vital aspect to be taken care. It was then the evolution of cloud computing that came into existence which provides the best methods to store data in a cost-effective way. The rapid progress of IT industries in different fields like medicine, engineering, business and research requires new technique for processing huge volume of data. Each of the specified field contains voluminous data which has to be managed and controlled for processing. To process and manage the data in an effective way certain mathematical models, data-intensive techniques are required together. A new emerging approach that is used for processing multidimensional data which combines mathematical models, data-intensive techniques is termed as big data computing (Kune et al., 2016).

Big data keeps the data safe and secure by utilizing different software tools (Venkatesh et al., 2015). Since data are stored on cloud, the three major criteria like speed, scalability and capacity to process the data are achieved. New business opportunities emerge by using big data as it enables the users to visualize the data. Data analytics is another advantage where the datasets are examined, and information's are obtained.

Section 2 introduces the background of big data. Section 3 discusses big data challenges. Section 4 describes the related work. Section 5 explains the future research directions. The conclusion of the chapter is described in Section 6.

2. BACKGROUND

In day-to-day life millions and billions of data are created everyday by people be it on any social networking sites, finance, medicine, sensors, mobile applications and so on. To manage, analyze and process all these data new processing methodologies, techniques and tools must be used. The information's are being flooded and are beyond a range, in which it cannot to measure. A best example is Facebook, where 100 Terabytes of data are uploaded every day. The term "Big data" came into emergence to store and process huge amount of data in a simple way. There are various definitions of big data stated by researches. According to McKinsey, Big data is a huge amount of data in which the size of the data is beyond the size of regular databases. O'Reilly states that big data is nothing but the data that exceeds the limit of normal database where the data or information is large and processed quickly. Hence new approaches have to be followed to process the information. According to Gartner, Enormous data means high volume, rapid speed and variety of data resources which needs new procedures and techniques to handle the data.

New approaches and techniques is difficult to apply on traditional databases by using simple software tools used in accessing the relational database. Data can be both structured as well as unstructured data collected from different resources. All the definitions lead to 5 V's which is Volume, Velocity, Variety, Veracity, Value.

Hence new approaches have to be followed to process the information. According to Gartner, Enormous data means high volume, rapid speed and variety of data resources which needs new procedures and techniques to handle the data. New approaches and techniques is difficult to apply on traditional databases by using simple software tools used in accessing the relational databases database. Data can be both structured as well as unstructured data collected from different resources (Sunny Sharma et al., 2016). All the definitions lead to 5 V's which is Volume, Velocity, Variety, Veracity, Value.

1. **Volume:** Large volume of data are collected from enterprises or organizations. These data are usually in form of terabytes ranges from 30-50 or even more TBs. The available storage cannot handle structure and unstructured data; this is an important challenge for organizations.
2. **Velocity:** Velocity describes the speed of data that an organization can handle and analyze to increase the profit of business before the value of information is lost.
3. **Variety:** Information can be structured, unstructured, semi structured or even the combination of all three. It comes in many forms like logs, tweets status, images, animations, audio, text files, PDF, click stream and so on.
4. **Veracity:** Data sources are of different qualities with differences accuracy, coverage and timeliness.
5. **Value:** The data collected are stored and has to reused whenever needed. Hence the data should not be outdated. The data has to be processed and produced quickly during analysis. The data are combined with other data-sets and reused for future reference. Based on the 5 V's big data can be classified under five categories:
    a. **Data Sources:** Includes internet data-for example social media, sensing data- example IoT, and transactional data- example financial data.
    b. **Content Format:** Since data are from different sources, they are of different format namely structured, unstructured and semi-structured data.
    c. **Data Stores:** The collected data are stored in either document database, column database, graph database, and key-value alternate to relational database.

d. **Data Staging:** In staging the unwanted or incomplete data are identified, then the data are transformed for analysis and finally normalization is done for minimizing duplicate, redundant data.
e. **Data Processing:** The collected data are processed by batch processing using Map-reduce techniques, and by certain big data tools (Ibrahim Abaker et al., 2015).

Since the huge amount of data collected are unstructured the concept of Big data emerged. A large amount of complex data, which can be captured, stored and analyzed in Real-Time. 570 new websites are developed every minute, 72 hours of video are uploaded in Youtube every second. Billions of data are added to Facebook every week and millions of tweets are created by user on each day. It is highly impossible. without big data for all these data to be stored, analyzed and managed.

As the amount of data grows, cloud computing is combined with big data technologies for managing and storing the large amount of data. In all the applications the information's are easily accessible. Hence the advantages of using cloud in the field of big data is in terms of Agility, Affordability, Data processing and feasibility (Ibrahim et al., 2015).

Agility: In organizations the normal databases is no longer compatible for storing and managing enormous data, as it is slower and is difficult to process the data. Hence cloud computing is used to provide resources to the organizations on demand. Storing information's on cloud database can enable the organization to have number of virtual servers which can manage, store and access data.

Affordability: Before cloud, the organizations invested huge amount of money to update the hardware and software they use. Now the resources are easily available on cloud and can be used by the organizations any time whenever need at any cost, that is they need to pay only for the resources they use, be it a storage space or power.

Data processing: Due to a drastic increase of data, processing became a little difficult. For example, Social media generates millions and trillions of data such as videos, photos, tweets, blogs, posts which cannot be analyzed and processed under a single class or category. Cloud computing makes use of map-reduce methodology on big data platform like Hadoop which helps to process the data in an easier and efficient way.

Feasibility: To increase the storage space and processing speed, large number of servers are required, whereas virtual characteristic of cloud helps to access the resources on demand, anywhere and at any time easily and quickly. Big data needs new methodologies for processing enormous data, hence cloud computing plays a vital role in providing the resources.

APPLICATIONS

The several areas of application where big data computing used are Education, Health care, sports, gaming, security, Financial and business analytics (Sabia et al., 2014).

In the Field of Education

Big data plays vital role in education. Educators can create an online forum for students be it a moodle or any online website. The educators or instructors can upload video, notes, lesson plan on all topics and activities can be given based on the topics related to video. The Students behavior such as their understanding of the topics can be evaluated by the activities done by the students. It can also identify the interest of student looking at time spent on online videos, notes, textbook. Smart classrooms are on board where the major base is big data.

Healthcare

The major goals in healthcare sectors is to enhance the quality and satisfaction of the patients experience in treatment, to reduce the cost, to use modern approaches to analyze and manage the patients records or information's. It is quite difficult to collect, store and manage the clinical data of all patients. Hence high-performance analytics and methods has to be used to manage the large amount data. Unstructured data can be extracted by performing text mining on patients record. Hence the data can be collected quickly and correctly without causing any difficulty to clinicians. In addition to it, making the information's regarding treatment of patients transparent, patients will be able to get their treatment through online health applications.

Network Security

Big data plays a vital role in security technologies. For example, credit card details given during online transactions can be hacked and used by an intruder. Big data makes use of fraud detection techniques to tackle the issue and prevents the intruder to access the personal card details. It is also being used in the field of forensics and SIEM.

Sports

Big data next interesting application is sports. Coaches, players and the leading minds in sports came together to discuss the potential of analytics and big data. For example, in athletics, the athletes are monitored frequently in terms of speed, performance, time, kilometers they run per day so on. The monitored data are stored on daily basis. Statistics of data collected are calculated to understand the capacity of the athletes. The benefit is, coaches can easily identify which player need additional support, training and guidance. This will surely help to increase the performance and progress of the player.

Gaming

Three main data such as game data, player data and session data are collected from the people playing video games. The volume of data that the players are generating every day is growing very quickly. To manage all these data a new big data technology which is "Hadoop" is used. It makes use of map-reduce concept to analyze collect and process the massive data. By analyzing the collected data like the user's behavior, rewards, activity, leader boards, character selections the game developers will be able to improve or upgrade the game options and versions. The up-gradation helps to improve the gaming experiences of the player.

Telecommunication

A very big challenge faced by telecommunication sector are volume, variety and complexity. To overcome this challenge "telcos" technology is used. It is actually the combination of ETL and traditional databases with big data technologies. Telcos combines huge volume of data generated by location sensors, IPv6 devices, clickstream, CDRs, 4G networks and machine to machine monitors information. It also handles multiple forms of unstructured data be it form mobile, web, mail and so on.

Emerging applications are continuously generating huge amount of structured and unstructured data hence advanced techniques like Hadoop has to be used to process and store the data. New tools and approaches has to adapted in near future to track, analysis share our personal data in a secure manner. All real-world applications are related to big data is one way or the other.

3. BIG DATA CHALLENGES

Several challenges need to be focused as big data deals with large amount of data. Based on the applications of big data the issues or challenges faced are broadly classified into two. The issues that are related to management activities like storage, scalability and efficiency are grouped under engineering category and the issues dealing with unstructured data are grouped under semantic challenges.

Since the application of big data ranges from Science to business, enormous amount of data needs to be stored analyzed and processed. As the result various challenges like Heterogeneity, Incompleteness, scalability, Timeliness, Privacy and Security are to be addressed.

Heterogeneity

Data collected are from various sources the major challenges lies on the format of data. Mostly the collected data will be in unstructured form. It may be in the form of email's, pdf file, graphics, audio, animations, medical x-rays, CT scans, voice mails and so on. Converting all these data into structured form is a major challenge where new technologies and methodologies has to be adopted to deal with the issues.

Incompleteness

Sometimes the data fields values entered would be missing. This creates uncertainty of data which is a major challenge to be addressed. The missing values can occur due to repair in sensor, system crash and so on. Incomplete data creates uncertainties during data analysis and it must be managed during data analysis. Various datamining algorithms are developed to deal with missing data or values. If the algorithms are not stated properly it would become a major drawback to collect and process the data correctly.

Scalability

Scalability is one of the serious issue which prevails for several years as big data deals with large amount data. Parallel data processing methods that were used in the past to maintain and process the data are no longer useful as the size of data keeps increasing rapidly day by day. New approaches have to be followed to maintain the growing size or elasticity of data.

Timeliness

The next serious issue is timeliness which means the request of the data has to processed much faster, but since the size of data is large it is difficult to scan the data and respond the query or request made by the user.

Security

Among all the issues the most serious issue that must be addressed is security. If security violation occurs, it will cause very serious damage and consequence on data that is stored and analyzed. In-order to maintain the data in a secured way we need to follow techniques and algorithms related to encryption, logging, honeypot, and fraud detection.

Management Challenges

As big-data deals with enormous amount of data several challenges related to data management like accessing, processing and governing the data arises. The repository of data which are otherwise called as data warehouse stores large amount of sensitive data related to medicine, insurance, diagnosis, end user's personal data etc. Hence all the data must be kept in a secure manner by the organizations and each user has to be given privilege only to view relevant data. Certain privacy rules have to be followed by the management to monitor the security of data, which means only the relevant data can be viewed and accessed by the employees of the organization. Broadly all these data management issues are divided into seven fields namely privacy, data and information sharing, cost, operational expenditures, data governance and data ownership (Stephen et al., 2013).

Data and Information Sharing

Each and every agency and departments, maintain their own data center, and data are kept confidentially. Certain data cannot be shared due to some privacy conditions in such cases data sharing becomes a challenge in smart city as data has to be shared among different devices. Different approaches need to be followed to achieve proper information sharing and exchange among different devices and departments. In addition to it, large amount of data are updated, and stored in different format every second on real time applications. Hence it is difficult to create a general format of data and extract information, directly from real time application.

Cost

Even if huge investments are made on certain projects to maintain privacy, it still remains to be greater challenge. For example, in smart cities sensors are used to capture each and every individual activity, which are accessed by several government and security agencies. As the result location based data are transferred over the network which is an important privacy concern.

Security and Privacy

Next major concern in big data is security. If security issues are not properly taken care, then it may lead to attacks like malware or it can be hacked by any third-party user. In certain applications as confidential data about people and government are collected and stored in the database, more security policies and procedures should be followed to keep the data protected from unauthorized user and from virus attack or bugs. Privacy rights of organizations and individuals has to be clearly stated and protected. In certain cases, like medical records, bank and financial records are viewed by the individual which violates the privacy rights hence better techniques has to be followed to rectify this issue.

Governance

Data quality must be met as importance of big data is increasing day by day. The major three issues in maintaining the quality of data are how data are analyzed, accessed and stored. A good big data governance strategy must be followed to ensure the quality of the data.

In addition to it, certain key challenges have been identified in big data management related to the cloud. The challenges include Data security and privacy. Security issues causes a major threat to business and cloud providers nowadays. Mostly transactional data carry sensitive information like details of credit and debit cards like numbers, address and so on. The intruders find new ways to hack the details of the system and find out the card details. Other security issues like ransomware, Denial of Service attacks, Phising attacks, Cloud abuse are of major concern which has to be addressed. Weak APIs and interfaces allows the hackers to hack the information's and misuse them in anyway.

Certain cloud models are still in development stage. Data-Acts is another major issue where the cloud providers except the datacenter to be closer to the user so that the data can be accessed easily. The next issue is data replication- more data are collected from various resources and devices it is necessary to avoid the duplication of data, as duplication results affects the analysis stage. Other issues include approximate results, Data exploration to enable deep analytics; Enterprise data enrichment with web and social media, Query optimization; and Performance isolation for multi-tenancy (Stephen et al., 2013).

Since large amount of data are used for storage, the cost for storing the enormous amount of data is still a challenge for medium and small organizations. In traditional method the storage is based on network-attached storage. To collect and store information or data large number of NAS need to be interconnected with one another to form cluster, which requires NAS pods. Hence the best option for medium and small organizations is to make use of cloud. The resources on demand will be provided by an outside entity, hence only, little management effort and cost need to be put by the small and medium sized organizations. (Bernice, 2012)

The way to deal with all these challenges is to implement new next-gen technologies which can identify the issue before it could cause damage to the data. Algorithms like fraud detection, encryptions can be used to protect the data from intruders.

4. RELATED WORK

Sameer Agarwal et.al. presents a BlinkDB, an approximate query engine for running collaborative SQL queries on large volume of data which is massively parallel. BlinkDB uses two key ideas such as an adaptive optimization framework that builds and maintains a set of multi-dimensional stratified samples from original data over time, and a dynamic sample selection strategy that selects an appropriately sized sample based on a query's accuracy or response time requirements.

Yingyi Bu et.al. have used a new technique called HaLoop that allows iterative applications to be assembled from existing Hadoop programs without modification, and significantly improves their efficiency by providing inter- iteration caching mechanisms and a loop-aware scheduler to exploit these caches. He presents the design, implementation, and evaluation of HaLoop, a novel parallel and distributed system that supports large-scale iterative data analysis applications.

Swanson et.al develops a new MapReduce scheduling technique to enhance map task's data locality. He has integrated this technique into Hadoop default FIFO scheduler and Hadoop fair scheduler.

Albert Bifet et.al. Stated that streaming data analysis in real time is becoming the fastest and most efficient way to obtain useful knowledge, allowing organizations to react quickly when problem appear or detect to improve performance. The tools used for mining big data are apache Hadoop, apache big, cascading, scribe, storm, apache HBase, apache mahout, MOA, R, etc.

5. BIG DATA ANALYTICS

Big data analytics deals with analyzing, inspecting, transforming large amount of data in order to find useful information and also use the data for decision making purposes. To get valuable information from the data it has to processed in a timely manner. Analytics plays a vital role in the field of business. To process the data efficiently the combination of three major parameters namely people, process, technology have to be considered compulsorily. In addition to it explanatory and predictive models are used for processing statistical and quantitative data in order to achieve effectiveness. The major benefits of using analytics in big data is it optimizes the process, combines internal and external data, helps organizations to meet client's requests, manage market related risks and as a whole converts useful information or data to intelligent data. Analytics is a huge area where it can be divided as text analysis, audio, video analysis, social media analysis and so on. Big data deals with all these fields.

Text analysis deals with textual data like news feeds, surveys, call and message logs, blogs, social media updates and posts. All these data are analyzed and helps in evidence related decision making. Analyzing text data helps in prediction purpose for example prediction of stock market. Audio usually comes under unstructured data. Call centers and healthcare are two major application of audio analytics. In call centers each and every hour, minutes, seconds, the calls are recorded which improves customers' demands, increases the sales profit rates, identify sales turnover etc. Few organizations use Interactive Voice Response (IVR) platforms to identify and handle frustrated callers in the field of medicine, the psychological behavior of patients can be identified, and treatment can be given based on the disease predicted (Hadi et al., 2014).

In video analytics the information is gathered from video streams. The vital issue in video analytics is the size of data from which the information is extracted, analyzed and processed. Social media analytics contains both structured as well as unstructured data. Maintaining both these data is a major task, which is done in an easier way by data analytics.

Predictive analytics comprise a variety of techniques that predict future outcomes based on historical and current data predictive analytics seek to uncover patterns and capture relationships in data. Predictive analytics techniques are sub divided into two groups. Some techniques, such as moving aver-ages, attempt to discover the historical patterns in the outcome variable(s) and extrapolate them to the future. Others, such as linear regression, aim to capture the inter dependencies between outcome variable(s) and explanatory variables, and exploit them to make predictions. Based on the underlying methodology, techniques can also be categorized into two groups: regression techniques and machine learning techniques.

6. FUTURE RESEARCH DIRECTIONS

Big data has become a great technology that is used by all organizations to analyze, store data. The huge amount of data obtained or gathered from different resources like mobile devices, sensors, social media, satellites helps organization to improve their decision making and take their organization to a higher level. Few issues are addressed which have to be taken into account to improve the quality of information given to the customers. Bigdata makes use of Hadoop at present to handle large amount of data, but it is becoming insufficient. Effective techniques and tools should be developed to overcome the issues faced by big data.

Future scope of big data relies on: (Samiddha Mukherjee et al., 2016)

1. **Data Volume Increases Rapidly:** As new smart applications are evolving rapidly enormous amount of data, will be collected from various internet collected devices hence as the result the volume of data will grow rapidly.
2. **Improve the Ways to Analyze the Data:** Traditional SQL database will be outdated, and several tools like Spark will be rapidly evolving for analyzing the data.
3. **Real-Time Streaming of Data:** Users will be able to process the real-time data for decision making using programs like kafka and spark.
4. **Machine Learning:** The advent of machine learning, will be helpful for data preparation and prediction analysis of applications.
5. **Privacy:** Since, all the data are shared online, the major challenge will be privacy. Organizations has to find way through new policies and regulations to address privacy controls and procedures.
6. **Autonomous Agents:** Automatic agents and things like robots, autonomous vehicles, virtual personal assistants, and smart advisers will be a new trend for the people.
7. The data-as-a-service business model is growing rapidly used for predictions in whether forecast.
8. New algorithms to support big data methodologies have to be developed. Existing algorithms like Algorithmia, Data Xu, and Kaggle can be expected to grow and multiply.

CONCLUSION

With the advent of the digital age, the amount of data being generated, stored and shared has been on the rise. The benefits and limitations of accessing the data are arguable in view of the fact that this analysis may involve access and analysis of medical records, social media interactions, financial data, government records and genetic sequences. The requirement of an efficient and effective analytics service, applications, programming tools and frameworks has given birth to the concept of big data Processing and Analytics. Big data analytics has found application in several domains and fields. Some of these applications include Education, Health care, sports, gaming, security, Financial and business analytics. Thus, this chapter describes a collaborative study on applications, general issues and challenges in big data and cloud computing and the future scope where this big data will take the organization in the near future.

REFERENCES

Abaker, I., Yaqoob, A., & Mokhtar, G. (2015). The rise of "big data" on cloud computing: Review and open research issues. *Information Systems*, *47*, 98–115. doi:10.1016/j.is.2014.07.006

Abawajy, J. (2015). Comprehensive analysis of big data variety landscape. *International Journal of Parallel, Emergent and Distributed Systems, 30*(1).

Agarwal, S. (2013). *BlinkDB: Queries with Bounded Errors and Bounded Response Times on Very Large Data*. ACM. doi:10.1145/2465351.2465355

Bifet, A. (2013). Mining Big Data. In *Real Time*. Informatica.

Big data and privacy. (n.d.). Standard Law School-The center for internet and society.

Condie, T. (2010). *Online Aggregation and Continuous Query support in MapReduce. In SIGMOD*. ACM.

Eldawy, A. (2013). A Demonstration of Spatial Hadoop: An Efficient MapReduce Framework for Spatial Data. *Proceedings of the VLDB Endowment International Conference on Very Large Data Bases*, *6*(12). doi:10.14778/2536274.2536283

Emani, C. K., Cullot, N., & Nicolle, C. (2015). Understandable Big Data: A survey. *Computer Science Review*, *17*, 70–81. doi:10.1016/j.cosrev.2015.05.002

Gandomi, A., & Haider, M. (2015). Beyond the hype: Big data concepts, methods, and analytics. *International Journal of Information Management*, *35*(2), 137–144. doi:10.1016/j.ijinfomgt.2014.10.007

Hadi, Shnain, Hadishaheed, & Ahmad. (2015). Big data and five v's characteristics. *International Journal of Advances in Electronics and Computer Science*, *2*(1).

Harshawardhan, S., & Gadekar, P. (2014). A Review Paper on Big Data and Hadoop. *International Journal of Scientific and Research Publications, 4*(10).

Kaisler, S., & Armour, E. (2013). Big Data: Issues and Challenges Moving Forward. *46th Hawaii International Conference on System Sciences*. 10.1109/HICSS.2013.645

Kune, Konugurthi, Chillarige, & Buyya. (2016). *The anatomy of big data computing, Software: Practice and Experience*. Wiley Online Library.

Lee & Choi. (2011). Parallel Data Processing with MapReduce: A Survey. SIGMOD Record, 40(4).

Loshin, D. (2014). *Addressing Five Emerging Challenges of Big Data*. Progress Software.

Marcos, Calheiros, Bianchi, Nettoc, & Buyya. (2015). Big Data computing and clouds: Trends and future directions. *Journal of Parallel and Distributed Computing*, 79–80.

Mukherjee & Shaw. (2016). Big Data – Concepts, Applications, Challenges and Future Scope. *International Journal of Advanced Research in Computer and Communication Engineering, 5*(2).

Narooka. (2016). Paradigm Shift of Big-Data Application in Cloud Computing. *International Journal of Advanced Research in Computer and Communication Engineering*, *5*(5).

Pansarel, N. (2011). *Online Aggregation for Large MapReduce Jobs*. ACM.

Phaneendra, V. S. (2013). Big Data- solutions for RDBMS problems- A survey. *12th IEEE/IFIP Network Operations & Management Symposium (NOMS 2010)*.

Purcell. (2012). Big data using cloud computing. *Journal of Technology Research*.

Purcell. (2013). The emergence of big data technology and analytics. *Journal of Technology Research*.

Sabia, S. K. (2014). Applications of big Data: Current Status and Future Scope. *International Journal on Advanced Computer Theory and Engineering, 3*(5).

Security and Privacy in the Era of Big Data. (n.d.). The SMW, a Technological Solution to the Challenge of Data Leakage, renci ncds.

Sivarajah, U., Kamal, M. M., Irani, Z., & Weerakkody, V. (2017). Critical analysis of Big Data challenges and analytical methods. *Journal of Business Research*, *70*, 263–286. doi:10.1016/j.jbusres.2016.08.001

Swapnil, A. (2014). Understanding the big data problems and their solutions using hadoop and map-reduce. International Journal of Application or Innovation in Engineering & Management, 3, 3.

Troester, M. (2013). *Big Data Meets Big Data Analytics*. White Paper.

Umasri, M.L. (2014). *Mining Big Data: Current status and forecast to the future*. Academic Press.

Venkatesh, Perur, & Jaliha. (2015). A Study on Use of Big Data in Cloud Computing Environment. *International Journal of Computer Science and Information Technologies, 6*.

Ying Lu, C. H., & Swanson, D. (2010). Matchmaking: A New MapReduce Scheduling. *10th IEEE International Conference on Computer and Information Technology (CIT'10)*.

Chapter 10
Using Social Media for Healthcare Recruiting

Susan Swayze
The George Washington University, USA

Thomas M. Gronow
University of Colorado Hospital, USA

Johanna Sweet
Roanoke College, USA

ABSTRACT

Healthcare organizations have turned to social media to attract applicants to hard-to-fill positions. This chapter is focused on the use of social media as part of e-recruiting strategies in two healthcare organizations—one located in the Rocky Mountain region and the other in the Mid-Atlantic region. Interviews with human resources recruiters and administrators provided insight into the mechanisms by which healthcare organizations are utilizing social media to move the needle within their organizations.

INTRODUCTION

Technology has changed the way organizations function in a myriad of ways – one such way is the recruitment of job candidates. Gone are the days of jobs posted on bulletin boards and paper applications. Current recruiting efforts rely heavily on the Internet for most aspects of the recruitment process. Typically, organizations amplify job postings on their company websites and job boards with social media posts. This strategy reaches both active and passive job candidates – those currently

DOI: 10.4018/978-1-5225-5829-3.ch010

in the market for a new position and those that may apply given the right job opening. Human resource functions within organizations utilize data analytics to understand and target candidate pools and applicant streams and to optimize recruiting processes. This chapter explores the use of social media and specific e-recruiting techniques utilized by two healthcare organizations in the United States – one located in the Rocky Mountain region and the other in the Mid-Atlantic region.

BACKGROUND

Often Internet-facilitated employee recruitment is referred to as electronic recruiting or e-recruiting (Galanaki, 2002; Stone, Deadrick, Lukaszewski, & Johnson, 2015; Waddill & Marquardt, 2011; Wozniak, 2014). E-recruiting emerged as a recruiting tool in the mid-1990s and thus has been utilized as a human resource tool for more than 20 years. What began as a competitive strategy has become a necessity for healthcare organizations that are trying to fill critical shortages in specific positions, such as nurses. But e-recruiting represents more than a human resource tool or strategy, but a "change in the culture" (Capelli, 2001) because e-recruiting fundamentally changed the recruitment process from batch submission and processing of applications to continuous submission and processing more aligned with the 24-7 nature of the technology-enabled or online environment (Lee, 2005). E-recruiting also contributed to greater efficiency in the recruitment and application process as Holm (2010) found in their qualitative study of three Danish companies; e-recruiting replaced the traditional process consisting of unique tasks into a process where some tasks could be performed concurrently resulting in greater efficiency of the recruitment and application process.

The progression of e-recruiting has moved from augmenting traditional recruitment methods (e.g., company website job postings and application submission) to developing a recruitment strategy on the foundation of social networks (Priyadarshini, Kumar, & Jha, 2017). What constitutes e-recruiting is wide-ranging and consists of posting open positions on job search websites such as Indeed or Glassdoor to utilizing social media applications including Facebook, Linkedin, and Twitter as well as real-time recruitment activities such as virtual career fairs and interactive dialogs. Stone et al. (2015) suggest that approximately 90% of large organizations engage in e-recruiting and allow online applications. The rise of e-recruiting can be aligned with the growth of the Internet as well as the increased use of handheld Internet-enabled devices, such as cell phones and tablets (Mackelden, 2013).

Organizations benefit from e-recruiting strategies because they make the recruitment process more efficient and effective, and reach a larger pool of potential candidates resulting in a larger volume of applications for open positions. Through the use of social media sites, such as Linkedin, recruiters can connect with a large number of passive job seekers (those who may already be employed but may apply for a new position if they see one of interest), screen candidates, and send targeted position announcements when an applicable position becomes available which has led to greater efficiency in hiring (Boscai, 2017; Gupta, 2016; Roth, Bobko, Van Iddekinge, & Thatcher, 2016; Van Iddekinge, Lanivich, Roth, & Junco, 2016). Additionally, the use of social media for job search and application is particularly beneficial for organizations seeking to attract younger job seekers, such as Generation Y or Millennials, who conduct the majority of their daily business via cell phone.

However, not all perspectives regarding e-recruiting are positive. In their mixed methods study consisting of interviews and surveys of private sector and service sector organizations in the UK, Parry and Tyson (2008) found that e-recruiting yielded a larger volume of applications but that many of those individuals did not meet qualifications and/or did not have permits to work in the UK requiring greater effort to analyze the applications and screen out candidates. In another international mixed methods study, du Plessis & Frederick (2012) found that in Auckland, New Zealand's business industry, "With smiles comes tears, with every action comes an equal and opposite reaction. Some managers and recruiters think that e-recruitment has allowed them to get applicants faster and cheaper but it has equally reduced the applicant's ability to express his or her individuality and character … " (p. 16) suggesting that candidates who may actually be a good fit for a position may be missed in the application process. Stone et al. (2015) suggest another drawback to e-recruiting suggesting that it can be "extremely impersonal, passive, and create an artificial distance between applicants and organizations" (p. 218). This, the authors state, is a function of

> *… current technologies [that] use static, or one-way communication processes that merely provide information to applicants about job openings and enable them [to] apply for jobs online (e.g., websites, job boards). These technologies do not give applicants the opportunity to ask questions or interact with organizational members. As a result, applicants do not have the opportunity to communicate with actual organizational members or clarify the nature of jobs or the benefits of working for the organization. (Stone et al., 2015, p. 218)*

The authors suggest that emerging technologies (e.g., virtual career fairs, interactive dialogs) and social media will contribute to a more personal relationship between the candidate and organization during the job search and application process. Thus, the question becomes: How do healthcare organizations leverage the benefits of e-recruiting while minimizing the shortcomings?

METHODOLOGY

In order to explore the mechanisms by which healthcare organizations leverage e-recruiting techniques, a case study research methodology (Merriam, 1998; Stake, 1995; Yin, 2014) was utilized. Site visits at two healthcare organizations – one located in the Rocky Mountain region and the other in the Mid-Atlantic region – were conducted to gather information firsthand. Interviews with members of the human resource functions in both organizations as well as internal reports were analyzed to unpack the dynamic and nuanced world of e-recruiting.

The Rocky Mountain Healthcare Organization (pseudonym, hereafter referred to as RMHO) is a nationally recognized healthcare organization that serves more than one million patients each year. RMHO consists of more than 10,000 employees working in numerous hospitals and clinics in the Rocky Mountain region. RMHO is undergoing rapid growth with nearly 5,000 external hires last year. The organization utilizes Linkedin, Glassdoor, and Facebook as channels to advertise open positions and communicate what the organization is doing and producing. Social media is an amplifier – with every post of a position description, a virtual career event, or a white paper, RMHO's organizational identity is also disseminated. And when the post is liked or shared, RMHO's identity is further propagated. RMHO expertly utilizes social media to mediate the relationship between itself and the public sphere.

The Mid-Atlantic Healthcare Organization (pseudonym, hereafter referred to as MAHO) is the largest employer in its metropolitan region with more than 10,000 employees. MAHO is comprised of numerous hospitals located in urban and rural areas. Each year the organization fills approximately 3,000 positions from approximately 45,000 applications. MAHO utilizes a variety of channels to promote open positions and relies heavily on social media to increase exposure for hard to fill positions. For positions where demand far exceeds supply, such as nurses, MAHO recruiters look far outside their geographic area for applicants. Through targeted recruitment fueled by social media, MAHO identifies and connects with potential candidates through the most appropriate means given their generation and geographic location. By leveraging each recruitment channel for everything that it is has to offer, MAHO has been able to hire qualified candidates in today's highly competitive healthcare market.

The researchers conducted interviews with eight members of RMHO's human resource department. The interviewees included recruiters and the director. The interviews were audio-recorded and transcribed. At MAHO, an interview with an analyst and the director were conducted. The resulting interview transcripts were supplemented with data from internal reports. Given the homogeneity of the interviewees, saturation was achieved after conducting the eight interviews at

RMHO. Thus, the data collected from MAHO was utilized for comparison and contrast purposes. These data provide a glimpse into the use of social media by human resource departments within two U.S. healthcare organizations.

FINDINGS

Rocky Mountain Healthcare Organization (RMHO)

RMHO utilizes social media to simultaneously recruit candidates and improve its organizational identity. The organization believes that by increasing the awareness of the organization in the public sphere, the network of passive candidates is also increased leading to more efficient recruitment. As the director stated: "Recruitment is filling a job. Talent acquisition is having a long-term strategy to develop a talent pipeline. Recruitment is a part of talent acquisition. But yes, the goal is that when a job opens, you already have a candidate in mind." RMHO utilizes social media to portray the organization, not just a particular job opening, as stated here: "… the social media campaigns are not necessarily stating, 'We have this job opening.', but they're giving RMHO a presence … it's helping brand at the same time as attracting talent to the organization." The short-term goal is to drive individuals to engage with the organization (awareness) while the long-range goal is to move the candidate from awareness to action – to submit an application when there is a suitable position opening. And the reach is beyond the Rocky Mountain region as stated here by a recruiter, "Social media gives us the ability to not necessarily be focused on this local clientele, but to really have a national footprint, and to really build our name on a national scale versus a local scale."

E-Recruiting: I Think You Could Just Drop the "E".

When asked the percentage of recruitment that is fueled by social media, RMHO recruiters gave a wide range of responses, including 30%, 80%, and 100%. The variety of responses is due, in part, to differing definitions of e-recruiting and differing application channels. The 30% perspective of RMHO's recruitment was fueled by the belief that a direct link between viewing a page on social media and submitting an online application is needed to associate social media with recruitment. Whereas the 80% response was based on the belief that 80% of positions were posted on social media thereby making 80% of RMHO's recruitment fueled by social media[1]. The 100% response was based on the belief that candidates are influenced by RMHO's social media presence regardless of how they came to learn about a position.

Regardless of actual percentage, RMHO's use of e-recruiting is critical to their recruitment strategy. However, there are varying definitions of e-recruiting held by the RMHO recruiters:

I would say my perspective on e-recruiting is anything that we do, outreach through the Internet, whether it be special job boards, social media, careers page, Internet-based career fairs, really anything that utilizes Internet technology for outreach.

I think you could just drop the "E". I feel like it is recruiting now, all the tools that we have, everything's electronic, everything flows through our career site. I think with technology, I think it's just recruiting now. ... social media's really changed the game.

... anything online, anything where you're not shaking hands with a candidate at a job fair, or marketing something to someone at a restaurant, or in your day-to-day life, I think, would be e-recruiting.

E-recruiting to me is anything that I can put online to inform people and communities about RMHO and interact with people. There's really no limits. It might not be the only strategy, that's along with a ton of other things, but we're using it all of the time.

Although the definitions of e-recruiting vary, they converge around the theme of online information that is not personal or individualized. The varying definitions of e-recruiting and the varying percentages of recruitment fueled by social media within one human resource department in one healthcare organization suggest a lack of consensus among the individuals carrying out these functions. How might a consistent definition of e-recruiting and an aligned perspective around the role of social media contribute to greater recruitment successes?

From Keyboard Clicks to a Network of Candidates

The RMHO interviews revealed the importance of a network of passive candidates – those who are not necessarily actively searching for a position but may be interested in a suitable open position. RMHO recruiters spoke to the different functions among the social media sites which is summarized in this statement:

Indeed and Glassdoor are essentially a social media network for careers. [They] are for active candidates where interested people can search for positions and submit resumes. ... Facebook and Linkedin and Twitter, that's more where we can actually communicate. We can build those passive networks, we can have interactions, share stories about what RMHO is doing or growth, new hospitals we're opening, new executives that are coming into the organization, whatever it happens to be to really build our brand.

In describing the power of passive networks, RMHO recruiters stated:

A lot of those folks aren't looking for jobs – it's more of a passive search to where you're just building your networks and candidate pipeline. Maybe they're not interested now, they'll be interested in the future. It's really your ability to have that outreach and that impact on a national scale ... and to be able to touch so many people with a couple keyboard clicks. It's something that doesn't happen overnight, your network. The more positions that you have that are hard to fill, and consistently the same positions, you end up building those networks ...

Passive recruiting. In my experience, the phenomenal, the game changers, as we like to call them, they aren't necessarily looking. It's building those networks ... so that when we have another position, we already have essentially a little bit of a network that I can go to and say, not only are you guys interested, but is anyone in your network interested? It's just a snowball effect.

RMHO began implementing their social media strategy in 2015. This social media strategy resulted in an increased number of passive candidates ready to apply for open positions thereby increasing applicant flow and reducing time to fill. RMHO credited these passive networks for measurable increases in applicant flow and a reduction in time to fill. RMHO experienced a 10% increase in applicant flow from 2015-2016 and 30% from 2016-2017. Additionally, during 2015-2017 RMHO experienced a 15% reduction in time to fill resulting in an average of less than 40 days.

Facebook & Linkedin: Personal Accounts With Professional Possibilities

In one quarter alone, the RMHO Facebook page and Linkedin page had approximately 250,000 and 125,000 impressions respectively. The Facebook and Linkedin pages had approximately 750 and 1250 engagements (e.g., likes, comments, shares) respectively. It is through these engagements that RMHO leverages the power of social media as stated here – "... how social media's working for us, right, is really in the shares ... or tagging their friend or their family member."

Facebook was created for personal social networking purposes while Linkedin was created for professional social networking purposes. However, organizations utilize both sites for professional networking purposes. RMHO recruiters maintain personal social media accounts in addition to the career pages maintained by the organization itself. The recruiters describe their use of social media accounts for professional purposes – either to build their network of passive candidates and/or share information regarding the organization. Facebook, in particular, has both personal and professional uses. One recruiter described the positive intersection of the two on her Facebook account:

I get Facebook on my phone, every time I'm there scrolling through my feed, something about RMHO pops up, whether it's a patient story or career event that we're having. We also post the patients' stories and the employee stories. I like that we use all of our social media platforms for everything. If we can get our employees to be more active on social media, then I think it will definitely support our hiring strategies going forward.

While this recruiter is touting employee amplification, another recruiter seems conflicted regarding the use of Facebook for professional purposes:

I actually don't have a Facebook profile anymore. I've actually backed off of Facebook. It's a weird balance that you have to strike in HR. You have to be extremely politically correct, while at the same time not offending anybody, and not bringing any sort of politics and deleting posts that may or may not touch on any of these protected classes, like race, or religion, or sex, or gender, you know, whatever it might be. If anybody even goes there, you can't really even talk about it. It might be showing that you're having biases one way or another. And everybody loves to bring it up on Facebook, especially, I find. So, it's almost to the point where you would need two separate Facebooks, one for yourself as a professional, and one for yourself as a friend, and then it's like, oh, do I even friend my real friends on this professional one? So, Facebook, I'm off of there right now.

As organizations work toward an increased social media presence, employee use of personal accounts for professional purposes will need to be explored further. As recent media stories have shown, personal communication via social media can have negative professional consequences.

Information Flows Both Ways on Social Media

Social media is an interactive channel through which information is exchanged. Glassdoor is an example of a social media site that is a two-way conduit of information as described here:

But really what social media is is a way for people to share data and share information online. That's all it is. But I consider Glassdoor social media because this is a space where people are absolutely sharing information online. Specifically, what they're doing on Glassdoor is they are sharing ... current and former employees are sharing information about our company. If you go to Glassdoor, that's an anonymous way for employees to give feedback, current and former employees about their employer and what their salary was for future candidates to look at. As much as we do get constructive feedback on those things, we're doing better than everybody else, and its unsolicited feedback through Glassdoor. Glassdoor was started as more of a feedback [channel], you know? This company is great, this company isn't, but it is starting to become a source for people looking for positions as well.

Although Glassdoor began as a place for applicants and employees to rate organizations, organizations have begun to leverage Glassdoor's popularity by posting pictures, video content, and links to career fairs and job announcements. Thereby making Glassdoor a one-stop-shop for information on the organization as well as position openings. Since 2015 RMHO has been proactive with posting content to Glassdoor and monitoring ratings and reviews on the site. Through this targeted use of Glassdoor, RMHO's Glassdoor rating increased 25% between 2015 and 2017. Currently, the organization has the highest overall Glassdoor rating among competitors in their market.

For the most part, RMHO recruiters utilize Linkedin to build networks and connect with candidates – both active and passive. Recruiters and candidates alike utilize Linkedin to research each other as described here:

Every application I get, I look that person up on Linkedin, just to see if things are consistent, see who else they're connected to. It helps me understand their networks, who these people are connected with, what kind of stuff they're following, what kind of articles they're sharing, to really hone in what their true interests are ...

So we really have to be on top of it, because I rarely talk to a candidate who hasn't like ... you can tell they've looked at your Linkedin profile ... they know how long you've been here, what you do.

These are a few examples of how social media sites have been utilized as information sources of both candidates and recruiters. The following statement encapsulates a RMHO recruiter's perspective regarding the two-way capabilities of social media:

I think social media's becoming one of the biggest outlets for recruitment. I think that transcends every industry too, especially in healthcare though. It's arguably one of the most competitive industries in the nation right now. At the age of the Internet now, you've got candidates out there that can research us. They can see our profile, our brands. Social media is an outlet that people are using to advertise our culture. You know, so people can log into these accounts and see what we're doing internally, and who we are as a company. As much as we're looking at their resume and vetting them ... It works both ways, and it's only going to continue getting deeper and deeper.

Most social media communication is asynchronous where content is posted and viewed or responded to later. Even though RMHO relies heavily on social media for talent acquisition, all recruiters also engage in human-to-human interaction. This is especially important given the 24-7 nature of the Internet that has contributed to expectations of rapid response time: "I mean, the trend is that people want to hear back really quickly, regardless of how they're contacted, or regardless of how they contact us. Whether they send me a message on one of these platforms, whether it's Twitter, or Facebook, or Linkedin, or actually directly applying to our applicant tracking system, the goal is the same." Once recruiters identify potential candidates for positions through social media sites, they follow up with the potential candidates via phone and email. Recruiters state that they also cold call individuals who they believe might be a good fit for hard to fill positions – they feel that such calls communicate volumes, "... people are very appreciative. They can hear, when I talk about this organization, they can hear my passion for it. They can hear that I believe in this organization, and that helps sell something you couldn't necessarily communicate over an email." RMHO recruiters use real time, human-to-human engagement to bridge the gap between candidates and the organization in the job search and application process.

E-Recruiting Doesn't Necessarily Save Time

The RMHO case demonstrates effective use of social media supplemented with human-to-human interaction for talent acquisition in the highly competitive healthcare market. One recruiter spoke of the generational shift that contributed to the evolution of recruitment:

We are going through a generational shift right now to where a lot of our Baby Boomer generation is stuck in their ways, at the end of their career, maybe phasing out, and our Millennial generation wants immediate career growth and work-life balance. We're seeing a Millennial gap to where we, as a healthcare organization, or industry rather, have to adapt, because the old ways just don't work.

It is likely that the reliance on social media for recruiting is here to stay as the workforce continues to rely more heavily on technology for all aspects of their lives. However, e-recruiting may not necessarily save time as the maintenance of the social media strategy as well as human-to-human interaction is time intensive as described here:

... the posting and praying and just sending candidates is much faster than trying to engage with candidates and find passive candidates and email them and connect with them and call them and have them call you back. That takes a lot longer, but that's the requirement now. It is good and I think we get top candidates, we get better talent in our mix, but it doesn't necessarily save time.

Since technological advances are not stagnant, it is imperative that organizations keep pace with what is new or emerging:

So it's a little bit of trial and error, a little bit. Just what's working, because the thing that worked a month ago may not be working this month. And whatever is new and greater next week, I mean, we don't know what's coming beyond Facebook and Glassdoor, and always kind of being up on the new technology and where we can get our jobs out ... we have a lot of managers out there, just asking like these are the big things, are we utilizing them?

The assumption is that as the workforce becomes more reliant on emerging technologies that these technologies will become part of organizational recruitment strategies. RMHO will continue to seek out and incorporate technological advances that will enable them to continue to excel at talent recruitment.

Mid-Atlantic Healthcare Organization (MAHO)

MAHO relies less heavily on social media for recruitment when compared to RMHO. MAHO utilizes career fairs, college recruiting, radio ads, billboards, newspaper ads, postcards, and employee referrals in addition to the company website and specialized job boards to fill open positions and relies more on social media to raise awareness for hard to fill positions. In addition, the organization sees the benefit of social media for organizational branding that will indirectly contribute to recruitment, "And I think that the way we would utilize social media both for recruiting and then also as a brand, so there's two different aspects to that. We want to maintain brand integrity and make sure that we're representing a good company and our values. Also, that will help attract the right candidates." MAHO defines e-recruiting as "...

pretty much anything that's on the Internet ..." and acknowledges the usefulness of e-recruiting in talent recruitment:

I think the majority of people are finding out about jobs through the Internet, especially as we try to expand and reach out to other cities, other states, and even occasionally to other countries, like Canada. I mean it's necessary that we have a robust presence through a lot of mediums on the Internet. We know if we increase our presence that can readily influence people's impression of our organization, which then would lead to the recruitment piece.

In contrast to RMHO, when asked what percentage of recruitment is fueled by social media, MAHO could not provide a specific percentage and stated, "Well, I think that it's definitely growing. I don't know if there's a definitive percentage that we've allocated to that. I think some of the areas that we're looking at is ... social media in current day, it's just prevalent everywhere. So, sometimes it's hard to directly measure the full of it and that's something that we're really looking at, how to quantify it."

Glassdoor: An Eye Into the Organization

Whereas RMHO relies heavily on Facebook and Linkedin, MAHO's social media presence is largely focused on Glassdoor – "Folks used to all go to Facebook to look at the organization. Some do, but now they're going to Glassdoor." The RMHO analyst described how a few changes resulted in improved page views: "I started to add content to our Glassdoor site, it was just simply text before I got here. Just by adding a few photos, news, we've seen a 400% increase in traffic. About every week we have on average 2-3 people leaving a review ... every four seconds someone was actually looking at our Glassdoor page." In the most recent year, the number of page views nearly doubled from 3,500 to approximately 7,000. Data analytics showed that an individual may visit Glassdoor multiple times during their career search – "They look at it right as they're starting off. They come to Glassdoor for an application, but then they look after the application to determine how should I prepare for the interview."

Glassdoor aligns with MAHO's strategy of transparency – showing candidates what is it like to work at the organization. MAHO believes that such transparency leads to attracting more qualified candidates, especially when trying to attract Millennials:

In today's market people can go out and get reviews on literally everything that they purchase. So, when they're making a career decision, social media is going to be able to help impact that because they're going to be able to see reviews of our company. So we are dealing with informed consumers. They're used to having choices. That's just the way that the world is now shifting to. We shouldn't expect anything less of job seekers. They know they have opportunities out of various different areas. They're going to go out and they're going to look at reviews. They're going to make informed decisions because it's all right there for them. So, we need to make sure that we're providing an accurate depiction of what our company is and showing them the value proposition of why they should come work for us. I think even making sure that ... some people will self select out if they don't think that they're a good fit for the organization. I think that that's even a positive thing. If they can see the organization and think maybe they don't want to work here and they wouldn't be a good fit, then we're getting the most qualified candidates – the ones that are going to stay around and are interested in a career versus just simply a job that they can work at for a little while.

If you want to attract the Millennials, you need to be able to offer the reputation of your company, personally, how will that help them in their career? How is it rewarding? How is it meaningful? I think you get there and you get that brand and you have that impact by telling your stories, by sharing what's going on within your organization ... By telling them we have an opening, there's so many choices, that's not going to get it. So, by telling the stories, we open their eyes ... You know it's more awareness of MAHO and then they may decide to come to work here.

MAHO credits their enhanced Glassdoor presence as contributing to their recent increase in hires as stated here: "The time to fill has not moved in a positive direction and that's because of the shortages. It was a record-breaking year for external RN hires – nearly 500. So the volume of the hires has increased. However, the time to fill due to the challenges in the market has not been reduced." Thus, even though time to fill has remained constant at near the healthcare average, MAHO considers their recruitment efforts successful because they were able to fill a larger number of hard to fill positions while maintaining a competitive time to fill metric.

Real Time Engagement in the 24-7 Environment

Like RMHO, MAHO feels the pressure of the 24-7 nature of the Internet. Candidates expect rapid responses and interaction from recruiters just as they would from friends on social media. MAHO implemented a Live Chat capability in order to provide real time engagement with potential candidates. Live Chat is available on all of the recruiters' computers. When a potential candidate clicks on Live Chat while on the company website, recruiters are alerted to connect with the candidate and begin a conversation. But the connectivity does not stop there. Leveraging data analytics,

MAHO recognized peak activity on the website outside of the standard office hours. To convert this activity into applications, MAHO created a Live Chat opportunity during this after hours, peak time. The organization makes a recruiter available during this after hours time period for the sole purpose of responding to Live Chat inquiries. MAHO credits Live Chat with converting interests into applications for hard to fill positions as stated here:

Since we realized that candidates really want to reach out and immediately be contacted with people we've implemented Live Chat for our candidates. For our high demand roles, like RNs, they're able to immediately connect with an RN recruiter and start talking about a job. And they can send their resume directly with dragging and dropping right to the recruiter there. We've seen that they can set up an interview within 15 minutes for a high demand role.

MAHO recruiters have engaged in nearly 1,000 chat sessions since implementing Live Chat earlier in the year.

MAHO provides another opportunity for real time engagement – texting recruiters.

We text back and forth ... Millennials, that's how they like to communicate ... we'll text for a while and then we try and convert them to maybe a phone call after a while. They want to do the whole selection process through a text ... We've added that to our job descriptions in saying text our recruiters as well. I realize nurses don't work a standard 9-5 job. If we can just get them in the door and they can just send a quick text after they're done with their shift or on a quick lunch break, then we can initiate conversation and go from there. So, it's really just getting our foot in the door with them.

The text option of connecting with recruiters provides another channel by which candidates for hard to fill positions can connect with recruiters. Unlike the after hours Live Chat that has a scheduled recruiter, candidates can text recruiters at all hours. As discussed in regard to RMHO and Facebook use, the lack of boundary between recruiters and candidates can be problematic. Add to this the 24-7 nature of texting to the equation and the problems may multiply. Providing real time engagement opportunities for candidates is likely to be a strategic advantage but may contribute to stress among recruiters.

MAHO describes their overall strategy as "candidate centric" and tailors the job search and application process to the candidate. This strategy results in a greater mix of mediums for advertising open job positions than RMHO and less of a reliance on e-recruiting. However, MAHO's real time engagement efforts for hard to fill positions are innovative ways to convert interested candidates into applicants. The RMHO director stated, "You may think you have it figured out … what works today, may not work tomorrow." and thus the organization is continually investigating innovative techniques that will help the organization fill open positions.

CONCLUSION

Today's healthcare recruitment is undeniably enhanced by the effective utilization of social media and e-recruitment. This chapter is focused on two healthcare organizations that utilize these tools as their primary means of finding candidates. Both healthcare organizations utilize social media applications for recruitment and talent acquisition as well as human-to-human interaction and real time engagement to convert potential candidates into applicants. And both human resource functions rely more heavily on e-recruitment and social media to identify and attract candidates for hard to fill positions such as nurses. The organizations, although similar in size and function, differ in their level of engagement with social media and real time dialog with candidates. Each case provides insight into the dynamics and nuances associated with e-recruitment and social media use in healthcare recruitment. There is no way to know what is on the horizon for the use of social media and e-recruitment in healthcare recruiting. However, it is likely that there will be greater use of online applications focused on human-to-human interaction and real time engagement as these are enhancements to the technology-infused talent recruitment process.

Future studies of social media and e-recruitment in healthcare organizations can focus on macro level issues such as changing societal and corporate views regarding the safety of online information (e.g., How will cyber threats affect the sharing of personal, individual information online?), organizational level issues surrounding work-life balance (e.g., How will organizations protect recruiters' personal time given the encroachments made possible by accessibility?), and micro level issues such as individuals' relationship with technology and the application process (e.g., How might one's gender, race, or culture influence engagement with social media for job application purposes?).

REFERENCES

Boscai, B. (2017). *The evolution of e-recruitment: the introduction of online recruiter*. Retrieved December 1, 2017 from http://real.mtak.hu/54549/1/162_Management_and_Organization-Pearson- 2017jún08-DOI_CrossRef-2017jún13f.pdf

Cappelli, P. (2001). Making the Most of on-Line Recruiting. *Harvard Business Review*, *79*(3), 139–146. PMID:11246921

du Plessis, A. J., & Frederick, H. (2012). Effectiveness of e-recruiting: Empirical evidence from the Rosebank business cluster in Auckland, New Zealand. *Science Journal of Business Management*, *126*, 1–21.

Gupta, Y. (2016). Literature review on e-recruitment: A step towards paperless HR. *International Journal of Advance Research in Computer Science and Management Studies*, *4*(1), 79–84.

Holm, A. (2010). The effect of e-recruitment on the recruitment process: evidence from case studies of three Danish MNCs. *Proceedings of the 3rd European Academic Workshop on Electronic Human Resource Management*, 91–111.

Lee, I. (2005). The evolution of e-recruiting: A content analysis of Fortune 100 career web sites. *Journal of Electronic Commerce in Organizations*, *3*(3), 57–68. doi:10.4018/jeco.2005070104

Mackelden, L. (2013). *How do big recruiters recruit online?* Retrieved December 1, 2017 from http://www.onrec.com/news/features/onrec-online-recruitmentmagazine-feature-how-do-big-recruiters-recruit-online

McCarthy, J., Bauer, T., Truxillo, D., Anderson, N., Costa, A., & Ahmed, S. (2017). Applicant perspectives during selection: A review addressing "so what?" "what's new?" and "where to next?". *Journal of Management*, *43*(6), 1693–1725. doi:10.1177/0149206316681846

Merriam, S. B. (1998). *Qualitative Research and Case Study Applications in Education*. San Francisco, CA: John Wiley & Sons.

Parry, E., & Tyson, S. (2008). An analysis of the use and success of online recruitment methods in the UK. *Human Resource Management Journal*, *18*(3), 257–274. doi:10.1111/j.1748-8583.2008.00070.x

Poisat, P., & Mey, M. (2017). Electronic human resource management: Enhancing or entrancing? *SA Journal of Human Resource Management*, *15*(0), 858. doi:10.4102ajhrm.v15i0.858

Priyadarshini, C., Kumar, Y. L. N., & Jha, R. R. (2017). Employer attractiveness through social media: A phenomenological study. *Qualitative Report*, *22*(4), 969–983.

Roth, P. L., Bobko, P., Van Iddekinge, C. H., & Thatcher, J. B. (2016). Social media in employee-selection-related decisions: A research agenda for uncharted territory. *Journal of Management*, *42*(1), 269–298. doi:10.1177/0149206313503018

RoyChowdhury, T., & Srimannarayana, M. (2013). Applicants' perceptions on online recruitment procedures. *Management and Labour Studies*, *38*(3), 185–199. doi:10.1177/0258042X13509737

Stake, R. E. (1995). *The Art of Case Study Research*. Thousand Oaks, CA: Sage Publications.

Stone, D., Deadrick, D., Lukaszewski, K., & Johnson, R. (2015). The influence of technology on the future of human resource management. *Human Resource Management Review*, *25*(2), 216–231. doi:10.1016/j.hrmr.2015.01.002

Van Iddekinge, C. H., Lanivich, S. E., Roth, P. L., & Junco, E. (2016). Social media for selection? Validity and adverse impact potential of a Facebook-based assessment. *Journal of Management*, *42*(7), 1811–1835. doi:10.1177/0149206313515524

Waddill, D. D., & Marquardt, M. J. (2011). *The e-HR Advantage: The complete handbook for technology-enabled human resources*. Boston, MA: Nicholas Brealey.

Wozniak, J. (2014). On e-recruitment and four ways of using its methods. *Proceedings of the 8th International Scientific Conference*.

Yin, R. K. (2014). *Case Study Research: Design and Methods*. Thousand Oaks, CA: Sage Publications.

ENDNOTE

1 RMHO occasionally uses print media, newspaper ads and flyers, for certain jobs at particular locations.

Chapter 11
Beyond SOA and REST for Distributed Application Integration

José Carlos Martins Delgado
Universidade de Lisboa, Portugal

ABSTRACT

The fundamental problem of distributed application integration is reducing application coupling as much as possible while still meeting the minimum interoperability requirements. Service-oriented architecture (SOA) and representational state transfer (REST) are the most used architectural styles to deal with this problem. This chapter performs a comparative study of these styles and shows that, while both solve basic interoperability, neither of them minimizes coupling, since data description schemas are shared by the interacting applications (symmetric interoperability). SOA is oriented towards behavior (services) and REST towards state (structured resources). Services have no structure and resources have a fixed service. This chapter proposes a new architectural style, structured services, that combines the best characteristics of SOA and REST (services can have structure and resources can implement application-specific services), while using asymmetric interoperability (schema compatibility is based on structural compliance and conformance) to minimize application coupling.

INTRODUCTION

A software application is usually complex and programming it involves modeling the entities of the problem domain by modules that need to interact to achieve the goals that justify the purpose of that application. In addition, the context and specifications of the problem are dynamic and typically change frequently. Complexity and

DOI: 10.4018/978-1-5225-5829-3.ch011

changeability have always been a huge challenge for software developers, affecting not only applications but also virtually all aspects of computer science.

The object-oriented modeling paradigm, in particular through the Unified Modeling Language (UML) (Dennis, Wixom, & Tegarden, 2015), has long been recognized as an adequate solution to these difficulties. The main tenet is to divide and conquer complexity by structuring programs into objects, according to principles that tend to limit the impact of a change, by reducing dependencies between objects, and allowing them to be incrementally adapted through inheritance. Table 1 describes the main relevant principles.

Ideally, one would like to extend these principles to interacting objects in a distributed environment. Unfortunately, most of the advantages of the object-oriented paradigm, namely inheritance and polymorphism, stem from the fact that the lifecycles of the objects are coupled, either at compile or link time, which is not the case for distributed applications. These are loosely coupled and evolve independently, but need nonetheless to interact and cooperate towards some common goals. As one application changes, all the others that use it must also be adapted, in order to maintain interoperability.

There is no universally accepted definition of interoperability, since its meaning can vary accordingly to the perspective, context or domain under consideration. Nevertheless, the ISO/IEC/IEEE 24765 standard (ISO, 2010) provides the seemingly most cited definition of interoperability: "*the ability of two or more systems or components to exchange information and to use the information that has been exchanged*".

Table 1. Main principles of object-oriented modeling

Id	Name	Description
P1	Least semantic gap	The entities in the problem and solution spaces should have a one to one mapping, by modeling each problem entity with a solution entity, with both state and related behavior, and corresponding structures.
P2	Information hiding	There must be a clear separation between interface (syntax and semantics) and its implementation. This reduces the change propagation effect. A change in one object affects those that use it only if its interface is affected.
P3	Substitution	An object X should be able to be used with its own implementation wherever an object Y is expected, as long as X conforms to Y, a form of polymorphism.
P4	Non-duplication of information	Objects with similar features (state or behavior) should factor these features and share a common definition, usually implemented by inheritance, instead of duplicating it.
P5	Open-closed	An object should be closed, so that it can be used, but at the same time open, so that it can be changed without having to close it. This means that it is possible to tune up objects by redefining operations, even if the source code is not available.

Therefore, distributed interoperability asserts the ability of two or more distributed systems to meaningfully understand each other's messages. Message interoperability, at the data level, has been solved with data description languages such as Extensible Markup Language (XML) (Fawcett, Ayers, & Quin, 2012) and JavaScript Object Notation (JSON) (Bassett, 2015), in which a schema, describing the data in a message, needs to be shared between the sender and receiver of that message.

The two main solutions for application interoperability, at the interface level, are based on the Service-Oriented Architecture (SOA) (Erl, Merson, & Stoffers, 2017) and Representational State Transfer (REST) (Fielding, Taylor, Erenkrantz, Gorlick, Whitehead, Khare, & Oreizy, 2017) architectural styles. Although both SOA and REST support distributed interoperability and can be used as the base to develop distributed applications, their underlying philosophies are rather different (Delgado, 2013).

The most common technologies that instantiate these architectural styles are Web Services (Zimmermann, Tomlinson, & Peuser, 2012) for SOA and RESTful APIs (Pautasso, 2014) for REST. Neither of these technologies satisfies adequately the principles enunciated by Table 1:

- Web Services satisfy reasonably only P1 (and just in terms of interface, not structure) and P2. The fact that the interacting applications must share the WSDL file (with its data schemas), which describes the service implemented by the object, hampers the other principles in SOA.
- RESTful APIs satisfy P1 only if the structure of the resources is similar to the structure of the problem's domain and the actions have essentially a CRUD (Create, Read, Update, Delete) nature, i.e., data structure manipulation. P2 is satisfied only partially, since it exposes structure. Substitution (P3) seems to be satisfied, since all resources have the same interface, but this can easily be done wrongly in a blind, not model-driven manner, precisely due to the universal interface. The need to share data schemas between the interacting applications greatly limits, in practice, the benefits of a universal interface.

Therefore, the main problems to solve are:

- Having to choose between SOA-based and REST-based solutions, each with its pros and cons. It should be possible to combine the two architectural styles, increasing the advantages and minimizing the disadvantages.
- Having to share data schemas. This not only introduces more coupling than actually needed (if not all values supported by a schema are used) but also hampers principles P3, P4 and P5.

This chapter proposes a new architectural style, Structural Services, with the goal of contributing to solve these problems.

The rest of this chapter is organized as follows. After reviewing the main existing technologies, the chapter establishes the fundamental problem of application integration, in terms of interoperability and coupling. The most common architectural styles for application integration, SOA and REST, are discussed and compared. The main characteristics of the proposed architectural style, Structural Services, are described, after envisaging a way of reducing coupling by using asymmetric interoperability based on compliance and conformance, as well as defining a model to encompass services, resources and processes. This new style is compared with SOA and REST. Finally, the chapter lays down the lines of future research and draws some conclusions.

BACKGROUND

Application integration requires the alliance of interoperability and low coupling to achieve effective cooperation. It has been studied in domains such as enterprise cooperation (Popplewell, 2014; Rezaei, Chiew, & Lee, 2014), e-government services (Sharma & Panigrahi, 2015), military operations (Hussain, Mehmood, Haq, Alnafjan, & Alghamdi, 2014), cloud computing (Zhang, Wu, & Cheung, 2013), healthcare applications (Robkin, Weininger, Preciado, & Goldman, 2015), digital libraries (Agosti, Ferro, & Silvello, 2016) and metadata (Chen, 2015).

Historically, interoperability has been the main goal in Web-based distributed systems, whereas coupling has been one of the top concerns in software engineering. Software development methods emphasize changeability and agility, which means structuring components of an application so that a change somewhere affects as little as possible the remaining components, and can be implemented in a very short time. Interoperability within an application is the easy part. Type names and inheritance are shared and there is usually a single programming language.

Distributed applications are a different matter. Interoperability is not as simple, since interacting applications are developed, compiled, and linked independently. This usually means different type names, inheritance hierarchies, programming languages, execution platforms and data formats. In this context, coupling has been treated as a best-effort endeavor, after achieving interoperability.

The two main technological solutions for distributed interoperability, Web Services (Zimmermann, Tomlinson, & Peuser, 2012) and RESTful APIs (Pautasso, 2014), are based on data description languages such as XML (Fawcett, Ayers, & Quin, 2012) and JSON (Bassett, 2015). Although they have been able to connect independent and heterogeneous systems, supporting distributed application interoperability, they are not brilliant solutions from the point of view of coupling.

The scientific community has engaged in a continuing debate over which architectural style, SOA (Erl, Merson, & Stoffers, 2017) or REST (Fielding, Taylor, Erenkrantz, Gorlick, Whitehead, Khare, & Oreizy, 2017), is more adequate for specific classes of applications. The literature comparing these styles is vast (Bora & Bezboruah, 2015; Kumari & Rath, 2015), usually with arguments more on technology issues than on conceptual and modeling arguments. There are also several proposals to integrate SOA and RESTful services (Dahiya, & Parmar, 2014; Sungkur, & Daiboo, 2015; Sungkur, & Daiboo, 2016; Thakar, Tiwari, & Varma, 2016).

XML-based interoperability, essential for Web Services, assumes that both interacting applications share the same schema, namely in WSDL documents and other data schemas. XML Schema and other schema languages are complex enough to award additional coupling concerns. Changing something in a schema affects all applications that use it, both servers and clients, entailing a significant coupling and reducing changeability.

Applications based on RESTful APIs follow the REST architectural style, developed by Fielding (2000), who claims that this style reduces coupling because the client does not depend on the server's specification, since all it needs to do is to traverse the structured data representation of the server, by following its links (URIs). If a change occurs at the server, it changes the data structured returned but, as long as the data types are the same, the client will still be able to traverse it without modification. However, this decoupling is limited to protocol and data syntax. The interacting applications still depend on the shared knowledge about the data types, not to mention higher-level semantics and behavior.

Several metrics have been proposed to assess the maintainability of service-based distributed applications, based essentially on structural features, namely for service coupling, cohesion and complexity (Babu, & Darsi, 2013). Other approaches focus on dynamic coupling, rather than static, with metrics for assessing coupling during program execution (Geetika, & Singh, 2014). There are also approaches trying to combine structural coupling with other levels of coupling, such as semantics (Alenezi, & Magel, 2014).

Compliance (Tran, Zdun, Oberortner, Mulo, & Dustdar, 2012) and conformance (Khalfallah, Figay, Barhamgi, & Ghodous, 2014) are concepts that can be used as the foundation mechanisms to ensure partial interoperability and thus minimize coupling.

THE PROBLEM OF APPLICATION INTEGRATION

Distributed Application Interaction

Distributed interoperability implies that interacting applications can use some network to send each other messages, which both sender and receiver need to understand and react to appropriately. A given application, in the role of server, publishes the set of messages that it is able to respond to, which defines the interface of the functionality offered by that application (its Application Programming Interface – API). In the role of client, another application may send one of the acceptable messages to the server and invoke the corresponding functionality. Applications can also express their APIs in terms of exposed features, such as operations. Each operation can accept its own set of messages.

Figure 1 illustrates a typical interaction, initiated by the client, which sends a request message to the server through the interconnecting network. This may cause the provider to answer with a response message, upon executing the request.

The server needs to be able to understand the client's request and to react and respond according to what the client expects. Otherwise, the interaction will not produce the intended effects.

In a distributed environment, interacting applications evolve independently from each other and cannot rely on shared data type names or inheritance hierarchies. However, exchanged messages must be correct and meaningful in both the contexts of the interacting applications. The goal of achieving a simple interaction such as the one depicted in Figure 1 can be decomposed into the following objectives:

- There must be an addressable interconnecting network and a message-based protocol, supporting a request-response message exchange pattern.
- The server needs to validate the request message, ensuring that it is one of those acceptable by the server's API. This validation must be done both at the syntactic and semantic levels.

Figure 1. Message-based interaction between two distributed applications

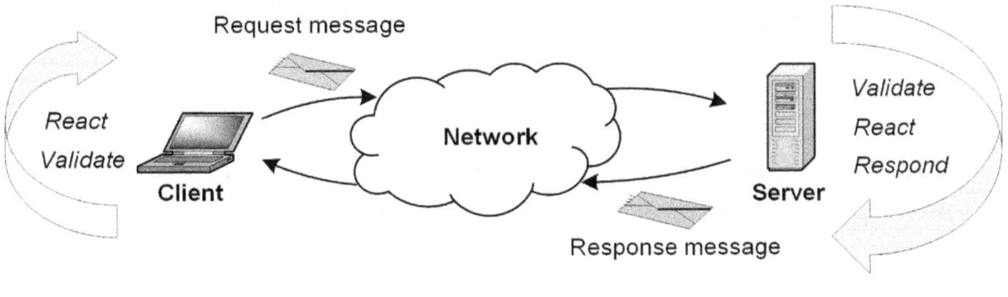

- The reaction of the server and the corresponding effects, as a consequence of executing the request message, must fulfil the expectations of the client regarding that reaction. The server needs to do what the client expects. This is a higher level than semantics, designated *pragmatics* (Athanasopoulos, 2017).
- The client needs to validate the eventual response message, ensuring that it is one of those acceptable by the client as a response. The validation must be done both at the syntactic and semantic levels.
- The client must react to the response appropriately, fulfilling the purpose of the server in sending that response, as well as completing the purpose of the client in initiating the interaction. Again, this is done at the pragmatic level.

This means that both request and response messages need to be validated and understood (correctly reacted upon) by the application that receives it. In addition, many other factors need to be taken into account as well, such as performance, scalability, reliability, and security, but this chapter focus on two main aspects:

- **Interoperability**: Guaranteeing that a service understands the requests of another and reacts according to what is expected.
- **Coupling**: Mutual dependencies between services, with the goal of reducing them as much as possible, to avoid unnecessary constraints to the evolution and variability of services.

A Layered Model of Interoperability

Most interoperability technologies, such as Web Services (Zimmermann, Tomlinson, & Peuser, 2012) and RESTful APIs (Pautasso, 2014), usually consider only the syntactic format of messages, or at most the semantics of its terms (Verborgh, Harth, Maleshkova, Stadtmüller, Steiner, Taheriyan, & Van de Walle, 2014). However, the ability to meaningfully interact involves higher levels, including naturally behavior. Table 2 establishes a linearized systematization of interoperability in several levels of abstraction. The higher levels are particularly relevant when complex, enterprise-class applications are involved.

The abstraction levels of interoperability can be described as follows:

- **Symbiotic:** Expresses the purpose and intent of two interacting applications to engage in a mutually beneficial agreement. This can entail a tight coordination under a common governance, a joint-venture agreement, a collaboration involving a partnership agreement, or a mere value chain cooperation.

Table 2. Abstraction levels and layers of interoperability in an application interaction

Abstraction level	Layers	Description
Symbiotic (purpose and intent)	• Coordination • Alignment • Collaboration • Cooperation	• Motivations to interact, with varying levels of mutual knowledge of governance, strategy and goals.
Pragmatic (reaction and effects)	• Contract • Workflow • Interface	• Management of the effects of the interaction at the levels of choreography, process and service.
Semantic (meaning of content)	• Inference • Knowledge • Ontology	• Interpretation of a message in context, at the levels of rule, known application components and relations, and definition of concepts.
Syntactic (notation of representation)	• Structure • Predefined type • Serialization	• Representation of application components, in terms of composition, primitive components and serialization format of messages.
Connective (transfer protocol)	• Messaging • Routing • Communication • Physics	• Lower level formats and network protocols involved in transferring a message from the context of the sender to that of the receiver.

- **Pragmatic:** The effect of an interaction between a client and a server is the outcome of a contract, which is implemented by a choreography that coordinates processes, which in turn implement workflow behavior by orchestrating service invocations.
- **Semantic:** Interacting applications must be able to understand the meaning of the content of the messages exchanged, both requests and responses. This implies interoperability in rules, knowledge and ontologies, so that meaning is not lost when transferring a message from the context of the sender to that of the receiver.
- **Syntactic:** Deals mainly with form, rather than content. Each message has a structure, composed of data (primitive resources) according to some structural definition (its schema). Data need to be serialized to be sent over the channel as messages.
- **Connective:** The main objective is to transfer a message from the context of one resource to the other's, regardless of its content. This usually involves enclosing that content in another message with control information and implementing a message protocol over a communications network according to its own protocol, possibly involving routing gateways.

All these abstraction levels are always present in all application interactions, even the simplest ones. However, what happens in practice is that some of these levels are catered for *tacitly* (implicitly assumed) or *empirically* (explicitly hidden behind some existing specification).

It is also important to realize that all these interoperability levels constitute an expression of application coupling. On the one hand, two uncoupled applications (with no interactions between them) can evolve freely and independently, which favors adaptability, changeability and even reliability (if one fails, there is no impact on the other). On the other hand, applications need to interact to cooperate towards common or complementary goals, which means that some degree of previously agreed mutual knowledge must exist. The more they share with the other, the easier interoperability becomes, but the greater coupling gets.

The Meaning of Coupling

Any interaction entails some form of dependency, stemming from the knowledge required to establish that interaction in a meaningful way (Figure 1), which translates to application coupling that expresses not only how much an application depends on (is affected by changes in) the servers it uses but also how much its clients depend on (are affected by changes in) it.

Coupling can be assessed by the fraction of the features of one application that impose constraints on another application. Features can be operations, data types, semantic terms, and so on. From the point of view of a given application, two coupling metrics can be defined:

- C_F (*forward coupling*), which expresses how much an application is dependent on its servers:

$$C_F = \frac{\sum_{i \in S} \frac{Us_i}{Ts_i \cdot N_i}}{|S|} \tag{1}$$

where:

S - Set of servers that this application uses, with $|S|$ as its cardinality

Us_i - Number of features that this application uses in server i

Ts_i - Total number of features that server i has

N_i - Number of servers with which this application is compatible as a client, in all uses of features of server i by this application

- C_B (*backward coupling*), which expresses how much impact an application has on its clients:

$$C_B = \frac{\sum_{i \in C} \frac{Uc_i}{Tc \cdot M}}{|C|} \tag{2}$$

where:

C - Set of clients that use this application as a server, with $|C|$ as its cardinality
Uc_i - Number of features of this application that client i uses
Tc - Total number of features that this application has
M - Number of known applications that are compatible with this application and can replace it, as a server

These coupling metrics yield values between 0, expressing completely unrelated and independent applications, and 1, in the case of completely dependent applications, constrained by all features.

Equation (1) indicates that the existence of alternative servers to a given application reduces its forward coupling C_F, since more applications with which this application is compatible, as a client, dilute the dependencies. On the other hand, equation (2) means that having alternatives to an application, in its role as a server, reduces the overall system dependency on it, thereby reducing the impact that application may have on its potential clients (its backward coupling C_B). Both equations (1) and (2) also express the fact that a smaller fraction of features used induces a lower coupling.

Alternative server applications can be found not only by designing and building them on purpose, but also by reducing the fraction of features needed for compatibility to the minimum required by the interaction between applications. The smaller the number of constraints, the greater the probability of finding applications that satisfy them.

Therefore, both factors on which coupling depends (the fraction of features used, as a client, and the number of server alternatives available) work in the same direction, with the first reinforcing the second. Reducing coupling means reducing the fraction of features used, or the knowledge of one application about another.

Technologies such as Web Services (Zimmermann, Tomlinson, & Peuser, 2012) and RESTful APIs (Pautasso, 2014) constitute poor solutions in terms of coupling, since Web Services rely on sharing a schema (a WSDL document) and RESTful

APIs are usually based on previously agreed upon media types. These technologies support the distributed interoperability problem, but do not solve the coupling problem.

The Fundamental Problem of Application Integration

Interoperability and coupling are two facets of the same problem, application integration, which revolves around two conflicting goals, interoperability (mutual knowledge is required for cooperation) and decoupling (mutual knowledge implies dependencies that may hamper evolution).

The fundamental problem of application integration is therefore how to provide *at most* the minimum coupling possible while ensuring *at least* the minimum interoperability requirements. The main goal is to ensure that each interacting application knows just enough about the others to be able to interoperate with them but no more than that. Unnecessary dependencies and constraints should be avoided. This is consistent with the information hiding principle (P2) in Table 1, which itself is an instance of the principle of least knowledge (Hendricksen, 2014).

Existing data interoperability technologies, such as XML and JSON, assume that interacting applications share the same message schema, as illustrated by Figure 2. This can be referred to as *symmetric interoperability* and is reminiscent of the first days of the Web and HTML documents, in which the client read the document produced by the server and both needed to use the same data specification. Today, data have been separated from their specification (schema), but both client and server still work on the same information. Coupling has not diminished.

Figure 2. Schema sharing in symmetric message-based interaction between two distributed applications

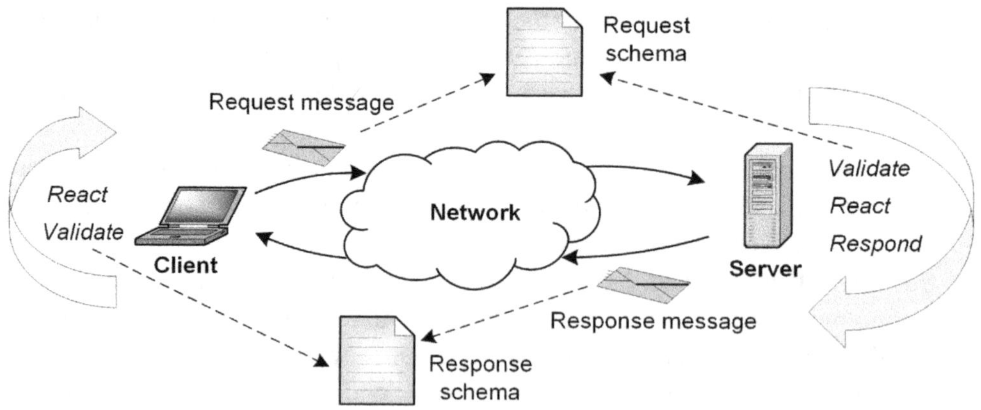

The problem, as hinted by equations (1) and (2), is that a server may need to serve several potentially different clients and a client may need to send requests to several potentially different servers. Sharing a schema couples both client and server for the whole set of messages that the schema can describe, even if the client only uses a subset of the admissible requests and the server only responds with a subset of the admissible responses.

The net effect of this symmetry is that in many cases client and server are more coupled than needed and changes in one application may very likely imply changing the other as well. Contributing to change these state of affairs is one of the major goals of this chapter.

Analysys of SOA and REST as Integration Solutions

The main integration solutions in use today are based on the SOA (Erl, Merson, & Stoffers, 2017) and REST (Fielding, Taylor, Erenkrantz, Gorlick, Whitehead, Khare, & Oreizy, 2017) architectural styles. An architectural style can be defined as a collection of design patterns, guidelines, and best practices to design the architecture of a system (Sharma, Kumar, & Agarwal, 2015). Each architectural style has an underlying modeling paradigm, which serves as a guiding tenet.

Although this section concentrates on SOA and REST, Table 3 illustrates the main characteristics of several architectural styles, also relevant to the discussion (Delgado, 2013).

Table 3. Main characteristics of several relevant architectural styles

Style	Brief description	Examples of characteristics or constraints
Object-Oriented	Applications follow the Object-Oriented paradigm.	• Application modules are modeled as classes. • References are pointers. • Reactions discretized into operations. • Polymorphism based on inheritance.
Distributed	Interacting applications have independent lifecycles.	• References are global, not local pointers. • Type checking cannot be name-based. • Different applications may use different technologies.
SOA	Style similar to Object-Oriented, but with distributed constraints.	• Services (interfaces of applications) have no structure. • Each application has its own interface. • No polymorphism. • Integration based on common schemas and ontologies.
Process	Behavior modeled as orchestrations and choreographies.	• Services are the units of behavior. • A process is an orchestration of services. • Processes must obey the rules of choreographies.
REST	Resources have structure but a fixed service.	• Clear distinction of the client and server roles. • Resources have a common set of operations. • Stateless interactions.

SOA is essentially the extension of the object-oriented paradigm to the distributed application world, losing some of the principles enunciated in Table 1. REST is essentially the extension of the WWW paradigm (client-server stateless interaction, fixed set of server operations) to generic application integration, again with limitations on the support of those principles. The Process architectural style models behavior as processes, which orchestrate the invocation of services (implemented using either SOA or REST).

SOA is easy to grasp, since it constitutes a natural evolution of the object-oriented style, with which analysts and programmers are already familiar. However, its Web Services instantiation, with WSDL, XML Schema and SOAP, is complex to use, especially without adequate tools that usually automate or hide most of the development process.

REST can be comparatively harder to master at first, in particular for people with an object-oriented mindset, who tend to slide to the probably more familiar RPC (Remote Procedure Call) style (Kukreja & Garg, 2014), with operation parameters instead of dynamic resource references, something long criticized by Fielding (2008), the original proponent of REST. On the other hand, its instantiation with HTTP is relatively straightforward to use, even without elaborate tools, since what is involved is essentially plain HTTP messaging.

The motivations behind the appearance of each style can be described in the following way:

- SOA appeared in the context of enterprise integration, with the main goal of achieving interoperability between existing enterprise applications with the then emerging XML-based technologies. It was a natural evolution of the object-oriented style, now in a distributed environment and with large-grained resources to integrate. Therefore, the emphasis was put on modeling applications as black boxes, exposing their external functionality with an interface composed of a set of operations, application dependent. Internal structure was avoided, as a measure to reduce coupling by applying the information hiding principle (P2 in Table 1).
- REST appeared in the context of Web applications, as a systematization of the underlying model of the Web and with scalability as the most relevant goal, since interoperability had already been solved by HTML (and, later, XML) and HTTP. As originally proposed by Fielding (2000), REST is based on six constraints. The most relevant are stateless interactions (only the client maintains the interaction state) and uniform interface (all resources have a service with the same set of operations, with variability on structure and with links to resources, rather than on service interface). These constraints have

decoupling as their main motivation, to support scalability. When potentially thousands of clients connect to a server, server applications need to scale and to evolve as needed and as independently as possible from the clients.

SOA is guided by behavior and REST by representation of state. In UML terminology, modeling with SOA favors a static class diagram, to specify which services are used and the set of operations provided by each, and a sequence diagram to specify their interactions along time. On the other hand, REST interactions can be modeled by a state diagram, without relevant concern about distinguishing which state belongs to which resource.

SOA hides service structure, considering it part of the implementation, whereas REST hides resource behavior (its service) by converting it into resource structure, since each operation is modeled as a resource.

SOA tries to minimize the semantic gap (Sikos, 2017) by modeling services as close as possible to real world entities. Since these are different from each other, offering a specific set of functionalities, the result is a set of services with different sets of operations. The client must know the specific interface of the server. This entails coupling and may only be acceptable if the number of clients for a given server is usually reasonably small and the system evolves slowly (to limit the maintenance effort).

The interface coupling is precisely what REST tries to avoid, with a simple idea: to decompose complex resources into smaller ones (with links to other resources), until they are so primitive and/or atomic that they can all be treated in the same way, with a common interface. The initial complexity is transferred to the richness of the structure of the links between resources. The most distinguishing feature of REST is this uniform interface for all resources, with a common set of operations. This corresponds to separating the mechanism of traversing a graph (the links between resources) from the treatment of each node (resource). The overall idea is that a universal link follow-up mechanism coupled with a universal resource interface leads to decoupling between clients and servers, allowing servers to change what they send back to the clients because they will adapt automatically, by just navigating the structure and following the links to progress in the interaction process.

SOA has no dynamic visibility control mechanism for operations. In contrast, REST limits what the client can do to the links contained in the resource representations retrieved from the server, which helps to increase the robustness of applications. The idea of providing only the currently allowable commands has been borrowed from the field of user interfaces and is known as *affordances* (Amundsen, 2014). This is a strong point in favor of the REST style.

Unfortunately, both SOA and REST have fallacies and limitations:

- SOA assumes that all services are at the same level and that exposing services is just providing some interface and the respective endpoint. The fallacy is to assert that structure is unimportant. This may be true when integrating very large-grained resources, but not in many applications that include lists of resources that need to expose their services individually. The limitation is in changeability. Changing the interface of the server will most likely require changes in the clients as well.
- REST imposes a uniform interface, which allows treating all the resources in the same way. The fallacy is to consider only a syntactic interface, or even semantic (Verborgh, Harth, Maleshkova, Stadtmüller, Steiner, Taheriyan, & Van de Walle, 2014), but forgetting about the pragmatic (behavior) and symbiotic (collaboration) abstraction levels, described in Table 2. The reaction of resources need to be considered, which means that following a link cannot be done blindly. The client needs to know which kind of reaction the server is going to have. In the same way, traversing a structured resource implies knowing the type of that resource, otherwise which link should be followed next may not be known. Since there is no declaration of resource types, all types of resources to be used must be known in advance, either standardized or previously agreed upon (with custom media types). This is a relevant limitation of REST. However, developers are more than happy to agree on simple resource structures and on an aligned API to match. REST advocates contend that an API should be represented simply by its initial link (an URI – Universal Resource Identifier, for example) and all the functionality should be dynamically discovered by the client by exploring links. This can only be done with a set of fixed resource types (predefined or previously agreed upon). Resource structure can vary, a good advantage of REST, but only within the boundaries of resource types known in advance.

SOA is a good option for large-grained, slowly-evolving complex services. REST is a good option for small-grained, structured resources that are relatively simple. In search for simplicity and maintainability, many companies have stopped using SOA APIs in favor of REST, by modeling operations as resources, using naturally occurring lists of resources as structured resources with links, and dynamically building URIs instead of resorting to operation parameters. However, decoupling in REST is not as good as its structure dynamicity seems to indicate. All the resource types (media types) must be known in advance and the client may break if a new media type unknown to the client is used by the server. In addition, even when the type is known, the client cannot invent what to do and which link to choose when it receives a resource representation of a given type. Collaboration requires that both server and client implement behavior and deal with its effects, which means that they cannot be completely agnostic of each other. Data schema coupling is still there.

BEYOND SOA AND REST: STRUCTURAL SERVICES

Both SOA and REST have advantages and limitations. The goal of this chapter is to derive an architectural style that emphasizes the advantages and reduces the limitations.

Reducing Coupling

The first step to go beyond SOA and REST is to reduce the coupling caused by the sharing of schemas between the client and the server, characteristic of symmetric interoperability, as illustrated by Figure 2.

To this end, interoperability should be *asymmetric*, in the following sense, illustrated by Figure 3:

- A server should accept any request message with a schema that satisfies the mandatory items of the server's schema. Optional items need not be present in the request message, with default values provided by the server's schema, and any item in the request message not contemplated by the server's schema should be ignored.
- The same applies to the response message and the client's schema, now reversing the roles of the client and server as sender and receiver of the message (details in this direction omitted in figure 3, for simplicity).
- Both client and server deal only with its own message schema. The translation between them, both in structural and semantic terms, should be done by a universal mechanism. There should be no stubs to adapt the client or the server to a common message schema.

The asymmetric message interoperability mechanism of Figure 3 can be described in the following way:

- The server publishes a request *type schema*, which describes the type of request message values that the server can accept.
- The actual request message, sent by the client, is described by a *value schema*. This is simply a self-description and, unlike type schemas, includes no variability (range of structured values).

Figure 3. Compliance in asymmetric interoperability; only the request message validation is shown

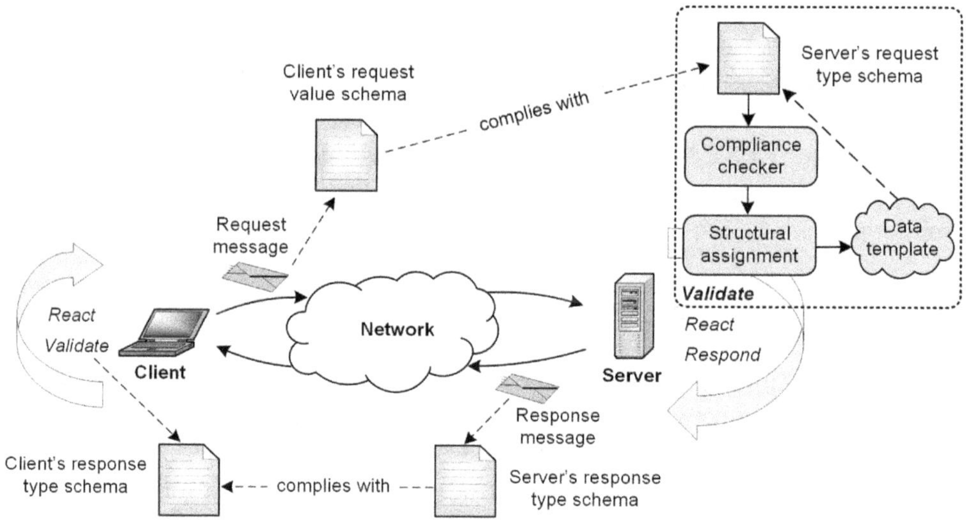

- When the request message arrives at the server, the message's value schema is validated by checking it for satisfaction of, or compliance with, the type schema of the server, in the *compliance checker*. If compliance holds, the request message is one of those that satisfy the server's request type schema and is accepted.
- The request message's value is structurally assigned to the *data template*, which is a data structure that satisfies the server's type schema and includes default values for the components in the type schema that are optional (minimum number of occurrences specified as zero).
- Structural assignment involves mapping the request message to the server's request type schema, by assigning the message to the data template, component by component, according to the following basic rules:
    - Components in the message that do not comply with any component in the data template are not assigned but simply ignored.
    - Components in the data template that are also present in the message have their values set to the corresponding message's component values, otherwise maintain their default values.
    - Structured components are assigned by recursive application of these rules.

After this, the data template is completely populated and ready to be accessed by the server. Each request message populates a new instance of the data template. Note that this mechanism is different from the usual data binding of existing technologies, since the server deals only with its own request message schema. It does not know the actual schema of the request message and there is no need for a data binding stub to deal with it. The mapping between the request message and the data template is done in a universal manner and does not depend on the schemas used by either the client or the server. As long as compliance holds, the structural assignment rules can be applied. This means that coupling is reduced in comparison with symmetric interoperability (Figure 2).

Conventionally, searching for an interoperable service is done by schema matching with similarity algorithms (Elshwimy, Algergawy, Sarhan, & Sallam, 2014) and ontology matching and mapping (Anam, Kim, Kang, & Liu, 2016). This may find similar server schemas, but does not ensure interoperability and manual adaptations are usually unavoidable.

Compliance (Tran, Zdun, Oberortner, Mulo, & Dustdar, 2012), a concept expressed in Figure 3, allows exact, not just approximate, interoperability even if the client and server schemas are not identical, as long as compliance requirements are verified. The main advantages of this are:

- Coupling is limited to the actually used features of a schema and not to the full set of features of that schema.
- A client is more likely to find suitable servers based on a smaller set of features, rather than on a full schema.
- A server will be able to serve a broader base of clients, since it will impose fewer restrictions on them.

In this respect, two application relationships are of relevance:

- **Client-Server**: Compliance (Tran, Zdun, Oberortner, Mulo, & Dustdar, 2012). The client must satisfy (*comply with*) the requirements established by the server to accept requests sent to it, without which these cannot be validated and executed (Figure 3). It is important to note that any client that complies with a given server can use it, independently of having been designed for interaction with it or not. The client and server need not share the same schema. The client's schema needs only to be compliant with the server's schema in the features that it actually uses. Since distributed applications have independent lifecycles, they cannot freely share names, and schema compliance must be tested structurally, feature by feature, between messages sent by the client and the interface offered by the server. Note that in a response the roles of schema compliance are reversed.

- **Server-Server**: The issue is to ascertain whether a server 1, serving a client, can be replaced by another server 2 such that the client-server relationship enjoyed by the client is not impaired. This is illustrated by Figure 4. In other words, the issue is whether server 2 is replacement compatible with server 1. Replacement compatibility between two servers is known as *conformance* (Khalfallah, Figay, Barhamgi, & Ghodous, 2014). Server 2 must possess all the characteristics of server 1 (and probably more), therefore being able to take the form of (*to conform to*) of server 1 and fulfill the expectations of the client regarding what it expects the server to be. In particular, the schema of server 2 cannot include any additional mandatory component, regarding the schema of server 1, otherwise it would impose more requirements on the client and the interoperability could break. The reasons for replacing a server with another may be varied, such as switching to an alternative in case of failure or lack of capacity, evolution (in which case server 2 would be the new version of server 1), or simply a management decision.

Given the huge variability possible in interfaces, compliance and conformance are not universal solutions to find a server adequate for any given client, but can cater for client and/or server variants and support the P3 (Substitution), P4 (Non-duplication of information) and P5 (Open-closed) principles of Table 1. These had been lost when moving from the object-oriented to the distributed architectural style. Now, an application can be replaced by another (P3), as a server, without breaking the service, delegation can be used to implement part of the interface that is missing (P4), and a server can remain in service while a variant serves new clients (P5).

Bringing Resources, Services and Processes Under a Common Model

Bridging SOA and REST requires an underlying model that encompasses the main architectural styles, namely those described by Table 3. In particular, SOA-like services should be able to be structured and REST-like resources should be able to have an application specific service interface. It is also important to recognize that services and processes are not dissociable. Processes cannot exist without services (the units of behavior that processes invoke) and services originate processes when the chain of service-to-service interactions is unraveled at any service's entry point. The relevant issue is which concept is at the top, process (activity perspective) or service (architectural perspective).

Figure 4. Compliance and conformance in application interoperability

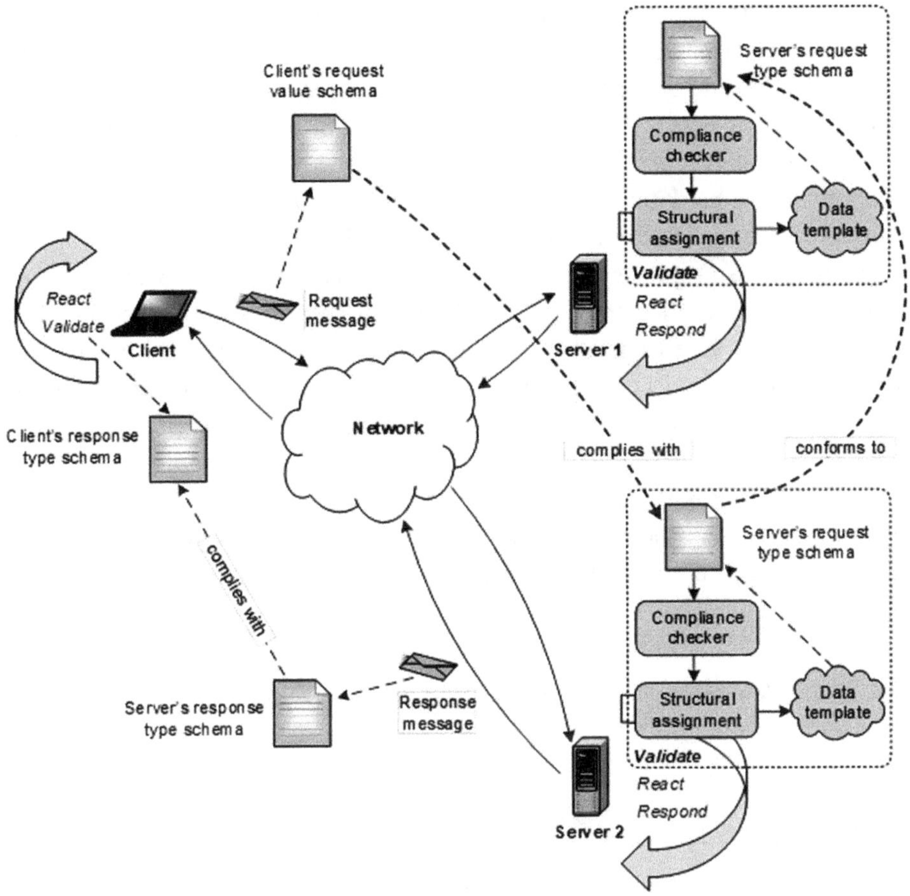

Services are essentially defined by their abstract interface, but need to be implemented by concrete entities, usually designated resources. In terms of modeling, resources correspond to distributed objects and these basic principles should also apply. The goal is to benefit from the advantages heralded by object-oriented programming in a distributed application context.

The relationship between resources, services and processes can be described in the following way:

- A service is a set of logically related operations of a resource, or a facet of that resource that makes sense in modeling terms. A service is pure behavior, albeit the implementation of concrete operations may depend on state, which needs a resource as an implementation platform.

- Resources interact by sending each other messages. A resource *X* that sends a message to a resource *Y* is in fact invoking the service of *Y*. This constitutes a service transaction between these two resources, in which the resources *X* and *Y* perform the role of service consumer (client) and service provider (server), respectively. A service transaction can entail other service transactions, as part of the chain reaction to the message on part of the service provider. A service should be defined in terms of reactions to messages (external view) and not in terms of state transitions or activity flows (internal view).
- A process is a graph of all service transactions that are allowed to occur, starting with a service transaction initiated at some resource *X* and ending with a final service transaction, which neither reacts back nor initiates new service transactions. The process corresponds to a use case of resource *X* and usually involves other resources as service transactions flow.

An abstract model is needed, to express the relationships between the entities described above, so that the interoperability of applications can be dealt with in a uniform way. Figure 5 depicts such a model, using UML (Unified Modeling Language)

Figure 5. A simple model of distributed application interaction

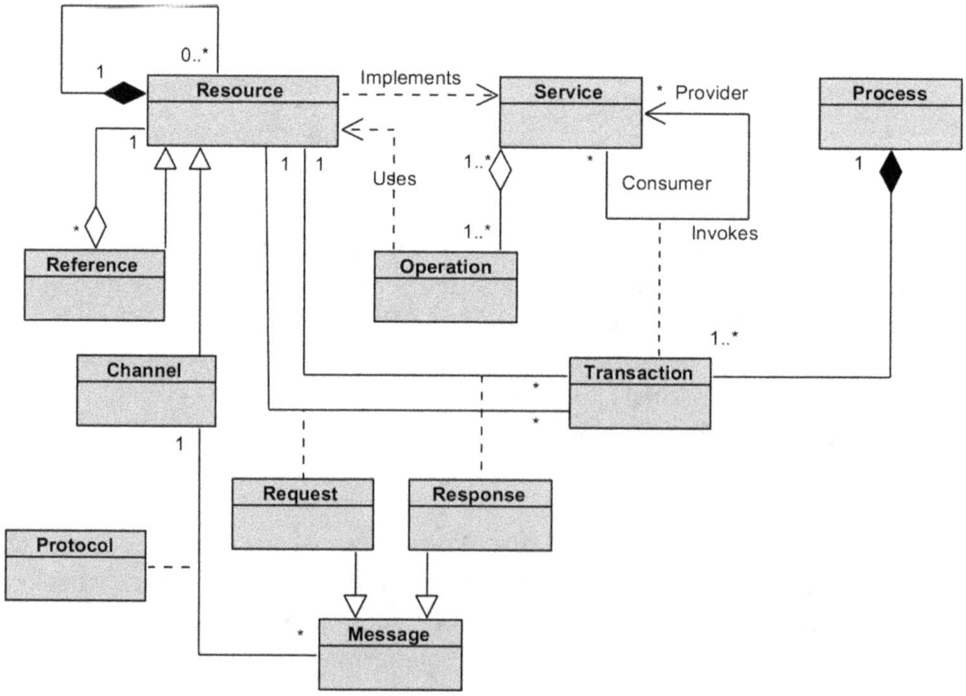

notation. A resource provides implementation for a service, namely its operations. Services invoke each other through service transactions, forming a process. Interaction is message based, assuming that an adequate channel and message protocol are available. Resources can be composed of other resources (composition) and have references to other resources (aggregation). Distributed references are themselves resources and included as components (but not the resources they reference) in their containers.

Association classes describe relationships (such as Transaction and the message Protocol) or roles, such as Message, which describes the roles (specialized by Request and Response) performed by resources when they are sent as messages.

The interaction between resources has been represented as an interaction between services, since the service represents the active part (behavior) of a resource and exposes its operations. The mention of interaction between resources actual refers to the interaction between the services that they implement.

Resources entail structure, state and behavior. Services refer only to behavior, without imposing a specific implementation. Processes are a view on the behavior sequencing and flow along services, which are implemented by resources. Services and processes are dual of each other, having resources as the structural entities. Where there is a service, there is a process and vice-versa. The question is which paradigm should be used first and foremost in modeling an enterprise's architecture, with the other derived from it. In a distributed application context, and in terms of modeling, adaptability and changeability, the service paradigm constitutes a better approach than the process paradigm (Baghdadi, 2014).

The Structural Services Architectural Style

In a local environment (application), the object-oriented paradigm is probably the best in the non-declarative world, with its low semantic gap, information reuse (inheritance), polymorphism and ability to expose both behavior and structure. Unfortunately, in a distributed environment pointers to objects can no longer be used and inheritance stops working, since the lifecycles of the objects are not synchronized (they can be modified, recompiled and linked independently).

Remote Procedure Call (Kukreja & Garg, 2014) was an early attempt to transport the object-oriented paradigm to the distributed world, but failed due to a very poor interoperability model, language specific. SOA was a much better interoperability solution (thanks to XML), but could not provide the mechanisms by which classes could expose structure and benefit from polymorphism.

REST went in the opposite direction, exposing only structure (actually, converting operations into resources, or behavior into structure), but also without a solution for polymorphism (media types need to be previously known).

The goal is to combine the best features of SOA and REST (Delgado, 2013), by allowing a resource:

- To refer to other resources through distributed references (e.g., URIs).
- To expose a universal set of common operations such as returning a description of itself, under request.
- To expose an additional, application-specific set of operations (service), as required for a low semantic gap in complex resource modeling.
- To expose structure, to easily model resources that are naturally structured.
- To base data interoperability on compliance and conformance, rather than of shared schemas. This allows using structural (rather than inheritance-based) polymorphism, for increased interoperability, adaptability and changeability, without the need to have resource types (schemas) necessarily shared or known beforehand.

In a sense, the ideal would be to have the object-oriented paradigm back, but now with distributed references, structural polymorphism and self-description. This is the essence of the *Structural Services* architectural style, proposed by this chapter. Table 4 summarizes its main differences and advantages regarding SOA and REST, in the light of the discussion already made in section “Analysys of SOA and REST as integration solutions”.

One of the advantages of the Structural Services style is the ability to lean more towards SOA or REST, according to modeling convenience, and mix several approaches and patterns in the same problem. In particular, it should be noted that, in the Object-Oriented style, inheritance-based polymorphism is based on the assumption that objects belonging to classes inheriting from a common base class share a common set of features (variables and operations of the base class). In Structural Services, resources do not belong to any class and there is no inheritance, but polymorphism still works on similar grounds, thanks to compliance. The server never deals with request messages, only with the data template (Figure 3). All the request messages that can be morphed into the data template (all for which compliance holds) will be seen as having a common set of features (those of the data template) and will be treated in the same way, exactly as in inheritance-based polymorphism, but now with the added advantage of supporting application distribution.

It is also important to acknowledge that the REST style requires a fixed set of operations, without stating which operations should be in that set. The HTTP implementations use some of the HTTP verbs, but this is just one possibility. The Structural Services style allows a further step in flexibility, by opening the possibility of using several fixed set of operations in the same problem. Now not only both extremes are possible (one different set for each resource, SOA style, or one common

Table 4. Comparison between SOA, REST and Structural Services

	SOA	REST	Structural Services
Basic tenet	Behavior.	Hypermedia (structure + links).	Tunable between pure behavior and pure hypermedia.
Distinguishing features	• Resource-specific interface. • Operations are entry points to a service. • Design-time service declaration.	• Uniform interface. • Operations are resources. • Clients react to structure received (do not invoke resource interfaces).	• Variable resource interface. • Resources are structured. • Operations are resources. • Links are resources. • Resource types need not be known at design time.
Best applicability	Large-grained resources (application integration).	Small-grained resources (CRUD-oriented APIs).	Wide range (small to large, behavior to structured-oriented).
Interoperability based on	Schema sharing.	Predefined media types.	Structural polymorphism (compliance and conformance).
Self-description	Repository (e.g., WSDL document).	Content type declaration in resource representations.	Included in each resource, message or application resource.
Main advantages	Low semantic gap (resources model closely real world entities).	Structured resources, with links to other resources (hypermedia).	• Low semantic gap. • Structured resources with links. • Polymorphism. • Self-description.
Main fallacy	Resource structure is unimportant.	Hypermedia increases decoupling.	None identified.
Main limitation	No polymorphism (coupling higher than needed).	Fixed interface (semantic gap higher than needed).	None identified.

set for all resources, REST style), but also any intermediate combination can be used, with different sets of operations for different sets of resources. This includes the distributed polymorphism mechanism based on compliance. Each server's type schema in Figure 3 specifies, in practice, a set of features common to all the resources that comply with that type schema.

FUTURE RESEARCH DIRECTIONS

The Structural Services architectural style, which can bridge the characteristics of SOA and REST and increase decoupling and the range of application interoperability, has the potential to improve substantially the current technological scenario, although much remains to be done before the architectural style is realistically tested and its capabilities demonstrated.

A comparative study needs to be carried out, including qualitative and quantitative assessment, between the Structural Services architectural style, SOA, and REST, with their instantiations (Web Services and RESTful APIs, respectively).

Compliance and conformance are basic concepts in interoperability and can be applied to all domains and levels of abstraction and complexity. Although work exists on its formal treatment in specific areas, such as choreographies (Yang, Ma, Deng, Liao, Yan, & Zhang, 2013), an encompassing and systematic study needs to be conducted regarding what is the formal meaning of compliance and conformance in each of the layers of Table 2. Their formal definition, across all layers, needs to be made in a systematic way.

Non-functional interoperability and coupling are also important, namely in context-aware applications and in those involving the design and management of SLR (Service Level Requirements). Detailing how compliance and conformance can be applied in these cases awards additional research. For example, response time conformance between an application and another that replaces it means that it is able to respond with a delay that must be within the delay interval of the original application.

CONCLUSION

The fundamental problem of application integration is how to achieve the minimum possible coupling, so that dependencies between applications that hinder changeability are kept to a minimum, while ensuring the minimum interoperability requirements, so that applications are able to effectively interact.

SOA and REST are the most common architectural styles used to address this problem, but they focus more on the interoperability side of the issue than on the coupling problem. Both require previous knowledge of the schemas of the messages exchanged in the interaction. On the one hand, SOA emphasizes behavior and does not contemplate service structure. On the other hand, REST supports structure but is not a good modeling match for complex applications, since these must be decomposed into simpler resources with a uniform syntactic interface (but different at higher levels, namely semantic, pragmatic and symbiotic).

The approach taken by this chapter was twofold:

- On the coupling side of the integration problem, the idea is to use structural compliance (Tran, Zdun, Oberortner, Mulo, & Dustdar, 2012) and conformance (Khalfallah, Figay, Barhamgi, & Ghodous, 2014) as the basis for relaxing the constraint of having to share message schemas. Two applications that share *at least* the characteristics required for interoperability can interoperate, independently of knowing the rest of the characteristics. This minimizes coupling, something that neither SOA nor REST is good at;

- On the interoperability side, syntax or even semantics are not enough. Higher levels (pragmatic and symbiotic) need to be considered as well, as shown by Table 2. This means that the principle of uniform interface of REST (trying to deal with resources in a universal way) is an illusion, achievable only at the syntactic level. As a consequence, REST is an incomplete solution for integration. Nevertheless, resource structure is fundamental. Many applications are naturally structured and depend on exposing and accessing that structure. Therefore, any integration solution must natively support resource structure. This means that SOA is also an incomplete solution to integration. To have a complete solution, the characteristics of SOA and REST need to be combined and complemented with others.

This chapter has described and proposed a new architectural style for integration, Structural Services, which combines the behavior flexibility of SOA, the structural hypermedia capabilities of REST, and the innovation of structural interoperability based on compliance and conformance.

These features are essential to the solution of the fundamental integration problem, resulting in a low modeling semantic gap (resources closely model real world entities, both in structure and behavior), while minimizing coupling for high adaptability, changeability and reliability.

The goal is not to replace SOA or REST, but rather to evaluate what can be gained by using a technology that natively supports the architectural style that has been proposed, instead of increasing the complexity resulting from the mismatch between this style and classical technologies such as HTTP, XML, and JSON.

REFERENCES

Agosti, M., Ferro, N., & Silvello, G. (2016). Digital library interoperability at high level of abstraction. *Future Generation Computer Systems*, *55*, 129–146. doi:10.1016/j.future.2015.09.020

Alenezi, M., & Magel, K. (2014). Empirical evaluation of a new coupling metric: Combining structural and semantic coupling. *International Journal of Computers and Applications*, *36*(1). doi:10.2316/Journal.202.2014.1.202-3902

Amundsen, M. (2014). APIs to Affordances: A New Paradigm for Services on the Web. In C. Pautasso, E. Wilde, & R. Alarcon (Eds.), *REST: Advanced Research Topics and Practical Applications* (pp. 91–106). New York, NY: Springer. doi:10.1007/978-1-4614-9299-3_6

Anam, S., Kim, Y., Kang, B., & Liu, Q. (2016). Adapting a knowledge-based schema matching system for ontology mapping. In *Proceedings of the Australasian Computer Science Week Multiconference* (p. 27). New York, NY: ACM Press. 10.1145/2843043.2843048

Athanasopoulos, D. (2017). Self-Adaptive Service Organization for Pragmatics-Aware Service Discovery. In *Proceedings of the IEEE International Conference on Services Computing* (pp. 164-171). Piscataway, NJ: IEEE Computer Society Press. 10.1109/SCC.2017.28

Babu, D., & Darsi, M. (2013). A Survey on Service Oriented Architecture and Metrics to Measure Coupling. *International Journal on Computer Science and Engineering*, *5*(8), 726–733.

Baghdadi, Y. (2014). Modelling business process with services: Towards agile enterprises. *International Journal of Business Information Systems*, *15*(4), 410–433. doi:10.1504/IJBIS.2014.060377

Bassett, L. (2015). *Introduction to JavaScript Object Notation: A to-the-point Guide to JSON*. Sebastopol, CA: O'Reilly Media, Inc.

Bora, A., & Bezboruah, T. (2015). A Comparative Investigation on Implementation of RESTful versus SOAP based Web Services. *International Journal of Database Theory and Application*, *8*(3), 297–312. doi:10.14257/ijdta.2015.8.3.26

Chen, Y. (2015). A RDF-based approach to metadata crosswalk for semantic interoperability at the data element level. *Library Hi Tech*, *33*(2), 175–194. doi:10.1108/LHT-08-2014-0078

Dahiya, N., & Parmar, N. (2014). SOA AND REST Synergistic Approach. *International Journal of Computer Science and Information Technologies*, *5*(6), 7045–7049.

Delgado, J. (2013). Architectural styles for distributed interoperability. *Information Resources Management Journal*, *26*(4), 40–65. doi:10.4018/irmj.2013100103

Dennis, A., Wixom, B., & Tegarden, D. (2015). *Systems analysis and design: An object-oriented approach with UML*. Indianapolis, IN: John Wiley & Sons.

Elshwimy, F., Algergawy, A., Sarhan, A., & Sallam, E. (2014). Aggregation of similarity measures in schema matching based on generalized mean. *Proceedings of the IEEE International Conference on Data Engineering Workshops* (pp. 74-79). Piscataway, NJ: IEEE Computer Society Press. 10.1109/ICDEW.2014.6818306

Erl, T., Merson, P., & Stoffers, R. (2017). *Service-oriented Architecture: Analysis and Design for Services and Microservices*. Upper Saddle River, NJ: Prentice Hall PTR.

Fawcett, J., Ayers, D., & Quin, L. (2012). *Beginning XML*. Indianapolis, IN: John Wiley & Sons.

Fielding, R. (2000). *Architectural Styles and the Design of Network-based Software Architectures* (Doctoral dissertation). University of California at Irvine, CA.

Fielding, R. (2008). REST APIs must be hypertext-driven. *Roy Fielding's blog: Untangled*. Retrieved November 13, 2017, from http://roy.gbiv.com/untangled/2008/rest-apis-must-be-hypertext-driven

Fielding, R., Taylor, R., Erenkrantz, J., Gorlick, M., Whitehead, J., Khare, R., & Oreizy, P. (2017). Reflections on the REST architectural style and principled design of the modern web architecture. In *Proceedings of the 2017 11th Joint Meeting on Foundations of Software Engineering* (pp. 4-14). New York, NY: ACM Press. 10.1145/3106237.3121282

Geetika, R., & Singh, P. (2014). Dynamic coupling metrics for object oriented software systems: A survey. *Software Engineering Notes, 39*(2), 1–8. doi:10.1145/2579281.2579296

Hendricksen, D. (2014). *12 More Essential Skills for Software Architects*. Upper Saddle River, NJ: Addison-Wesley Professional.

Hussain, T., Mehmood, R., Haq, A., Alnafjan, K., & Alghamdi, A. (2014). Designing framework for the interoperability of C4I systems. In *International Conference on Computational Science and Computational Intelligence* (pp. 102–106). Piscataway, NJ: IEEE Computer Society Press. 10.1109/CSCI.2014.102

ISO. (2010). *Systems and software engineering – Vocabulary. ISO/IEC/IEEE 24765:2010(E) International Standard*. Geneva, Switzerland: International Organization for Standardization.

Khalfallah, M., Figay, N., Barhamgi, M., & Ghodous, P. (2014). Model driven conformance testing for standardized services. In *IEEE International Conference on Services Computing* (pp. 400–407). Piscataway, NJ: IEEE Computer Society Press. 10.1109/SCC.2014.60

Kukreja, R., & Garg, N. (2014). Remote Procedure Call: Limitations and Drawbacks. *International Journal of Research, 1*(10), 914–917.

Kumari, S., & Rath, S. (2015). Performance comparison of SOAP and REST based Web Services for Enterprise Application Integration. In *International Conference on Advances in Computing, Communications and Informatics* (pp. 1656–1660). Piscataway, NJ: IEEE Computer Society Press. 10.1109/ICACCI.2015.7275851

Pautasso, C. (2014). RESTful web services: principles, patterns, emerging technologies. In Web Services Foundations (pp. 31-51). New York, NY: Springer. doi:10.1007/978-1-4614-7518-7_2

Popplewell, K. (2014). Enterprise interoperability science base structure. In K. Mertins, F. Bénaben, R. Poler, & J. Bourrières (Eds.), *Enterprise Interoperability VI: Interoperability for Agility, Resilience and Plasticity of Collaborations* (pp. 417–427). Cham, Switzerland: Springer International Publishing. doi:10.1007/978-3-319-04948-9_35

Rezaei, R., Chiew, T., & Lee, S. (2014). A review on E-business interoperability frameworks. *Journal of Systems and Software, 93*, 199–216. doi:10.1016/j.jss.2014.02.004

Robkin, M., Weininger, S., Preciado, B., & Goldman, J. (2015). Levels of conceptual interoperability model for healthcare framework for safe medical device interoperability. In *Symposium on Product Compliance Engineering* (pp. 1–8). Piscataway, NJ: IEEE Computer Society Press. 10.1109/ISPCE.2015.7138703

Sharma, A., Kumar, M., & Agarwal, S. (2015). A Complete Survey on Software Architectural Styles and Patterns. *Procedia Computer Science, 70*, 16–28. doi:10.1016/j.procs.2015.10.019

Sharma, R., & Panigrahi, P. (2015). Developing a roadmap for planning and implementation of interoperability capability in e-government. *Transforming Government: People, Process and Policy, 9*(4), 426–447.

Sikos, L. (2017). The Semantic Gap. In *Description Logics in Multimedia Reasoning* (pp. 51–66). Cham, Switzerland: Springer. doi:10.1007/978-3-319-54066-5_3

Sungkur, R., & Daiboo, S. (2015). SOREST, A Novel Framework Combining SOAP and REST for Implementing Web Services. In *Proceedings of the Second International Conference on Data Mining, Internet Computing, and Big Data* (pp. 22-34). Red Hook, NY: Curran Associates, Inc.

Sungkur, R., & Daiboo, S. (2016). Combining the Best Features of SOAP and REST for the Implementation of Web Services. *International Journal of Digital Information and Wireless Communications*, *6*(1), 21–33. doi:10.17781/P001923

Thakar, U., Tiwari, A., & Varma, S. (2016). On Composition of SOAP Based and RESTful Services. In *Proceedings of the 6th International Conference on Advanced Computing* (pp. 500-505). Piscataway, NJ: IEEE Computer Society Press. 10.1109/IACC.2016.99

Tran, H., Zdun, U., Oberortner, E., Mulo, E., & Dustdar, S. (2012). Compliance in service-oriented architectures: A model-driven and view-based approach. *Information and Software Technology*, *54*(6), 531–552. doi:10.1016/j.infsof.2012.01.001

Verborgh, R., Harth, A., Maleshkova, M., Stadtmüller, S., Steiner, T., Taheriyan, M., & Van de Walle, R. (2014). Survey of semantic description of REST APIs. In C. Pautasso, E. Wilde, & R. Alarcon (Eds.), *REST: Advanced Research Topics and Practical Applications* (pp. 69–89). New York, NY: Springer. doi:10.1007/978-1-4614-9299-3_5

Yang, H., Ma, K., Deng, C., Liao, H., Yan, J., & Zhang, J. (2013). Towards conformance testing of choreography based on scenario. In *Proceedings of the International Symposium on Theoretical Aspects of Software Engineering* (pp. 59-62). Piscataway, NJ: IEEE Computer Society Press. 10.1109/TASE.2013.23

Zhang, Z., Wu, C., & Cheung, D. (2013). A survey on cloud interoperability: Taxonomies, standards, and practice. *Performance Evaluation Review*, *40*(4), 13–22. doi:10.1145/2479942.2479945

Zimmermann, O., Tomlinson, M., & Peuser, S. (2012). *Perspectives on Web Services: Applying SOAP, WSDL and UDDI to Real-World Projects*. Berlin: Springer-Verlag.

Chapter 12
Information Technology Security as Scored by Management Budget

Tiina K. O. Rodrigue
The George Washington University, USA

ABSTRACT

In information technology security as scored by management budget, the author examines information technology (IT) security in the context of organizational management, business, complexity leadership theories, and current IT security scholarship. Based on well-known organizational power and politics theory as well as accounting, budget, and management literature, the chapter examines what is known about the impact of power and politics on IT security and the importance of budgetary gamesmanship as illustrated by understanding that the budget as a game, the politics of allocation within an organization, the influence of budgetary bias and how it shapes what CISOs must understand and master, the unfunded mandate impediment through which each the organization picks winners and losers under the auspices of "doing more with less." The author suggests a future framework for IT security-management-budget review that includes measures that track expenditure versus the power alignment and how to gauge the net effect on an organization's information-technology security posture.

INTRODUCTION

Ever wonder how Chief Information Security Officers (CISOs) justify the spending of tens of billions of dollars (Selyukh, Shalal, and Mason, 2015) annually? More importantly, have CISOs created a more protected, safer organization and world with the money spent – have the CISOs scored well with the allocations gained

DOI: 10.4018/978-1-5225-5829-3.ch012

or gamed? There exists an industry-wide agreement that the attack vector from IT threats is very dangerous (Contreras, Denardis, and Teplinsky, 2013). Are the dangers sufficiently abated with the money spent on IT security?

For the purpose of this discussion, IT security ensures data and system "... availability, integrity, authentication, confidentiality and nonrepudiation..." (Wilson, 2013, p. 44). IT security sufficiency is based on the presence of four different systems to constitute a comprehensive IT security posture. Each of the IT security posture systems: people, process, policy and technology – could be compared to a loosely coupled system which interacts with each other and adapts to create a stronger or weaker holonic set of systems (Orton & Weick, 1990). If all four components are represented in the IT security posture budget and actual final spend, then the IT security posture could be considered comprehensive (Bagchi-Sen, Rao, Upadhyaya, & Chai, 2010). If a component is not represented in the budget nor the actual spending, then the IT security posture could be inherently lacking (Batteau, 2011). This assertion is based on the premise that as IT threats are constantly evolving and growing (Chang, 2013; Hathaway, 2012), corporations and federal agencies must invest each year in all four aspects of an IT security posture, just to maintain comprehensive IT security protection (Bagchi-Sen et al., 2010; Libicki, Ablon, & Webb, 2015).

For example, technology alone is ineffective IT security, as argued by Batteau (2011) . IT security could be examined holonically (McHugh, 1996), similar to a complex adaptive system made up of multiple, smaller systems as defined by Uhl-Bien, Marion, & McKelvey in 2007. IT security is most effective when the IT security posture is upheld by resilient, complex adaptive systems (Egli, 2013). A complex adaptive system is more than just hardware and software (Uhl-Bien et al., 2007). This approach could shift the perspective of IT security as a simple system where a holistic view might suffice (McMahon, 2016), to expand the understanding that each component in and of itself is a complex system, affecting multiple other complex systems, each adapting to multiple other systems (Uhl-Bien et al., 2007).

BACKGROUND

A compromise to national security due to a neglected component of an IT security posture could cause death, damage to trust and reputation, undermining the critical infrastructure of America (Pawlak and Wendling, 2013). On the corporate side, we have seen the impact of a major breach with Equifax, a single instance losing millions of records and costing shareholders $4B in market capitalization, with more loss expected in the hundreds of pending lawsuits ("Equifax Breach: Cyber Insurance To The Rescue?!," 2017). With such severe consequences, why would there be any hesitation to fund IT security in all four components?

An answer can be found in the theory of budgeting as a political game of power and influence that exists in both the public and private sectors (Mintzberg, 1985). This gamed approach would run counter to the logical, technically driven approach typified in IT security. In the fields of organizational theory, management, accounting, governance, business anthropology and others; the presence of organizational power (French and Raven, 1959; March, 1966; Mintzberg, 1983) is well-established. In the federal space, either wing's partisan agenda is also a clear scholarly topic on influence on budgeting (Andrews, 2011; Epp, Lovett, and Baumgartner, 2014; Lapsley, Midwinter, Nambiar, and Steccolini, 2011; Williams, Macintosh, and Moore, 1990). Within the budgeting process, gamesmanship was acknowledged not only in establishing and managing of budgets but in the subsequent allocating and controlling of budgets, as well (Buchanan, 2008; Libby and Lindsay, 2009; Lukka, 1988). The whole of IT may remain under-protected because of aged security approaches in the new IT era (Batteau, 2011; Egli, 2013) coupled with organizational games of power and politics (Mintzberg, 1985).

By measuring the influence of individual and group power on budgets, expenditures and resulting effectiveness (Glaser, Lopez-De-Silanes, and Sautner, 2013) in the IT security arena, the degree of the problem of power and politics in capital allocation could be measured, and then, mitigated and controlled. Notionally, the top-level executive of IT security activities, the CISO, makes the financial investment decisions regarding an organization's IT operation and leverages his or her management abilities, capacity to master the technical, as well as strategic, decision making (Berghel, 2014, p.66).

CISOs are more than orchestra directors. To be effective; CISOs must challenge the status quo; subscribe to contrarianism - leveraging creativity, abstract thinking, imagination, and innovation - while still embracing self-doubt, second guessing, in the context of IT subtleties and nuances (Berghel, 2014, p.66) to:

merge broad IT knowledge with high-level understanding of physical security, including forensic skills; privacy management (or fields such as finance and healthcare); business contingency; legal matters, including policy creation and enforcement...network security (and) engineering, data security operations, investigations, information system security and risk management. (Bagchi-Sen et al., 2010, p. 25).

By adding the financial investment and spending decision making to this definition, the CISO must achieve IT security effectiveness which can be difficult to judge, as thwarted attacks and averted impacts are almost impossible to measure (Libicki et al., 2015, p. 12) while continuing to secure the funds for the operation ("2015 Risk Practices Survey Summary Report," 2015).

The CISO role was invented in the commercial world, when Citigroup created the position and hired the very first CISO in 1995, after the bank suffered a $10M breach that was largely unrecovered (Goodchild, 2009, p. 1). In the federal space, the IT leader role, Chief Information Officer (CIO), was established for the public sector in the Clinger-Cohen Act of 1996, which further established that agency heads were ultimately responsible for IT security.(*Clinger Cohen Act of 1996*, 1996). Under FISMA in 2002, the IT security effort was delegated to senior information security officers who report to the CIO (*Federal Information Security Management Act of 2002 (FISMA)*, 2002, sec. 3544, subsec. a.3.A). Now termed CISOs in the federal space too, IT security executive leaders fulfill a broad list of IT security standards from the National Institute of Standards and Testing (NIST). The FISMA-enforced NIST standards cover policy, procedures, practices, and plans (subsection c.2) with "...the resources, including budget, staffing, and training, that are necessary to implement the program required..." (subsection d.1.B). The NIST approach parallels the four components in the suggested comprehensive information-technology security posture.

One of the realities CISOs face is that IT space boundaries are socially constructed, state independent, increasingly complex and more rapidly adaptive than modern corporate or government decision-making and response (Pawlak and Wendling, 2013, p. 537). Contemporary IT security concerns itself with more than just individual and organizational attacks, but also organizational resistance (Burke, 2011; Klein, 1989), up to and including the real prospect of IT war from nation state and other actors (Pawlak and Wendling, 2013).

How do organizations ensure CISOs are receiving sufficient resources? In the area of IT security, the primary stakeholders are the CISOs who need to leverage the budgetary gamesmanship (Buchanan, 2008) to ensure sufficient resources, assuming that the CISO may both request and spend whatever budget is allotted for IT security. Given that all organizations have finite resources, the budget decision maker, such as Chief Executive Officer (CEO) or the agency head, become the secondary stakeholder in this problem area. Often ill-represented in the executive boardroom, the tertiary stakeholders are all humans regardless of role; humans whose life and livelihood are protected by the IT security posture created by the CISOs. There is no guarantee that the CISO isn't using outdated thought (Berghel, 2014) and 20th-century mechanisms instead of addressing the contemporary complexity that befits the evolving danger of IT threats (Egli, 2013).

TO WHAT EXTENT DOES POWER AND POLITICS IMPACT IT SECURITY MANAGEMENT BUDGETS?

Controversies and Problems Are Opportunities, If You Know the Game

Although there are tremendous bodies of knowledge within the worlds of IT security, as well as the organizational aspects of power and politics, these worlds of research are almost entirely separate. The different areas of focus – hardline, technical, computer science vs humanistic social science may seem at odds or ill-suited for comparative discussion; however without the normative authority of the social aspects and context, the technologist will only be half prepared, and the traditional leader will be lost without subject matter expertise (Engle and Guttmann, 2014). As discovered by this author, human and organizational research rarely cross paths with IT security research. Neither of these silos individually distinguishes between the hard choices that leaders face: limited resources, gamesmanship, and the ongoing tussle that is every day power and politics of organizational interactions. There is concern that purely rational plays of a technologist CISO have little chance of strategic resource victory in the aggressive yet covert world of politically savvy leaders (Mintzberg, 1985). Therefore, this disparity demonstrates a clear gap between IT security research and organizational research, as well as the political and comprehension gap between CISOs and CEOs or agency heads. Significant problems arise for CISOs are unable to gather the power or play politics to have an effective IT security budget or worse, to have an insufficient IT security and not realize the inadvertent organizational sabotage.

If CISOs are unable to secure the means to influence and change the established action, as predicted by Mintzberg (1979, 1983, 1985); then CISOs will be ineffective in getting the necessary resources to both improve the ongoing organizational dynamic and to provide sufficient protection from the increasingly complex and difficult cyberthreats that are prevalent (Kuhn, 2010). Moreover, as the threats are escalating, becoming more mobile, and ubiquitous, this challenge affects not just CISOs but every organization, leader and person from presidents to entrepreneurs and professors to students (Chang, 2013, p. 3; Kuhn, 2010). While the leaders and participants may not be able to prevent political influence and power games, the degree of influence could be established and the appropriate skills, countermeasures and mitigations could be determined to ensure that the data, systems and services that make up the corporation, enterprise, agency or organization have sufficient if not munificent resources needed to ensure confidentiality, availability, integrity, authentication and nonrepudiation (Wilson, 2013).

This discussion will extend the current technical focus of the cybersecurity literature to include the known theories of human and organizational power and politics; management and leadership complexity theory; and budgeting and accounting theory. CISOs will know the score, be able to keep score and realize how to play the game, as well as a traditional leader, to keep IT Security scoring management budget allocations.

The Importance of Budgetary Gamesmanship

The Budget as a Game

In IT security articles that mention budgeting, such as Smeraldi and Malacaria (2014) the focus was on selection criteria to choose between technology options in order to find the appropriate level of expenditure on the best IT security hardware and software possible within a given budget amount. The underlying assumption remains that the answer to any IT security issue is more technology. Further, the article has no after-action budgetary assessment of efficacy or adaptation to a rapidly changing threat environment which literature suggests is important in the IT arena (Batteau, 2011; Chang, 2013; Egli, 2013; Epp et al., 2014; Kuhn, 2010; Pawlak and Wendling, 2013; Wilson, 2013). The standard budgetary approach does not account for uncertainty or conditional shifts in the IT threat situation.

The IT security industry extends the technology-based approaches to logically mitigate the budgetary question by using mathematical formulas to maximize the result from minimum input, as shown in Smeraldi and Malacaria (2014). The normal negotiation in establishing appropriate controls involves the five competing measures of risk management (Wilson, 2013). When coupled with cost-benefit analysis, such as by Garvey, Moynihan and Servi (2011) risk management in IT security literature provides a method to assess the efficacy of multiple options to find the most efficient technology solution, given the potential impact of an intrusion or incident to the organization from a transactional and technology focus, especially in corporations.

Disparate from the corporate world approach, the combination of risk management, cost-benefit analysis and economic impact may have limited application in the federal space as the threat of a single data record exposure can negatively impact reputation and the organization depending on the sensitivity of the record. Where the corporate IT security standard accepts some risk; within some areas of the federal government, there is no acceptable probability of exposure. While an elevated level of protection will not hold for all federal data or corporate data (*Federal Information Security Modernization Act of 2014 (FISMA REFORM*, 2014), the absolute protection model requires a different type of undiscussed analysis. A precautionary principle (Stone, 2012) demonstrates some data are significant enough to demand the highest protection. Money, lives and liberty are spent to ensure the ongoing well-being of America, her data and her citizens.

Standard corporate budgeting is driven by current company goals and vision; federal budgeting, based on disparate ideals, has created a dysfunctional, crisis-driven environment (Andrews, 2011, p. 345). Federal budgeting is essentially an institution with imbedded process seemingly impervious to financial reforms (Andrews, 2011, p.348). Literature creates a link between federal institutional theory and the complex game of federal budgets with regulatory, cultural and normative rules (Andrews, 2011) which parallel the budgetary gamesmanship articles in management, accounting and leadership to similar articles in the federal budgetary arena. For example, Brogan (2012) reviewed the error rate among three budget forecast approaches to determine the influence by competing political (state and national) actors attempting to shape the budget into a form most amenable to their needs (p.85). Brogan's analysis concurs with Mintzberg (1985) that budgets are a political tool, especially during election cycles. Therefore, Brogan (2012) was not only examining internal organizational politics but partisan politics between institutional forces at a state and national level. Mintzberg called the organization an arena in 1985, and budget games have only gotten more cagey and ruthless over time. Where IT security literature focuses on logical measures to optimize the budget spend on even more technology; organizational, leadership, budget, accounting and federal literature focus on maximizing the share allocated.

The Politics of Allocation

Resource allocation as a political move is mentioned as a gap in the regulatory framework to unite nations against IT incidents (Pawlak & Wendling, 2013). Given the current examples of nation-state-initiated security attacks (p. 539), there may be some time before an international consensus on IT security crime is reached. The IT security problem demands nimble response to rapid growth, crisis management, transformation and the need for enhanced renewal. IT security requires more than technology but additionally, human and organizational aspects such as a resilient mindset, culture, organization, process, budget, and solution set (Egli, 2013).

When looking at organizations, Brogan incorporated Corina and team's 2004 finding that competition between political institutions has a significant impact on the accuracy of revenue forecasts, even after economic and other stresses were factored (2012, p. 89). The statistical approach indicated the degree and significance of political institutional sway on forecast and expenditure error, and therefore the impact of politics on budgets (Brogan, 2012). Brogan's 2012 work linked partisan political institutional variables to internal organizational political variables in alignment with the other scholarly work. Political behavior happens not only at the institutional level as shown by Buchanan, 2008. Budgetary political behavior has left a changed impression on individual participants and the followers and groups affected by them. Buchanan (2008) demonstrated how politically-oriented behavior in past research was once equated with immoral or evil behavior; however, the contemporary interpretation from the participant or spectator perspective appears less condemning. Buchanan (2008) and other authors (Libby and Lindsay, 2009; Lukka, 1988) agree that politics is a necessity to ensure sufficient allocation of resources. Further, the literature suggests that politics may actually be more than needed but also enjoyable for the participant (Buchanan, 2008, p. 61) as political play is now expected in current organizational life.

The phenomenon of budgetary allocations and politics was studied longitudinally; Epp et al., (2014) found minimal influence of left- and right-wing priorities in twenty-nine countries as the political fiscal changes were statistically insignificant regardless of ideology. Partisan politics were essentially unable to bring about strong, clear and immediate shifts on the multiple-country federal-level budgeting process (Epp et al., 2014, p. 877) as examined in participative democracies around the globe. Epp et al., (2014) argued that in the budgetary process, the non-discretionary aspects of federal budgeting and the counter-vailing need to address the economic, social and emergent needs demanded federal response regardless of ideological base (Epp, et al., 2014). Similarly, other literature considered the mandatory allocations on social, defense and other programs as relatively unchanged by politics (Lapsley et al., 2011).

Both Epp et al., (2014) and Lapsley et al., (2011) noted the effects of crisis as well as the institutionalized methodologies and mindsets as mentioned by Andrews (2011). Epp et al., (2014) confirmed that the best determinant of the next year's budget was spending level of the previous year (p. 869). Therefore, current literature suggests IT security budgeting may be less affected by partisan influence unless the left- or right-wing control is undivided, uncontestable. Even in that circumstance, the controlling political party could only modify discretionary spending and not the budgetary allocations (Epp et al., 2014).

When Lapsley et al., (2011) examined power influences due to different political influences in the Scottish Parliamentary budgeting process; the focus was on coalition and minority governments. This aspect was also covered in the Epp et al., (2014) work, to distinguish to what degree power directed the budgeting process in different government bases. Similar to Brogan (2012), Lapsley et al., (2011) found that budgetary allocations and political ideology was balanced against the need to respond to situations and govern. Additionally, the works of Lapsley et al., (2011) and Brogan (2012) both found that the two primary political parties were essentially not statistically different over time when establishing budgetary allocation priorities. The Lapsley et al., (2011) work also agreed with the findings of Epp et al., (2014) that the less concentrated the power base of the government, the less influential and able to change the discretionary budget, or new monies. Lapsley et al., (2011) do not depart from the other managerial accounting research. Therefore, while politics often attempts to sway the budgetary allocations as tool, unless undivided control is achieved first; the net results will be insignificant.

The Influence of Budgetary Bias

Budgetary bias became a leading finding that influenced other decisions in Libby and Lindsay (2009) survey of budgeting practices in the United States and Canada with a critical eye towards whether or not budget processes restrain organizational flexibility and gathered data on budget outcomes, patterns, practices and associated managerial beliefs on the value of continuing participative and performance-based budgets and managerial accounting (Libby and Lindsay, 2009). Much like the other budgetary literature, Libby and Lindsay (2009) piece found that budgetary bias and gamesmanship was prevalent and included at least five different types, including sandbagging. Budgetary gamesmanship aligns with the Glaser et al., (2013) finding that managerial staff often created slack in their proposed budgets to create cash windfalls for reallocation. The literature suggests that the budgetary process will not be eliminated any time soon, thus the budget political game plays a significant factor in the IT security budgetary arena. Libby and Lindsay (2009) suggested need for better governance for continued study, for example, in important subareas such as IT security budgeting, as agreed by Brogan (2012).

In another study, Lukka (1988) explained the potential for budgetary bias in an organizational structure and examined power and gamesmanship, in alignment with other budgetary literature works (Andrews, 2011; Buchanan, 2008; Brogan, 2012; Egli, 2013; Epp, et al., 2014; Glaser et al., 2013; Lapsley et al., 2011; Libby and Lindsay, 2009). Lukka (1998) provided new ideas in the budgetary creation and control as both areas contained elements of gamesmanship. Lukka (1998) included as a new basis of underlying factors that explained why bias and gamesmanship were ubiquitous, as also found by Libby and Lindsay (2009). In fact, Lukka (1998) found that managers would decry budgeting bias on one hand and create bias with the other (p. 297), in alignment with Buchanan's (2008) finding that gamesmanship was a normal part of the managerial role and Mintzberg's (1985) description of budgets as one of many games in the political arena of an organization. IT security budget research could leverage the cited literature to explain the why logic-based, technical approaches often fail in the face of multiple types of gamesmanship. Budgetary bias provides a clear understanding to the conscious and subconscious rationale that creates the individual and group mentalities that perpetuate political ploys as everyday plays. More than just obligatory, Mintzberg (1985) indicated the positive function of organizational politics as disruptors to the dysfunctional legitimate, expertise and ideology bases of power (p. 148) used by various groups and individuals. The Mintzberg (1985) literature could be extended to argue the positive potential of the pursuit of power and politics of IT security budgeting by CISOs. If budgets are just a game in a larger organizational arena that seeks to consolidate power (Mintzberg, 1985), how does a CISO score a hit for IT security?

The Unfunded Mandate Impediment

Unlike some corporations, the federal government recognizes that unfunded mandates create crisis and has passed legislation to minimize the impact via the Unfunded Mandate Reform Act (UMRA) (Gullo, 2004). However, this Act only looks at the federal unfunded mandates that exceed a threshold beyond current direct costs of above $77 million for intergovernmental efforts (Congressional Budget Office, 2016). Therefore, if an existing budget has been allocated for a purely federal endeavor with no state or regional intergovernmental requirement, there may be an assumption that the agency will reprioritize and include this new effort, just as happened with the 2014 FISMA expansion (Pickford, Wheelock, & Gullo, 2014) and is typical in corporate organizations. However, with sequestration in 2013 and now ongoing budget cuts, underfunding has become the modern modus operandi - "Because organizations and agencies are not performing cost-cutting initiatives, they focus on making funding cuts rather than reducing actual costs. The goal seems to be to produce a lower funding amount here and now."(Lippuner, 2011, p. 28). Former Federal CIO VanRoekel shared that lowered funding amounts lead to poor innovation and in IT security, as well as reduced vigilance (Hoover, 2013).

For example, while the federal FY17 $19B budget for IT security could seem to be the exception to the 'doing more with less' initiatives (Lippuner, 2011; Lyngaas, 2016), the reality is that when the budget was established, the president himself shared that without additional measures that America is at "the height of irresponsibility to leave a digital backdoor wide open for IT adversaries." (Dixon, 2012, p. 37). When the federal CIO, Tony Scott, appointed the first federal CISO, Brigadier General (retired) Gregory J. Tohill (Scott & Daniel, 2016), this created a juxtaposition of continued emphasis on improving federal IT security despite the multiple unfunded mandates that can only provide lip service national action. In the corporate world, this emphasis on excellence while not providing sufficient resources may be viewed as an acceptable paradox (Burke, 2011). In short, while corporations or agencies may proactively establish a reprioritized budget in response to an unfunded mandate, more often in the author's experience, the first reaction is to ignore the mandate if there are not additional moneys attached to the requirement.

The Future Framework for IT Security Budgeting

Mintzberg's (1985) literature connects power and budgets:

- to complexity leadership theory (Uhl-Bien, Marion, and Mckelvey, 2007), and
- to government and management accounting (Andrews, 2011; Brogan, 2012; Epp et al., 2014; Glaser et al., 2013; Lapsley et al., 2011; Libby and Lindsay, 2009; Lukka, 1988; Williams et al., 1990), and
- cross-pollination with medical ethics and ecological adaption (Brogan, 2012; Egli, 2013).

The future framework of power and politics is already in play; although unrecognized in IT security scholarly work. Williams et al., (1990) studied Canadian public-sector managers' impact on budget-related behavior within organizational budgets in public sector environments to determine if the public sector is more susceptible to political factors (p. 221). Williams et al., (1990) noted that expectation of budgetary behavior became a self-fulfilling prophecy in the public sector that drove future budgetary allocation (p. 239), similar to Mintzberg (1985) and Glaser et al., (2013).

The literature of budgetary gamesmanship in the public and private sectors validates that the influence of power and politics as a known, accepted principle. Further, the budgetary gamesmanship is has transformed into an essential part of any manager's position, including the CISO role.; Unlike the logical approaches found in IT security literature; the human and organizational approach of power and politics won't change or reform any time soon. While awareness and governance may mitigate the impact of power and politics, CISOs need to be very aware of budgetary games among technological, cultural, legal and other factors that are now part of the new style of leadership needed in the IT security space.

Expenditure and Power Alignment

The importance of power and money are relevant factors and underlying facets in current IT security leadership. Batteau (2011) reviewed the importance of trust in IT security leadership from multiple levels of analysis. Batteau showed a culture of IT security can be cultivated by a CISO, in the same sense that a gardener cultivates a flower garden (p.45, 2011). Conversely, distrust and cynicism in leadership have created the largest known federal IT security breaches. In the examination of WikiLeaks, Batteau (2011) explored IT security leadership mistakes; and found, for example, negative reciprocity led to unremediated insider disillusionment and reaction (p. 39). Berghel similarly explored a different federal IT security breach, caused by Snowden (2014, p. 65) as an illustration of disillusionment with leadership that made real the insider threat. Put more simply, current IT security leadership ignores power and politics to its detriment. Moreover, outdated, power-based, IT security leadership approaches as argued by Egli, (2013) underscore additional, related issues to power and IT security leadership. Egli's (2013) argument aligns with Berghel's (2014) suggestion that security is not created via an over-reliance on firepower.

A historical example of over-reliance in the kinetic-war space would be the billions spent on Maginot line (Trueman, 2015). Misplaced trust and the resulting devastation of the German blitzkrieg led to the subsequent surrender of France (Trueman, 2015). Hardware-based approaches directly parallel the IT security argument of old-fashioned over-reliance on technology as forwarded by Batteau (2011), who argues the reliance on technology leaves an organization less secure, just as France was unwittingly made less secure by the investment Maginot line. By assuming more technology is the answer, current IT security scholarship and leadership demonstrates a serious gap in understanding the role and importance of power and politics – and that gap has already resulted in the largest, most impactful breaches to IT and national security.

Just as technology alone cannot fulfill all of IT security because human intelligence vectors will discover the limitations of technology and evade the controls, Berghel's (2014) focus on failures of leadership and power links an underlying theme of needed new IT security leadership – no 'yes men' or simply the politically faithful. The importance of clear CISO empowerment and leadership to obtain budgets and spend wisely are implicated by Berghel (2014). In contrast, the insufficient or wasteful impact when a CISO's leadership is inefficient or lacks IT Security expertise:

Due to exceedingly poor leadership, our intelligence agencies have wasted hundreds of billions of dollars on a brutish surveillance panopticon, whereas more talented and refined intellects could have invented and deployed constitutionally compatible alternatives at a fraction of the cost (p.67)

The human elements of power and politics have tremendous influence on both people and process (Mintzberg, 1985). Batteau (2011) argues that current IT security leadership approach leaves at least 2/3^{rds} of IT security under or entirely unaddressed (p. 37). Similarly, Berghel (2014) explored how the current leadership criteria do not produce excellent CISOs and moreover, "Effective cyber security leadership is hard to find because of finely interwoven technical, legal, and ethical dimensions involved." (p.65). Berghel (2014) deconstructs the elements that define success in current security leadership and reveals that today's leader-selection criteria produce the opposite of an effective IT leader or CISO.

Net Effect on IT Security Posture

Egli (2013) best summarized the underlying leadership issue:

...while we live in an interconnected world of complex 21st century vulnerabilities, we often employ 20th century ways of thinking and planning for security – allocating resources for physical protection based on the most senior member on the congressional committee, best written grant proposal, or a bias for "fixing things" to relieve the most immediate pain. (p.33)

Egli (2013) leveraged the Gunderson, Holling and Ludwig 2002 study of ecological and social systems to form the proposal of a similar adaptive cycle in physical and IT security. Through a cycle of growth, crisis, transformation and renewal, systems flex and become stronger through adversity to promote resilience at all levels, through awareness, planning, resource allocation and leadership (p. 44). IT security and leadership mindset are among the many elements included by Egli (2013) as complex factors that needs to change in order to create a resilient system at all levels – physical, virtual, economic - for local, regional, state and national issues. Egli, (2013) demonstrated that the current resource allocation approach in the federal budgetary approach seems to be stuck on crisis, in agreement with Andrews (2011) assessment. Organizational resistance (Burke, 2011; Klein, 1989) prevents progression through the adaptive steps of transformation and renewal – therefore according to Egli's (2013) logic; the ongoing budget adversity continues to weaken and degrade the IT security system, as well as the federal budget process as a whole.

Egli's 2013 analysis agrees with the Friedman (2011) article, which examined the United States federal homeland security approach and found the perpetuation and exacerbation of fear to further political and funding goals. Friedman (2011) acknowledged IT threats as a possible avenue of harm. However, IT threats not only hypothetical – as the current agency head of the IRS, John Koskinen, recently observed:

Every day, federal departments and agencies face sophisticated and persistent IT threats that pose strategic, economic, and security challenges to our nation. Addressing these IT threats has required a bold reassessment of the way we approach security in the digital age and a significant investment... (Otto, 2016, p. 1)

However, similar to Egli (2013), and Koskinen (Otto, 2016), Friedman advocates not only a change in IT leadership, but also communications, risk management and cost-benefit analysis (2011) in parallel to the IT security budgetary literature (Garvey et al., 2011; Smeraldi and Malacaria, 2014). Friedman illustrated that current approaches are the worst of both worlds, where IT security remains poor and people are more afraid than ever. Friedman lays the result at the feet of intentional antagonism of politicians, institutions, think tanks, subject matter experts and those who benefit from fear mongering (2011, p.94). In agreement with Andrew (2011), Freidman described the situation as an institutional one, which emphasizes crisis and vulnerability rather than strength (2011). Further, much like Epp et al., (2014) Friedman (2011) argues that ongoing problems, like IT security can require a national response however, that almost any response can be sold as the correct one to furthering political objectives. Poor IT security built by a yes-man CISO may use outmoded thinking, overreliance on perimeter hardware-approaches, and intentional antagonism of fear without ending the crisis - all the makings of a digital Maginot line that leaves an organization feeling falsely secure but crushingly vulnerable to invasion and collapse.

New IT security leadership needs to understand that the power and political connectedness of a CISO influences budget and funding decisions, much like the private sector study by Glaser, Lopez-De-Silanes and Sautner (2013). Glaser et al., (2013) established metrics to measure not only the power and connectedness of each leader, but the degree of capital allocation, the degree of investment and the performance of each budgetary decision and specifically included IT and computer investments as one of the areas included in the study (p. 1608). The Glaser et al., (2013) methodology outlined the clear distinction between planned capital vs ad-hoc budgetary decisions in parallel to the mandatory vs discretionary budgetary status within large organizations and federal government (Brogan, 2012). Glaser et al., (2013) recognized the budgetary game (Libby and Lindsay, 2009; Lukka, 1988) as the basis of empire building similar to Mintzberg (1985). The cited literature can be extrapolated to IT security budgeting and funding as the literature discusses the same problem area that affects both. Corporations and public sector need a new style of CISO to overcome complex challenges that outdated thinking and antiquated approaches simply perpetuate or worsen with unsound investments.

SOLUTIONS AND RECOMMENDATIONS

The CISO needs to understand the influence of power and politics to cultivate IT security via cultural as well as technological changes (Batteau, 2011) while creating an innovative IT leadership style that creates appropriate decisions; unaffected by current standards of status and prestige (Berghel, 2014).

Within the budgeting process, a CISO needs to know the game to score not only in budgetary establishment and management but in funding and control, as well (Buchanan, 2008; Libby and Lindsay, 2009; Lukka, 1988). A CISO can't ignore of organizational power and politics and must recognize that partisan agendas endeavor to influence budgeting, as well (Andrews, 2011; Epp et al., 2014; Lapsley et al., 2011; Williams et al., 1990). Excellent CISOs must become familiar with the fields of organizational theory, management, accounting, public administration, business anthropology and organizational power (French and Raven, 1959; March, 1966; Mintzberg, 1983). The theory of budgeting as a political game in both the public and private sectors arose within multiple references in the literature and therefore must be incorporated in the IT security strategy of the CISO (Clegg, 1989; Lapsley et al., 2011; Mintzberg, 1985). If a CISO does less, the result is in an organization that remains under-protected because of application of aged approaches in a new era, regardless of how much money is spent (Batteau, 2011; Berghel, 2014; Egli, 2013).

The real impact affects all Americans today regardless of role, whose life and livelihood are protected by CISOs, CEOs and agency heads who may be using outdated thought (Berghel, 2014) and 20th-century mechanisms instead of addressing the contemporary complexity that befits the ongoing danger of IT threats (Egli, 2013; Otto, 2016). CISOs must address IT security holonically (McHugh, 1996) via a complex adaptive systems (Egli, 2013; Uhl-Bien et al., 2007) of technology, people, policy and process (Bagchi-Sen et al., 2010; Batteau, 2011). Exploring power and politics as an influence in budgeting will ensure the most effective IT security countermeasures are selected (Garvey et al., 2011) by the leader with skills with the IT decision making as well as power and politics to ensure sufficiency. The literature has made clear that power and politics are affecting the efficacy of the IT security, despite the best intentions of the logic of IT security scholarship.

Poor IT security posture undermines the critical infrastructure of America and the world (Pawlak and Wendling, 2013). While there is an industry-wide agreement that IT threats (Contreras, Denardis, and Teplinsky, 2013) are dangerous, this agreement doesn't ensure the appropriate spending or results are created.

Conceptual Framework

In IT security, the potential positive or negative impact of organizational power and politics could be traced by examining the net effect on the organizational IT security posture. It could be interesting to examine if the monies were used to establish or improve the people, process, policy or technology protections of the IT security posture. If there are gaps in the comprehensive coverage a loss of funds or poor allocation may have a net zero or potentially a negative impact. The following conceptual framework is built on the streams of IT security, power and politics and budgeting/ management academic literature.

The Glaser et al., (2013) theoretical frame could be expanded to look at intergroup contact, partisan alignment, agency participation and other measures which indicate political fellowship and power dynamics (van Dick et al., 2004). The power dynamics are represented by the original request and the cash windfalls potentially influenced by power and politics as a type of score as measured by the management budget and actual spend. The subsequent allocation onto the operating plan can represent application of influences to affect the original allocation to shift between IT security and other budgetary aspects. The factor of cash windfalls in parallel to the Glaser et al., (2013) study could be examined for the alignment to the power dynamic, which could be the same as discretionary or ad-hoc capital expenditure in the IT security sphere (Egli, 2013; Epp et al., 2014; Lapsley et al., 2011). Those seeking data protection and those endeavoring to protect data will have a unified benefit as the human systems; technical solutions; policies and enforcement; new, refined, or established processes will be more likely to have appropriate, sufficient resources and will not be undermined by games with the management budget.

Figure 1.

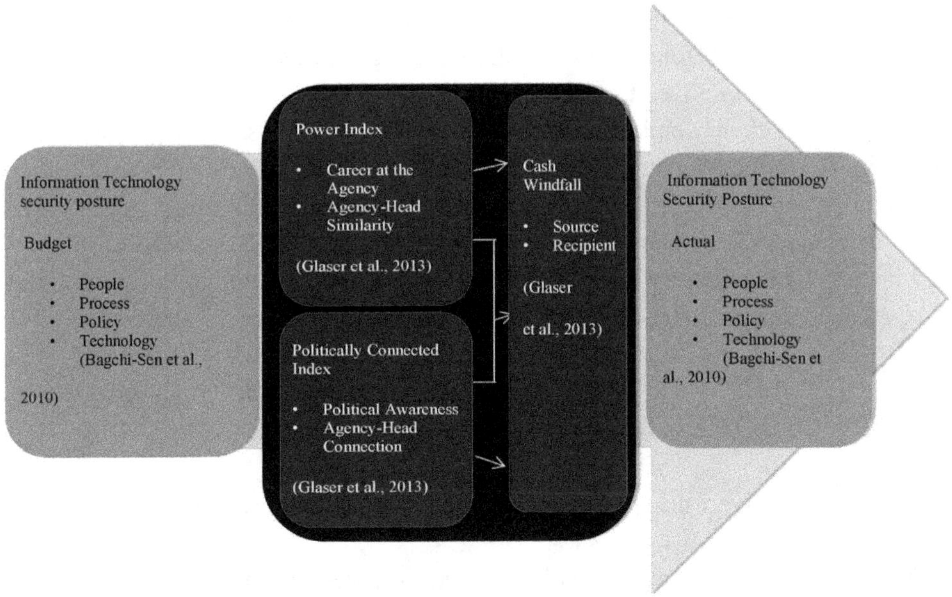

FUTURE RESEARCH DIRECTION

The research suggests that literature from disparate human and organizational, business and other fields can be applied to IT security, therefore the first future research direction would be to validate that suggestion. Additionally, the solutions and recommendations do not assert an optimal balance is between investment in the four holonic systems of people, process, policy and technology, which could be a direction of future research. Lastly, while this research calls for a new style of CISO with different criteria for selection and leadership, there are no established measures to validate this assertion, which could be researched subsequently.

CONCLUSION

This research asked many questions, and was able to discover answers to many of those questions posed. New CISOs must be aware of power and politics to score hits for IT security in the game of budgets in the organizational arena (Mintzberg, 1985). This is a critical understanding for CISOs and the CEOs or agency heads who must ensure IT security initiatives are receiving sufficient resources. The extent to which organizational power and politics influences CEOs or agency heads and CISOs is unclear, therefore also unclear is if a more protected, safer America can be created via the current budget, allocation, sweep and spend approach for IT security by CISOs, given the fragmented IT security leadership cadre of today. The consequences of breach are severe, therefore CISOs and CEOs or agency heads must work together to fund IT security in all four components.

While CISOs clearly endeavor to create a more protected, safer organization and world with the money spent; they may be using ineffective mindsets, ignore culture and focus on adding more technology which could waste the allocations CISOs gained or gamed. CISOs spending of tens of billions of dollars (Selyukh, Shalal, and Mason, 2015) annually to counter the very real attacks that are ongoing today (Otto, 2016) must ensure the budget results in comprehensive IT security.

ACKNOWLEDGMENT

This research received no specific grant from any funding agency in the public, corporate or not-for-profit sectors.

The author received a scholarship to attend George Washington University as part of a grant to create a doctoral CyberCorp from National Science Foundation and is ever so grateful for the honor.

REFERENCES

ACM Joint Task Force on Cybersecurity Education. (2016). *Defining Cybersecurity*. Retrieved from http://www.csec2017.org/

Andrews, M. (2011). The (il)logics of federal budgeting, and why crisis must come. *Public Administration Review, 70*(2), 345–348.

Bagchi-Sen, S., Rao, H. R., Upadhyaya, S. J., & Chai, S. (2010). Women in cybersecurity: A study of career advancement. *IT Professional*, *12*(February), 24–31. doi:10.1109/MITP.2010.39

Batteau, A. W. (2011). Creating a culture of enterprise cybersecurity. *International Journal of Business Anthropology*, *2*(2), 36–47. Retrieved from http://ezproxy.net.ucf.edu/login?url=http://search.ebscohost.com/login.aspx?direct=true&db=buh&AN=67474318&site=ehost-live

Berghel, H. (2014). Leadership failures in the national security complex. *Computer*, *47*(6), 64–71. doi:10.1109/MC.2014.152

Breach, E. (2017). *Cyber Insurance To The Rescue?!* Retrieved from https://www.riskbasedsecurity.com/2017/09/equifax-breach-cyber-insurance-to-the-rescue/

Brogan, M. (2012). The politics of budgeting: Evaluating the effects of the political election cycle on state-level budget forecast errors. *Public Administration Review*, *71*(3), 345–348.

Buchanan, D. A. (2008). You stab my back, I'll stab yours: Management experience and perceptions of organization political behaviour. *British Journal of Management*, *19*(1), 49–64. doi:10.1111/j.1467-8551.2007.00533.x

Burke, W. W. (2011). A Perspective on the Field of Organization Development and Change: The Zeigarnik Effect. *The Journal of Applied Behavioral Science*, *47*(2), 143–167. doi:10.1177/0021886310388161

Chang, J. M. (2013). New trends in cybersecurity. *IT Professional*, 2–3.

Clegg, S. (1989). Circuits of Power: a Framework for Analysis. In *Frameworks of Power* (pp. 187–239). London: Sage Publications. doi:10.4135/9781446279267.n8

Clinger Cohen Act of 1996. (1996). United States: U.S.C. Retrieved from http://uscode.house.gov/download/title_40.shtml

Congressional Budget Office. (2016). *Bills Reviewed by CBO That Contained Mandates | Congressional Budget Office*. Retrieved from https://www.cbo.gov/umra-search

Contreras, J. L., Denardis, L., & Teplinsky, M. (2013). Mapping today's cybersecurity landscape. *The American University Law Review*, *62*(5), 1113–1130. Retrieved from http://search.proquest.com/docview/1443695399?accountid=11243

Dixon, H. B. (2012). Cybersecurity...how important is it? *51. The Judges' Journal*, 36–39.

Egli, D. S. (2013). Beyond the storms: Strengthening preparedness, response, & resilience in the 21st century. *Journal of Strategic Security*, *6*(2), 32–45. doi:10.5038/1944-0472.6.2.3

Engle, B., & Guttmann, R. (2014). The evolution of the CISO role and organizational readiness. *CSO*. Retrieved from https://www.csoonline.com/article/2838371/security-leadership/the-evolution-of-the-ciso-role-and-organizational-readiness.html

Epp, D. A., Lovett, J., & Baumgartner, F. R. (2014). Partisan priorities and public budgeting. *Political Research Quarterly*, *67*(4), 864–878. doi:10.1177/1065912914550045

(2011). French, J. R., & Raven, B. (1959). *The bases of social power*. InCartwright, D. (Ed.), *Studies in social power* (pp. 150–167). Ann Arbor, MI: Research Center for Group Dynamics, Institute for Social Research, University of Michigan reprinted in Shafritz, J. M., Ott, J. S., & Jang, Y. S.

Garvey, P. R., Moynihan, R. A., & Servi, L. (2011). A macro method for measuring economic-benefit returns on cybersecurity investments: The table top approach. *Systems Engineering*, *14*, 305–326. doi:10.1002ys

Glaser, M., Lopez-De-Silanes, F., & Sautner, Z. (2013). Opening the black box: Internal capital markets and managerial power. *The Journal of Finance*, *68*(4), 1577–1631. doi:10.1111/jofi.12046

Goldman, E. H. (2012). The effect of acquisition decision making on security posture. *Information Management & Computer Security*, *205*(5), 350–363. doi:10.1108/09685221211286520

Goodchild, J. (2009). *The Unique Story and Evolution of the CSO Role*. Retrieved from https://www.cio.com/article/2427347/security0/the-unique-story-and-evolution-of-the-cso-role.html

Gullo, T. (2004). History and evaluation of the Unfunded Mandates Reform Act. *National Tax Journal*, *57*(3), 559–570. doi:10.17310/ntj.2004.3.04

Hathaway, M. (2012, December). Creating the demand curve for cybersecurity. *Georgetown Jounral of International Affairs*, 163–170.

Hoover, J. N. (2013). Federal CIO Details Concerns On Looming Budget Cuts. *Information Week, 1*. Retrieved from http://www.informationweek.com/regulations/federal-cio-details-concerns-on-looming-budget-cuts/d/d-id/1108634

Jenkins, R. (2009). The ways and means of power: Efficacy and resources. In S. Clegg & M. Haugaard (Eds.), *The SAGE Handbook of Power* (pp. 140–157). London: Sage Publications. doi:10.4135/9780857021014.n8

Klein, D. (1989). Some notes on the dynamics of resistance to change: The defender role. In Diagnostics of Planned Change (pp. 98–105). Academic Press.

Kuhn, R. (2010, August). Cybersecurity. *IT Professional, IEEE*, 18–20.

Lapsley, I., Midwinter, A., Nambiar, T., & Steccolini, I. (2011). Government budgeting, power and negotiated order. *Management Accounting Research*, *22*(1), 16–25. doi:10.1016/j.mar.2010.10.009

Libby, T., & Lindsay, R. M. (2009). Beyond budgeting or budgeting reconsidered? A survey of North-American budgeting practice. *Management Accounting Research*, *21*(1), 56–75. doi:10.1016/j.mar.2009.10.003

Libicki, M. C., Ablon, L., & Webb, T. (2015). *The defender's dilemma - Charting a course toward cybersecurity*. Santa Monica, CA: RAND Corporation.

Lippuner, D. (2011). Something's gotta give! *Journal of Government Financial Management*, *63*(1), 26–30.

Lukka, K. (1988). Budgetary biasing in organizations: Theoretical framework and empirical evidence. *Accounting, Organizations and Society*, *13*(3), 281–301. doi:10.1016/0361-3682(88)90005-0

Lyngaas, S. (2016, February). Cybersecurity: White House wants $19B for cyber in FY 2017. *FCW: The Business of Federal Technology Federal Computer Weekly*, 1. Retrieved from https://fcw.com/articles/2016/02/09/cyber-budget-lyngaas.aspx

March, J. G. (1966). The power of power. In D. Easton (Ed.), *Varieties of political theory* (pp. 39-70). Englewood Cliffs, NJ: Prentice-Hall.

McHugh, N. D. (1996). Book reviews - Beyond business process re-eingineering:Towards the holonic enterprise.pdf. *International Journal of Production Research*, *34*(12), 3515–3517. doi:10.1080/00207549608905103

McMahon, M. (2016). *What is Holistic Security?* Retrieved from http://www.wisegeek.com/what-is-holistic-security.htm

Mintzberg, H. (1979). The structure of organizations: A synthesis of the research. Upper Saddle River, NJ: Prentice-Hall.

Mintzberg, H. (1983). Power in and around organizations. Englewood Cliffs, NJ: Prentice-Hall.

Mintzberg, H. (1985). The organization as political arena. *Journal of Management Studies*, *22*(2), 133–154. doi:10.1111/j.1467-6486.1985.tb00069.x

NIST NVD - Control - AU-10 - NON-REPUDIATION. (2017). Retrieved from https://nvd.nist.gov/800-53/Rev4/control/AU-10

Orton, J. D., & Weick, K. E. (1990). Loosely coupled systems: A reconceptualization. *Academy of Management Review*, *15*(2), 203–223.

Otto, G. (2016, July). White House releases federal cybersecurity workforce strategy. *Fedscoop*, 1. Retrieved from http://fedscoop.com/us-government-cybersecurity-workforce-strategy

Pawlak, P., & Wendling, C. (2013). Trends in cyberspace: Can governments keep up? *Environment Systems & Decisions*, *33*(4), 536–543. doi:10.100710669-013-9470-5

Pickford, M., Wheelock, J., & Gullo, T. (2014). *Congressional budget office cost estimate: S. 2521 Federal Information Security Modernization Act of 2014*. Retrieved from https://www.cbo.gov/sites/default/files/113th-congress-2013-2014/costestimate/s25211.pdf

Public Law 107-347 - Federal Information Security Management Act of 2002 (FISMA), Federal Information Security Modernization Act. (2002). U.S.C. Retrieved from http://csrc.nist.gov/drivers/documents/FISMA-final.pdf

Public Law 113-283 - Federal Information Security Modernization Act of 2014 (FISMA REFORM), Pub. L. No. 3073. (2014). United States of America: U.S.C. Retrieved from https://www.congress.gov/bill/113th-congress/senate-bill/2521

2015. Risk Practices Survey Summary Report. (2015). *Bank Director*.

Scott, T., & Daniel, J. M. (2016). *Announcing the first federal Chief Information Security Officer | whitehouse.gov*. Retrieved from https://www.whitehouse.gov/blog/2016/09/08/announcing-first-federal-chief-information-security-officer

Selyukh, A., Shalal, A., & Mason, J. (2015). *Obama seeks $14 billion to boost U.S. cybersecurity defenses*. Reuters. Retrieved from http://www.reuters.com/article/2015/02/02/us-usa-budget-cybersecurity-idUSKBN0L61WQ20150202

Smeraldi, F., & Malacaria, P. (2014). How to spend it: Optimal investment for cybersecurity position paper. *ACySE '14 Proceedings of the 1st International Workshop on Agents and CyberSecurity,* 1–4.

Stone, D. (2012). Security. In Policy Paradox (3rd ed.; pp. 129–153). New York, NY: W.W. Norton and Company.

Trueman, C. N. (2015). *The Maginot Line - History Learning Site*. Retrieved from http://www.historylearningsite.co.uk/world-war-two/world-war-two-in-western-europe/the-attack-on-western-europe/the-maginot-line/

Uhl-Bien, M., Marion, R., & Mckelvey, B. (2007). Complexity leadership theory: Shifting leadership from the industrial age to the knowledge era. *The Leadership Quarterly, 18*(4), 298–318. doi:10.1016/j.leaqua.2007.04.002

van Dick, R., Wagner, U., Pettigrew, T. F., Christ, O., Wolf, C., Petzel, T., ... Jackson, J. S. (2004). Role of Perceived Importance in Intergroup Contact. *Journal of Personality and Social Psychology, 87*(2), 211–227. doi:10.1037/0022-3514.87.2.211 PMID:15301628

Williams, J. J., Macintosh, N. B., & Moore, J. C. (1990). Budget-related behavior in public sector organizations: Some empirical evidence. *Accounting, Organizations and Society, 15*(3), 221–246. doi:10.1016/0361-3682(90)90006-G

Wilson, K. S. (2013). Conflicts among the pillars of information assurance. *IT Professional, IEEE, 15*(August), 44–49. doi:10.1109/MITP.2012.24

ADDITIONAL READING

Denison, D. R., & Mishra, A. K. (1995). Toward a theory of organizational culture and effectiveness. *Organization Science, 6*(2), 204–222. doi:10.1287/orsc.6.2.204

Hatch, M. J. (2004). Dynamics in organizational culture. In M. S. Poole & A. Van de Ven (Eds.), *Handbook of organizational change and innovation* (pp. 190–211). Oxford University Press.

Hatch, M. J. (2010). Material and meaning in the dynamics of organizational culture and identity with implications for leadership of organizational change. In N. Ashkanasy, C. Wilderom, & M. Peterson (Eds.), *The handbook of organizational culture and climate* (2nd ed., pp. 341–348). Thousand Oaks, CA: Sage.

Lewis, M. W. (2000). Exploring paradox: Toward a more comprehensive guide. *Academy of Management Review, 25*(4), 760–776.

Luscher, L. S., & Lewis, M. W. (2008). Organizational change and managerial sensemaking: Working through paradox. *Academy of Management Journal*, *51*(2), 221–240. doi:10.5465/AMJ.2008.31767217

Markus, M. L., & Robey, D. (1988). Information technology and organizational change: Causal structure in theory and research. *Management Science*, *34*(5), 583–598. doi:10.1287/mnsc.34.5.583

Morrison, E. W., & Milliken, F. J. (2000). Organizational silence: A barrier to change and development in a pluralistic world. *Academy of Management Review*, *25*(4), 706–725.

Orlikowski, W. J. (1992). The duality of technology: Rethinking the concept of technology in organizations. *Organization Science*, *3*(3), 398–427. doi:10.1287/orsc.3.3.398

Piderit, S. K. (2000). Rethinking resistance and recognizing ambivalence: A multidimensional view of attitudes toward an organizational change. *Academy of Management Review*, *25*(4), 783–794.

Schein, E. H. (2010). The Concept of Organizational Culture: Why Bother? (chapter 1, pp. 7-22); The Three Levels of Culture (chapter 2, pp. 23-34). In Organizational culture and leadership (2nd Ed.). San Francisco: Jossey-Bass.

Schwandt, D. R., & Szabla, D. (2007). Systems and Leadership: Coevolution or Mutual Evolution towards Complexity? In J. K. Hazy, J. A. Goldstein, & B. B. Lichtenstein (Eds.), *Complex Systems Leadership Theory* (pp. 35–60). Marblehead, MA: ISCE Publishing.

Compilation of References

2015 Risk Practices Survey Summary Report. (2015). *Bank Director.*

Abaker, I., Yaqoob, A., & Mokhtar, G. (2015). The rise of "big data" on cloud computing: Review and open research issues. *Information Systems, 47*, 98–115. doi:10.1016/j.is.2014.07.006

Abawajy, J. (2015). Comprehensive analysis of big data variety landscape. *International Journal of Parallel, Emergent and Distributed Systems, 30*(1).

Abdel-Kader, M., & Nguyen, T. P. (2011). An investigation of enterprise resource planning implementation in a small firm: A study of problems encountered and successes achieved. *International Journal of Enterprise Information Systems, 7*(1), 18–40. doi:10.4018/jeis.2011010102

Abii, F., Ogula, D. C. N., & Rose, J. M. (2013). Effects Of Individual And Organizational Factors On The Turnover Intentions Of Information Technology Professionals. *International Journal of Management, 30*(2), 740–756.

Abraham, R., Tribolet, J., & Winter, R. (2013). Transformation of multi-level systems: Theoretical grounding and consequences for Enterprise Architecture Management. In D. Aveiro & K. Galoul (Eds.), Advances in Enterprise Engineering VII (Vol. 146). Springer Berlin.

ACM Joint Task Force on Cybersecurity Education. (2016). *Defining Cybersecurity*. Retrieved from http://www.csec2017.org/

Agarwal, R., & Karahanna, E. (2000). Time flies when you're having fun: Cognitive absorption and beliefs about information technology usage. *Management Information Systems Quarterly, 24*(4), 665–694. doi:10.2307/3250951

Agarwal, S. (2013). *BlinkDB: Queries with Bounded Errors and Bounded Response Times on Very Large Data*. ACM. doi:10.1145/2465351.2465355

Agosti, M., Ferro, N., & Silvello, G. (2016). Digital library interoperability at high level of abstraction. *Future Generation Computer Systems, 55*, 129–146. doi:10.1016/j.future.2015.09.020

Ahn, T., Ryu, S., & Han, I. (2007). The impact of Web quality and playfulness on user acceptance of online retailing. *Information & Management, 44*(3), 263–275. doi:10.1016/j.im.2006.12.008

Ajzen, I. (1991). The Theory Of Planned Behavior. *Organizational Behavior and Human Decision Processes, 50*(2), 179–211. doi:10.1016/0749-5978(91)90020-T

Akkermans, H. A., Bogerd, P., Yücesan, E., & Van Wassenhove, L. N. (2003). The impact of ERP on supply chain management: Exploratory findings from a European Delphi study. *European Journal of Operational Research, 146*(2), 284–301. doi:10.1016/S0377-2217(02)00550-7

Alamri, M. (2011). Higher education in Saudi Arabia. *Journal of Higher Education Theory and Practice, 11*(4), 88.

Alarcon, G. M. (2011). A Meta-Analysis Of Burnout With Job Demands, Resources, And Attitudes. *Journal of Vocational Behavior, 79*(2), 549–562. doi:10.1016/j.jvb.2011.03.007

Al-Debei, M. M., Akroush, M. N., & Ashouri, M. I. (2015). Consumer attitudes towards online shopping: The effects of trust, perceived benefits, and perceived web quality. *Internet Research, 25*(5), 707–733. doi:10.1108/IntR-05-2014-0146

Alenezi, A. M. (2012). *Faculty members' perception of E-Learning in higher education in the Kingdom of Saudi Arabia (KSA)* (Doctoral dissertation). Texas Tech University.

Alenezi, M., & Magel, K. (2014). Empirical evaluation of a new coupling metric: Combining structural and semantic coupling. *International Journal of Computers and Applications, 36*(1). doi:10.2316/Journal.202.2014.1.202-3902

Alexopoulou, N., Nikolaidou, M., Kanellis, P., Mantzana, V., Anagnostopoulos, D., & Martakos, D. (2010). Infusing agility in business processes through an event-centric approach. *International Journal of Business Information Systems, 6*(1), 21. doi:10.1504/IJBIS.2010.034005

Al-Gahtani, S. S. (2016). Empirical investigation of E-Learning acceptance and assimilation: a structural equation model. *Applied Computing and Informatics, 12*(1), 27e50. 10.1016/j.aci.2014.09.001

Al-Gahtani, S. S. (2011). Modeling the electronic transactions acceptance using an extended technology acceptance model. *Applied Computing and Informatics, 9*(1), 47–77. doi:10.1016/j.aci.2009.04.001

Al-Ghaith, W., Sanzogni, L., & Sandhu, K. (2010). Factors influencing the adoption and usage of online services in Saudi Arabia. *EJISDC: The Electronic Journal on Information Systems in Developing Countries,* (40), 1.

Al-Harbi, K. A. S. (2011). E-Learning in the Saudi tertiary education: Potential and challenges. *Applied Computing and Informatics, 9*(1), 31–46. doi:10.1016/j.aci.2010.03.002

Al-Hujran, O., Al-Lozi, E., & Al-Debei, M. M. (2014). "Get Ready to Mobile Learning": Examining Factors Affecting College Students' Behavioral Intentions to Use M-Learning in Saudi Arabia. *Jordan Journal of Business Administration, 10*(1).

Al-Mashari, M., Al-Mudimigh, A., & Zairi, M. (2003). Enterprise resource planning: A taxonomy of critical factors. *European Journal of Operational Research, 146*(2), 352–364. doi:10.1016/S0377-2217(02)00554-4

Al-Mashari, M., & Zairi, M. (2000). Supply-chain re-engineering using enterprise resource planning (ERP) systems: An analysis of a SAP R/3 implementation case. *International Journal of Physical Distribution & Logistics Management, 30*(3/4), 296–313. doi:10.1108/09600030010326064

Al-Saleem, S., & Ullah, H. (2014). Security considerations and recommendations in computer based testing. *The Scientific World Journal, 2014*, 1–7. doi:10.1155/2014/562787 PMID:25254250

Al-Sarrani, N. (2010). *Concerns and professional development needs of science faculty at Taibah university in adopting blended learning* (Doctoral dissertation). Kansas State University. Retrieved Mar 9th, 2016 from: http://krex.kstate.edu/dspace/bitstream/2097/3887/1/NauafAl-Sarrani2010

Al-Zamil, O. A. (2003). *High School Social Studies Teachers' Attitudes and Usage of Instructional Technology in Saudi Arabia* (Unpublished doctoral dissertation). University of Arkansas.

Alzamil, Z. A. (2006). Students' perception towards the E-Learning at the GOTEVOT and the Arab Open University in Riyadh. *Journal of King Saud University: Educational Sciences and Islamic Studies, 18*(2), 655–698.

Amid, A., Moalagh, M., & Ravasan, A. Z. (2012). Identification and classification of ERP critical failure factors in Iranian industries. *Information Systems, 37*(3), 227–237. doi:10.1016/j.is.2011.10.010

Amundsen, M. (2014). APIs to Affordances: A New Paradigm for Services on the Web. In C. Pautasso, E. Wilde, & R. Alarcon (Eds.), *REST: Advanced Research Topics and Practical Applications* (pp. 91–106). New York, NY: Springer. doi:10.1007/978-1-4614-9299-3_6

Anam, S., Kim, Y., Kang, B., & Liu, Q. (2016). Adapting a knowledge-based schema matching system for ontology mapping. In *Proceedings of the Australasian Computer Science Week Multiconference* (p. 27). New York, NY: ACM Press. 10.1145/2843043.2843048

Andrews, M. (2011). The (il)logics of federal budgeting, and why crisis must come. *Public Administration Review, 70*(2), 345–348.

Armstrong, D. J., & Riemenschneider, C. K. (2011). *The Influence Of Demands And Resources On Emotional Exhaustion With The Information Systems Profession. Paper Presented At The Thirty Second International Conference On Information Systems*, Shanghai, China.

Ashford, B., Kreiner, G., & Fugate, M. (2000). All in a Day's Work: Boundaries and Micro Role Transitions. *Academy of Management Review, 25*(3), 472–491.

Asiri, M. J. S., Mahmud, R. B., Abu Bakar, K., & Mohd Ayub, A. F. B. (2012). Factors influencing the use of learning management system in Saudi Arabian higher education: A theoretical framework. *Higher Education Studies, 2*(2), 125. doi:10.5539/hes.v2n2p125

Athanasopoulos, D. (2017). Self-Adaptive Service Organization for Pragmatics-Aware Service Discovery. In *Proceedings of the IEEE International Conference on Services Computing* (pp. 164-171). Piscataway, NJ: IEEE Computer Society Press. 10.1109/SCC.2017.28

Ayag, Z., & Özdemir, R. (2007). An intelligent approach to ERP software selection through fuzzy ANP. *International Journal of Production Research*, *45*(10), 2169–2194. doi:10.1080/00207540600724849

Babu, D., & Darsi, M. (2013). A Survey on Service Oriented Architecture and Metrics to Measure Coupling. *International Journal on Computer Science and Engineering*, *5*(8), 726–733.

Baddeley, A. (1986). *Working memory*. Oxford, UK: Oxford University Press.

Bagchi-Sen, S., Rao, H. R., Upadhyaya, S. J., & Chai, S. (2010). Women in cybersecurity: A study of career advancement. *IT Professional*, *12*(February), 24–31. doi:10.1109/MITP.2010.39

Baghdadi, Y. (2014). Modelling business process with services: Towards agile enterprises. *International Journal of Business Information Systems*, *15*(4), 410–433. doi:10.1504/IJBIS.2014.060377

Bakker, A. B., Demerouti, E., & Sanz-Vergel, A. I. (2014). Burnout And Work Engagement: The JD-R Approach. *Annual Review of Organizational Psychology and Organizational Behavior*, *1*(1), 389–411. doi:10.1146/annurev-orgpsych-031413-091235

Bakker, A. B., Demerouti, E., & Verbeke, W. (2004). Using The Job Demands-Resources Model To Predict Burnout And Performance. *Human Resource Management*, *43*(1), 83–104. doi:10.1002/hrm.20004

Bakker, A. B., Hakanen, J. J., Demerouti, E., & Xanthopoulou, D. (2007). Job Resources Boost Work Engagement, Particulary When Job Demands Are High. *Journal of Educational Psychology*, *99*(2), 274–284. doi:10.1037/0022-0663.99.2.274

Bassett, L. (2015). *Introduction to JavaScript Object Notation: A to-the-point Guide to JSON*. Sebastopol, CA: O'Reilly Media, Inc.

Batteau, A. W. (2011). Creating a culture of enterprise cybersecurity. *International Journal of Business Anthropology*, *2*(2), 36–47. Retrieved from http://ezproxy.net.ucf.edu/login?url=http://search.ebscohost.com/login.aspx?direct=true&db=buh&AN=67474318&site=ehost-live

Beck, K. (2001). *Manifesto for Agile Software Development*. Retrieved from http://www.agilemanifesto.org/principles.html

Beheshti, H. M., & Beheshti, C. M. (2010). Improving productivity and firm performance with enterprise resource planning. *Enterprise Information Systems*, *4*(4), 445–472. doi:10.1080/17517575.2010.511276

Bejar, I. (2012). Item generation: Implications for a validity argument. In M. Gierl & T. Haladyna (Eds.), *Automatic item generation: Theory and practice* (pp. 40–56). New York: Routledge.

Bejar, I. I. (1993). A generative approach to psychological and educational measurement. In N. Frederiskson, R. J. Mislevy, & I. I. Bejar (Eds.), *Test theory for a new generation of tests* (pp. 323–359). Mahwah, NJ: Lawrence Erlbaum Associates.

Bendoly, E., & Schoenherr, T. (2005). ERP system and implementation-process benefits: Implications for B2B e-procurement. *International Journal of Operations & Production Management*, *25*(4), 304–319. doi:10.1108/01443570510585516

Bennis, W. G. (1966). Changing organizations. *The Journal of Applied Behavioral Science*, *2*(3), 247–263. doi:10.1177/002188636600200301

Bentler, P., & Bonett, D. (1980). Significance tests and goodness of fit in the analysis of covariance structures. *Psychological Bulletin*, *88*(3), 588–606. doi:10.1037/0033-2909.88.3.588

Berghel, H. (2014). Leadership failures in the national security complex. *Computer*, *47*(6), 64–71. doi:10.1109/MC.2014.152

Bider, I., & Jalali, A. (2016). Agile business process development: Why, how and when—applying Nonaka's theory of knowledge transformation to business process development. *Information Systems and e-Business Management*, *14*(4), 693–731. doi:10.100710257-014-0256-1

Bifet, A. (2013). Mining Big Data. In *Real Time*. Informatica.

Big data and privacy. (n.d.). Standard Law School-The center for internet and society.

Blumenthal, D. (2004). Launching HITECH. *The New England Journal of Medicine*, *362*(5), 382–385. doi:10.1056/NEJMp0912825 PMID:20042745

Blumenthal, D. (2009). Stimulating the adoption of health information technology. *The New England Journal of Medicine*, *360*(15), 1477–1499. doi:10.1056/NEJMp0901592 PMID:19321856

Blumenthal, D. (2011). Implementation of the federal health information technology initiative. *The New England Journal of Medicine*, *365*(25), 2426–2431. doi:10.1056/NEJMsr1112158 PMID:22187990

Bora, A., & Bezboruah, T. (2015). A Comparative Investigation on Implementation of RESTful versus SOAP based Web Services. *International Journal of Database Theory and Application*, *8*(3), 297–312. doi:10.14257/ijdta.2015.8.3.26

Bormuth, J. R., & Menzel, P. (1970). *On the theory of achievement test items*. Chicago: University of Chicago Press.

Boscai, B. (2017). *The evolution of e-recruitment: the introduction of online recruiter*. Retrieved December 1, 2017 from http://real.mtak.hu/54549/1/162_Management_and_Organization-Pearson- 2017jún08-DOI_CrossRef-2017jún13f.pdf

Boswell, W. R., & Olson-Buchanan, J. B. (2007). The Use of Communication Technologies After Hours: The Role of Work Attitudes and Work-Life Conflict. *Journal of Management*, *33*(4), 592–610. doi:10.1177/0149206307302552

Botta-Genoulaz, V., & Millet, P. A. (2005). A classification for better use of ERP systems. *Computers in Industry*, *56*(6), 573–587. doi:10.1016/j.compind.2005.02.007

Botta-Genoulaz, V., & Millet, P. A. (2006). An investigation into the use of ERP systems in the service sector. *International Journal of Production Economics*, *99*(1-2), 202–221. doi:10.1016/j.ijpe.2004.12.015

Brailer, D., & Thompson, T. (2004). *Health IT strategic framework*. Washington, DC: Department of Health and Human Services.

Bratton, J., & Gold, J. (2012). *Human Resource Management: Theory and Practice*. Basingstoke, UK: Palgrave Macmillan. doi:10.1007/978-1-137-00095-8

Breach, E. (2017). *Cyber Insurance To The Rescue?!* Retrieved from https://www.riskbasedsecurity.com/2017/09/equifax-breach-cyber-insurance-to-the-rescue/

Brezillon, P. (2003). Using context for supporting users efficiently. *Proceedings of the 36th Annual Hawaii International Conference on System Sciences*.

Bridges, W. (2004). *Transitions: Making sense of life's changes*. Cambridge, MA: De Capo Press.

Bridges, W. (2010). *Managing Transition: Making the Most of Change*. Philadelphia, PA: Accessible Publishing Systems.

Bridges, W. (2013). *Managing Transition: Bridges transition model*. Philadelphia, PA: Accessible Publishing Systems.

Brogan, M. (2012). The politics of budgeting: Evaluating the effects of the political election cycle on state-level budget forecast errors. *Public Administration Review*, *71*(3), 345–348.

Brotheridge, C. M., & Lee, R. T. (2002). Testing A Conservation Of Resources Model Of The Dynamics Of Emotional Labor. *Journal of Occupational Health Psychology*, *7*(1), 57–67. doi:10.1037/1076-8998.7.1.57 PMID:11827234

Buchanan, D. A. (2008). You stab my back, I'll stab yours: Management experience and perceptions of organization political behaviour. *British Journal of Management*, *19*(1), 49–64. doi:10.1111/j.1467-8551.2007.00533.x

Bulger, C. A., Matthews, R. A., & Hoffman, M. E. (2007). Work and Personal Life Boundary Management: Boundary Strength, Work/Personal Life Balance, and the Segmentation-Integration Continuum. *Jounral of Occupational Health Pscyhology*, *12*(4), 365–375. doi:10.1037/1076-8998.12.4.365 PMID:17953495

Buntin, M. B., Jain, S. H., & Blumenthal, D. (2010). Health information technology: Laying the infrastructure for national health reform. *Health Affairs*, *29*(6), 1214–1219. doi:10.1377/hlthaff.2010.0503 PMID:20530358

Burke, W. W. (2011). A Perspective on the Field of Organization Development and Change: The Zeigarnik Effect. *The Journal of Applied Behavioral Science*, *47*(2), 143–167. doi:10.1177/0021886310388161

Burke, W. W. (2013). *Organization Change: Theory and practice*. New York, NY: Sage Publications.

Burrell, S. (2014). *IT Staff Turnover Intentions, Job Modification And The Effects Of Work Recognition At Large Higher Education Public Institutions* (Ed.D. Dissertation). Georgia Southern University.

Cappelli, P. (2001). Making the Most of on-Line Recruiting. *Harvard Business Review*, *79*(3), 139–146. PMID:11246921

Carlson, D. S., Grzywacz, J. G., & Kacmar, K. M. (2010). The Relationship of Schedule Flexibility and Outcomes via the Work-Family Interface. *Journal of Managerial Psychology*, *25*(4), 330–355. doi:10.1108/02683941011035278

Carr, P. (2017). *NAEP Special Interest Group Business Meeting*. Presented at the *annual meeting of the American Educational Research Association*, San Antonio, TX.

Carucci, R. (2016). *Organizations Can't Change If Leaders Can't Change with Them*. Retrieved from https://hbr.org/2016/10/organizations-cant-change-if-leaders-cant-

Castela, N., Dias, P., Zacarias, M., & Tribolet, J. (2012). Collaborative maintenance of business process models. *International Journal of Organisational Design and Engineering*, *2*(1), 61–84. doi:10.1504/IJODE.2012.045903

Central Intelligence Agency (CIA). (2015). *The world factbook*. Retrieved from https://www.cia.gov/library/publications/resources/the-world-factbook/index.html

Chalofsky, N., & Krishna, V. (2009). Meaningfulness, Commitment, And Engagement: The Intersection Of A Deeper Level Of Intrinsic Motivation. *Advances in Developing Human Resources*, *11*(2), 189–203. doi:10.1177/1523422309333147

Chang, J. M. (2013). New trends in cybersecurity. *IT Professional*, 2–3.

Chang, B. L. P. (2002). Career Goals And Career Management Strategy Among Information Technology Professionals. *Career Development International*, *7*(1), 6–13. doi:10.1108/13620430210414829

Chang, C. L. (2010). The Study Of The Turnover Of MIS Professionals--The Gap Between Taiwanese And US Societies. *International Journal of Information Management*, *30*(4), 301–314. doi:10.1016/j.ijinfomgt.2009.11.002

Chaudhry, B., Wang, J., Wu, S., Maglione, M., Mojlca, W., Roth, E., ... Shekelle, P. G. (2006). Systematic review: Impact of health information technology on quality, efficiency, and costs of medical care. *Annals of Internal Medicine*, *144*(10), 742–752. doi:10.7326/0003-4819-144-10-200605160-00125 PMID:16702590

Chau, P. (1997). Reexamining a model for evaluating information center success using a structural equation modeling approach. *Decision Sciences, 28*(2), 309–334. doi:10.1111/j.1540-5915.1997.tb01313.x

Chen, A., & Karahanna, E. (2014). Boundaryless Technology: Understanding The Effects Of Technology-Mediated Interruptions Across The Boundaries Between Work And Personal Life. *AIS Transactions On Human-Computer Interaction, 6*(2), 16–36. doi:10.17705/1thci.00059

Chen, C. M., Lee, H. M., & Chen, Y. H. (2005). Personalized E-Learning system using item response theory. *Computers & Education, 44*(3), 237–255. doi:10.1016/j.compedu.2004.01.006

Cheng, I., & Basu, A. (2009). Interactive graphics for computer adaptive testing. *Computer Graphics Forum, 28*(8), 2033–2045. doi:10.1111/j.1467-8659.2009.01427.x

Chen, Y. (2015). A RDF-based approach to metadata crosswalk for semantic interoperability at the data element level. *Library Hi Tech, 33*(2), 175–194. doi:10.1108/LHT-08-2014-0078

Chien, S. W., & Tsaur, S. M. (2007). Investigating the success of ERP systems: Case studies in three Taiwanese high-tech industries. *Computers in Industry, 58*(8-9), 783–793. doi:10.1016/j.compind.2007.02.001

Chin, W. (1998). Issues and opinion on structural equation modeling. *Management Information Systems Quarterly, 22*(1), 7–16.

Choi, J. (2017a). Next Generation Item and Test Development: A Practical Introduction to Automatic Item Generation. Washington, DC: Assessment, Testing and Measurement Technical Report Serics, The George Washington University.

Choi, J. (2017b). Next generation item and test development: A practical introduction to Automatic Item Generation. Washington, DC: Assessment, Testing, and Measurement Technical Report Series, The George Washington University.

Choi, J. (2017b, April). *Assessments on Textbook: Psychometric Implications on Next Generation Digital Textbook based on Automatic Item Generation*. Paper presented at the 2016 meeting of the Korean Society for Educational Evaluation, Seoul, South Korea.

Choi, J. (2017a). *Introduction to assessment engineering lectures*. Washington, DC: Personal Collection of J. Choi, The George Washington University.

Choi, J., Kim, S., & Yoon, K. (2012). CAFA automatic item generation: Vol. 1. *0 beta) system: Computer adaptive formative assessment client application for automatic item generation* [computer system]. CAFA Lab, Inc.

Choi, J., Kim, S., & Yoon, K. (2016). *K-Math Workbook Grade 6*. Clarksville, MD: CAFA Lab, Inc.

Choi, J., Kim, S., & Yoon, K. (2017). *K-Math Workbook Grade 7*. Clarksville, MD: CAFA Lab, Inc.

Choi, J., & Li, L. (2016). *Automatic item generation: Beyond cost efficiency*. Presented at *Annual Meeting of Korean-American Educational Researchers Association*, Washington, DC.

Clegg, S. (1989). Circuits of Power: a Framework for Analysis. In *Frameworks of Power* (pp. 187–239). London: Sage Publications. doi:10.4135/9781446279267.n8

Clinger Cohen Act of 1996. (1996). United States: U.S.C. Retrieved from http://uscode.house.gov/download/title_40.shtml

Cloninger, P. A., Selvarajan, T. T., Singh, B., & Huang, S. (2015). The Mediating Influence of Work-Family Conflict and the Moderating Influence of Gender on Employee Outcomes. *International Journal of Human Resource Management*, *26*(8), 2269–2287. doi:10.1080/09585192.2015.1004101

Cohen, G., Blake, R. S., & Goodman, D. (2016). Does Turnover Intention Matter? Evaluating The Usefulness Of Turnover Intention Rate As A Predictor Of Actual Turnover Rate. *Review of Public Personnel Administration*, *36*(3), 240–263. doi:10.1177/0734371X15581850

Communications and Information Technology Commission (CITC). (2012). *Internet Usage Study in Saudi Arabia*. Retrieved from http://www.internet.sa/en/internet-usage-study/#more-120

Communications and Information Technology Commission (CITU). (2013). *Electronic newsletter*. Retrieved from http://www.citc.gov.sa/English/MediaCenter/Newsletter/Documents/PR_ENL_017.pdf

Condie, T. (2010). *Online Aggregation and Continuous Query support in MapReduce. In SIGMOD*. ACM.

Congressional Budget Office. (2016). *Bills Reviewed by CBO That Contained Mandates | Congressional Budget Office*. Retrieved from https://www.cbo.gov/umra-search

ConsumerReports.org. (2012). *Update on Health Care Reform; Many updates are already here, though major ones come in 2014*. Retrieved from http://www.consumerreports.org/cro/2012/06/update-on-health-care-reform/index.htm

Contreras, J. L., Denardis, L., & Teplinsky, M. (2013). Mapping today's cybersecurity landscape. *The American University Law Review*, *62*(5), 1113–1130. Retrieved from http://search.proquest.com/docview/1443695399?accountid=11243

Cousins, K., & Robey, D. (2015). Managing Work-Life Boundaries with Mobile Technologies. *Information Technology & People*, *28*(1), 34–71. doi:10.1108/ITP-08-2013-0155

Cronbach, L., & Meehl, P. (1968). Construct validity in psychological tests. *The Foundations of Science and the Concepts of Psychology and Psychoanalysis*, 174-204.

Cronbach, L. (1951). Coefficient alpha and the internal structure of tests. *Psychometrika*, *16*(3), 297–334. doi:10.1007/BF02310555

Cropanzano, R., Rupp, D. E., & Byrne, Z. S. (2003). The Relationship Of Emotional Exhaustion To Work Attitudes, Job Performance, And Organizational Citizenship Behaviors. *The Journal of Applied Psychology*, *88*(1), 160–169. doi:10.1037/0021-9010.88.1.160 PMID:12675403

Dağhan, G., & Akkoyunlu, B. (2016). Modeling the continuance usage intention of online learning environments. *Computers in Human Behavior, 60*, 198–211. doi:10.1016/j.chb.2016.02.066

Dahiya, N., & Parmar, N. (2014). SOA AND REST Synergistic Approach. *International Journal of Computer Science and Information Technologies, 5*(6), 7045–7049.

Daniel, S., & Sonnetag, S. (2015). Crossing the Borders: The Relationship Between Boundary Management, Work-Family Enrichment and Job Satisfaction. *International Journal of Human Resource Management, 27*(4), 407–426. doi:10.1080/09585192.2015.1020826

Dardick, W., & Choi, J. (2016). Teacher Empowered Assessment System: Assessment for the 21st Century. *Journal of Applied Educational and Policy Research, 2*(2).

Davenport, T. (1998). Putting the enterprise into the enterprise system. *Harvard Business Review, 76*(4). PMID:10181586

Davenport, T. (2000). *Mission critical: Realizing the promise of enterprise systems*. Harvard Business Press.

Davenport, T., & Brooks, J. D. (2004). Enterprise systems and the supply chain. *Journal of Enterprise Information Management, 17*(1), 8–19. doi:10.1108/09576050410510917

Davis, F. D., Bagozzi, R. P., & Warshaw, P. R. (1989). User acceptance of computer technology: A comparison of two theoretical models. *Management Science, 35*(8), 982–1003. doi:10.1287/mnsc.35.8.982

Delgado, J. (2013). Architectural styles for distributed interoperability. *Information Resources Management Journal, 26*(4), 40–65. doi:10.4018/irmj.2013100103

Delone, W., & McLean, E. (1992). Information systems success: The quest for the dependent variable. *Information Systems Research, 3*(1), 60–95. doi:10.1287/isre.3.1.60

Delone, W., & McLean, E. (2003). The DeLone and McLean model of information systems success: A ten-year update. *Journal of Management Information Systems, 19*(4), 9–30. doi:10.1080/07421222.2003.11045748

Demerouti, E. (2015). Strategies Used By Individuals To Prevent Burnout *Stichting European Society For Clinical Investigation Journal Foundation*, 1106-1112. Retrieved From www.ejci-online.com

Demerouti, E., & Bakker, A. B. (2008). The Oldenburg Burnout Inventory: A Good Alternative To Measure Burnout And Engagement. In J. R. B. Halbesleben (Ed.), *Stress And Burnout In Health Care* (pp. 65–78). Happauge, NY: Nova Sciences.

Demerouti, E., Bakker, A. B., Nachreiner, F., & Schaufeli, W. B. (2001). The Job Demands-Resources Model Of Burnout. *The Journal of Applied Psychology, 86*(3), 499–512. doi:10.1037/0021-9010.86.3.499 PMID:11419809

DeMers, J. (2016). *7 Technology Trends That Will Dominate 2017*. Retrieved from https://www.forbes.com/sites/jaysondemers/2016/11/16/7-technology-trends-that-will-dominate-2017/1#95695054a51d

Deng, L., Turner, D. E., Gehling, R., & Prince, B. (2010). User experience, satisfaction, and continual usage intention of IT. *European Journal of Information Systems*, *19*(1), 60–75.

Den-Nagy, I. (2014). A Double Edged Sword? A Critical Evaluation of the Mobile Phone in Creating Work-Life Balance. *New Technology, Work and Employment*, *29*(2), 193–211. doi:10.1111/ntwe.12031

Dennis, A., Wixom, B., & Tegarden, D. (2015). *Systems analysis and design: An object-oriented approach with UML*. Indianapolis, IN: John Wiley & Sons.

Derks, D., Bakker, A. B., Peters, P., & van Wingerden, P. (2016). Work-Related Smartphone Use, Work-Family Conflict and Family Role Performance: The Role of Segmentation Preference. *Human Relations*, *69*(5), 1045–1068. doi:10.1177/0018726715601890

Desrochers, S., Hilton, J. M., & Larwood, L. (2005). Preliminary Validation of the Work-Family Integration-Blurring Scale. *Journal of Family Issues*, *26*(4), 442–466. doi:10.1177/0192513X04272438

Diaz, I., Chiaburu, D. S., Zimmerman, R. D., & Boswell, W. R. (2012). Communication Technology: Pros and Cons of Constant Connections to Work. *Journal of Vocational Behavior*, *80*(2), 500–508. doi:10.1016/j.jvb.2011.08.007

Diener, E., Suh, E., Lucas, R., & Smith, H. (1999). Subjective Well-Being: Three Decades Of Progress. *Psychological Bulletin*, *125*(2), 276–302. doi:10.1037/0033-2909.125.2.276

Dinger, M., Thatcher, J. B., Stepina, L. P., & Craig, K. (2012). The Grass Is Always Greener On The Other Side: A Test Of Present And Alternative Job Utility On IT Professionals' Turnover. *IEEE Transactions on Engineering Management*, *59*(3), 364–378. doi:10.1109/TEM.2011.2153204

Dixon, S. (2016). *Retention Of Information Technology Employees*. Walden University. Retrieved From http://scholarworks.walden.edu/dissertations

Dixon, H. B. (2012). Cybersecurity...how important is it? *51. The Judges' Journal*, 36–39.

Djamasbi, S., Strong, D., Wilson, E. V., & Ruiz, C. (2016). *Designing and Testing User-Centric Systems with both User Experience and Design Science Research Principles*. Academic Press.

Drasgow, F., Luecht, R. M., & Bennett, R. E. (2006). Technology and testing. In S. H. Irvine & P. C. Kyllonen (Eds.), *Educational measurement* (4th ed.; pp. 471–516). Washington, DC: American Council on Education.

du Plessis, A. J., & Frederick, H. (2012). Effectiveness of e-recruiting: Empirical evidence from the Rosebank business cluster in Auckland, New Zealand. *Science Journal of Business Management*, *126*, 1–21.

Eagle, B. W., Icenogle, M. L., Maes, J. D., & Miles, E. W. (1998). The Importance of Employee Demographic Profiles for Understanding Experiences of Work-Family Interrole Conflicts. *The Journal of Social Psychology, 138*(6), 690–709. doi:10.1080/00224549809603255 PMID:9872064

Egli, D. S. (2013). Beyond the storms: Strengthening preparedness, response, & resilience in the 21st century. *Journal of Strategic Security, 6*(2), 32–45. doi:10.5038/1944-0472.6.2.3

Eldawy, A. (2013). A Demonstration of Spatial Hadoop: An Efficient MapReduce Framework for Spatial Data. *Proceedings of the VLDB Endowment International Conference on Very Large Data Bases, 6*(12). doi:10.14778/2536274.2536283

Elshwimy, F., Algergawy, A., Sarhan, A., & Sallam, E. (2014). Aggregation of similarity measures in schema matching based on generalized mean. *Proceedings of the IEEE International Conference on Data Engineering Workshops* (pp. 74-79). Piscataway, NJ: IEEE Computer Society Press. 10.1109/ICDEW.2014.6818306

Emani, C. K., Cullot, N., & Nicolle, C. (2015). Understandable Big Data: A survey. *Computer Science Review, 17*, 70–81. doi:10.1016/j.cosrev.2015.05.002

Embretson, S. E., & Yang, X. (2007). Automatic item generation and cognitive psychology. In C. R. Rao & S. Sinharay (Eds.), *Handbook of statistics: Psychometrics* (vol. 26, pp. 747-768). North Holland, UK: Elsevier. doi: 26023-110.1016/s0169-7161(06)

Embretson, S. E. (1998). A cognitive design system approach to generating valid tests: Application to abstract reasoning. *Psychological Methods, 3*(3), 380–396. doi:10.1037/1082-989X.3.3.380

Engle, B., & Guttmann, R. (2014). The evolution of the CISO role and organizational readiness. *CSO*. Retrieved from https://www.csoonline.com/article/2838371/security-leadership/the-evolution-of-the-ciso-role-and-organizational-readiness.html

Epp, D. A., Lovett, J., & Baumgartner, F. R. (2014). Partisan priorities and public budgeting. *Political Research Quarterly, 67*(4), 864–878. doi:10.1177/1065912914550045

Ericsson, K., Krampe, R., & Tesch-Römer, C. (1993). The role of deliberate practice in the acquisition of expert performance. *Psychological Review, 100*(3), 363–406. doi:10.1037/0033-295X.100.3.363

Erl, T., Merson, P., & Stoffers, R. (2017). *Service-oriented Architecture: Analysis and Design for Services and Microservices*. Upper Saddle River, NJ: Prentice Hall PTR.

Fawcett, J., Ayers, D., & Quin, L. (2012). *Beginning XML*. Indianapolis, IN: John Wiley & Sons.

Ferratt, T. W., Agarwal, R., Brown, C. V., & Moore, J. E. (2005). IT Human Resource Management Configurations And IT Turnover: Theoretical Synthesis And Empirical Analysis. *Information Systems Research, 16*(3), 237–255. doi:10.1287/isre.1050.0057

Fielding, R. (2000). *Architectural Styles and the Design of Network-based Software Architectures* (Doctoral dissertation). University of California at Irvine, CA.

Fielding, R. (2008). REST APIs must be hypertext-driven. *Roy Fielding's blog: Untangled.* Retrieved November 13, 2017, from http://roy.gbiv.com/untangled/2008/rest-apis-must-be-hypertext-driven

Fielding, R., Taylor, R., Erenkrantz, J., Gorlick, M., Whitehead, J., Khare, R., & Oreizy, P. (2017). Reflections on the REST architectural style and principled design of the modern web architecture. In *Proceedings of the 2017 11th Joint Meeting on Foundations of Software Engineering* (pp. 4-14). New York, NY: ACM Press. 10.1145/3106237.3121282

Ford, V. (2012). *An Exploratory Investigation Of The Relationship Between Turnover Intentions, Work Exhaustion And Disengagement Among IT Professionals In A Single Institution Of Higher Education In A Major Metropolitan Area* (Dissertation). The George Washington University.

Ford, V., Swayze, S., & Burley, D. L. (2012). An Exploratory Investigation Of The Relationship Between Disengagement, Exhaustion And Turnover Intentions Among University IT Professionals. *Information Resources Management Journal, 26*(3), 55–68. doi:10.4018/irmj.2013070104

Fornell, C., & Larcker, D. (1981). Evaluating structural equation models with unobservable variables and measurement error. *JMR, Journal of Marketing Research, 18*(1), 39–50. doi:10.2307/3151312

Fraillon, J., Schulz, W., & Ainley, J. (2013). International Computer and Information Literacy Study assessment framework. Amsterdam: International Association for the Evaluation of Educational Achievement (IEA).

Freudenberger, H. J. (1974). Staff Burn-Out. *The Journal of Social Issues, 30*(1), 159–165. doi:10.1111/j.1540-4560.1974.tb00706.x

Friedman, S., & Greenhaus, J. (2000). *Work and Family - Allies or Enemies?: What Happens When Business Professionals Confront Life Choices*. Oxford University Press. doi:10.1093/acprof:oso/9780195112757.001.0001

Friedman, S., & Westring, A. (2015). Empowering Individuals to Integrate Work and Life: Insights for Management Development. *Journal of Management Development, 34*(3), 299–315. doi:10.1108/JMD-11-2012-0144

Frone, M. R., Russell, M., & Cooper, M. L. (1992). Antecedents and Outcomes of Work-Family Conflict: Testing a Model of the Work-Family Interface. *The Journal of Applied Psychology, 77*(1), 65–78. doi:10.1037/0021-9010.77.1.65 PMID:1556042

Gable, G., Sedera, D., & Chan, T. (2003). Enterprise systems success: a measurement model. *Proceedings of the 24th International Conference on Information Systems*.

Gable, G., Sedera, D., & Chan, T. (2008). Re-conceptualizing information system success: The IS-impact measurement model. *Journal of the Association for Information Systems, 9*(7), 377–408. doi:10.17705/1jais.00164

Gandomi, A., & Haider, M. (2015). Beyond the hype: Big data concepts, methods, and analytics. *International Journal of Information Management, 35*(2), 137–144. doi:10.1016/j.ijinfomgt.2014.10.007

Gargeya, V. B., & Brady, C. (2005). Success and failure factors of adopting SAP in ERP system implementation. *Business Process Management Journal*, *11*(5), 501–516. doi:10.1108/14637150510619858

Garrison, D. R. (2011). *E-Learning in the 21st century: A framework for research and practice*. Academic Press.

Garvey, P. R., Moynihan, R. A., & Servi, L. (2011). A macro method for measuring economic-benefit returns on cybersecurity investments: The table top approach. *Systems Engineering*, *14*, 305–326. doi:10.1002ys

Geetika, R., & Singh, P. (2014). Dynamic coupling metrics for object oriented software systems: A survey. *Software Engineering Notes*, *39*(2), 1–8. doi:10.1145/2579281.2579296

Gefen, D., & Straub, D. (2005). A practical guide to factorial validity using PLS-Graph: Tutorial and annotated example. *Communications of the AIS*, *16*(5), 91–109.

Gierl, M. J., & Haladyna, T. M. (2013). *Automatic item generation: Theory and practice*. New York, NY: Routledge.

Gierl, M., Lai, H., & Turner, S. (2012). Using automatic item generation to create multiple-choice test items. *Medical Education*, *46*(8), 757–765. doi:10.1111/j.1365-2923.2012.04289.x PMID:22803753

Glaser, M., Lopez-De-Silanes, F., & Sautner, Z. (2013). Opening the black box: Internal capital markets and managerial power. *The Journal of Finance*, *68*(4), 1577–1631. doi:10.1111/jofi.12046

Golden, A. G., & Geisler, C. (2007). Work-Life Boundary Management and the Personal Digital Assistant. *Human Relations*, *60*(3), 519–551. doi:10.1177/0018726707076698

Goldman, E. H. (2012). The effect of acquisition decision making on security posture. *Information Management & Computer Security*, *205*(5), 350–363. doi:10.1108/09685221211286520

Gollner, J. A., & Baumane-Vitolina, I. (2016). Measurement of ERP-Project Success: Findings from Germany and Austria. *The Engineering Economist*, *27*(5), 498–508.

Goodchild, J. (2009). *The Unique Story and Evolution of the CSO Role*. Retrieved from https://www.cio.com/article/2427347/security0/the-unique-story-and-evolution-of-the-cso-role.html

Goodman, E., & Loh, L. (2011). Organizational change: A critical challenge for team effectiveness. *Business Information Review*, *28*, 242–250. doi:10.1177/0266382111427087

Gorla, N., Somers, T., & Wong, B. (2010). Organizational impact of system quality, information quality, and service quality. *The Journal of Strategic Information Systems*, *19*(3), 207–228. doi:10.1016/j.jsis.2010.05.001

Grandey, A. A., & Cropanzano, R. (1999). The Conservation Of Resources Model Applied To Work-Family Conflict And Strain. *Journal of Vocational Behavior*, *54*(2), 350–370. doi:10.1006/jvbe.1998.1666

Green, F. (2012). Employee Involvement, Technology and Evolution in Job Skills: A Task-Based Analysis. *Industrial & Labor Relations Review*, *65*(1), 36–67. doi:10.1177/001979391206500103

Greenhaus, J., & Beutell, N. (1985). Sources of Conflict Between Work and Family Roles. *Academy of Management Review*, *10*(1), 76–89.

Greenhaus, J., & Powell, G. (1985). When Work and Family are Allies: A Theory of Work-Family Enrichments. *Academy of Management Review*, *31*(1), 72–92. doi:10.5465/AMR.2006.19379625

Greenspoon, P., & Saklofske, D. (1998). Confirmatory factor analysis of the multidimensional students' life satisfaction scale. *Personality and Individual Differences*, *25*(5), 965–971. doi:10.1016/S0191-8869(98)00115-9

Gullo, T. (2004). History and evaluation of the Unfunded Mandates Reform Act. *National Tax Journal*, *57*(3), 559–570. doi:10.17310/ntj.2004.3.04

Gupta, Y. (2016). Literature review on e-recruitment: A step towards paperless HR. *International Journal of Advance Research in Computer Science and Management Studies*, *4*(1), 79–84.

Hackman, J., & Oldham, G. (1975). Development of the Job Diagnostic Survey. *The Journal of Applied Psychology*, *60*(2), 159–170. doi:10.1037/h0076546

Hadi, Shnain, Hadishaheed, & Ahmad. (2015). Big data and five v's characteristics. *International Journal of Advances in Electronics and Computer Science*, *2*(1).

Hair, J. F., Black, W. C., Babin, B. J., & Anderson, R. E. (2010). Multivariate data analysis (Vol. 7). Prentice Hall.

Halbesleben, J. R. B., & Buckley, M. R. (2004). Burnout In Organizational Life. *Journal of Management*, *30*(6), 859–879. doi:10.1016/j.jm.2004.06.004

Halbesleben, J. R. B., & Demerouti, E. (2005). The Construct Validity Of An Alternative Measure Of Burnout: Investigating The English Translation Of The Oldenburg Burnout Inventory. *Work and Stress*, *19*(3), 208–220. doi:10.1080/02678370500340728

Hanafizadeh, P., Gholami, R., Dadbin, S., & Standage, N. (2010). The core critical success factors in implementation of enterprise resource planning systems. *International Journal of Enterprise Information Systems*, *6*(2), 82–111. doi:10.4018/jeis.2010040105

Harju, L. K., Hakanen, J. J., & Schaufeli, W. B. (2016). Can Job Crafting Reduce Job Boredom And Increase Work Engagement? A Three-Year Cross-Lagged Panel Study. *Journal of Vocational Behavior*, *95-96*, 11–20. doi:10.1016/j.jvb.2016.07.001

Harshawardhan, S., & Gadekar, P. (2014). A Review Paper on Big Data and Hadoop. *International Journal of Scientific and Research Publications, 4*(10).

Harter, J. K. (2008). Why People Change Jobs? *Gallup Management Journal*. Retrieved From Http://Gmj.Gallup.Com/Content/106912/Turning-Around-Your-Turnover-Problem.Aspx

Harter, J. K., Schmidt, F. L., & Hayes, T. L. (2002). Business-Unit-Level Relationship Between Employee Satisfaction, Employee Engagement, And Business Outcomes: A Meta-Analysis. *The Journal of Applied Psychology*, *87*(2), 268–279. doi:10.1037/0021-9010.87.2.268 PMID:12002955

Hatcher, L. (1994). *A step-by-step approach to using the SAS system for factor analysis and structural equation modeling*. SAS Publishing.

Hathaway, M. (2012, December). Creating the demand curve for cybersecurity. *Georgetown Jounral of International Affairs*, 163–170.

Hatzithomas, L., Stamelos, I., Fotiadis, T., & Mylonakis, J. (2011). Quality And Effectiveness Of Enterprise Resource Planning–Customer Relationship Management Systems: Implications For Information Systems Marketing Strategies. *Journal of Applied Business Research*, *23*(3). doi:10.19030/jabr.v23i3.1389

Hecht, T. D., & Allen, N. J. (2009). A Longitudinal Examination of the Work-Nonwork Boundary Strength Construct. *Journal of Organizational Behavior*, *30*(7), 839–862. doi:10.1002/job.579

Henderson, R. (2012). Industry Employment And Output Projections To 2020. *Monthly Labor Review*, 65–83.

Hendricksen, D. (2014). *12 More Essential Skills for Software Architects*. Upper Saddle River, NJ: Addison-Wesley Professional.

Hersh, W. (2010). The Health Information Technology Workforce. *Applied Clinical Informatics*, *1*(2), 197–212. doi:10.4338/ACI-2009-11-R-0011 PMID:23616836

Hevner, A., March, S., Park, J., & Ram, S. (2004). Design Science in Information Systems Research. *Management Information Systems Quarterly*, *28*(1), 75–105. doi:10.2307/25148625

Hobfoll, S. E. (1989). Conservation Of Resources: A New Attempt At Conceptualizing Stress. *The American Psychologist*, *44*(3), 513–524. doi:10.1037/0003-066X.44.3.513 PMID:2648906

Hobfoll, S. E. (2002). Social And Psychological Resources And Adaptation. *Review of General Psychology*, *6*(4), 307–324. doi:10.1037/1089-2680.6.4.307

Hollingaworth, D. (2004). The Workflow Reference Model: 10 Years On. In L. Fischer (Ed.), *Workflow Handboook 2004* (pp. 295–312). Future Strategies Inc.

Holm, A. (2010). The effect of e-recruitment on the recruitment process: evidence from case studies of three Danish MNCs. *Proceedings of the 3rd European Academic Workshop on Electronic Human Resource Management*, 91–111.

Holsapple, C. W., & Sena, M. P. (2005). ERP plans and decision-support benefits. *Decision Support Systems*, *38*(4), 575–590. doi:10.1016/j.dss.2003.07.001

Hoover, J. N. (2013). Federal CIO Details Concerns On Looming Budget Cuts. *Information Week*, *1*. Retrieved from http://www.informationweek.com/regulations/federal-cio-details-concerns-on-looming-budget-cuts/d/d-id/1108634

Hoyt, R. E., & Liebenberg, A. P. (2011). The Value of Enterprise Risk Management. *The Journal of Risk and Insurance*, *78*(4), 795–822. doi:10.1111/j.1539-6975.2011.01413.x

Hsu, C. L., & Lu, H. P. (2004). Why do people play on-line games? An extended TAM with social influences and flow experience. *Information & Management*, *41*(7), 853–868.

Hsu, L. L., & Chen, M. (2004). Impacts of ERP systems on the integrated-interaction performance of manufacturing and marketing. *Industrial Management & Data Systems*, *104*(1), 42–55. doi:10.1108/02635570410514089

Huang, Y., Lin, Y., & Cheng, S. (2009). An adaptive testing system for supporting versatile educational assessment. *Computers & Education*, *52*(1), 53–67. doi:10.1016/j.compedu.2008.06.007

Hu, L., & Bentler, P. (1998). Fit indices in covariance structure modeling: Sensitivity to underparameterized model misspecification. *Psychological Methods*, *3*(4), 424–453. doi:10.1037/1082-989X.3.4.424

Hulin, C. L., Roznowski, M., & Hachiya, D. (1985). Alternative Opportunities And Withdrawal Decisions: Empirical And Theoretical Discrepancies And An Integration. *Psychological Bulletin*, *97*(2), 233–250. doi:10.1037/0033-2909.97.2.233

Hu, P. J.-H., Clark, T. H. K., & Ma, W. W. (2003). Examining technology acceptance by school teachers: A longitudinal study. *Information & Management*, *41*(2), 227–241. doi:10.1016/S0378-7206(03)00050-8

Hussain, T., Mehmood, R., Haq, A., Alnafjan, K., & Alghamdi, A. (2014). Designing framework for the interoperability of C4I systems. In *International Conference on Computational Science and Computational Intelligence* (pp. 102–106). Piscataway, NJ: IEEE Computer Society Press. 10.1109/CSCI.2014.102

Hussein, H. B. (2011). Attitudes of Saudi universities faculty members towards using learning management system (JUSUR). *TOJET: The Turkish Online Journal of Educational Technology*, *10*(2).

Ifinedo, P., & Nahar, N. (2007). ERP systems success: An empirical analysis of how two organizational stakeholder groups prioritize and evaluate relevant measures. *Enterprise Information Systems*, *1*(1), 25–48. doi:10.1080/17517570601088539

Ifinedo, P., Rapp, B., Ifinedo, A., & Sundberg, K. (2010). Relationships among ERP post-implementation success constructs: An analysis at the organizational level. *Computers in Human Behavior*, *26*(5), 1136–1148. doi:10.1016/j.chb.2010.03.020

Iivari, J. (2005a). An empirical test of the DeLone-McLean model of information system success. *ACM SIGMIS Database*, *36*(2), 8–27. doi:10.1145/1066149.1066152

Irvine, S. H., & Kyllonen, P. C. (Eds.). (2002). *Item generation for test development*. Mahwah, NJ: Lawrence Erlbaum Associates.

ISO. (2010). *Systems and software engineering – Vocabulary. ISO/IEC/IEEE 24765:2010(E) International Standard*. Geneva, Switzerland: International Organization for Standardization.

Iverson, R. D., Olekalns, M., & Erwin, P. J. (1998). Affectivity, Organizational Stressors, And Absenteeism: A Causal Model Of Burnout And Its Consequences. *Journal of Vocational Behavior*, *52*(1), 1–23. doi:10.1006/jvbe.1996.1556

Ives, B., Hamilton, S., & Davis, G. (1980). A framework for research in computer-based management information systems. *Management Science*, *26*(9), 910–934. doi:10.1287/mnsc.26.9.910

Jackson, M. B. (2012). Agile: A decade in. *PM Network, 26*(4), 58–62. Retrieved from https://www.pmi.org/learning/library/agile-manifesto-software-development-impact-2284

Jeffrey, K., Mahony, S., Michaelson, J., & Abdallah, S. (2014). The NEF Report On Well-Being. New Economics Foundation.

Jenkins, R. (2009). The ways and means of power: Efficacy and resources. In S. Clegg & M. Haugaard (Eds.), *The SAGE Handbook of Power* (pp. 140–157). London: Sage Publications. doi:10.4135/9780857021014.n8

Jöreskog, K., & Sörbom, D. (1989). *LISREL 7: A guide to the program and applications*. Chicago: SPSS.

Joseph, D., & Ang, S. (2003). *Turnover Of IT Professionals: A Quantitative Analysis Of The Literature. Paper Presented At The SIGMIS Conference*, Philadelphia, PA. 10.1145/761849.761872

Joseph, D., Ng, K., Koh, C., & Ang, S. (2007). Turnover Of Information Technology Professionals: A Narrative Review, Meta-Analytic Structural Equation Modeling, And Model Development. *Management Information Systems Quarterly*, *31*(3), 547–577. doi:10.2307/25148807

Judge, T., Boudreau, J., & Bretz, R. (1994). Job and Life Attitudes of Male Executives. *The Journal of Applied Psychology*, *79*(5), 767–782. doi:10.1037/0021-9010.79.5.767 PMID:7989277

Kahn, W. A. (1990). Psychological Conditions Of Personal Engagement And Disengagement At Work. *Academy of Management Journal*, *33*(4), 692–724. doi:10.2307/256287

Kaiser, H. F. (1974). An index of factorial simplicity. *Psychometrika*, *39*(1), 31–36. doi:10.1007/BF02291575

Kaisler, S., & Armour, E. (2013). Big Data: Issues and Challenges Moving Forward. *46th Hawaii International Conference on System Sciences*. 10.1109/HICSS.2013.645

Kalakota, R., & Robinson, M. (2001). *E-business 2.0: Roadmap for Success*. Addison-Wesley Professional.

Kalimo, R., & Toppinen, S. (1995). *Burnout In Computer Professionals*. Paper Presented At The Work, Stress And Health 1995: Creating Healthier Workplaces, Washington, DC.

Karahanna, E., Straub, D. W., & Chervany, N. L. (1999). Information technology adoption across time: A cross-sectional comparison of pre-adoption and post-adoption beliefs. *Management Information Systems Quarterly*, *23*(2), 183–213. doi:10.2307/249751

Karapanos, E. (2013). User experience over time. In Modeling Users' Experiences with Interactive Systems (pp. 57-83). Springer Berlin Heidelberg. doi:10.1007/978-3-642-31000-3_4

Kasper, H., Meyer, M., & Schmidt, A. (2005). Mangers Dealing with Work-Family Conflict: An Exploratory Analysis. *Journal of Managerial Psychology*, *20*(5), 440–461. doi:10.1108/02683940510602978

Kattenbach, R., Demerouti, E., & Nachreiner, F. (2010). Flexible Working Times: Effects on Employees' Exhaustion, Work-Nonwork Conflict and Job Performance. *Career Development International*, *15*(3), 279–295. doi:10.1108/13620431011053749

Kearney, K. S. (2002). *A study of the emotional effects on employees who remain through organizational change: A view through Kübler-Ross (1969) in an educational institution.* Oklahoma State University. Retrieved from ProQuest Dissertations and Theses: http://search.proquest.com/docview/276207296?accountid=11243 (276207296)

Kelloway, E. (1998). *Using LISREL for structural equation modeling: A researcher's guide.* Sage Publications, Inc.

Kemp, M., & Low, G. C. (2008). ERP innovation implementation model incorporating change management. *Business Process Management Journal*, *14*(2), 228–242. doi:10.1108/14637150810864952

Khalfallah, M., Figay, N., Barhamgi, M., & Ghodous, P. (2014). Model driven conformance testing for standardized services. In *IEEE International Conference on Services Computing* (pp. 400–407). Piscataway, NJ: IEEE Computer Society Press. 10.1109/SCC.2014.60

Khattak, M. A. O., She, Y., Memon, Z. A., Syed, N., Hussain, S., & Irfan, M. (2013). Investigating Critical Success Factors Affecting ERP Implementation in Chinese and Pakistani Enterprises. *International Journal of Enterprise Information Systems*, *9*(3), 39–76. doi:10.4018/jeis.2013070103

Kim, S., & Wright, B. E. (2007). IT Employee Work Exhaustion: Toward An Integrated Model Of Antecedents And Consequences. *Review of Public Personnel Administration*, *27*(2), 147–170. doi:10.1177/0734371X06290775

Kim, T. (2010). A self-directed dynamic web-based learning environment: Proposal for personalized learning framework. *Journal of Security Engineering*, *9*(2), 177–187.

Kini, R. B., & Basaviah, S. (2013). Critical Success Factors in the Implementation of Enterprise Resource Planning Systems in Small and Midsize Businesses: Microsoft Navision Implementation. *International Journal of Enterprise Information Systems*, *9*(1), 97–117. doi:10.4018/jeis.2013010106

Klaus, H., Rosemann, M., & Gable, G. (2000). What is ERP? *Information Systems Frontiers*, *2*(2), 141–162. doi:10.1023/A:1026543906354

Klein, D. (1989). Some notes on the dynamics of resistance to change: The defender role. In Diagnostics of Planned Change (pp. 98–105). Academic Press.

Koay, K., Soh, P., & Chew, K. (2017). Do Employees' Private Demands Lead to Cyberloafing? The Mediating Role of Job Stress. *Management Research Review*, *40*(9), 1025–1038. doi:10.1108/MRR-11-2016-0252

Kopelman, R., Greenhaus, J., & Connoly, T. (1983). A Model of Work, Family and Interrole Conflict: A Construct Validation Study. *Organizational Behavior and Human Performance*, *32*(2), 198–215. doi:10.1016/0030-5073(83)90147-2

Kossek, E. E., Ruderman, M. N., Braddy, P. W., & Hannum, K. M. (2012). Work-Nonwork Boundary Management Profiles: A Person-Centered Approach. *Journal of Vocational Behavior*, *81*(1), 112–128. doi:10.1016/j.jvb.2012.04.003

KPMG.com. (2014). *Business Transformation and the Corporate Agenda*. Retrieved from: http://www.kpmginfo.com/Transformation/assets/pdf/business-transformation-corporate-agenda.pdf

KPMG.com. (2016). *Evolution of an industry: Spotlight on Ed-tech*. Retrieved from:https://home.kpmg.com/xx/en/home/insights/2016/02/evolution-of-an-industry.html

Kreiner, G., Hollensbe, E., & Shee, M. (2009). Balancing Borders and Bridges: Negotiating the Work-Home Interface via Boundary Work Tactics. *Academy of Management Journal*, *52*(4), 704–730. doi:10.5465/AMJ.2009.43669916

Kübler-Ross, E. (1969). *On death and dying*. New York, NY: Touchstone.

Kuhn, R. (2010, August). Cybersecurity. *IT Professional, IEEE*, 18–20.

Kukreja, R., & Garg, N. (2014). Remote Procedure Call: Limitations and Drawbacks. *International Journal of Research*, *1*(10), 914–917.

Kumari, S., & Rath, S. (2015). Performance comparison of SOAP and REST based Web Services for Enterprise Application Integration. In *International Conference on Advances in Computing, Communications and Informatics* (pp. 1656–1660). Piscataway, NJ: IEEE Computer Society Press. 10.1109/ICACCI.2015.7275851

Kumar, V., Maheshwari, B., & Kumar, U. (2003). An investigation of critical management issues in ERP implementation: Emperical evidence from Canadian organizations. *Technovation*, *23*(10), 793–808. doi:10.1016/S0166-4972(02)00015-9

Kumar, V., & Pansari, A. (2015). Measuring The Benefits Of Employee Engagement. *MIT Sloan Management Review*, *56*(4), 67–72.

Kune, Konugurthi, Chillarige, & Buyya. (2016). *The anatomy of big data computing, Software: Practice and Experience*. Wiley Online Library.

Kwahk, K. (2006). ERP acceptance: organizational change perspective. In R. H. Sprague Jr. (Ed.), *Proceedings of the 39th Hawaii International Conference on System Sciences*. Hawaii, HI: IEEE Computer Society Press.

Lacity, M. C., Iyer, V. V., & Rudramuniyaiah, P. S. (2008). Turnover Intentions Of Indian IS Professionals. *Information Systems Frontiers On Outsourcing*, *10*(2), 225–241. doi:10.100710796-007-9062-3

Lai, H., Gierl, M. J., & Alves, C. (2009, June). *Development of an item model taxonomy for automatic item generation in computer adaptive testing*. Poster presented at the GMAC Conference on Computerized Adaptive Testing, Minneapolis, MN.

Lai, H., & Gierl, M. J. (2013). Generating items under the assessment engineering framework. In M. J. Gierl & T. Haladyna (Eds.), *Automatic item generation: Theory and practice* (pp. 77–101). New York, NY: Routledge.

Lapsley, I., Midwinter, A., Nambiar, T., & Steccolini, I. (2011). Government budgeting, power and negotiated order. *Management Accounting Research*, *22*(1), 16–25. doi:10.1016/j.mar.2010.10.009

Larry, L. (2017). *A qualitative study of the experience of individuals within information technology teams during transition using the kübler-ross grief construct and the bridges transition model* (Order No. 10615376). Available from ProQuest Dissertations & Theses Global. (1944510678). Retrieved from http://proxygw.wrlc.org/login?url=https://search-proquest-com.proxygw.wrlc.org/docview/1944510678?accountid=11243

Lavanya, N., & Malarvizhi, T. (2008). *Risk analysis and management—a vital key to effective project management.* Paper presented at PMI® Global Congress 2008—Asia Pacific, Sydney, Australia.

Law, C. C. H., Chen, C. C., & Wu, B. J. P. (2010). Managing the full ERP life-cycle: Considerations of maintenance and support requirements and IT governance practice as integral elements of the formula for successful ERP adoption. *Computers in Industry*, *61*(3), 297–308. doi:10.1016/j.compind.2009.10.004

Leavitt, H. J., & Whistler, T. L. (1958). Management in the 1980s. *Harvard Business Review*, *36*, 41–48.

Lee & Choi. (2011). Parallel Data Processing with MapReduce: A Survey. SIGMOD Record, 40(4).

Lee, I. (2005). The evolution of e-recruiting: A content analysis of Fortune 100 career web sites. *Journal of Electronic Commerce in Organizations*, *3*(3), 57–68. doi:10.4018/jeco.2005070104

Lee, M. C. (2009). Factors influencing the adoption of internet banking: An integration of TAM and TPB with perceived risk and perceived benefit. *Electronic Commerce Research and Applications*, *8*(3), 130–141. doi:10.1016/j.elerap.2008.11.006

Lee, Y., Hsieh, Y., & Chen, Y. (2013). An investigation of employees' use of E-Learning systems: Applying the technology acceptance model. *Behaviour & Information Technology*, *32*(2), 173–189. doi:10.1080/0144929X.2011.577190

Leon, J. (2015). *The True Cost of a Software Bug: Part One*. Retrieved from http://blog.celerity.com/the-true-cost-of-a-software-bug

Liaw, S. S., & Huang, H. M. (2003). An investigation of user attitudes toward search engines as an information retrieval tool. *Computers in Human Behavior, 19*(6), 751–765. doi:10.1016/S0747-5632(03)00009-8

Libby, T., & Lindsay, R. M. (2009). Beyond budgeting or budgeting reconsidered? A survey of North-American budgeting practice. *Management Accounting Research, 21*(1), 56–75. doi:10.1016/j.mar.2009.10.003

Libicki, M. C., Ablon, L., & Webb, T. (2015). *The defender's dilemma - Charting a course toward cybersecurity*. Santa Monica, CA: RAND Corporation.

Lin, H. F., & Lee, G. C. (2006). Determinants of success for online communities: An empirical study. *Behaviour & Information Technology, 25*(6), 479–488. doi:10.1080/01449290500330422

Lippitt, W., & Watson, J. (1958). *Westley, the dynamics of planned change*. New York, NY: HBJ.

Lippuner, D. (2011). Something's gotta give! *Journal of Government Financial Management, 63*(1), 26–30.

Litwin, A. S. (2011). Technological Change at Work: The Impact of Employee Involvement on the Effectiveness of Health Information Technology. *Industrial & Labor Relations Review, 64*(5), 863–888. doi:10.1177/001979391106400502

Lo, J. (2015). The Information Technology Workforce: A Review And Assessment Of Voluntary Turnover Research. *Information Systems Frontiers, 17*(2), 387–411. doi:10.100710796-013-9408-y

Loshin, D. (2014). *Addressing Five Emerging Challenges of Big Data*. Progress Software.

Luecht, R. (2014). Assessment Engineering Task Model Maps, Task Models and Templates as a New Way to Develop and Implement Test Specifications. *Journal Of Applied Testing Technology, 1*(1), 1–38. Retrieved from http://www.jattjournal.com/index.php/atp/article/view/45254

Lu, H., Hu, Y., Gao, J., & Kinshuk. (2016). The effects of computer self-efficacy, training satisfaction and test anxiety on attitude and performance in computerized adaptive testing. *Computers & Education, 100*, 45–55. doi:10.1016/j.compedu.2016.04.012

Lukka, K. (1988). Budgetary biasing in organizations: Theoretical framework and empirical evidence. *Accounting, Organizations and Society, 13*(3), 281–301. doi:10.1016/0361-3682(88)90005-0

Lyngaas, S. (2016, February). Cybersecurity: White House wants $19B for cyber in FY 2017. *FCW: The Business of Federal Technology Federal Computer Weekly*, 1. Retrieved from https://fcw.com/articles/2016/02/09/cyber-budget-lyngaas.aspx

Mackelden, L. (2013). *How do big recruiters recruit online?* Retrieved December 1, 2017 from http://www.onrec.com/news/features/onrec-online-recruitmentmagazine-feature-how-do-big-recruiters-recruit-online

Maier, C., Laumer, S., & Echardt, A. (2015). Information Technology As Daily Stressor: Pinning Down The Causes Of Burnout. *Journal Of Business Economics*, *85*(4), 349–387. doi:10.100711573-014-0759-8

Mandal, P., & Gunasekaran, A. (2003). Issues in implementing ERP: A case study. *European Journal of Operational Research*, *146*(2), 274–283. doi:10.1016/S0377-2217(02)00549-0

March, J. G. (1966). The power of power. In D. Easton (Ed.), *Varieties of political theory* (pp. 39-70). Englewood Cliffs, NJ: Prentice-Hall.

Marcos, Calheiros, Bianchi, Nettoc, & Buyya. (2015). Big Data computing and clouds: Trends and future directions. *Journal of Parallel and Distributed Computing*, 79–80.

Markus, M., & Tanis, C. (2000). The enterprise systems experience-from adoption to success. *Framing the domains of IT research: Glimpsing the future through the past, 173*, 207-173.

Martin, R. G. (2012). Factors affecting the usefulness of social networking in elearning at German university of technology in Oman. *International Journal of e-Education, e-Business, e-Management and e-Learning, 2*(6), 498–502.

Maslach, C., & Leiter, P. L. (Eds.). (1999). Burnout And Engagement In The Workplace: A Contextual Analysis (Vol. 11). Stamford, CT: JAI Press.

Maslach, C. (1982). *Burnout: The Cost Of Caring*. Englewood Cliffs, NJ: Prentice Hall.

Maslach, C. (2003). Job Burnout: New Directions In Research And Intervention. *Current Directions in Psychological Science*, *12*(12), 189–192. doi:10.1111/1467-8721.01258

Maslach, C., & Goldberg, J. (1998). Prevention Of Burnout: New Perspectives. *Applied & Preventive Psychology*, *7*(1), 63–74. doi:10.1016/S0962-1849(98)80022-X

Maslach, C., & Jackson, S. E. (1981). The Measurement Of Experienced Burnout. *Journal of Occupational Behaviour*, *2*(99), 113.

Maslach, C., & Leiter, M. P. (1997). *The Truth About Burnout*. San Francisco, CA: Jossey-Bass.

Maslach, C., & Leiter, M. P. (2008). Early Predictors Of Job Burnout And Engagement. *The Journal of Applied Psychology*, *93*(3), 498–512. doi:10.1037/0021-9010.93.3.498 PMID:18457483

Maslach, C., & Leiter, P. L. (2016). Understanding The Burnout Experience: Recent Research And Its Implications For Psychiatry. *World Psychiatry; Official Journal of the World Psychiatric Association (WPA)*, *15*(2), 103–111. doi:10.1002/wps.20311 PMID:27265691

Maslach, C., Schaufeli, W. B., & Leiter, M. P. (2001). Job Burnout. *Annual Review of Psychology*, *52*(1), 397–422. doi:10.1146/annurev.psych.52.1.397 PMID:11148311

May, D. R., Gilson, R. L., & Harter, L. M. (2004). The Psychological Conditions Of Meaningfulness, Safety And Availability And The Engagement Of The Human Spirit At Work. *Journal of Occupational and Organizational Psychology*, *77*(1), 11–37. doi:10.1348/096317904322915892

Mayer, R. (2005). *The Cambridge handbook of multimedia learning*. New York: University of Cambridge Press. doi:10.1017/CBO9780511816819

McCarthy, J., Bauer, T., Truxillo, D., Anderson, N., Costa, A., & Ahmed, S. (2017). Applicant perspectives during selection: A review addressing "so what?" "what's new?" and "where to next?". *Journal of Management*, *43*(6), 1693–1725. doi:10.1177/0149206316681846

McCloskey, D. (2016). Finding Work-Life Balance in a Digital Age: An Exploratory Study of Boundary Flexibility and Permeability. *Information Resources Management Journal*, *29*(3), 53–70. doi:10.4018/IRMJ.2016070104

McDonagh, J., & Coghlan, D. (2006). Information technology and the lure of integrated change: A neglected role for organizational development? *Public Administration Quarterly*, *30*(1), 22–55.

Mcgee, M. K. (1996). Hot Skills In '96: Internet, Client-Server, And Networking Experts Top Lists Of The Most Wanted. *Information Week*, 560–564.

McHugh, N. D. (1996). Book reviews - Beyond business process re-eingineering:Towards the holonic enterprise.pdf. *International Journal of Production Research*, *34*(12), 3515–3517. doi:10.1080/00207549608905103

Mcknight, D. H., Phillips, B., & Hardgrave, B. C. (2009). Which Reduces IT Turnover Intention The Most: Workplace Characteristics Or Job Characteristics? *Information & Management*, *46*(3), 167–174. doi:10.1016/j.im.2009.01.002

McMahon, M. (2016). *What is Holistic Security?* Retrieved from http://www.wisegeek.com/what-is-holistic-security.htm

Merriam, S. B. (1998). *Qualitative Research and Case Study Applications in Education*. San Francisco, CA: John Wiley & Sons.

Methot, J. R., & LePine, J. A. (2016). Too Close for Comfort? Investigating the Nature and Functioning of Work and Non-Work Role Segmentation Preferences. *Journal of Business and Psychology*, *31*(1), 103–123. doi:10.100710869-015-9402-0

Ministry of Education. (2005). *The executive summary of the Ministry of Education ten-year plan*. Ministry of Education in Saudi Arabia.

Mintzberg, H. (1979). The structure of organizations: A synthesis of the research. Upper Saddle River, NJ: Prentice-Hall.

Mintzberg, H. (1983). Power in and around organizations. Englewood Cliffs, NJ: Prentice-Hall.

Mintzberg, H. (1985). The organization as political arena. *Journal of Management Studies*, *22*(2), 133–154. doi:10.1111/j.1467-6486.1985.tb00069.x

Mislevy, R. J., Almond, R. G., & Lukas, J. F. (2004). *A Brief Introduction to Evidence-Centered Design (CSE Report 632)*. Center for Research on Evaluation, Standards, and Student Testing.

Moalagh, M., & Zare Ravasan, A. (2012). Developing a practical framework for assessing ERP post-implementation success using fuzzy analytic network process. *International Journal of Production Research*, *51*(4), 1236–1257. doi:10.1080/00207543.2012.698318

Moeini, A., Farahani Farmahini, A., & Zare Ravasan, A. (2013). The Consistency of Virtual Organizations Enabling Capabilities and Improvements in Knowledge Management Performance. *International Journal of Enterprise Information Systems*, *9*(2), 20–43. doi:10.4018/jeis.2013040102

Mohd Said, M. N. H., Ali, M. F., Sidek, R. Z. H., & Md Noor, N. (2005). *The application of e learning in supporting teaching and learning: An overview*. The 3rd International Seminar on Learning and Motivation Enhancing Student Engagement, Langkawi, Malaysia.

Moore, J. E. (2000a). One Road To Turnover: An Examination Of Work Exhaustion In Technology Professionals. *Management Information Systems Quarterly*, *24*(1), 141–168. doi:10.2307/3250982

Moore, J. E. (2000b). Why Is This Happening? A Causal Attribution Approach To Work Exhaustion Consequences. *Academy of Management Review*, *25*(2), 335–349.

Mueller, R. (1996). *Basic principles of structural equation modeling: An introduction to LISREL and EQS*. Springer Verlag. doi:10.1007/978-1-4612-3974-1

Mukherjee & Shaw. (2016). Big Data – Concepts, Applications, Challenges and Future Scope. *International Journal of Advanced Research in Computer and Communication Engineering*, *5*(2).

Mutschler, B., Weber, B., & Reichert, M. (2008). Workflow management versus case handling: results from a controlled software experiment. *Proceedings of the 2008 ACM symposium on Applied computing*. 10.1145/1363686.1363711

Narooka. (2016). Paradigm Shift of Big-Data Application in Cloud Computing. *International Journal of Advanced Research in Computer and Communication Engineering*, *5*(5).

Netemeyer, R. G., Boles, J. S., & McMurrian, R. (1995). Development and Validation of Work-Family Conflict and Family-Work Conflict Scales. *The Journal of Applied Psychology*, *81*(4), 400–410. doi:10.1037/0021-9010.81.4.400

Nicolaou, A. I., & Bhattacharya, S. (2006). Organizational performance effects of ERP systems usage: The impact of post implementation changes. *International Journal of Accounting Information Systems*, *7*(1), 18–35. doi:10.1016/j.accinf.2005.12.002

Nikookar, G., Yahya Safavi, S., Hakim, A., & Homayoun, A. (2010). Competitive advantage of enterprise resource planning vendors in Iran. *Information Systems*, *35*(3), 271–277. doi:10.1016/j.is.2009.09.002

NIST NVD - Control - AU-10 - NON-REPUDIATION. (2017). Retrieved from https://nvd.nist.gov/800-53/Rev4/control/AU-10

Nizamani, S., Khoumbati, K., Ismaili, I. A., Nizamani, S., Nizamani, S., & Basir, N. (2017). Testing and validating the ERP success evaluation model for higher education institutes of Pakistan. *International Journal of Business Information Systems, 25*(2), 165–191. doi:10.1504/IJBIS.2017.083682

Nour, M. A., & Mouakket, S. (2011). A classification framework of critical success factors for ERP systems implementation: A multi-stakeholder perspective. *International Journal of Enterprise Information Systems, 7*(1), 56–71. doi:10.4018/jeis.2011010104

Novak, T.P., & Hoffman, D.L. (2001). *Profitability on the Web: Business Models and Revenue Streams*. Owen Graduate School of Management, Vanderbilt University, eLab Position Paper, January.

Nunnally, J. (1978). *Psychometric theory*. McGraw-Hill.

Olhager, J., & Selldin, E. (2003). Enterprise resource planning survey of Swedish manufacturing firms. *European Journal of Operational Research, 146*(2), 365–373. doi:10.1016/S0377-2217(02)00555-6

Olson-Buchanan, J. B., & Boswell, W. R. (2006). Blurring Boundaries: Correlates of Integration and Segmentation Between Work and Nonwork. *Journal of Vocational Behavior, 68*(3), 432–445. doi:10.1016/j.jvb.2005.10.006

Organisation for Economic Co-operation and Development. (2017). *Beyond PISA 2015: A Longer-Term Strategy of PISA*. Retrieved from http://www.oecd.org/pisa/pisaproducts/Longer-term-strategy-of-PISA.pdf

Orton, J. D., & Weick, K. E. (1990). Loosely coupled systems: A reconceptualization. *Academy of Management Review, 15*(2), 203–223.

Osburn, H. (1968). Item sampling for achievement testing. *Educational and Psychological Measurement, 28*(1), 95–104. doi:10.1177/001316446802800109

Otto, G. (2016, July). White House releases federal cybersecurity workforce strategy. *Fedscoop*, 1. Retrieved from http://fedscoop.com/us-government-cybersecurity-workforce-strategy

Oxford Press Dictionary. (2017). *Oxford Dictionaries*. Retrieved from https://www.oxforddictionaries.com/

Oxford University. (2015). *A Dictionary of Physics* (6th ed.). New York, NY: Oxford University Press.

Paivio, A. (1986). *Mental representations*. New York: Oxford University Press.

Pansarel, N. (2011). *Online Aggregation for Large MapReduce Jobs*. ACM.

Parry, E., & Tyson, S. (2008). An analysis of the use and success of online recruitment methods in the UK. *Human Resource Management Journal, 18*(3), 257–274. doi:10.1111/j.1748-8583.2008.00070.x

Pautasso, C. (2014). RESTful web services: principles, patterns, emerging technologies. In Web Services Foundations (pp. 31-51). New York, NY: Springer. doi:10.1007/978-1-4614-7518-7_2

Pawlak, P., & Wendling, C. (2013). Trends in cyberspace: Can governments keep up? *Environment Systems & Decisions*, *33*(4), 536–543. doi:10.100710669-013-9470-5

Pawlowski, S., Kaganer, E., & Cater, J. III. (2004). Mapping Perceptions Of Burnout In The Information Technology Profession: A Study Using Social Representations Theory. *Paper Presented At The International Conference On Information Systems (ICIS).*

Petter, S., DeLone, W., & McLean, E. (2008). Measuring information systems success: Models, dimensions, measures, and interrelationships. *European Journal of Information Systems*, *17*(3), 236–263. doi:10.1057/ejis.2008.15

Pfeffer, J. (2009). *Building Sustainable Organizations: The Human Factor*. Stanford, CA: Foundations Of Human Ecology.

Phaneendra, V. S. (2013). Big Data- solutions for RDBMS problems- A survey. *12th IEEE/IFIP Network Operations & Management Symposium (NOMS 2010).*

Pickford, M., Wheelock, J., & Gullo, T. (2014). *Congressional budget office cost estimate: S. 2521 Federal Information Security Modernization Act of 2014*. Retrieved from https://www.cbo.gov/sites/default/files/113th-congress-2013-2014/costestimate/s25211.pdf

Piszczek, M. (2017). Boundary Control and Controlled Boundaries: Organizational Expectations for Technology Use at the Work-Family Interface. *Journal of Organizational Behavior*, *38*(4), 592–611. doi:10.1002/job.2153

Piszczek, M., & Berg, P. (2014). Expanding the Boundaries of Boundary Theory: Regulative Institutions and Work-Family Role Management. *Human Relations*, *67*(12), 1491–1512. doi:10.1177/0018726714524241

Poisat, P., & Mey, M. (2017). Electronic human resource management: Enhancing or entrancing? *SA Journal of Human Resource Management*, *15*(0), 858. doi:10.4102ajhrm.v15i0.858

Pomerol, J. C., & Brézillon, P. (2011). About some relationships between knowledge and context. *Proceedings of the Third International and Interdisciplinary Conference on Modeling and Using Context.*

Popplewell, K. (2014). Enterprise interoperability science base structure. In K. Mertins, F. Bénaben, R. Poler, & J. Bourrières (Eds.), *Enterprise Interoperability VI: Interoperability for Agility, Resilience and Plasticity of Collaborations* (pp. 417–427). Cham, Switzerland: Springer International Publishing. doi:10.1007/978-3-319-04948-9_35

Porter, S., & Ayman, R. (2010). Work Flexibility as a Mediator of the Relationship Between Work-Family Conflict and Intention to Quit. *Journal of Management & Organization*, *16*(3), 411–424.

Powell, A., & Craig, L. (2015). Gender Differences in Working at Home and Time Use Patterns: Evidence from Australia. *Work, Employment and Society*, *29*(4), 571–589. doi:10.1177/0950017014568140

Pressman, R. (2009). *Software Engineering: A Practitioner's Approach*. Columbus, OH: McGraw-Hill.

Priyadarshini, C., Kumar, Y. L. N., & Jha, R. R. (2017). Employer attractiveness through social media: A phenomenological study. *Qualitative Report*, *22*(4), 969–983.

Project Management Institute. (2009). *Practice Standard for Project Risk Management*. Newtown Square, PA: Project Management Institute.

Project Management Institute. (2017a). *Project Management*. Retrieved from https://search.pmi.org/default.aspx?q=Project%20Management

Project Management Institute. (2017b). *Requirements Management*. Retrieved from https://search.pmi.org/default.aspx?q=Requirements%20Management

Public Law 107-347 - Federal Information Security Management Act of 2002 (FISMA), Federal Information Security Modernization Act. (2002). U.S.C. Retrieved from http://csrc.nist.gov/drivers/documents/FISMA-final.pdf

Public Law 113-283 - Federal Information Security Modernization Act of 2014 (FISMA REFORM), Pub. L. No. 3073. (2014). United States of America: U.S.C. Retrieved from https://www.congress.gov/bill/113th-congress/senate-bill/2521

Purcell. (2012). Big data using cloud computing. *Journal of Technology Research*.

Purcell. (2013). The emergence of big data technology and analytics. *Journal of Technology Research*.

Purnomo, S. H., & Lee, Y. (2013). E-Learning adoption in the banking workplace in Indonesia: An empirical study. *Information Development*, *29*(2), 138–153. doi:10.1177/0266666912448258

Rana, N. P., Dwivedi, Y. K., Williams, M. D., & Weerakkody, V. (2015). Investigating success of an e-government initiative: Validation of an integrated IS success model. *Information Systems Frontiers*, *17*(1), 127–142. doi:10.100710796-014-9504-7

Reichert, M., Dadam, P., Jurisch, M., Kreher, U., & Goser, K. (2008). *Architectural Design of Flexible Process Management Technology*. Paper presented at the PRIMIUM Subconference at the Multikonferenz Wirtschaftsinformatik (MKWI), Garching, Germany.

Reyt, J., & Weisenfeld, B. M. (2015). Seeing The Forest For The Trees: Exploratory Learning, Mobile Technology, And Knowledge Workers' Role Integration Behaviors. *Academy of Management Journal*, *58*(3), 739–762. doi:10.5465/amj.2013.0991

Rezaei, R., Chiew, T., & Lee, S. (2014). A review on E-business interoperability frameworks. *Journal of Systems and Software*, *93*, 199–216. doi:10.1016/j.jss.2014.02.004

Robkin, M., Weininger, S., Preciado, B., & Goldman, J. (2015). Levels of conceptual interoperability model for healthcare framework for safe medical device interoperability. In *Symposium on Product Compliance Engineering* (pp. 1–8). Piscataway, NJ: IEEE Computer Society Press. 10.1109/ISPCE.2015.7138703

Roca, J. C., Chiu, C. M., & Martinez, F. J. (2006). Understanding E-Learning continuance intention: An extension of the technology acceptance model. *International Journal of Human-Computer Studies*, *64*(8), 683–696. doi:10.1016/j.ijhcs.2006.01.003

Rothmann, S. (2008). Job Satisfaction, Occupational Stress, Burnout And Work Engagement As Components Of Work-Related Wellbeing. *SA Journal of Industrial Psychology*, *34*(3), 11–16. doi:10.4102ajip.v34i3.424

Roth, P. L., Bobko, P., Van Iddekinge, C. H., & Thatcher, J. B. (2016). Social media in employee-selection-related decisions: A research agenda for uncharted territory. *Journal of Management*, *42*(1), 269–298. doi:10.1177/0149206313503018

Rouhani, S., Ashrafi, A., & Afshari, S. (2013). Segmenting critical success factors for ERP implementation using an integrated fuzzy AHP and fuzzy DEMATEL approach. *World Applied Sciences Journal*, *22*(8), 1066–1079.

RoyChowdhury, T., & Srimannarayana, M. (2013). Applicants' perceptions on online recruitment procedures. *Management and Labour Studies*, *38*(3), 185–199. doi:10.1177/0258042X13509737

Sabia, S. K. (2014). Applications of big Data: Current Status and Future Scope. *International Journal on Advanced Computer Theory and Engineering, 3*(5).

Saks, A. M. (2006). Antecedents And Consequences Of Employee Engagement. *Journal of Managerial Psychology*, *21*(7), 600–619. doi:10.1108/02683940610690169

Saldaña, J. (2011). *Fundamentals of Qualitative Research*. New York, NY: Oxford University Press.

Saldaña, J. (2013). *The Coding Manual for Qualitative Researchers*. Thousand Oaks, CA: Sage Publications, Inc.

Schaufeli, W. B., & Salanova, M. (2014). Burnout, Boredom And Engagement In The Workplace. In M. C. W. Peeters, J. D. Jonge, & T. W. Taris (Eds.), An Introduction To Contemporary Work Psychology (pp. 293-320). John Wiley & Sons, Ltd.

Schaufeli, W. B. (2012). Work Engagement. What Do We Know And Where Do We Go? *Romanian Journal of Applied Psychology*, *14*(1), 3–10.

Schaufeli, W. B., & Bakker, A. B. (2004). Job Demands, Job Resources, And Their Relationship With Burnout And Engagement: A Multi-Sample Study. *Journal of Organizational Behavior*, *25*(3), 293–315. doi:10.1002/job.248

Schaufeli, W. B., Bakker, A. B., & Van Rhenen, W. (2009). How Changes In Job Demands And Resources Predict Burnout, Work Engagement, And Sickness Absenteeism. *Journal of Organizational Behavior*, *30*(7), 893–917. doi:10.1002/job.595

Schaufeli, W. B., Leiter, M. P., & Maslach, C. (2009). Burnout: 35 Years Of Research And Practice. *Career Development International*, *14*(3), 204–220. doi:10.1108/13620430910966406

Scheuer, F., & Smetters, K. (2014). *Could a Website Really Have Doomed the Health Exchanges? Multiple Equilibria, Initial Conditions and the Construction of the Fine (No. w19835)*. National Bureau of Economic Research. doi:10.3386/w19835

Schneider, B., Macey, W. H., & Barbera, K. (2006). Employee Engagement. Academic Press.

Scott, T., & Daniel, J. M. (2016). *Announcing the first federal Chief Information Security Officer | whitehouse.gov*. Retrieved from https://www.whitehouse.gov/blog/2016/09/08/announcing-first-federal-chief-information-security-officer

Security and Privacy in the Era of Big Data. (n.d.). The SMW, a Technological Solution to the Challenge of Data Leakage, renci ncds.

Seddon, P. (1997). A respecification and extension of the Delone and McLean model of IS success. *Information Systems Research*, *8*(3), 240–253. doi:10.1287/isre.8.3.240

Sedera, D., Gable, G., & Chan, T. (2004). *A factor and structural equation analysis of the enterprise systems success measurement model*. Paper presented at the 25th international conference on information systems, Washington, DC.

Segars, A., & Grover, V. (1993). Re-examining perceived ease of use and usefulness: A confirmatory factor analysis. *MIS Quarterly Executive*, *17*(4), 517–525. doi:10.2307/249590

Selyukh, A., Shalal, A., & Mason, J. (2015). *Obama seeks $14 billion to boost U.S. cybersecurity defenses*. Reuters. Retrieved from http://www.reuters.com/article/2015/02/02/us-usa-budget-cybersecurity-idUSKBN0L61WQ20150202

Sethi, V., Barrier, T., & King, R. C. (1999). An Examination Of The Correlates Of Burnout In Information Systems Professionals. *Information Resources Management Journal*, *12*(3), 5–13. doi:10.4018/irmj.1999070101

Sharma, A., Kumar, M., & Agarwal, S. (2015). A Complete Survey on Software Architectural Styles and Patterns. *Procedia Computer Science*, *70*, 16–28. doi:10.1016/j.procs.2015.10.019

Sharma, R., & Panigrahi, P. (2015). Developing a roadmap for planning and implementation of interoperability capability in e-government. *Transforming Government: People, Process and Policy*, *9*(4), 426–447.

Shelly, G. B., Cashman, T. J., Adamski, J., & Adamski, J. J. (1995). *Systems Analysis and Design*. Danvers, MA: Boyd and Fraser Publishing Company.

Shih, H. P. (2004). An empirical study on predicting user acceptance of e-shopping on the web. *Information & Management*, *41*(3), 351–368. doi:10.1016/S0378-7206(03)00079-X

Shih, S.-P., Jiang, J. J., Klein, G., & Wang, E. (2011). Learning Demand And Job Autonomy Of IT Personnel: Impact On Turnover Intention. *Computers in Human Behavior*, *27*(6), 2301–2307. doi:10.1016/j.chb.2011.07.009

Shuck, B., & Reio, T. Jr. (2014). Employee Engagement And Well-Being: A Moderation Model And Implications For Practice. *Journal of Leadership & Organizational Studies*, *21*(1), 43–58. doi:10.1177/1548051813494240

Shumaker, J., Ward, K., Petter, S., & Riley, J. (2017). Mitigating The Threat Of Lost Knowledge Within Information Technology Departments. *Proceedings Of The 50th Hawaii International Conference On System Sciences.*

Sierhuis, M., Clancey, W. J., Hoof, R. V., & Hoog, R. D. (2000). *Modeling and simulating work practices from Apollo 12*. Paper presented at the International Workshop on Simulation for European Space programmes, ESTEC.

Sierhuis, M., Clancey, W. J., van Hoof, R., & de Hoog, R. (2000). *Modeling and simulating human activity*. Paper presented at the AAAI Fall Symposium on Simulating Human Agents, North Falmouth, MA.

Sikka, R., Dhankhar, A., & Rana, C. (2012). A survey paper on E-Learning recommender system. *International Journal of Computers and Applications*, *47*(9), 27–30. doi:10.5120/7218-0024

Sikos, L. (2017). The Semantic Gap. In *Description Logics in Multimedia Reasoning* (pp. 51–66). Cham, Switzerland: Springer. doi:10.1007/978-3-319-54066-5_3

Sivarajah, U., Kamal, M. M., Irani, Z., & Weerakkody, V. (2017). Critical analysis of Big Data challenges and analytical methods. *Journal of Business Research*, *70*, 263–286. doi:10.1016/j.jbusres.2016.08.001

Smeraldi, F., & Malacaria, P. (2014). How to spend it: Optimal investment for cybersecurity position paper. *ACySE '14 Proceedings of the 1st International Workshop on Agents and CyberSecurity,* 1–4.

Soja, P. (2008). Examining the conditions of ERP implementations: Lessons learnt from adopters. *Business Process Management Journal*, *14*(1), 105–121. doi:10.1108/14637150810849445

Soltani, S., Elkhani, N., & Bardsiri, V. K. (2014). The Effects of Perceived Organizational Support and Organizational Citizenship Behaviors on Continuance Intention of Enterprise Resource Planning. *International Journal of Enterprise Information Systems*, *10*(2), 81–102. doi:10.4018/ijeis.2014040105

Spathis, C., & Ananiadis, J. (2005). Assessing the benefits of using an enterprise system in accounting information and management. *Journal of Enterprise Information Management*, *18*(2), 195–210. doi:10.1108/17410390510579918

Spathis, C., & Constantinides, S. (2003). The usefulness of ERP systems for effective management. *Industrial Management & Data Systems*, *103*(9), 677–685. doi:10.1108/02635570310506098

Spewak, S. H., & Hill, S. C. (1993). *Enterprise architecture planning: developing a blueprint for data, applications and technology*. QED Information Sciences, Inc.

Stake, R. E. (1995). *The Art of Case Study Research*. Thousand Oaks, CA: Sage Publications.

Stone, D. (2012). Security. In Policy Paradox (3rd ed.; pp. 129–153). New York, NY: W.W. Norton and Company.

Stone, D., Deadrick, D., Lukaszewski, K., & Johnson, R. (2015). The influence of technology on the future of human resource management. *Human Resource Management Review*, *25*(2), 216–231. doi:10.1016/j.hrmr.2015.01.002

Straub, D. (1989). Validating instruments in MIS research. *MIS Quarterly Executive*, *13*(2), 147–169. doi:10.2307/248922

Subramanianh, G., & Hoffers, C. (2005). An exploratory case study of enterprise resource planning implementation. *International Journal of Enterprise Information Systems*, *1*(1), 23–38. doi:10.4018/jeis.2005010102

Sungkur, R., & Daiboo, S. (2015). SOREST, A Novel Framework Combining SOAP and REST for Implementing Web Services. In *Proceedings of the Second International Conference on Data Mining, Internet Computing, and Big Data* (pp. 22-34). Red Hook, NY: Curran Associates, Inc.

Sungkur, R., & Daiboo, S. (2016). Combining the Best Features of SOAP and REST for the Implementation of Web Services. *International Journal of Digital Information and Wireless Communications*, *6*(1), 21–33. doi:10.17781/P001923

Su, Y., & Yang, C. (2010). A structural equation model for analyzing the impact of ERP on SCM. *Expert Systems with Applications*, *37*(1), 456–469. doi:10.1016/j.eswa.2009.05.061

Swapnil, A. (2014). Understanding the big data problems and their solutions using hadoop and map-reduce. International Journal of Application or Innovation in Engineering & Management, 3, 3.

Syrek, C. J., Apostel, E., & Antoni, C. H. (2013). Stress In Highly Demanding IT Jobs: Transformational Leadership Moderates The Impact Of Time Pressure On Exhaustion And Work-Life Balance. *Journal of Occupational Health Psychology*, *18*(3), 252–261. doi:10.1037/a0033085 PMID:23834443

Tan, C., & Pan, S. (2002). *ERP success: the search for a comprehensive framework*. In R. D. Banker, H. Chang & Y-C. Kao (Eds.), *Proceedings of the 8th. Americas Conference on Information Systems*. Dallas, TX: AMCIS Press (AIS e-Library).

Taris, T. W., & Schaufeli, W. B. (2015). Individual Well-Being And Performance At Work: A Conceptual And Theoretical Overview. In M. V. V. R. Peccei (Ed.), *Well-Being And Performance At Work: The Role Of Context* (pp. 15–34). London: Taylor & Francis.

Tasir, Z., Al-Dheleai, Y., Harun, J., & Shukor, A. N. (2011). Students perception towards the use of social networking as an E-Learning platform. *Proceeding of the 10th WSEAS International Conference on Education and Educational Technology '11*.

Taylor, S., & Todd, P. A. (1995). Understanding information technology usage: A test of competing models. *Information Systems Research*, *6*(2), 144–176. doi:10.1287/isre.6.2.144

Terzis, V., Moridis, C. N., & Economides, A. A. (2013). Continuance acceptance of computer based assessment through the integration of user's expectations and perceptions. *Computers & Education*, *62*, 50–61. doi:10.1016/j.compedu.2012.10.018

Thai-Nghe, N., Drumond, L., Krohn-Grimberghe, A., & Schmidt-Thieme, L. (2010). Recommender system for predicting student performance. *Procedia Computer Science*, *1*(2), 2811–2819. doi:10.1016/j.procs.2010.08.006

Thakar, U., Tiwari, A., & Varma, S. (2016). On Composition of SOAP Based and RESTful Services. In *Proceedings of the 6th International Conference on Advanced Computing* (pp. 500-505). Piscataway, NJ: IEEE Computer Society Press. 10.1109/IACC.2016.99

The Open Group. (2011). *TOGAF® Version 9.1*. Van Haren Publishing.

Thwala, D. W., Ajagbe, A. M., Long, C. S., Bilau, A. A., & Enegbuma, W. I. (2012). Sdanese Small And Medium Sized Construction Firms: An Empirical Survey Of Job Turnover. *Journal of Basic and Applied Scientific Research*, *2*(8), 7414.

TIMSS 2011 Assessment. (2013). *International Association for the Evaluation of Educational Achievement (IEA)*. TIMSS & PIRLS International Study Center, Lynch School of Education, Boston College, Chestnut Hill, MA and International Association for the Evaluation of Educational Achievement (IEA), IEA Secretariat, Amsterdam, The Netherlands.

TIMSS. (2017). *International Association for the Evaluation of Educational Achievement (IEA)*. Retrieved 12 September 2017, from http://www.iea.nl/timss-2015

Tran, H., Zdun, U., Oberortner, E., Mulo, E., & Dustdar, S. (2012). Compliance in service-oriented architectures: A model-driven and view-based approach. *Information and Software Technology*, *54*(6), 531–552. doi:10.1016/j.infsof.2012.01.001

Tremblay, D.-G., & Genin, E. (2008). Permeability between Work and Non-Work: The Case of Self-Employed IT Workers. *Canadian Journal of Communication*, *33*(4), 701–720. doi:10.22230/cjc.2008v33n4a1994

Troester, M. (2013). *Big Data Meets Big Data Analytics.* White Paper.

Trueman, C. N. (2015). *The Maginot Line - History Learning Site*. Retrieved from http://www.historylearningsite.co.uk/world-war-two/world-war-two-in-western-europe/the-attack-on-western-europe/the-maginot-line/

Uhl-Bien, M., Marion, R., & Mckelvey, B. (2007). Complexity leadership theory: Shifting leadership from the industrial age to the knowledge era. *The Leadership Quarterly*, *18*(4), 298–318. doi:10.1016/j.leaqua.2007.04.002

Umasri, M.L. (2014). *Mining Big Data: Current status and forecast to the future*. Academic Press.

Van Den Broek, A., Elst, T. V., Baillien, E., Sercu, M., Schouteden, M., De Witte, H. L., & … . (2017). Job Demands, Job Resources, Burnout, Work Engagement, And Their Relationships: An Analysis Across Sectors., 59(4), 369-376. *Journal of Occupational and Environmental Medicine*, *59*(4), 369–376. doi:10.1097/JOM.0000000000000964 PMID:28157768

van Dick, R., Wagner, U., Pettigrew, T. F., Christ, O., Wolf, C., Petzel, T., ... Jackson, J. S. (2004). Role of Perceived Importance in Intergroup Contact. *Journal of Personality and Social Psychology*, *87*(2), 211–227. doi:10.1037/0022-3514.87.2.211 PMID:15301628

Van Heerden, J. (2015). *The Impact Of Job Engagement And Job Resources On Work Engagement And Turnover Intentions Within The Information Technology Division Of A South African Bank* (Unpublished Doctoral Dissertation). University Of The Western Cape.

Van Iddekinge, C. H., Lanivich, S. E., Roth, P. L., & Junco, E. (2016). Social media for selection? Validity and adverse impact potential of a Facebook-based assessment. *Journal of Management*, *42*(7), 1811–1835. doi:10.1177/0149206313515524

Venkatesh, Perur, & Jaliha. (2015). A Study on Use of Big Data in Cloud Computing Environment. *International Journal of Computer Science and Information Technologies, 6.*

Venkatesh, V., Morris, M. G., Davis, G. B., & Davis, F. D. (2003). User acceptance of information technology: Towards a unified view. *Management Information Systems Quarterly*, *27*(3), 425–478. doi:10.2307/30036540

Verborgh, R., Harth, A., Maleshkova, M., Stadtmüller, S., Steiner, T., Taheriyan, M., & Van de Walle, R. (2014). Survey of semantic description of REST APIs. In C. Pautasso, E. Wilde, & R. Alarcon (Eds.), *REST: Advanced Research Topics and Practical Applications* (pp. 69–89). New York, NY: Springer. doi:10.1007/978-1-4614-9299-3_5

Verner, L. (2004). BPM: The Promise and the Challenge. *Queue*, *2*(1), 82–91. doi:10.1145/984458.984503

Vivian, P., & Hormann, S. (2015). Persistent Traumatization In Nonprofit Organizations. *OD Practitioner*, *47*(1), 25–30.

Von Canon, W. A. (2017). *Personal correspondence. President*. Fairfax, VA: Business Intelligence, Incorporated.

Waddill, D. D., & Marquardt, M. J. (2011). *The e-HR Advantage: The complete handbook for technology-enabled human resources*. Boston, MA: Nicholas Brealey.

Wainer, H., & Kiely, G. L. (1987). Item clusters and computerized adaptive testing: A case for testlets. *Journal of Educational Measurement*, *24*(3), 185–201. doi:10.1111/j.1745-3984.1987.tb00274.x

Wang, E., Shih, S., Jiang, J., & Klein, G. (2008). The consistency among facilitating factors and ERP implementation success: A holistic view of fit. *Journal of Systems and Software*, *81*(9), 1609–1621. doi:10.1016/j.jss.2007.11.722

Weinert, C., Maier, C., Laumer, S., & Weitzel, T. (2015). *Extending Moore's Exhaustion Model: Including Further Dimensions Of Burnout And Investigating Their Influence On Turnover Intention Among IT Professionals. Paper Presented At The ACM SIGMIS Conference On Management Information Systems*, Newport Beach, CA. 10.1145/2751957.2751975

White, E., Anderson, J., Schroeder, R., & Tupy, S. (1982). A study of the MRP implementation process. *Journal of Operations Management*, *2*(3), 145–153. doi:10.1016/0272-6963(82)90002-X

Williams, J. J., Macintosh, N. B., & Moore, J. C. (1990). Budget-related behavior in public sector organizations: Some empirical evidence. *Accounting, Organizations and Society*, *15*(3), 221–246. doi:10.1016/0361-3682(90)90006-G

Willoughby, T. C. (1977). Computing Personnel Turnover: A Review Of The Literature. In *Proceedings of the 1977 Annual Conference*. Seattle, WA: ACM. 10.1145/800179.810204

Wilson, K. S. (2013). Conflicts among the pillars of information assurance. *IT Professional, IEEE*, *15*(August), 44–49. doi:10.1109/MITP.2012.24

Wixom, B. H., & Todd, P. A. (2005). A theoretical integration of user satisfaction and technology acceptance. *Information Systems Research, 16*, 85.

Wozniak, J. (2014). On e-recruitment and four ways of using its methods. *Proceedings of the 8th International Scientific Conference.*

Wright, T. A., & Cropanzano, R. (2000). Psychological Well-Being And Job Satisfaction As Predictors Of Job Performance. *Journal of Occupational Health Psychology*, *5*(1), 84–94. doi:10.1037/1076-8998.5.1.84 PMID:10658888

Wu, J., & Wang, Y. (2006). Measuring ERP success: The ultimate users' view. *International Journal of Operations & Production Management*, *26*(8), 882–903. doi:10.1108/01443570610678657

Xiong, W., Zhao, X., Yuan, J.-F., & Luo, S. (2017). Ex Post Risk Management in Public-Private Partnership Infrastructure Projects. *Project Management Journal*, *48*(3), 76–89.

Xu, G. (2011). *Social networking sites, Web 2.0 technologies and E-Learning* (Master thesis). Retrieved from http://hdl.handle.net/10652/1864

Xu, Y., Yen, D. C., Lin, B., & Chou, D. C. (2002). Adopting customer relationship management technology. *Industrial Management & Data Systems*, *102*(8), 442–452. doi:10.1108/02635570210445871

Yang, H., Ma, K., Deng, C., Liao, H., Yan, J., & Zhang, J. (2013). Towards conformance testing of choreography based on scenario. In *Proceedings of the International Symposium on Theoretical Aspects of Software Engineering* (pp. 59-62). Piscataway, NJ: IEEE Computer Society Press. 10.1109/TASE.2013.23

Ying Lu, C. H., & Swanson, D. (2010). Matchmaking: A New MapReduce Scheduling. *10th IEEE International Conference on Computer and Information Technology (CIT'10).*

Yin, R. K. (2014). *Case Study Research: Design and Methods*. Thousand Oaks, CA: Sage Publications.

Yu, C. S. (2005). Causes influencing the effectiveness of the post-implementation ERP system. *Industrial Management & Data Systems*, *105*(1), 115–132. doi:10.1108/02635570510575225

Yusuf, Y., Gunasekaran, A., & Abthorpe, M. (2004). Enterprise information systems project implementation: A case study of ERP in Rolls-Royce. *International Journal of Production Economics*, *87*(3), 251–266. doi:10.1016/j.ijpe.2003.10.004

Zacarias, M., & Martins, P. V. (2014). Business alignment methodology: The discovery phase. *Information Resources Management Journal*, *27*(1), 1–20. doi:10.4018/irmj.2014010101

Zacarias, M., Serendero, P., Pinto, H. S., & Tribolet, J. (2008). Capturing and modeling work practice: A context-based approach. *Revue d'Intelligence Artificialle*, *5*(22), 669–688. doi:10.3166/ria.22.669-689

Zare, A., & Ravasan, A. Z. (2014). An extended framework for ERP post-implementation success assessment. *Information Resources Management Journal*, *27*(4), 45–65. doi:10.4018/irmj.2014100103

Zaza, I., & Armstrong, D. (2016). *Turnover Intention Among Information Technology Professionals: A Meta-Analytical Perspective. Paper Presented At The Thirty Seventh International Conference On Information Systems*, Dublin, Ireland.

Zhang, Z., Lee, M., Huang, P., Zhang, L., & Huang, X. (2005). A framework of ERP systems implementation success in China: An empirical study. *International Journal of Production Economics*, *98*(1), 56–80. doi:10.1016/j.ijpe.2004.09.004

Zhang, Z., Wu, C., & Cheung, D. (2013). A survey on cloud interoperability: Taxonomies, standards, and practice. *Performance Evaluation Review*, *40*(4), 13–22. doi:10.1145/2479942.2479945

Zheng, C., Molineux, J., Mirshekary, S., & Scarparo, S. (2015). Developing Individual and Organisational Work-Life Balance Strategies to Improve Employee Health and Wellbeing. *Employee Relations*, *37*(3), 354–379. doi:10.1108/ER-10-2013-0142

Zheng, Y., Zhao, K., & Stylianou, A. (2013). The impacts of information quality and system quality on users' continuance intention in information-exchange virtual communities: An empirical investigation. *Decision Support Systems*, *56*, 513–524. doi:10.1016/j.dss.2012.11.008

Zimmermann, O., Tomlinson, M., & Peuser, S. (2012). *Perspectives on Web Services: Applying SOAP, WSDL and UDDI to Real-World Projects*. Berlin: Springer-Verlag.

About the Contributors

Susan Swayze, Ph.D., M.B.A., is an accomplished scholar and consultant who leverages her qualitative and quantitative research expertise in teaching, curriculum development, and organizational development. Dr. Swayze conducts research and evaluation studies for government and corporate clients. Additionally, she speaks regularly at conferences, reviews manuscripts for journals and book publishers, and publishes in the areas of diversity and inclusion, pedagogy and andragogy in the online environment, and data-driven decision-making.

Valerie Ford earned her doctorate in human and organizational learning from The George Washington University in Washington, DC. Her research interests comprise a broad range of topics, including how data and information technology change behaviors and processes in organizations, understanding the changing nature of organizations, teams, crowds and markets in the 21st century, effectively using decision analytics and 'big data' to build collective intelligence, and fostering organizational creativity and innovation to generate new processes and products. Her experience in MIS has given her a keen awareness of the technology issues in corporate environments and she feels fortunate to experience and investigate technology in organizations as both a scholar and a practitioner.

* * *

Jaehwa Choi is Associate Professor and Program Director of the Assessment, Testing, and Measurement Program in the Department of Educational Leadership (The George Washington University). He is also the Executive Director of the Computer Adaptive Formative Assessment (CAFA) Laboratory (CAFA Lab, Inc.) and has conducted various Information and Communication Technology (ICT)-based assessment projects in collaboration with Samsung Electronics (Intelligence Solution Team), Korea Institute for Curriculum and Evaluation (KICE; Assessment Advancement Team), Korea Research Institute for Educational Assessment (KRIEA), Cisco systems, and others.

José C. Delgado is an Associate Professor at the Computer Science and Engineering Department of the Instituto Superior Técnico (University of Lisbon), in Lisbon, Portugal, where he earned the Ph.D. degree in 1988. He lectures courses in the areas of Computer Architecture, Information Technology and Service Engineering. He has performed several management roles in his faculty, namely Director of the Taguspark campus, near Lisbon, and Coordinator of the B.Sc. and M.Sc. in Computer Science and Engineering at that campus. He has been the coordinator of and researcher in several international research projects. As an author, his publications include one book, 20 book chapters and more than 50 papers in international refereed conferences and journals.

Thomas M. Gronow, M.H.A., Ed.D.(c), currently serves as chief operating officer (COO) at University of Colorado Hospital (UCH). A Florida native, Tom started his career in aviation and holds his commercial/multi-engine rating. Tom's experience in aviation has enabled him to serve as a subject matter expert in communication, reliability, quality, and patient safety design. In his role as COO, Tom oversees key areas such as trauma, transplant, emergency, perioperative, oncology, ambulatory, and diagnostic services. Tom has been with UCH since 2014. Prior to that, Tom served as vice president of operations at UPMC Mercy in Pittsburgh, PA. Tom started his healthcare career at UPMC as an administrative fellow in 2007.

Seyed Mojtaba Hosseini Bamakan received his Ph.D. degree in Management Science and Engineering from University of Chinese Academy of Sciences (UCAS) in 2017, and his master degree in IT management field from Allameh Tabataba'i University (ATU), Iran in 2009. He is currently a postdoctoral scholar at Shenzhen Institute of Advanced Technology, Chinese Academy of Sciences, Shenzhen, China. His current research interests include information security, business intelligence, big data mining and intelligent optimization techniques.

Jayashree K. is an Engineer by qualification, having done her Doctorate in the area of Web services Fault Management from Anna University, Chennai and Masters in Embedded System Technologies from Anna University and Bachelors in Computer Science and Engineering from Madras University. She is presently Associate Professor in the Department of Computer Science and Engineering at Rajalakshmi Engineering College, affiliated to Anna University Chennai. Her areas of interest include Web services, Cloud Computing, Data Mining and distributed computing. She is a member of ACM and CSI.

Letitia Larry is a talented and accomplished executive, with 20+ years of demonstrated career success developing and executing operational strategies to promote organizational growth and optimal utilization of existing and emerging technologies. Experienced in multiple industries and disciplines with specialization in organizational change/transition/transformation.

Paula Ventura Martins is an assistant professor of the Electronics and Computers Engineering Department of Faculty of Sciences and Technology, University of Algarve, and a member of Research Centre for Spatial and Organizational Dynamics (CIEO). She has a PhD degree in Computer Science and Engineering from the "Instituto Superior Técnico da Universidade Técnica de Lisboa" (IST/ULT). In 2000, she got the Master's degree in Computer Science and Engineering from the "Faculdade de Ciências e Tecnologia da Universidade Nova de Lisboa" (FCT/UNL). She concluded her undergraduate course in Computer Science and Engineering on 1992, in the same institution. Her personal interests are Software Process Improvement, Software Development Processes, Domain Specific Languages, Modelling Languages and Business Process Modelling.

Donna Weaver McCloskey, Ph.D., is an Associate Professor at Widener University in Chester, Pennsylvania. She holds a B.S. in Finance and Management Information Systems (MIS) from the University of Delaware, an M.B.A. from Widener University; and a Ph.D. in Decision Sciences / MIS from Drexel University. She has earned the Project Management Professional (PMP) credential from the Project Management Institute (PMI) and is active in a number of professional organizations. The recipient of multiple teaching awards, Dr. McCloskey enjoys teaching at both the graduate and undergraduate level. Dr. McCloskey's research interests include the impact of technology on work-life balance, outcomes of telecommuting, the adoption of electronic commerce and data analytics. Her work has been published in numerous journals including Journal of End User Computing, Enterprise Operations Management, Information Resources Management Journal, Journal of Information Systems Education and Journal of Electronic Commerce in Organizations. Additionally, she written over 7 book chapters and has presented her research at both national and international conferences.

Abirami R. is currently working as Assistant Professor in Department of Computer Science and Engineering at Rajalakshmi Engineering College, Chennai. She pursued her Master degree in Computer Science and Engineering in Rajalakshmi Engineering College and completed the course in 2016. She received a gold medal for her outstanding performance in academics. She has a keen interest in Computer Science and passion for research in the field of Big-data.

Tiina Rodrigue leverages her more than 25 years of experience to guide interdepartmental cybersecurity efforts with government entities to establish an industry-wide professionalized cyber workforce, meaningful metrics and ground-truth security. Previously, Ms. Rodrigue was the Program Director, Professional Services at CipherCloud (San Jose, CA) where she supervised concurrent teams deploying globally the policy-based, on-the fly encryption product in financial and health-care environments for data protection in clouds such as Salesforce, O365, Box, Adobe, Amazon Web Service, Google, and Dropbox. Prior to CipherCloud, Ms. Rodrigue served as the Chief Information Security Officer (CISO) for U.S. Citizenship and Immigration Services (USCIS), a component of the Department of Homeland Security (DHS). During her tenure at DHS she was promoted to Chief Technology Officer (CTO) at USCIS, bridging the technology concerns of security, infrastructure, change, architecture and capability management. Tiina was selected to perform a similar function in support of Transportation Security Administration (TSA), where she ran projects focusing on improvements in security, innovation, culture, software development and capability. Previous to her federal service, she served in several senior positions at Cisco and multiple consulting firms. Ms. Rodrigue holds a Bachelor's from the University of Wisconsin, a Master's degree in Management Information Technology from the University of Virginia and currently a candidate in The George Washington University's Executive Cyber Corps Doctoral program. Her dissertation quantitatively examines the power and politics of cybersecurity within an organizational environment. Ms. Rodrigue is a wife and mother of six, enjoying running her farm of goats, chickens, and bees.

Kamaljeet Sandhu's teaching and research expertise are in Information Systems Adoption, Management Accounting and Corporate Governance Adoption, and E-Learning Acceptance at Universities.

Johanna Sweet is an Assistant Professor of Business Administration at Roanoke College, and oversees the Human Resource Management Concentration. Dr. Sweet has her Ed.D. in Human and Organizational Learning from the Executive Leadership Program at The George Washington University, an M.B.A. from East Carolina University, and a B.A. from UNC-Wilmington. She is a Senior Professional in Human Resources (SPHR, SHRM-SCP) and has over ten years of experience as a human resource professional in the healthcare industry. Her research interests include psychological capital, self-authorship, motivation, and learning organizations.

William Von Canon, Jr. is a member of the principle management team at Business Intelligence and has developed and led numerous business service activities for the company and helped grow revenue yearly to the current $16M base. Dr. Von Canon supports a variety of business programs and works directly with C-level Federal executives in building program strategies and managing program execution. Dr. Von Canon has a diverse business management, information technology and systems integration background focused on strategic planning, business operations, program execution, and systems delivery to a variety of Government and private-sector clients. Considered an expert in the field of shared services, Dr. Von Canon has developed and managed multiple program management offices within major Federal customers delivering transition of major internal system applications and business operations to both public and private shared service providers.

Danielle Young is a Research Associate for international assessments and other education research studies at Westat in Rockville, MD. She will complete the Assessment, Testing, and Measurement in Education Master's degree at George Washington University in 2018.

Marielba Zacarias is a Computer Engineering (1982) with a MSc degree in Systems Engineering (1996) from "Universidad Simón Bolívar de Venezuela" (USB), and a PhD in Informatics and Computers Engineering (2008) from "Instituto Superior Técnico da Universidade Técnica de Lisboa" (IST/ULT) . She has a professional experience of 35 year in Information Systems. From 1983 to 2001, she first worked as software developer and later as a software project manager. In 2001 she moved to Portugal where she is dedicated exclusively to teaching and research activities. Currently, she is an assistant professor of the Electronics and Computers Engineering Department of Faculty of Sciences and Technology, University of Algarve, and a member of Research Centre for Spatial and Organizational Dynamics (CIEO). Her research experience includes over 60 scientific papers in the topics of enterprise modeling and ontologies, process modeling and context modeling. She has participated in several organization and scientific committees of international events on these topics. She has also supervised 2 PhD students on related areas, as well as several master and pre-graduate students.

Ali Zare holds a master degree in Management from Shahid Beheshti University, Tehran, Iran. His research interests include Enterprise Resource Planning systems, business intelligence, and IT Service management.

Ahad Zare Ravasan is an Assisstant Professor of Information Systems at MehrAlborz University, Tehran, Iran. He received his MSc and PhD in Information Technology Management at Allameh Tabataba'i University, Tehran, Iran. Ahad has published a number of papers in acclaimed journals, such as the Expert Systems with Applications, Information Systems, International Journal of Production Research, Telecommunication Systems, Production Planning and Control, Scientia Iranica, International Journal of Data Warehousing and Mining, Journal of Enterprise Information Management, Journal of Global Operations and Strategic Sourcing and International Journal of Enterprise Information Systems to name only a few. His key research interests include ERPs, artificial neural networks' applications in practice, business process outsourcing, business intelligence, Requirements Engineering, and IT Service management.

Index

S

T

U

V

W

www.ingramcontent.com/pod-product-compliance
Lightning Source LLC
LaVergne TN
LVHW080557300926
849162LV00005B/972